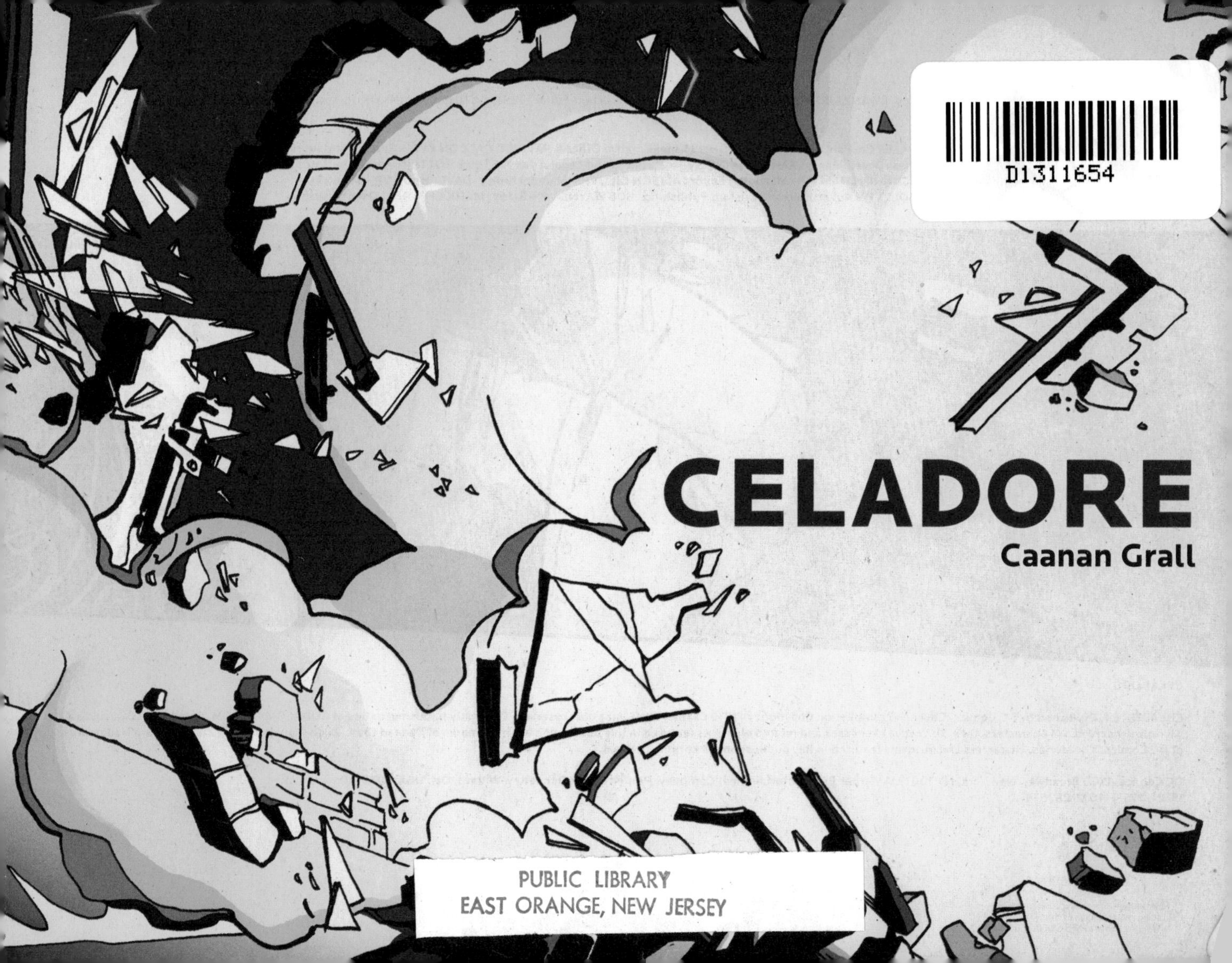

CELADORE

Caanan Grall

RON PERAZZA Editorial Director – Zuda Comics   KWANZA JOHNSON Editor   NIKA VAGNER Assistant Editor   JESSICA NUMSUWANKIJKUL Assistant Editor, Book Edition

DC COMICS
DIANE NELSON President   DAN DIDIO and JIM LEE Co-Publishers   GEOFF JOHNS Chief Creative Officer   PATRICK CALDON EVP – Finance and Administration
JOHN ROOD EVP – Sales, Marketing and Business Development   AMY GENKINS SVP – Business and Legal Affairs   STEVE ROTTERDAM SVP – Sales and Marketing
JOHN CUNNINGHAM VP – Marketing   TERRI CUNNINGHAM VP – Managing Editor   ALISON GILL VP – Manufacturing   DAVID HYDE VP – Publicity
SUE POHJA VP – Book Trade Sales   ALYSSE SOLL VP – Advertising and Custom Publishing   BOB WAYNE VP – Sales   MARK CHIARELLO Art Director

CELADORE

DC Comics, 1700 Broadway, New York, NY 10019. A Warner Bros. Entertainment Company. Printed by RR Donnelley, Willard, OH, USA. 9/15/10.
ISBN: 978-1-4012-2835-4

SUSTAINABLE
FORESTRY
INITIATIVE

Certified Fiber Sourcing
www.sfiprogram.org

Fiber used in this product line meets the
sourcing requirements of the SFI program.
www.sfiprogram.org NFS-SPIC0C-C0001801

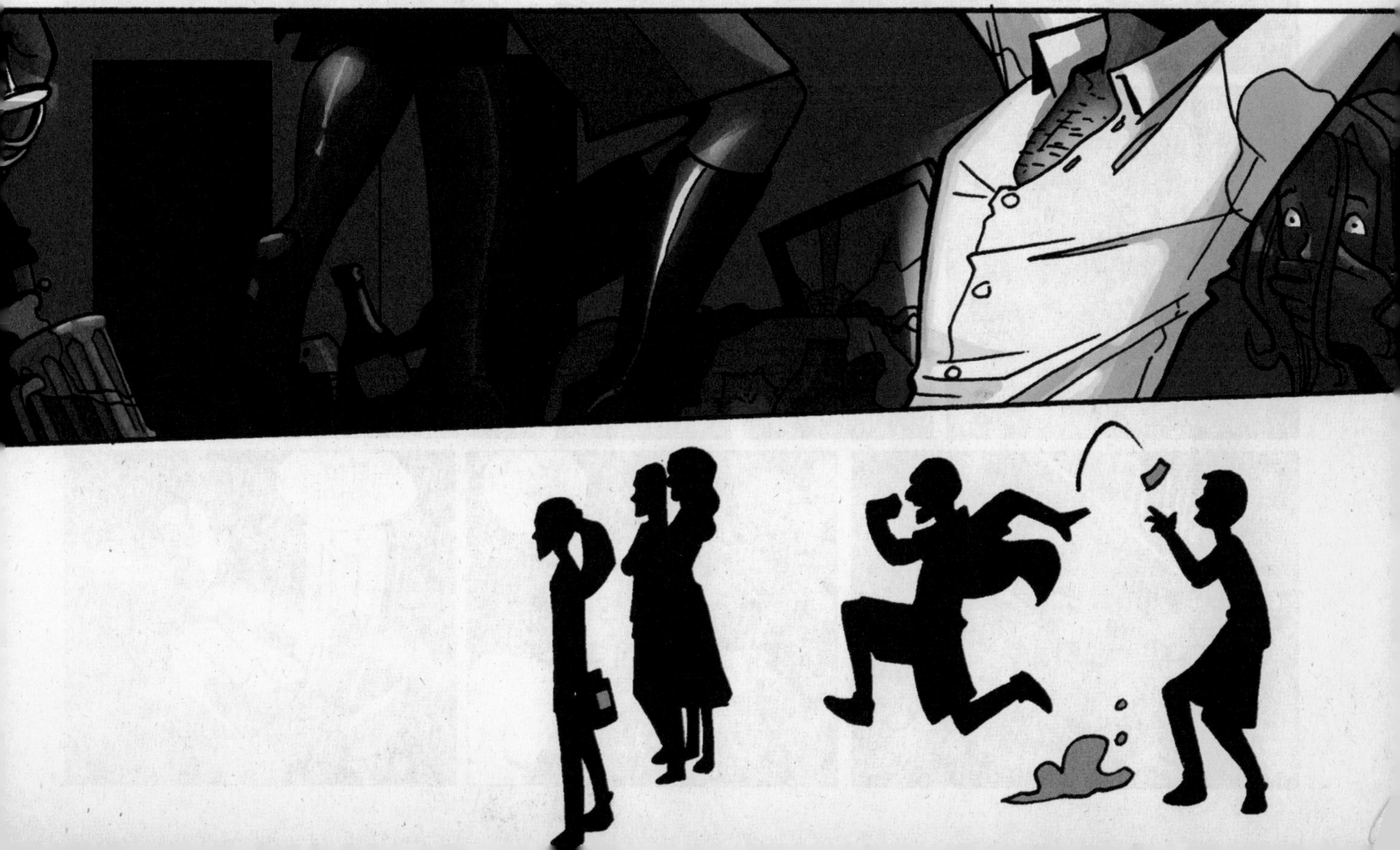

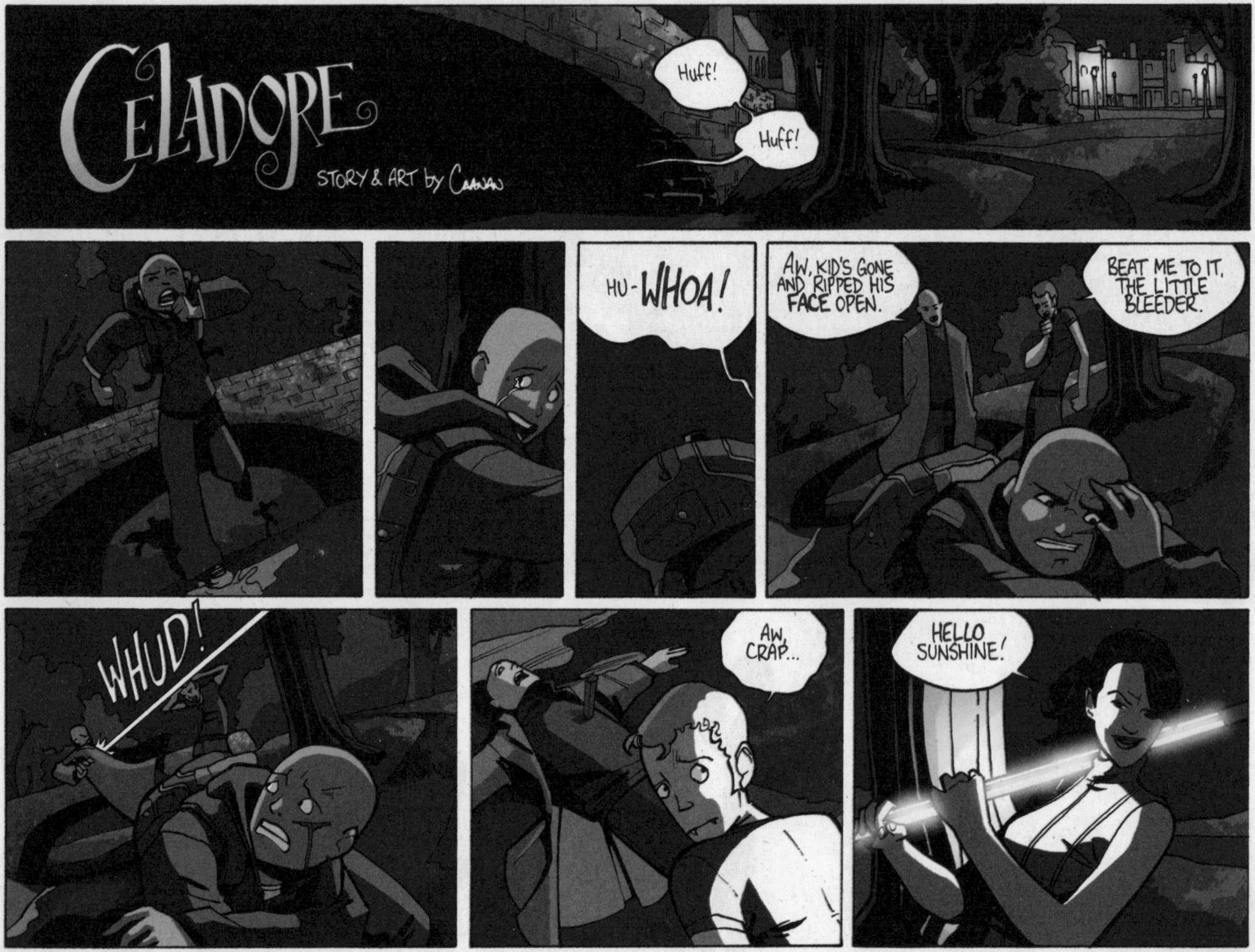
CELADORE
STORY & ART by CAANAN
Huff!
Huff!
HU-WHOA!
AW, KID'S GONE AND RIPPED HIS FACE OPEN.
BEAT ME TO IT, THE LITTLE BLEEDER.
WHUD!
AW, CRAP...
HELLO SUNSHINE!

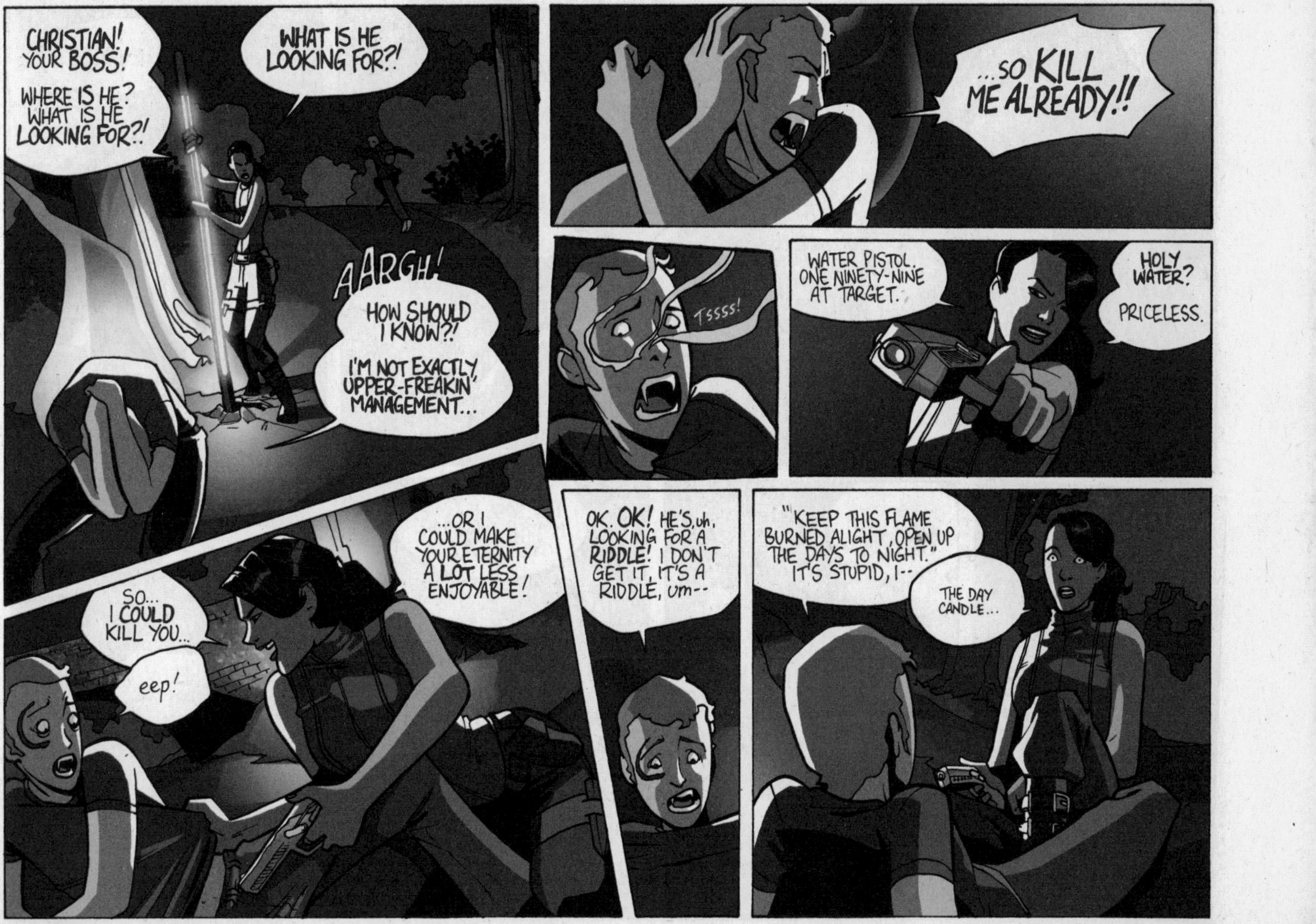
CHRISTIAN! YOUR BOSS!
WHERE IS HE? WHAT IS HE LOOKING FOR?!
WHAT IS HE LOOKING FOR?!
AARGH!
HOW SHOULD I KNOW?!
I'M NOT EXACTLY UPPER-FREAKIN' MANAGEMENT...
...SO KILL ME ALREADY!!
TSSSS!
WATER PISTOL. ONE NINETY-NINE AT TARGET.
HOLY WATER?
PRICELESS.
SO... I COULD KILL YOU...
eep!
...OR I COULD MAKE YOUR ETERNITY A LOT LESS ENJOYABLE!
OK. OK! HE'S, uh, LOOKING FOR A RIDDLE! I DON'T GET IT, IT'S A RIDDLE, um--
"KEEP THIS FLAME BURNED ALIGHT, OPEN UP THE DAYS TO NIGHT." IT'S STUPID, I--
THE DAY CANDLE...

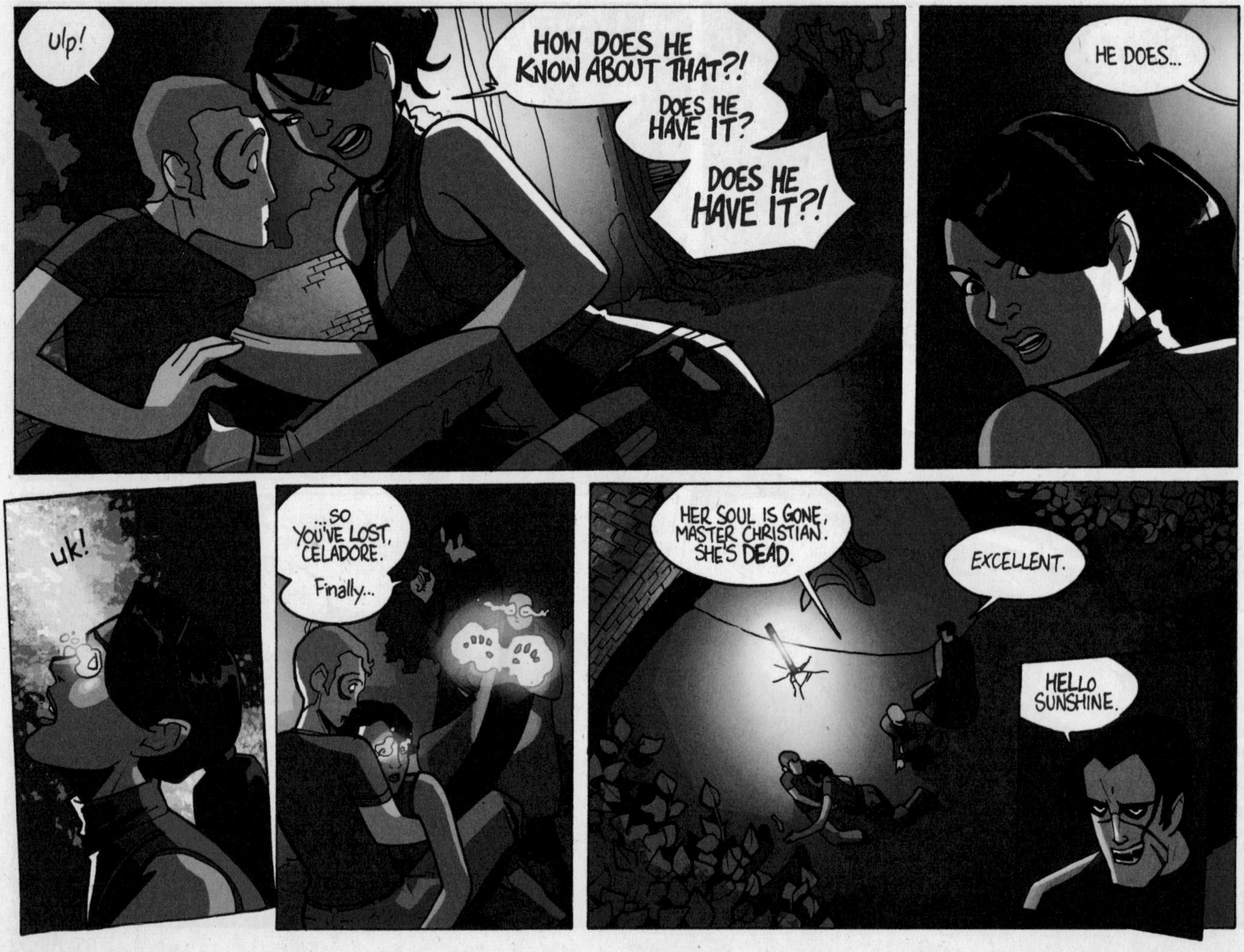
Ulp!
HOW DOES HE KNOW ABOUT THAT?!
DOES HE HAVE IT?
DOES HE HAVE IT?!
HE DOES...
uk!
...SO YOU'VE LOST, CELADORE.
Finally...
HER SOUL IS GONE, MASTER CHRISTIAN. SHE'S DEAD.
EXCELLENT.
HELLO SUNSHINE.

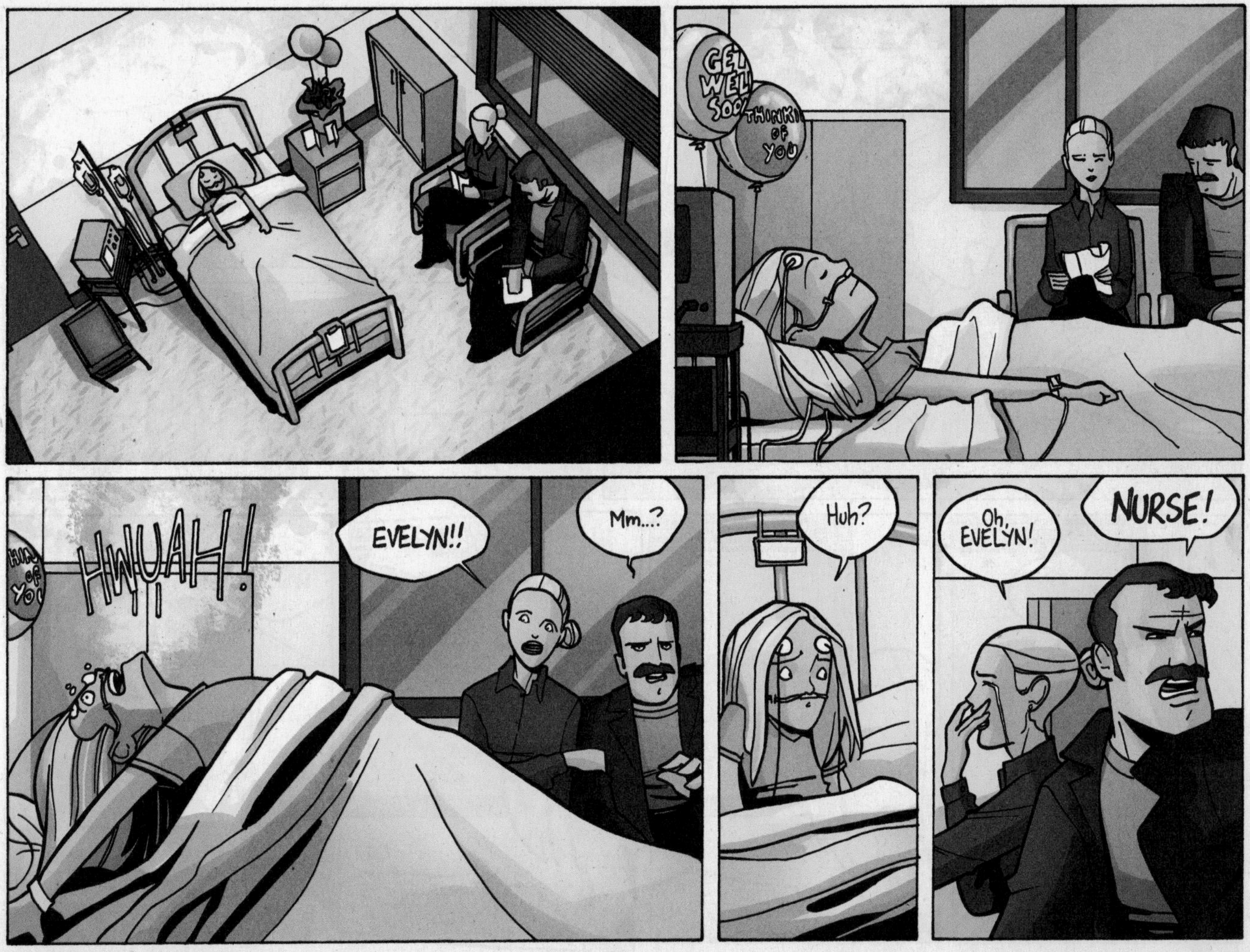
GET WELL SOON
THINKING OF YOU
HWUAH!
EVELYN!!
Mm...?
Huh?
Oh, EVELYN!
NURSE!

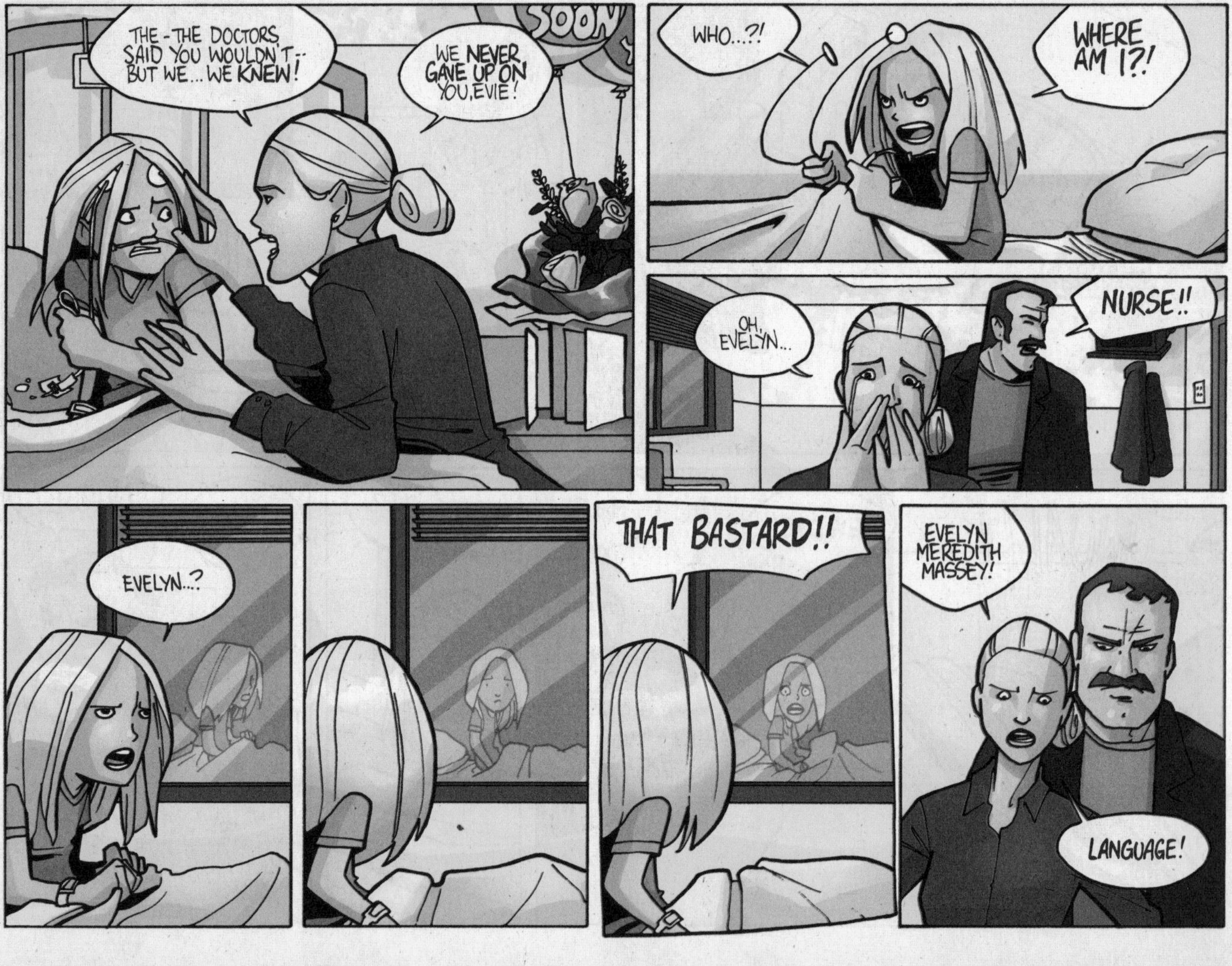
SOON
THE - THE DOCTORS SAID YOU WOULDN'T.. BUT WE... WE KNEW!
WE NEVER GAVE UP ON YOU, EVIE!
WHO...?!
WHERE AM I?!
OH, EVELYN...
NURSE!!
EVELYN...?
THAT BASTARD!!
EVELYN MEREDITH MASSEY!
LANGUAGE!

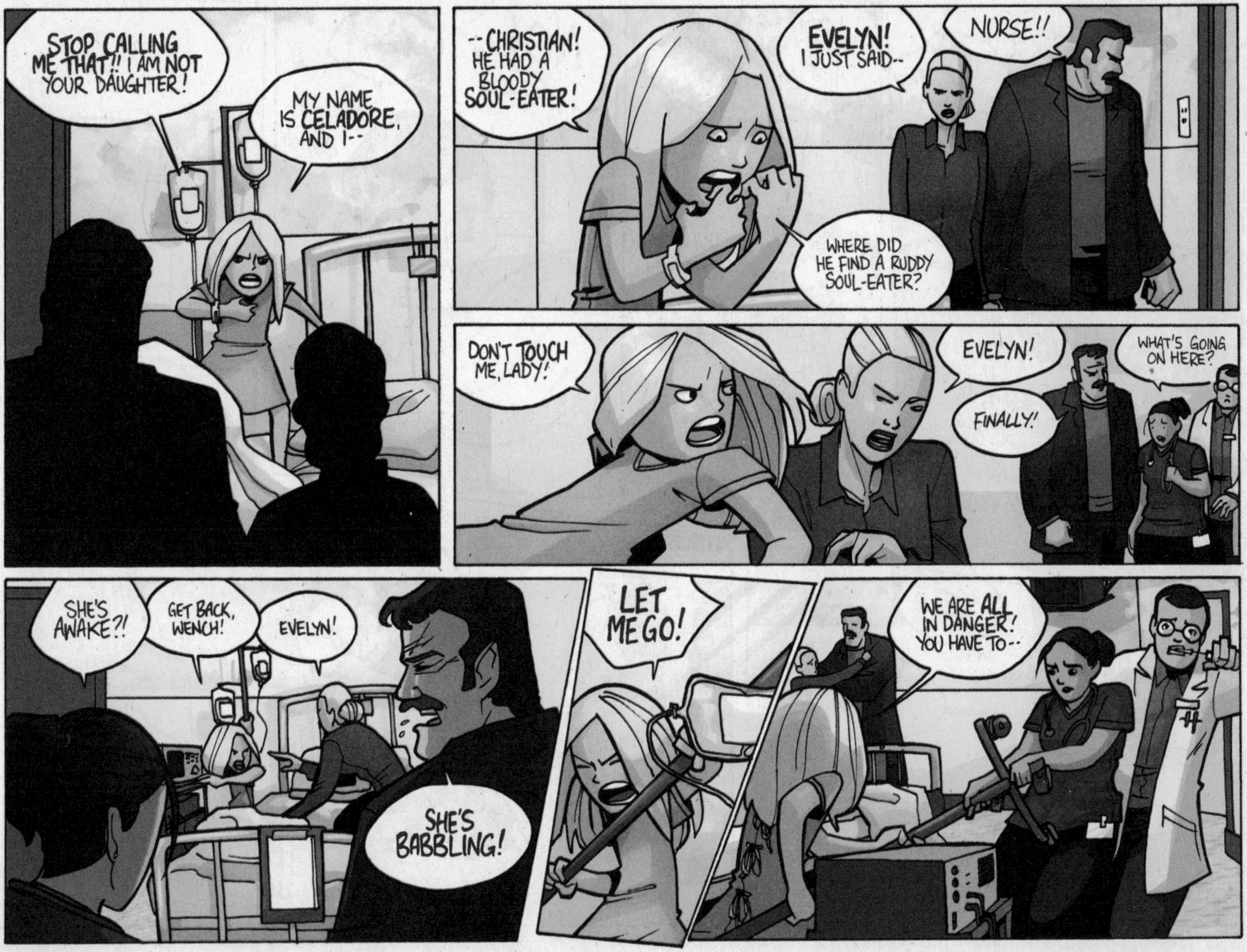
STOP CALLING ME THAT!! I AM NOT YOUR DAUGHTER!
MY NAME IS CELADORE, AND I--
--CHRISTIAN! HE HAD A BLOODY SOUL-EATER!
EVELYN! I JUST SAID--
NURSE!!
WHERE DID HE FIND A RUDDY SOUL-EATER?
DON'T TOUCH ME, LADY!
EVELYN!
FINALLY!
WHAT'S GOING ON HERE?
SHE'S AWAKE?!
GET BACK, WENCH!
EVELYN!
SHE'S BABBLING!
LET ME GO!
WE ARE ALL IN DANGER! YOU HAVE TO--

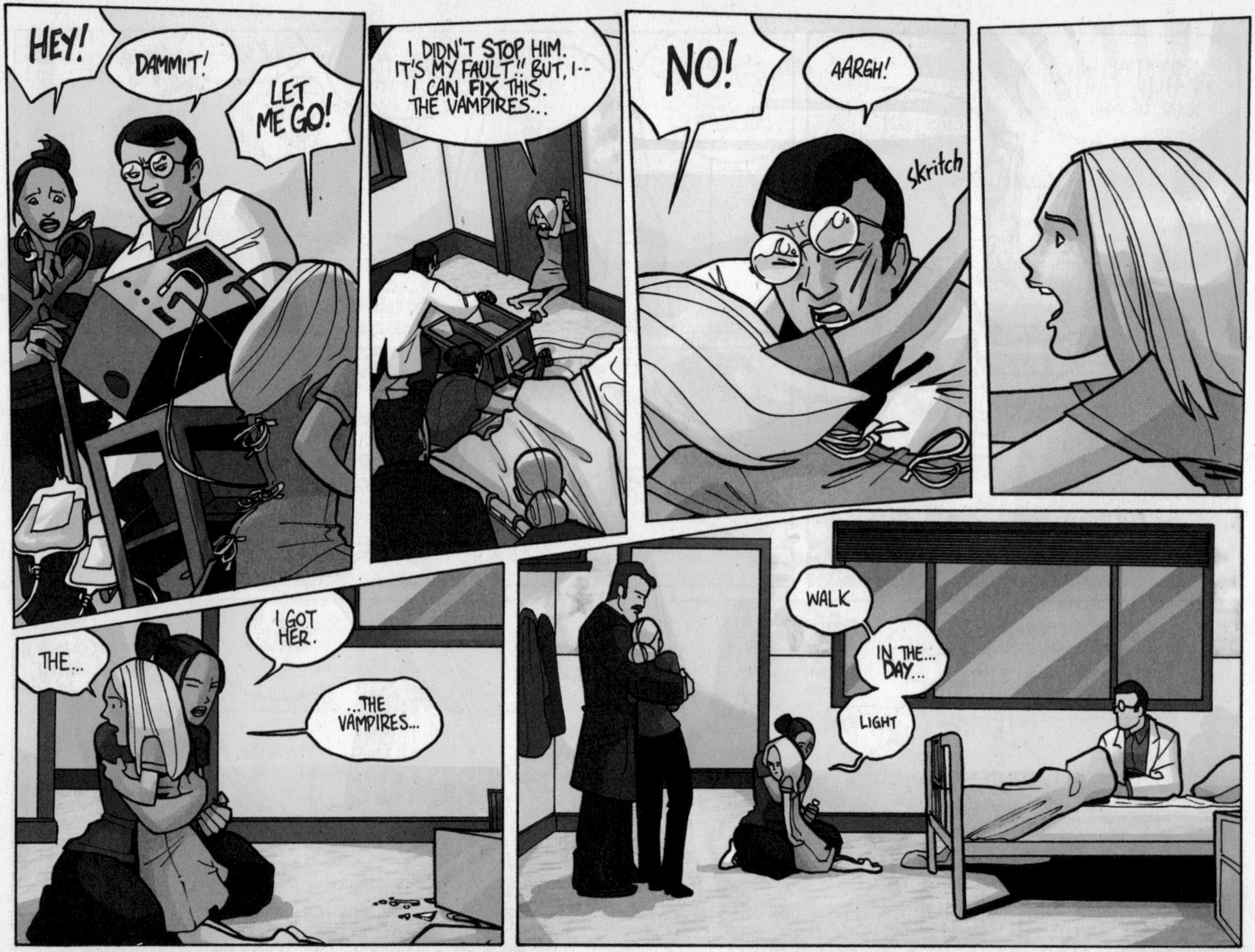
HEY!
DAMMIT!
LET ME GO!
I DIDN'T STOP HIM. IT'S MY FAULT!! BUT, I-- I CAN FIX THIS. THE VAMPIRES...
NO!
AARGH!
SKRITCH
THE...
I GOT HER.
...THE VAMPIRES...
WALK
IN THE... DAY...
LIGHT

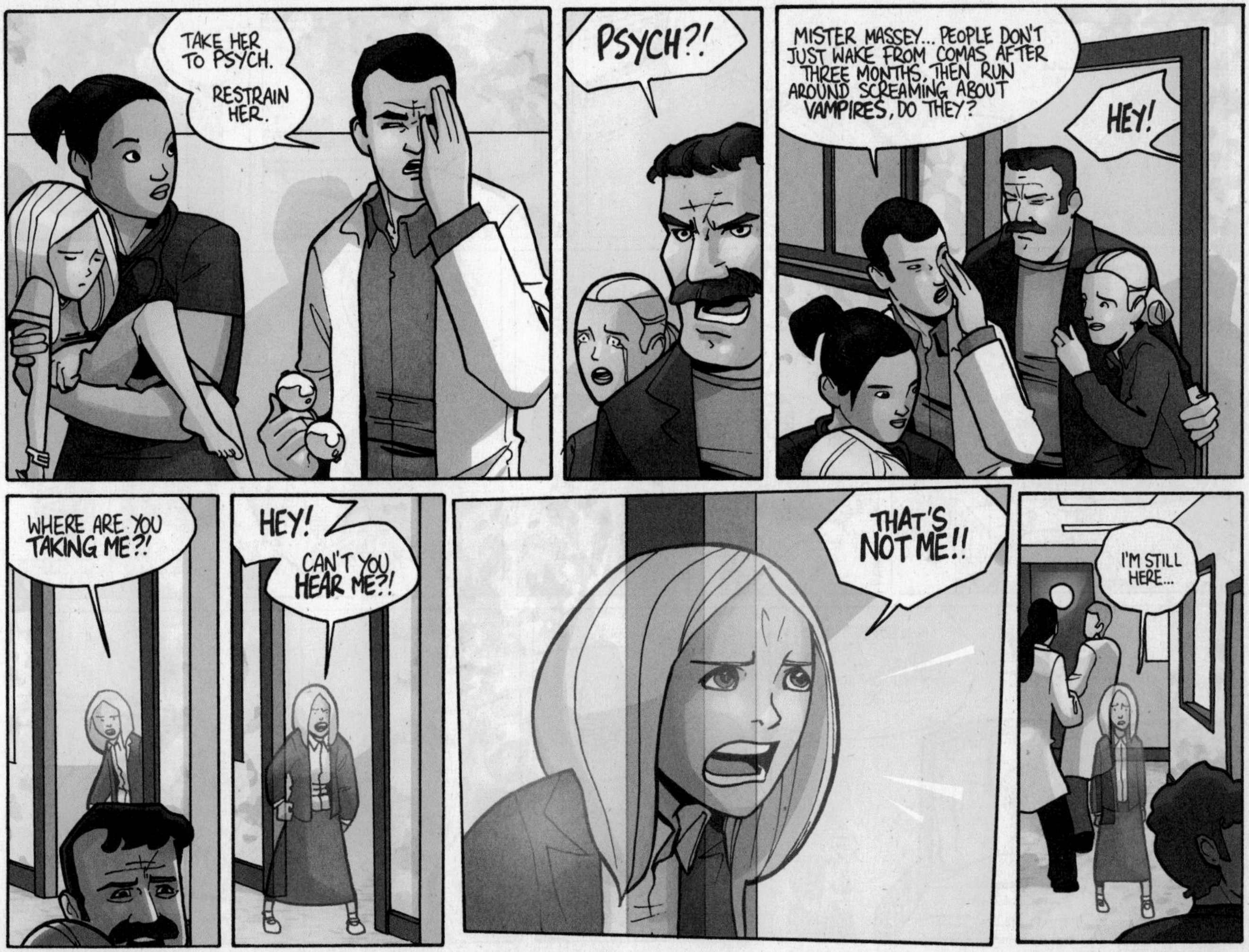
TAKE HER TO PSYCH.
RESTRAIN HER.
PSYCH?!
MISTER MASSEY... PEOPLE DON'T JUST WAKE FROM COMAS AFTER THREE MONTHS, THEN RUN AROUND SCREAMING ABOUT VAMPIRES, DO THEY?
HEY!
WHERE ARE YOU TAKING ME?!
HEY!
CAN'T YOU HEAR ME?!
THAT'S NOT ME!!
I'M STILL HERE...

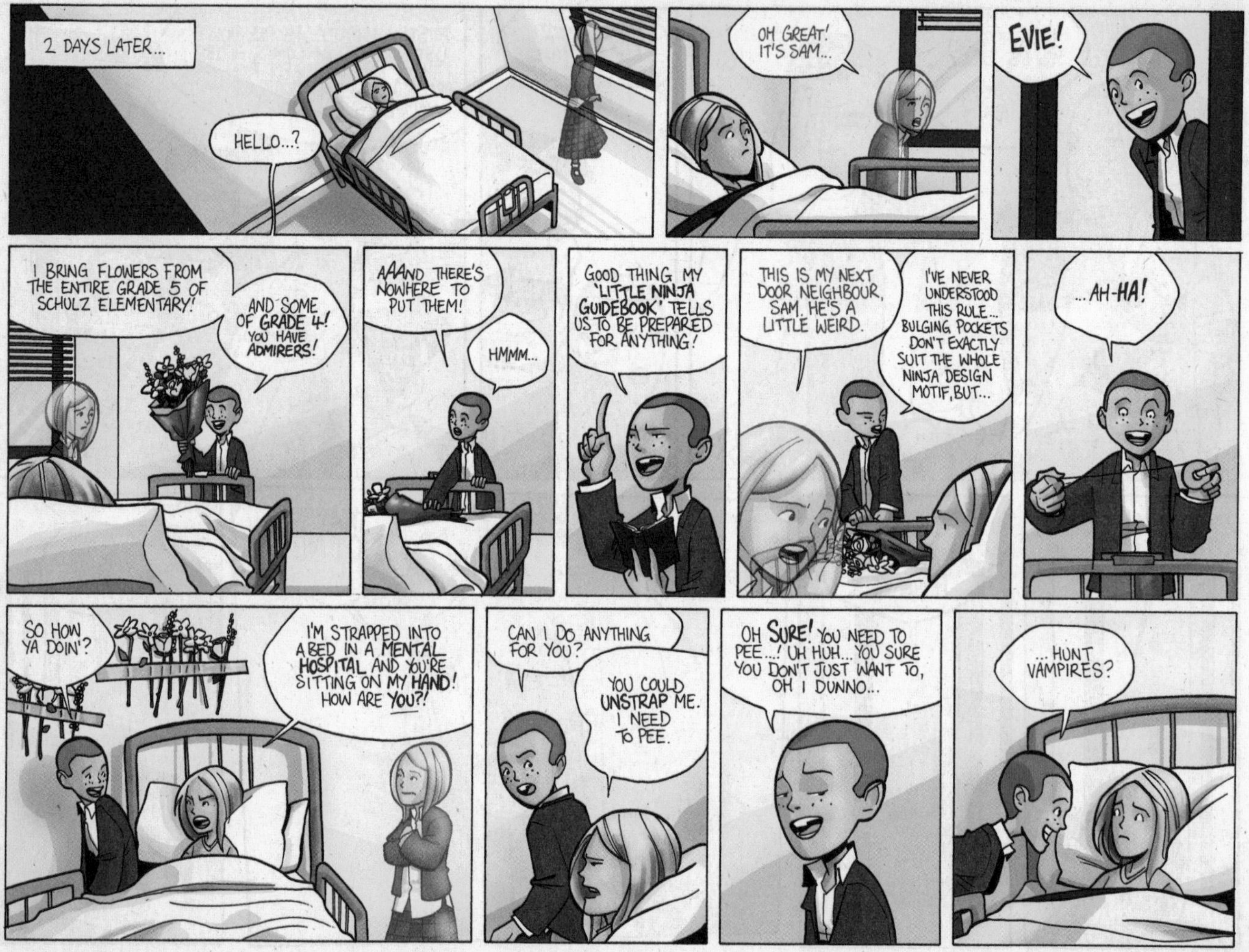
2 DAYS LATER...
HELLO...?
OH GREAT! IT'S SAM...
EVIE!
I BRING FLOWERS FROM THE ENTIRE GRADE 5 OF SCHULZ ELEMENTARY!
AND SOME OF GRADE 4! YOU HAVE ADMIRERS!
AAAND THERE'S NOWHERE TO PUT THEM!
HMMM...
GOOD THING MY 'LITTLE NINJA GUIDEBOOK' TELLS US TO BE PREPARED FOR ANYTHING!
THIS IS MY NEXT DOOR NEIGHBOUR, SAM. HE'S A LITTLE WEIRD.
I'VE NEVER UNDERSTOOD THIS RULE... BULGING POCKETS DON'T EXACTLY SUIT THE WHOLE NINJA DESIGN MOTIF, BUT...
...AH-HA!
SO HOW YA DOIN'?
I'M STRAPPED INTO A BED IN A MENTAL HOSPITAL AND YOU'RE SITTING ON MY HAND! HOW ARE YOU?!
CAN I DO ANYTHING FOR YOU?
YOU COULD UNSTRAP ME. I NEED TO PEE.
OH SURE! YOU NEED TO PEE...! UH HUH... YOU SURE YOU DON'T JUST WANT TO, OH I DUNNO...
... HUNT VAMPIRES?

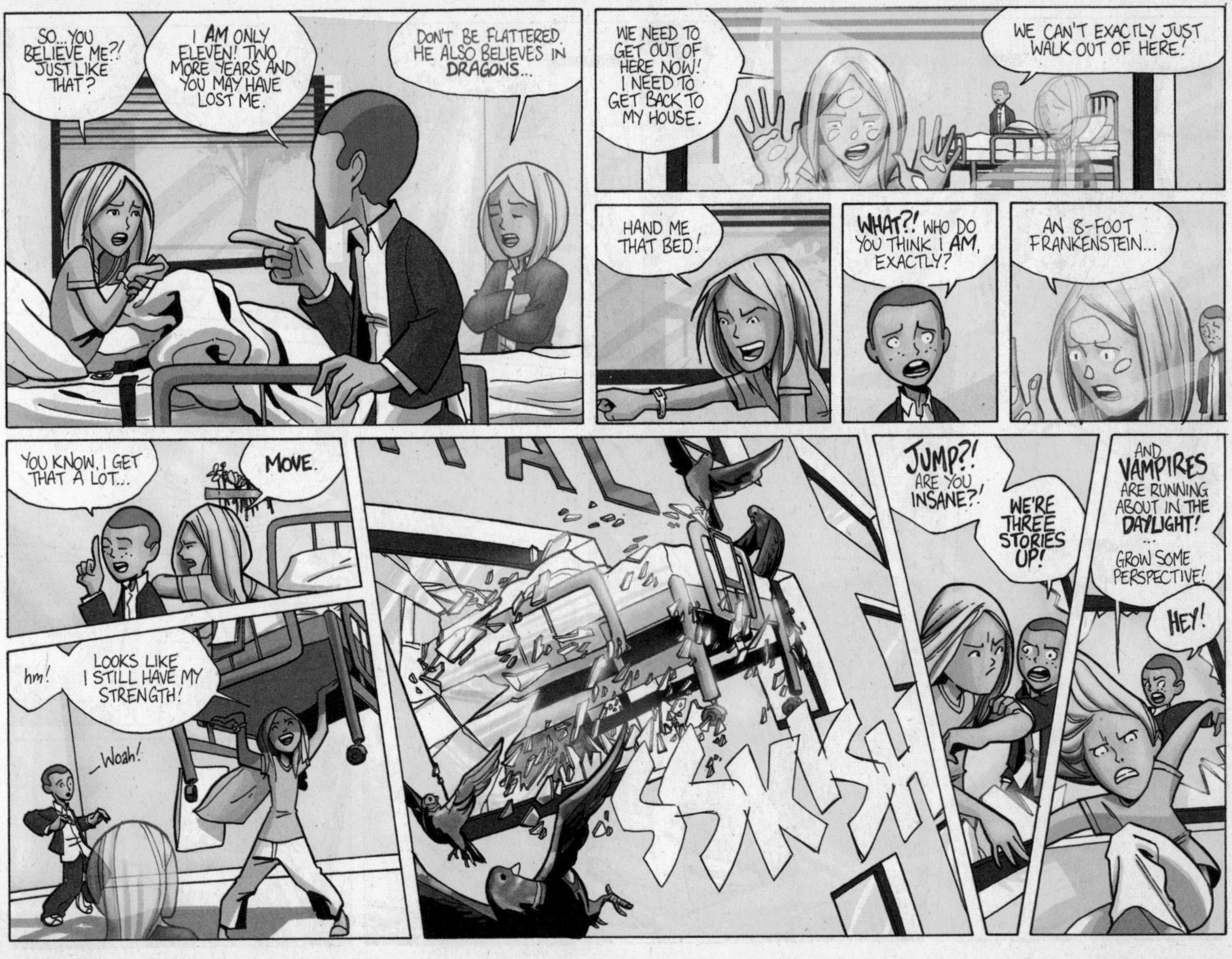
SO... YOU BELIEVE ME?! JUST LIKE THAT?
I AM ONLY ELEVEN! TWO MORE YEARS AND YOU MAY HAVE LOST ME.
DON'T BE FLATTERED. HE ALSO BELIEVES IN DRAGONS...
WE NEED TO GET OUT OF HERE NOW! I NEED TO GET BACK TO MY HOUSE.
WE CAN'T EXACTLY JUST WALK OUT OF HERE!
HAND ME THAT BED!
WHAT?! WHO DO YOU THINK I AM, EXACTLY?
AN 8-FOOT FRANKENSTEIN...
YOU KNOW, I GET THAT A LOT...
MOVE.
hm!
LOOKS LIKE I STILL HAVE MY STRENGTH!
Woah!
JUMP?! ARE YOU INSANE?!
WE'RE THREE STORIES UP!
AND VAMPIRES ARE RUNNING ABOUT IN THE DAYLIGHT! ... GROW SOME PERSPECTIVE!
HEY!

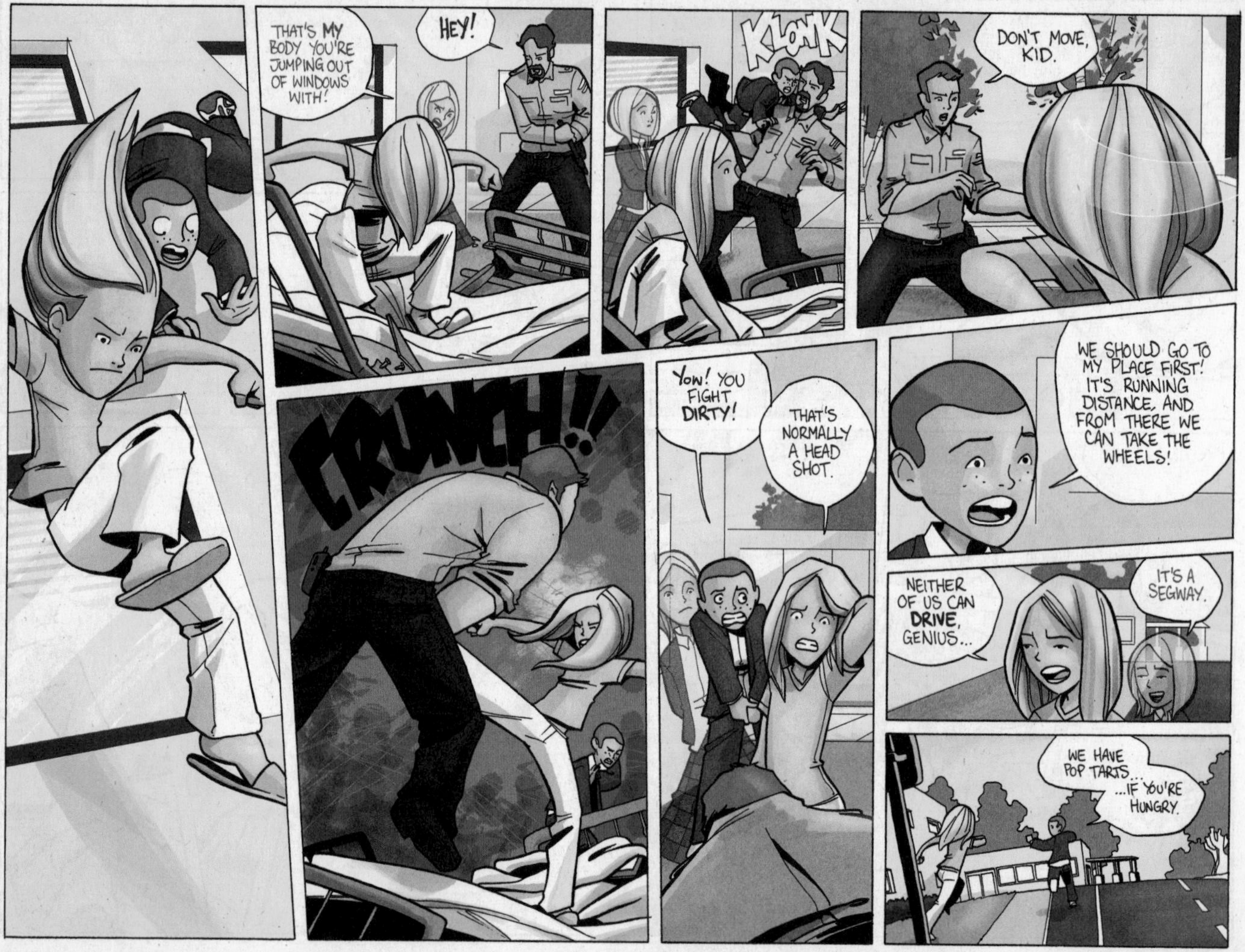
THAT'S MY BODY YOU'RE JUMPING OUT OF WINDOWS WITH!
HEY!
KLONK
DON'T MOVE, KID.
CRUNCH!!!
YOW! YOU FIGHT DIRTY!
THAT'S NORMALLY A HEAD SHOT.
WE SHOULD GO TO MY PLACE FIRST! IT'S RUNNING DISTANCE, AND FROM THERE WE CAN TAKE THE WHEELS!
NEITHER OF US CAN DRIVE, GENIUS...
IT'S A SEGWAY.
WE HAVE POP TARTS...
...IF YOU'RE HUNGRY.

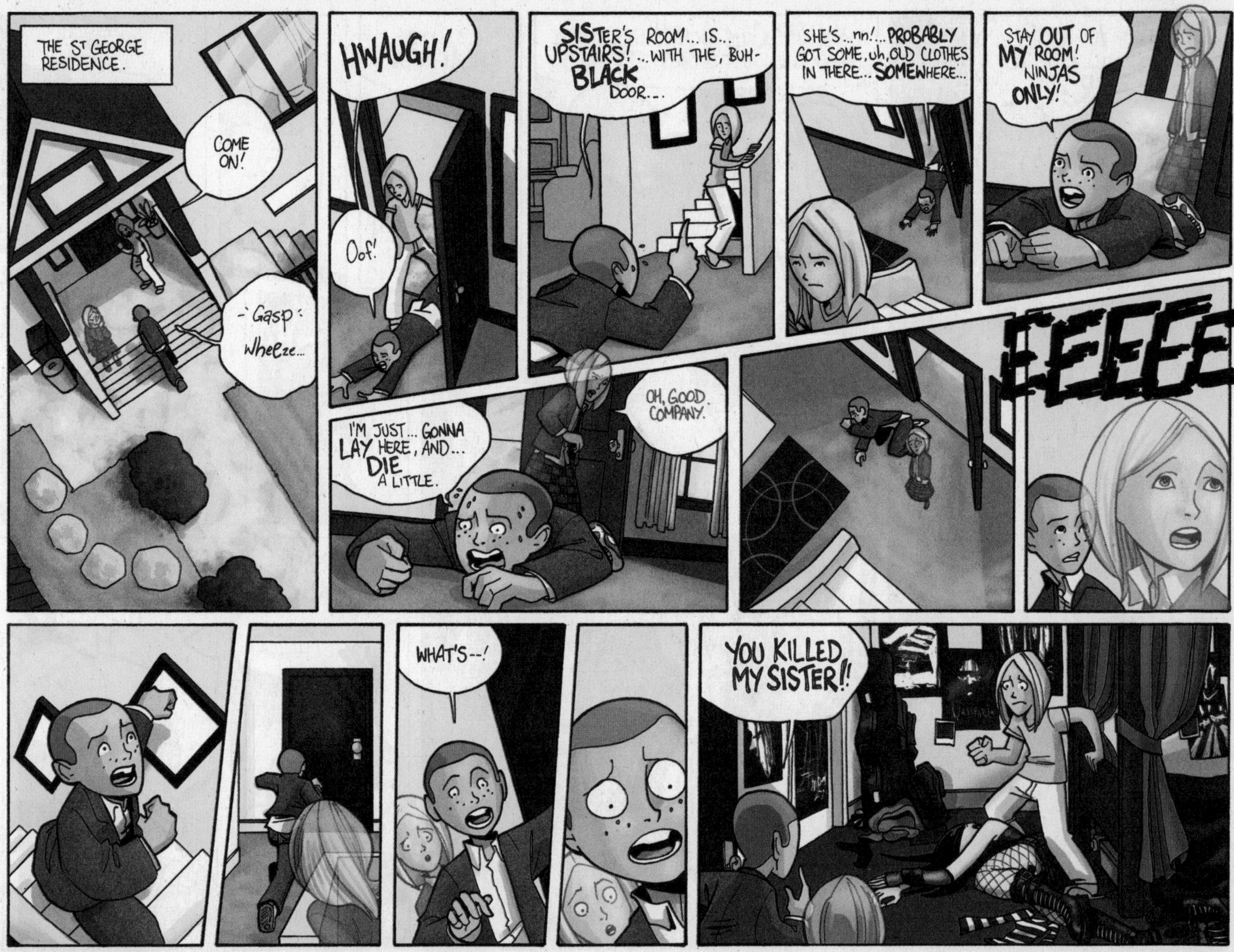
THE St GEORGE RESIDENCE.
COME ON!
-Gasp-
wheeze...
HWAUGH!
Oof!
SISTER'S ROOM... IS... UPSTAIRS! ...WITH THE, BUH- BLACK DOOR...
SHE'S ...nn!...PROBABLY GOT SOME, uh, OLD CLOTHES IN THERE... SOMEWHERE...
STAY OUT OF MY ROOM! NINJAS ONLY!
I'M JUST... GONNA LAY HERE, AND... DIE A LITTLE.
OH, GOOD. COMPANY.
EEEEE
WHAT'S--!
YOU KILLED MY SISTER!!

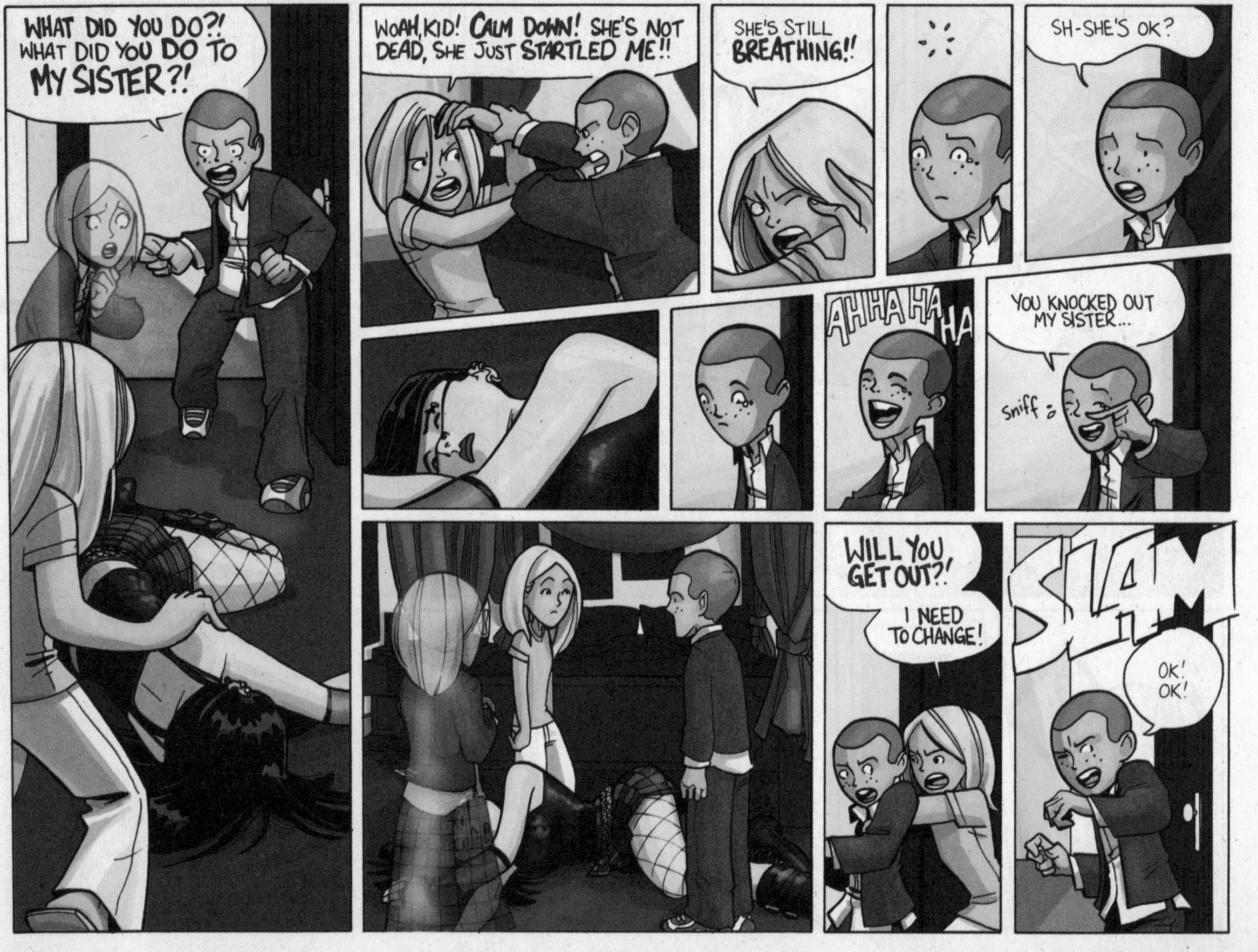
WHAT DID YOU DO?! WHAT DID YOU DO TO MY SISTER?!
WOAH, KID! CALM DOWN! SHE'S NOT DEAD, SHE JUST STARTLED ME!!
SHE'S STILL BREATHING!!
SH-SHE'S OK?
AHHAHAHA HA
YOU KNOCKED OUT MY SISTER...
Sniff
WILL YOU GET OUT?!
I NEED TO CHANGE!
SLAM
OK! OK!

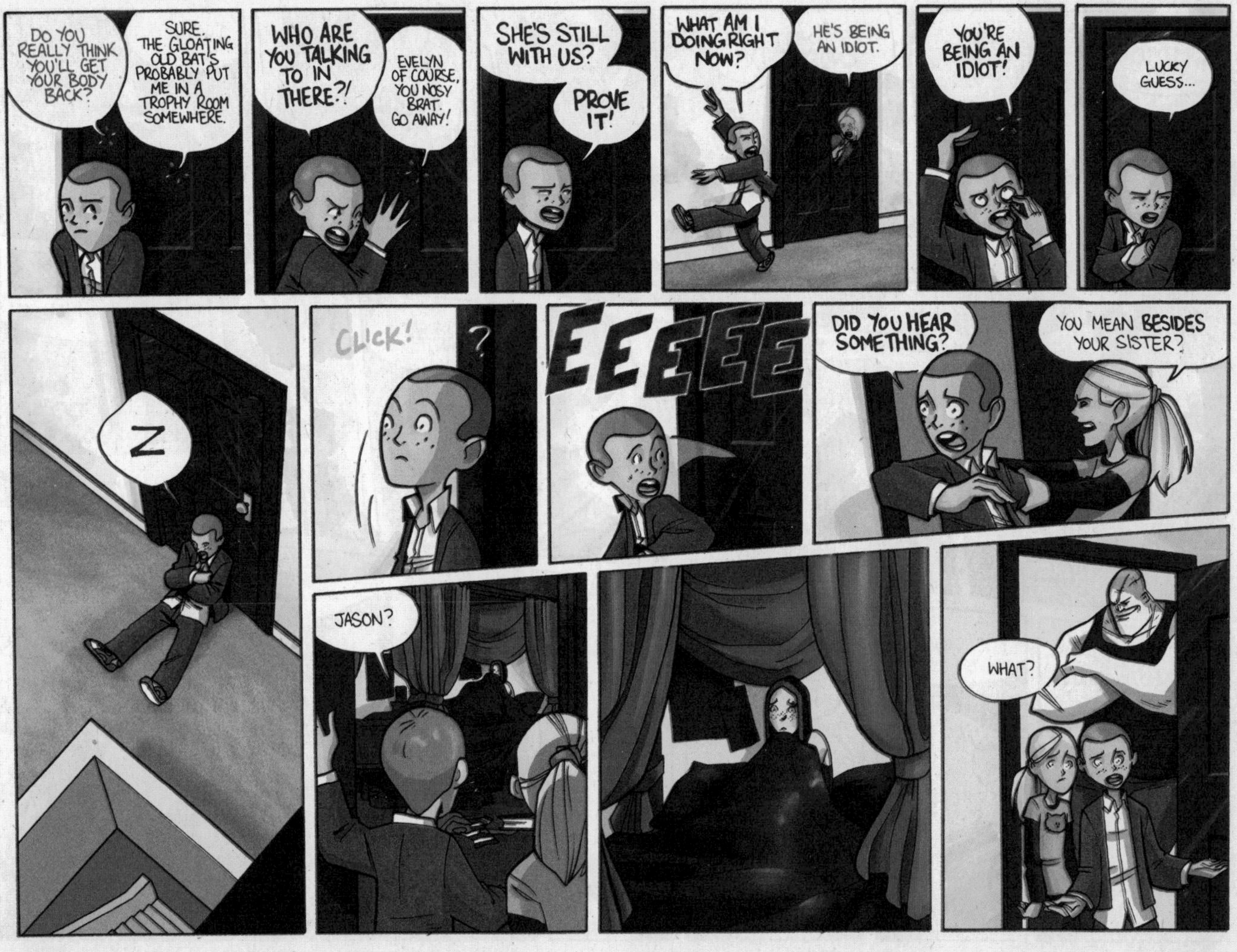
DO YOU REALLY THINK YOU'LL GET YOUR BODY BACK?
SURE. THE GLOATING OLD BAT'S PROBABLY PUT ME IN A TROPHY ROOM SOMEWHERE.
WHO ARE YOU TALKING TO IN THERE?!
EVELYN OF COURSE, YOU NOSY BRAT. GO AWAY!
SHE'S STILL WITH US?
PROVE IT!
WHAT AM I DOING RIGHT NOW?
HE'S BEING AN IDIOT.
YOU'RE BEING AN IDIOT!
LUCKY GUESS...
Z
CLICK!
?
EEEEE
DID YOU HEAR SOMETHING?
YOU MEAN BESIDES YOUR SISTER?
JASON?
WHAT?

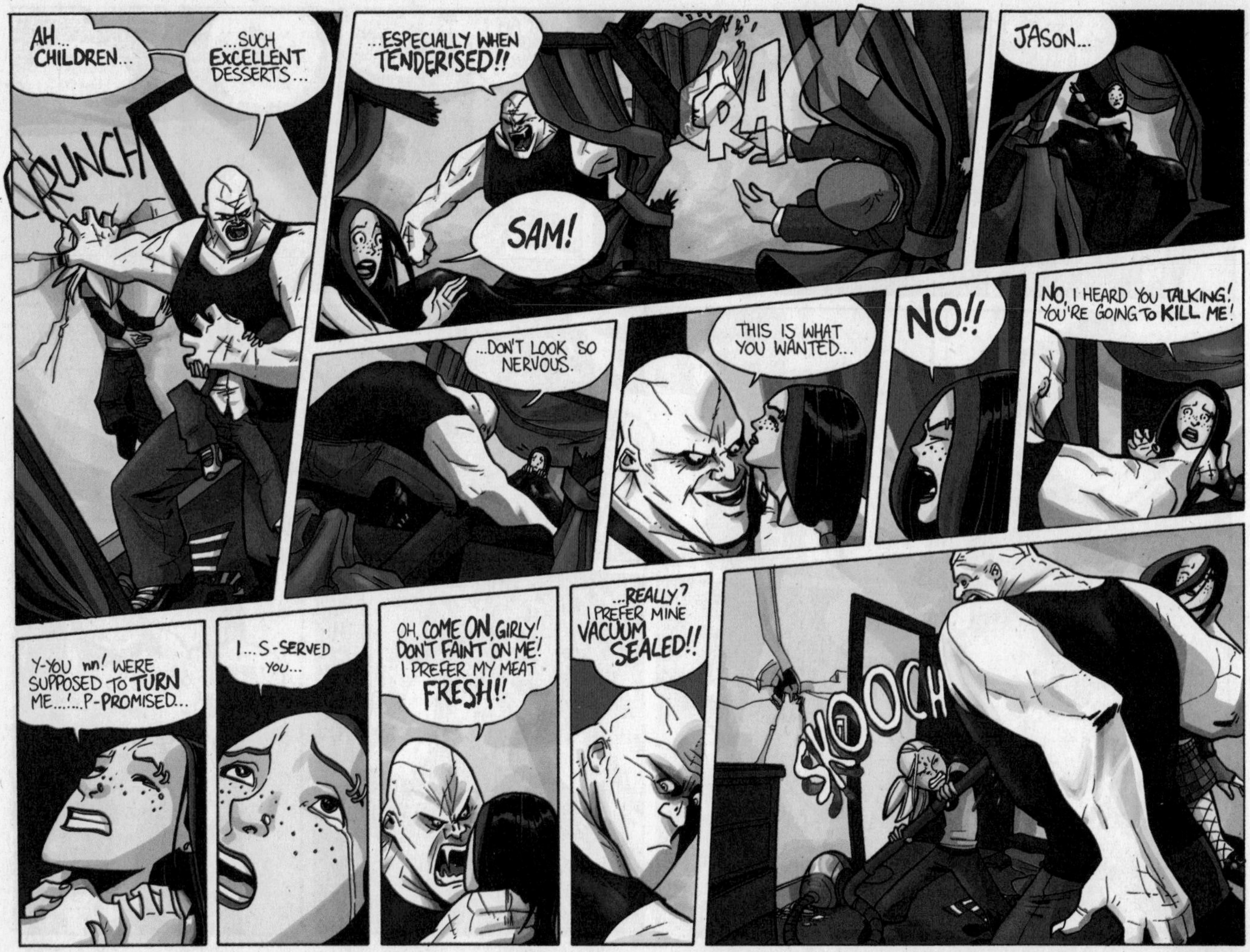
AH... CHILDREN...
...SUCH EXCELLENT DESSERTS...
CRUNCH
...ESPECIALLY WHEN TENDERISED!!
SAM!
CRACK
JASON...
...DON'T LOOK SO NERVOUS.
THIS IS WHAT YOU WANTED...
NO!!
NO, I HEARD YOU TALKING! YOU'RE GOING TO KILL ME!
Y-YOU mn! WERE SUPPOSED TO TURN ME...!...P-PROMISED...
I...S-SERVED YOU...
OH, COME ON, GIRLY! DON'T FAINT ON ME! I PREFER MY MEAT FRESH!!
...REALLY? I PREFER MINE VACUUM SEALED!!
SHLOOOCH

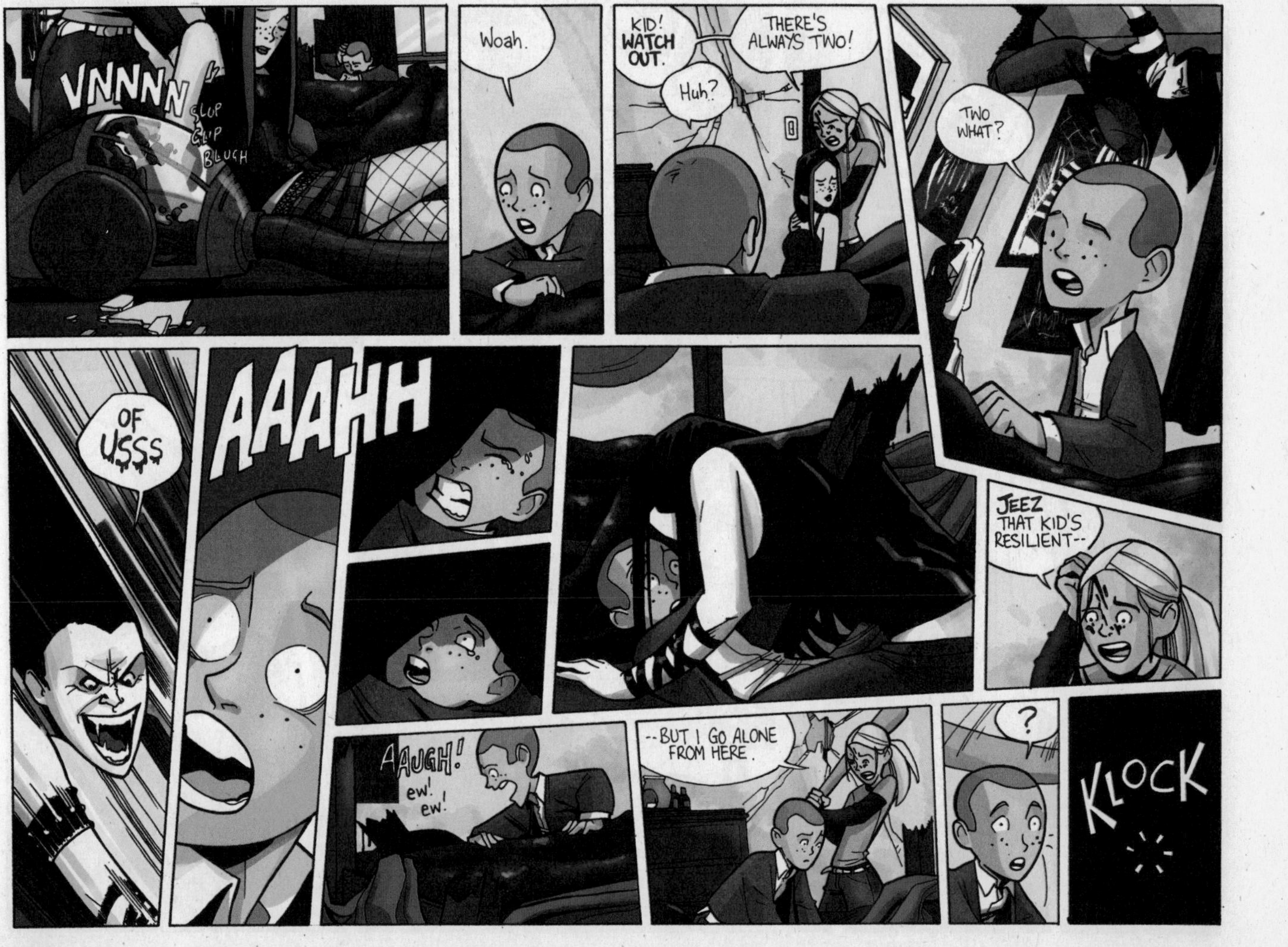
VNNNN
SLUP
GLIP
BLUGH
Woah.
KID! WATCH OUT.
THERE'S ALWAYS TWO!
Huh?
TWO WHAT?
OF USSS
AAAHH
JEEZ THAT KID'S RESILIENT--
AAUGH!
ew!
ew!
--BUT I GO ALONE FROM HERE.
?
KLOCK

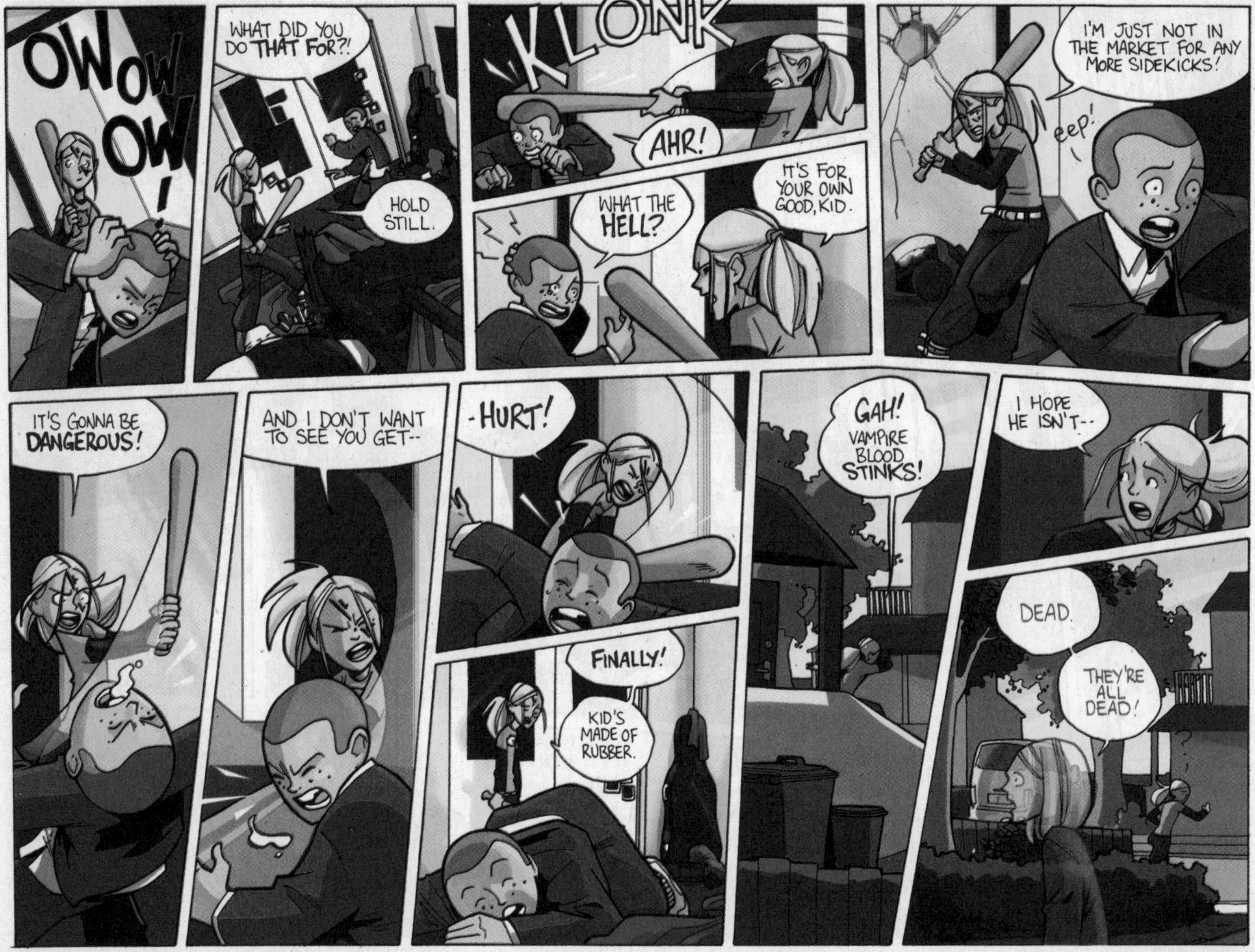
OW OW OW!
WHAT DID YOU DO THAT FOR?!
HOLD STILL.
KLONK
AHR!
WHAT THE HELL?
IT'S FOR YOUR OWN GOOD, KID.
I'M JUST NOT IN THE MARKET FOR ANY MORE SIDEKICKS!
eep!
IT'S GONNA BE DANGEROUS!
AND I DON'T WANT TO SEE YOU GET--
-HURT!
FINALLY!
KID'S MADE OF RUBBER.
GAH! VAMPIRE BLOOD STINKS!
I HOPE HE ISN'T--
DEAD.
THEY'RE ALL DEAD!

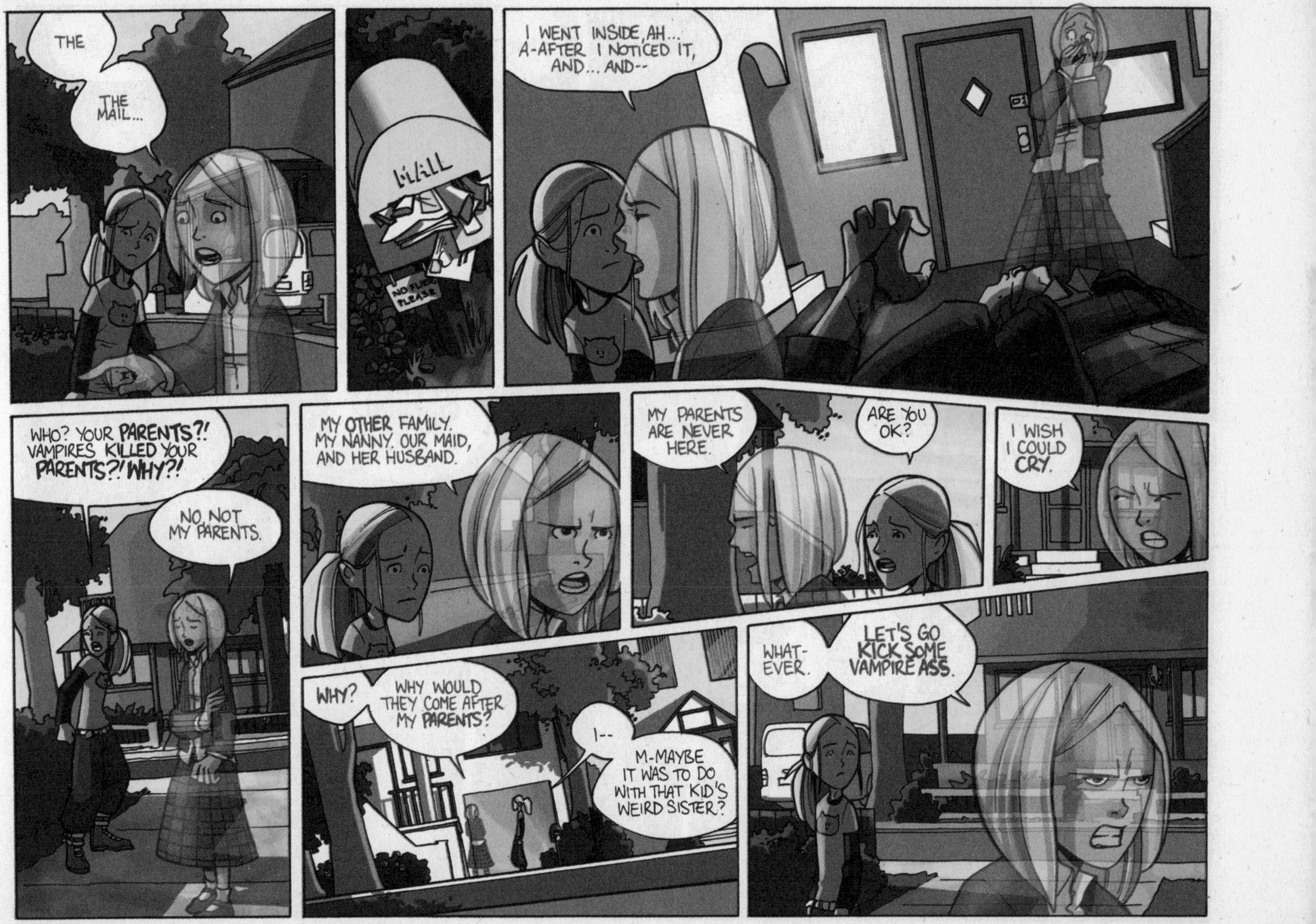
THE
THE MAIL...
MAIL
NO FLIERS PLEASE
I WENT INSIDE, AH... A-AFTER I NOTICED IT, AND... AND--
WHO? YOUR PARENTS?! VAMPIRES KILLED YOUR PARENTS?! WHY?!
NO, NOT MY PARENTS.
MY OTHER FAMILY. MY NANNY. OUR MAID, AND HER HUSBAND.
MY PARENTS ARE NEVER HERE.
ARE YOU OK?
I WISH I COULD CRY.
WHY?
WHY WOULD THEY COME AFTER MY PARENTS?
I--
M-MAYBE IT WAS TO DO WITH THAT KID'S WEIRD SISTER?
WHAT-EVER.
LET'S GO KICK SOME VAMPIRE ASS.

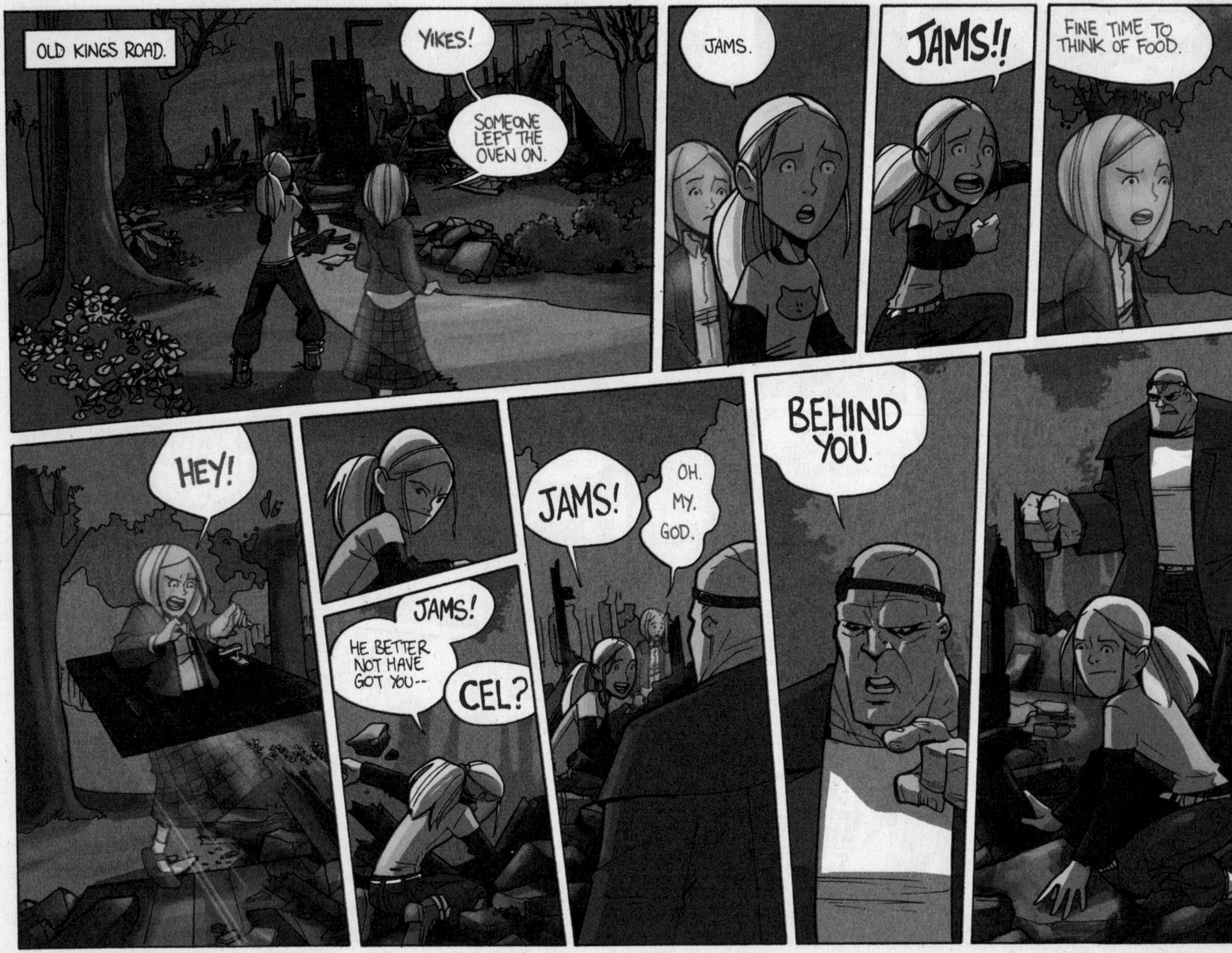
OLD KINGS ROAD.
YIKES!
SOMEONE LEFT THE OVEN ON.
JAMS.
JAMS!!
FINE TIME TO THINK OF FOOD.
HEY!
JAMS!
HE BETTER NOT HAVE GOT YOU--
CEL?
JAMS!
OH. MY. GOD.
BEHIND YOU.

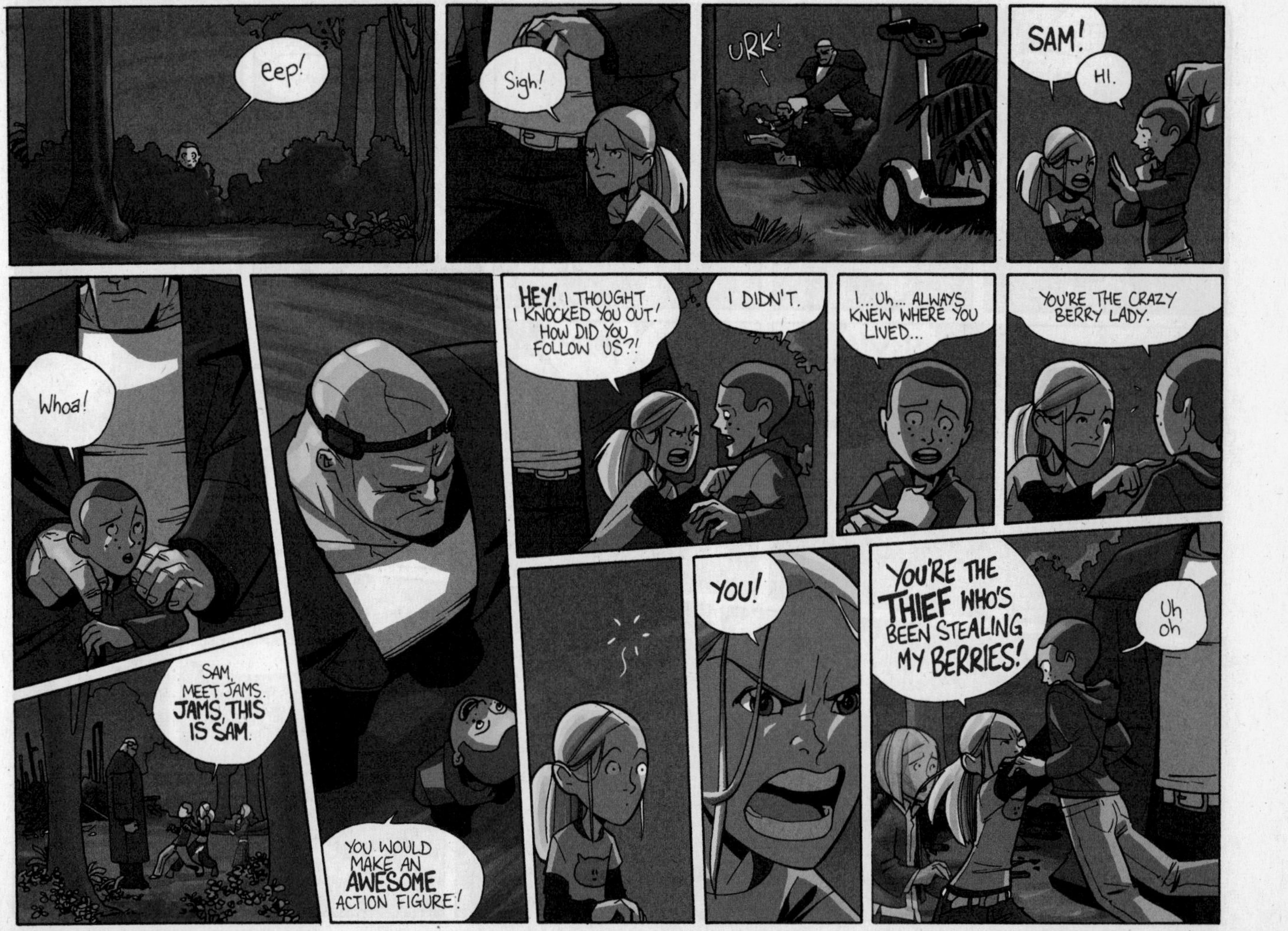
eep!
Sigh!
URK!
SAM!
HI.
Whoa!
HEY! I THOUGHT I KNOCKED YOU OUT! HOW DID YOU FOLLOW US?!
I DIDN'T.
I... Uh... ALWAYS KNEW WHERE YOU LIVED...
YOU'RE THE CRAZY BERRY LADY.
SAM, MEET JAMS. JAMS, THIS IS SAM.
YOU WOULD MAKE AN AWESOME ACTION FIGURE!
YOU!
YOU'RE THE THIEF WHO'S BEEN STEALING MY BERRIES!
Uh oh

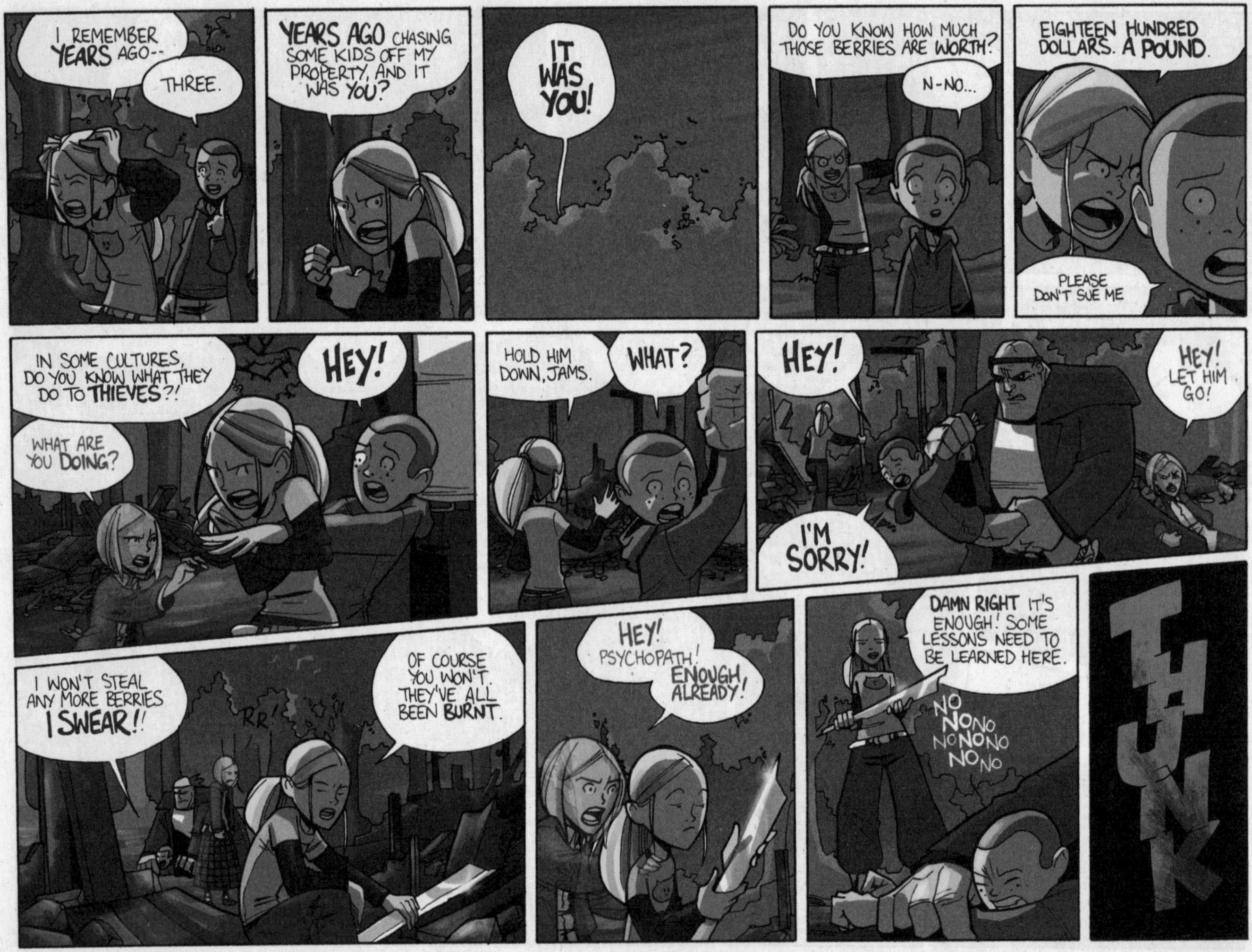
I REMEMBER YEARS AGO--
THREE.
YEARS AGO CHASING SOME KIDS OFF MY PROPERTY, AND IT WAS YOU?
IT WAS YOU!
DO YOU KNOW HOW MUCH THOSE BERRIES ARE WORTH?
N-NO...
EIGHTEEN HUNDRED DOLLARS. A POUND.
PLEASE DON'T SUE ME
IN SOME CULTURES, DO YOU KNOW WHAT THEY DO TO THIEVES?!
HEY!
WHAT ARE YOU DOING?
HOLD HIM DOWN, JAMS.
WHAT?
HEY!
HEY! LET HIM GO!
I'M SORRY!
I WON'T STEAL ANY MORE BERRIES I SWEAR!!
RR!
OF COURSE YOU WON'T. THEY'VE ALL BEEN BURNT.
HEY! PSYCHOPATH! ENOUGH ALREADY!
DAMN RIGHT IT'S ENOUGH! SOME LESSONS NEED TO BE LEARNED HERE.
NO NONO NONONO NONO
THUNK

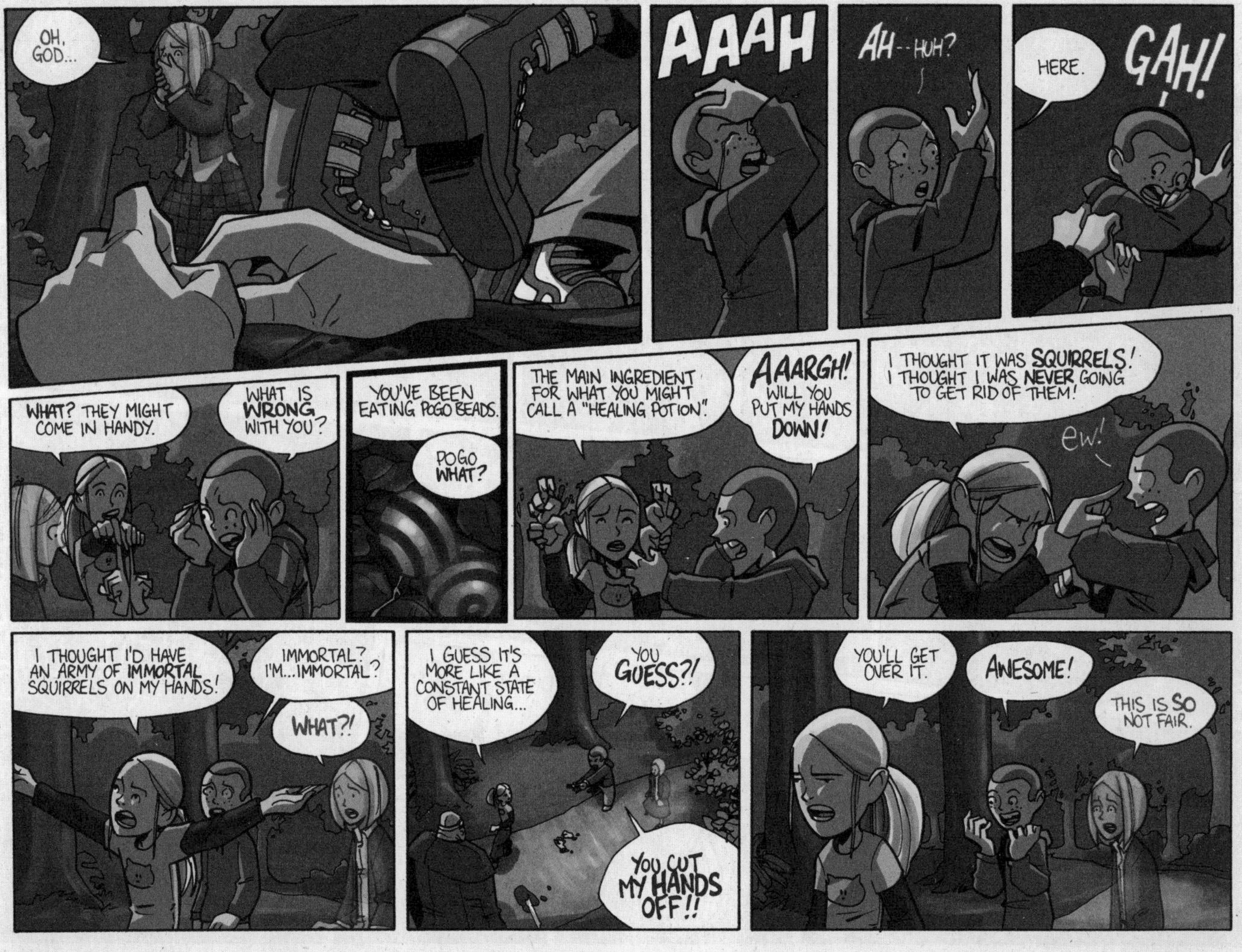
OH, GOD...
AAAH
AH--HUH?
HERE.
GAH!
WHAT? THEY MIGHT COME IN HANDY.
WHAT IS WRONG WITH YOU?
YOU'VE BEEN EATING POGO BEADS.
POGO WHAT?
THE MAIN INGREDIENT FOR WHAT YOU MIGHT CALL A "HEALING POTION".
AAARGH! WILL YOU PUT MY HANDS DOWN!
I THOUGHT IT WAS SQUIRRELS! I THOUGHT I WAS NEVER GOING TO GET RID OF THEM!
EW!
I THOUGHT I'D HAVE AN ARMY OF IMMORTAL SQUIRRELS ON MY HANDS!
IMMORTAL? I'M...IMMORTAL?
WHAT?!
I GUESS IT'S MORE LIKE A CONSTANT STATE OF HEALING...
YOU GUESS?!
YOU CUT MY HANDS OFF!!
YOU'LL GET OVER IT.
AWESOME!
THIS IS SO NOT FAIR.

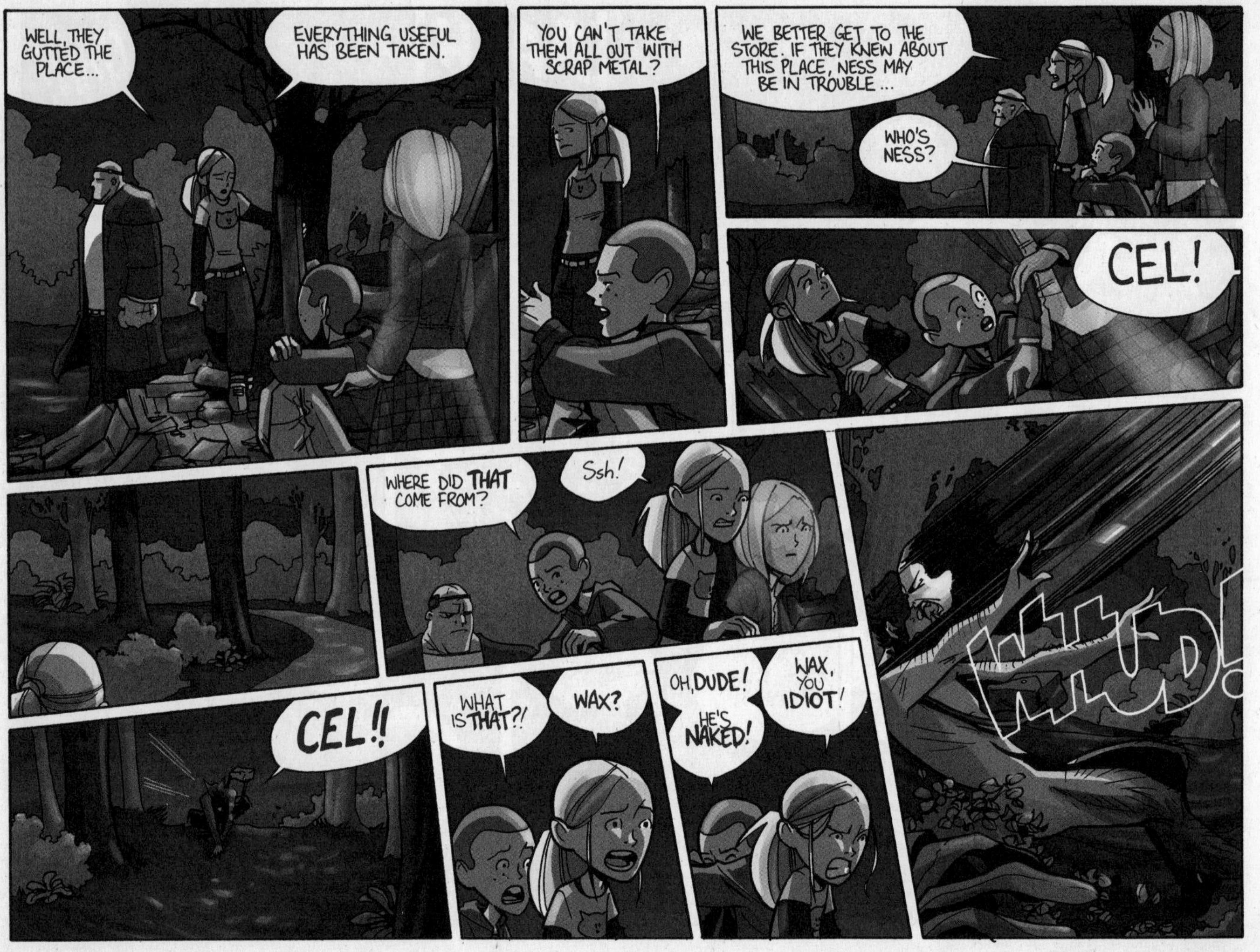
WELL, THEY GUTTED THE PLACE...
EVERYTHING USEFUL HAS BEEN TAKEN.
YOU CAN'T TAKE THEM ALL OUT WITH SCRAP METAL?
WE BETTER GET TO THE STORE. IF THEY KNEW ABOUT THIS PLACE, NESS MAY BE IN TROUBLE ...
WHO'S NESS?
CEL!
WHERE DID THAT COME FROM?
Ssh!
CEL!!
WHAT IS THAT?!
WAX?
OH, DUDE!
HE'S NAKED!
WAX, YOU IDIOT!
WHUD!

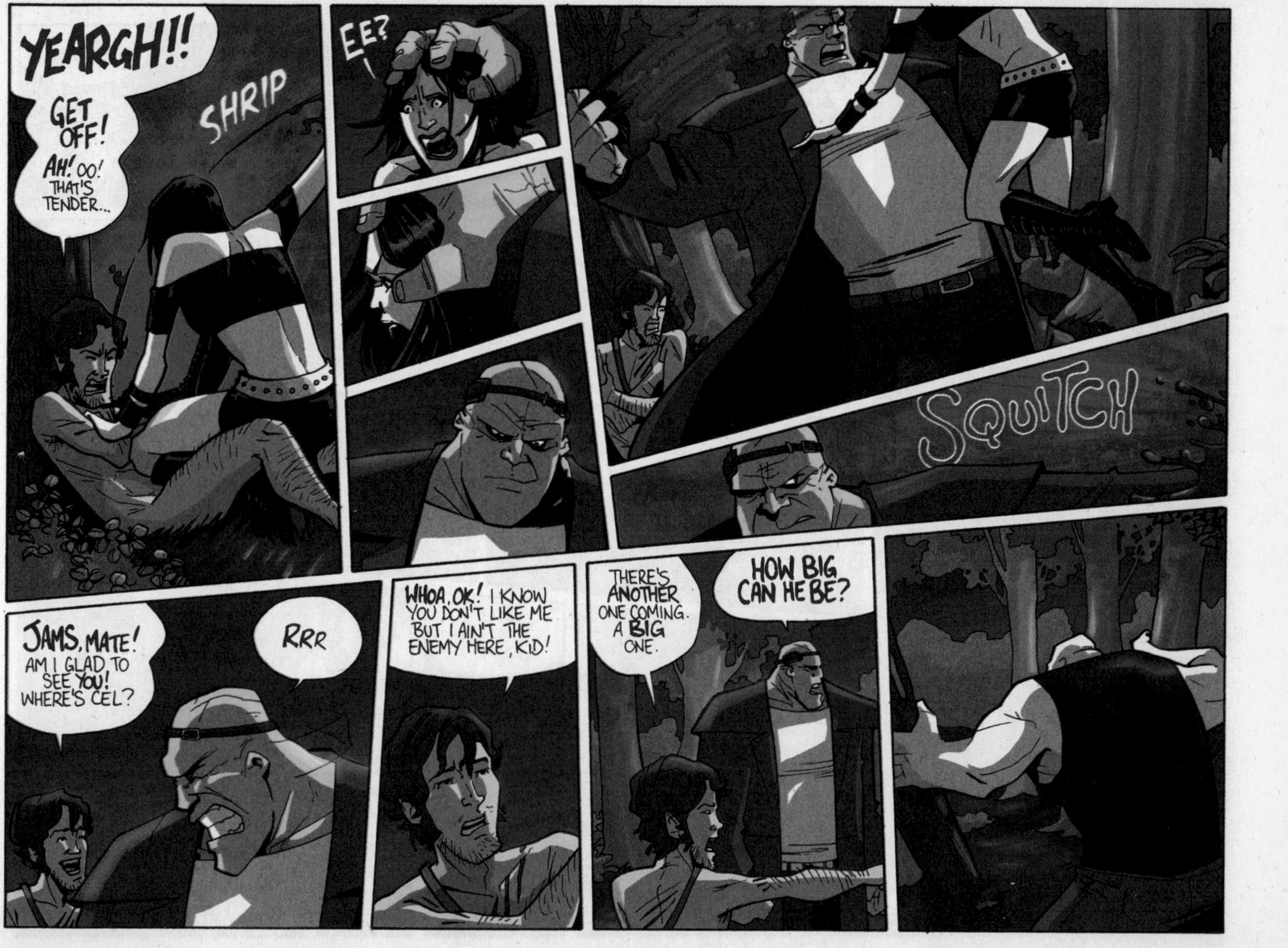
YEARGH!!
GET OFF!
AH! OO! THAT'S TENDER...
SHRIP
EE?
SQUITCH
JAMS, MATE! AM I GLAD TO SEE YOU! WHERE'S CEL?
RRR
WHOA, OK! I KNOW YOU DON'T LIKE ME BUT I AIN'T THE ENEMY HERE, KID!
THERE'S ANOTHER ONE COMING. A BIG ONE.
HOW BIG CAN HE BE?

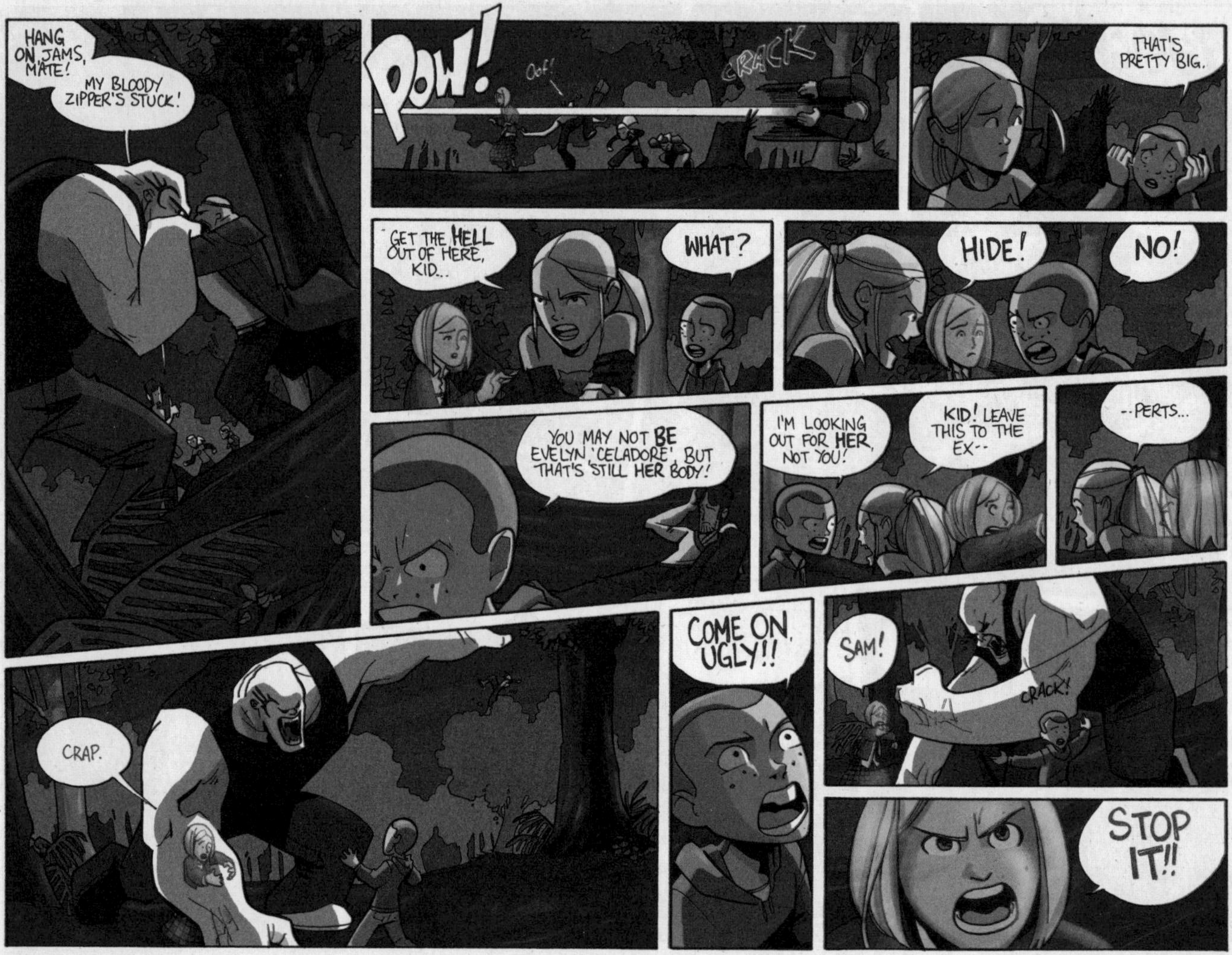
HANG ON JAMS, MATE!
MY BLOODY ZIPPER'S STUCK!
POW!
Oof!
CRACK
THAT'S PRETTY BIG.
GET THE HELL OUT OF HERE, KID...
WHAT?
HIDE!
NO!
YOU MAY NOT BE EVELYN 'CELADORE', BUT THAT'S STILL HER BODY!
I'M LOOKING OUT FOR HER, NOT YOU!
KID! LEAVE THIS TO THE EX--
--PERTS...
CRAP.
COME ON, UGLY!!
SAM!
CRACK!
STOP IT!!

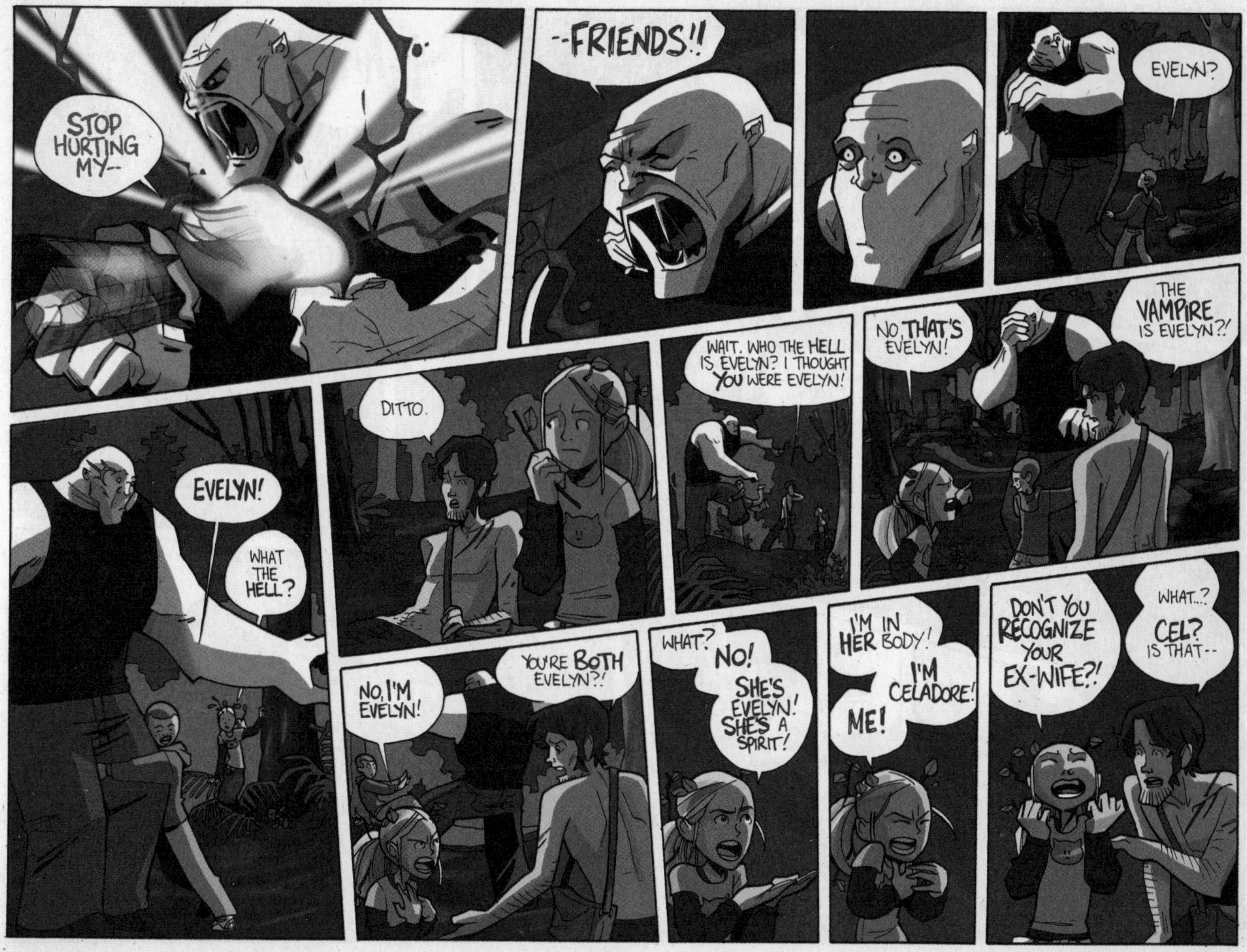
STOP HURTING MY--
--FRIENDS!!
EVELYN?
THE VAMPIRE IS EVELYN?!
NO, THAT'S EVELYN!
WAIT. WHO THE HELL IS EVELYN? I THOUGHT YOU WERE EVELYN!
DITTO.
EVELYN!
WHAT THE HELL?
YOU'RE BOTH EVELYN?!
NO, I'M EVELYN!
WHAT? NO!
SHE'S EVELYN! SHE'S A SPIRIT!
I'M IN HER BODY!
I'M CELADORE!
ME!
WHAT...?
CEL? IS THAT--
DON'T YOU RECOGNIZE YOUR EX-WIFE?!

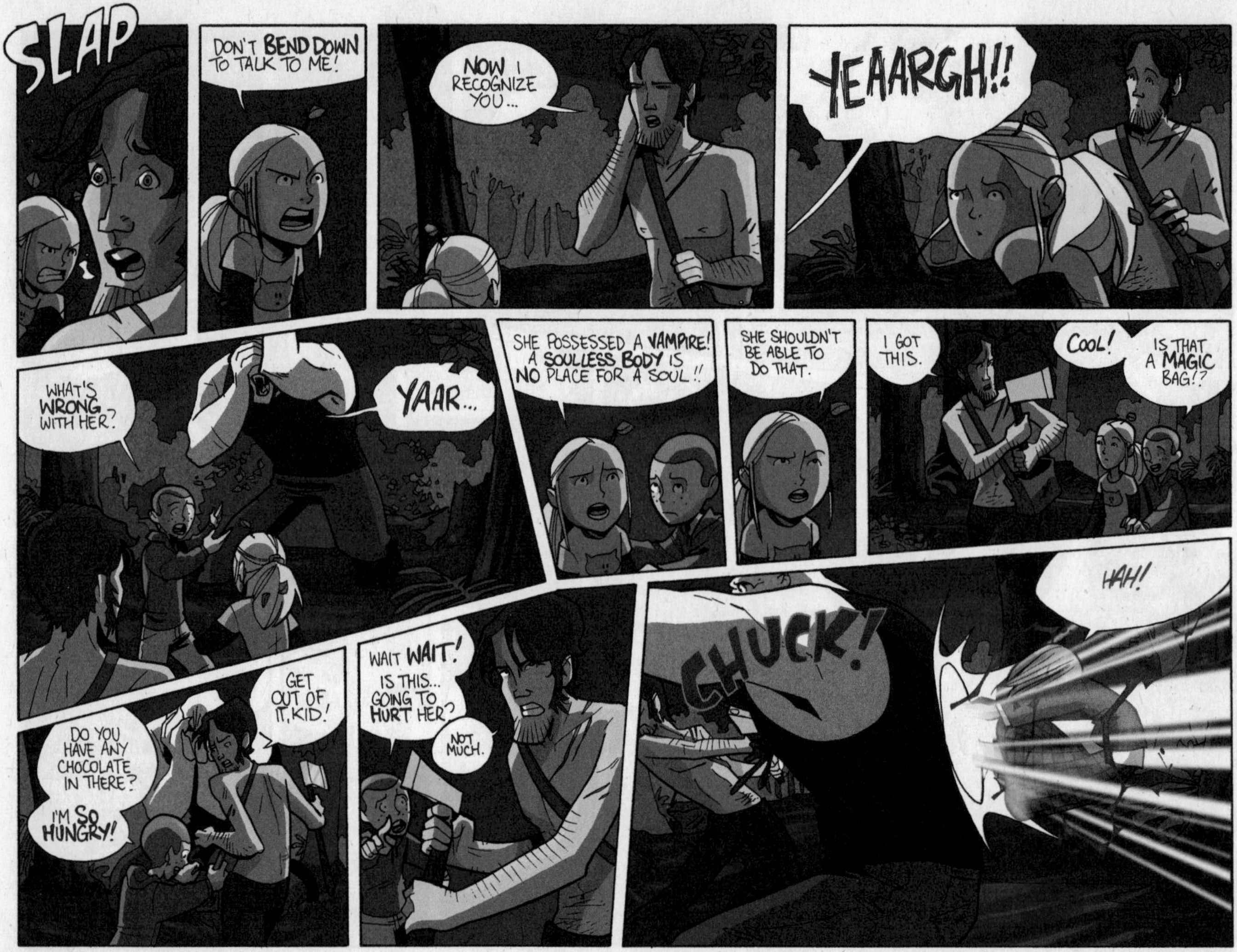
SLAP
DON'T BEND DOWN TO TALK TO ME!
NOW I RECOGNIZE YOU...
YEAARGH!!
WHAT'S WRONG WITH HER?
YAAR...
SHE POSSESSED A VAMPIRE! A SOULLESS BODY IS NO PLACE FOR A SOUL!!
SHE SHOULDN'T BE ABLE TO DO THAT.
I GOT THIS.
COOL!
IS THAT A MAGIC BAG!?
DO YOU HAVE ANY CHOCOLATE IN THERE?
I'M SO HUNGRY!
GET OUT OF IT, KID!
WAIT WAIT! IS THIS... GOING TO HURT HER?
NOT MUCH.
CHUCK!
HAH!

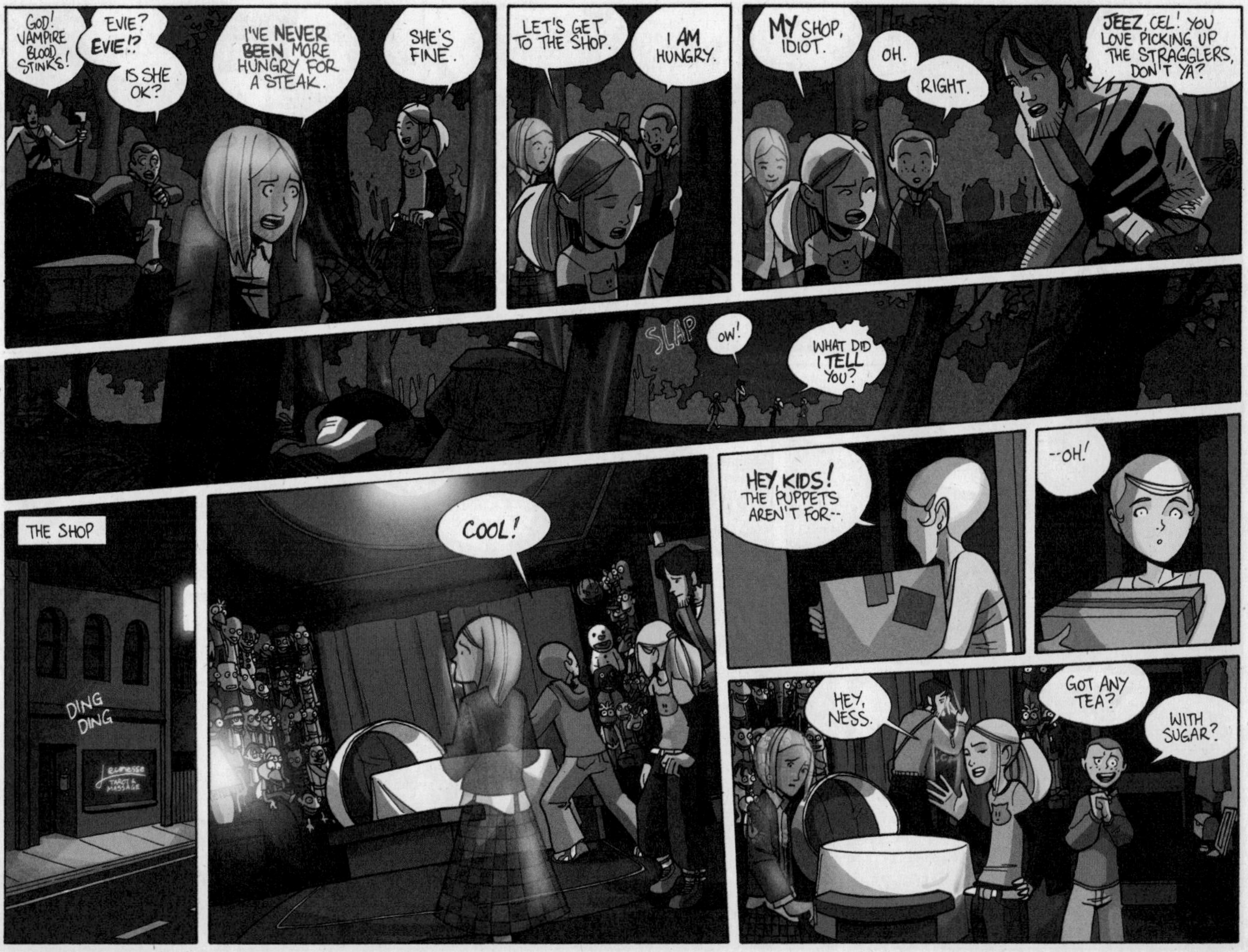
GOD! VAMPIRE BLOOD STINKS!
EVIE? EVIE!?
IS SHE OK?
I'VE NEVER BEEN MORE HUNGRY FOR A STEAK.
SHE'S FINE.
LET'S GET TO THE SHOP.
I AM HUNGRY.
MY SHOP, IDIOT.
OH.
RIGHT.
JEEZ, CEL! YOU LOVE PICKING UP THE STRAGGLERS, DON'T YA?
SLAP
OW!
WHAT DID I TELL YOU?
THE SHOP
DING DING
COOL!
HEY, KIDS! THE PUPPETS AREN'T FOR--
--OH!
HEY, NESS.
GOT ANY TEA?
WITH SUGAR?

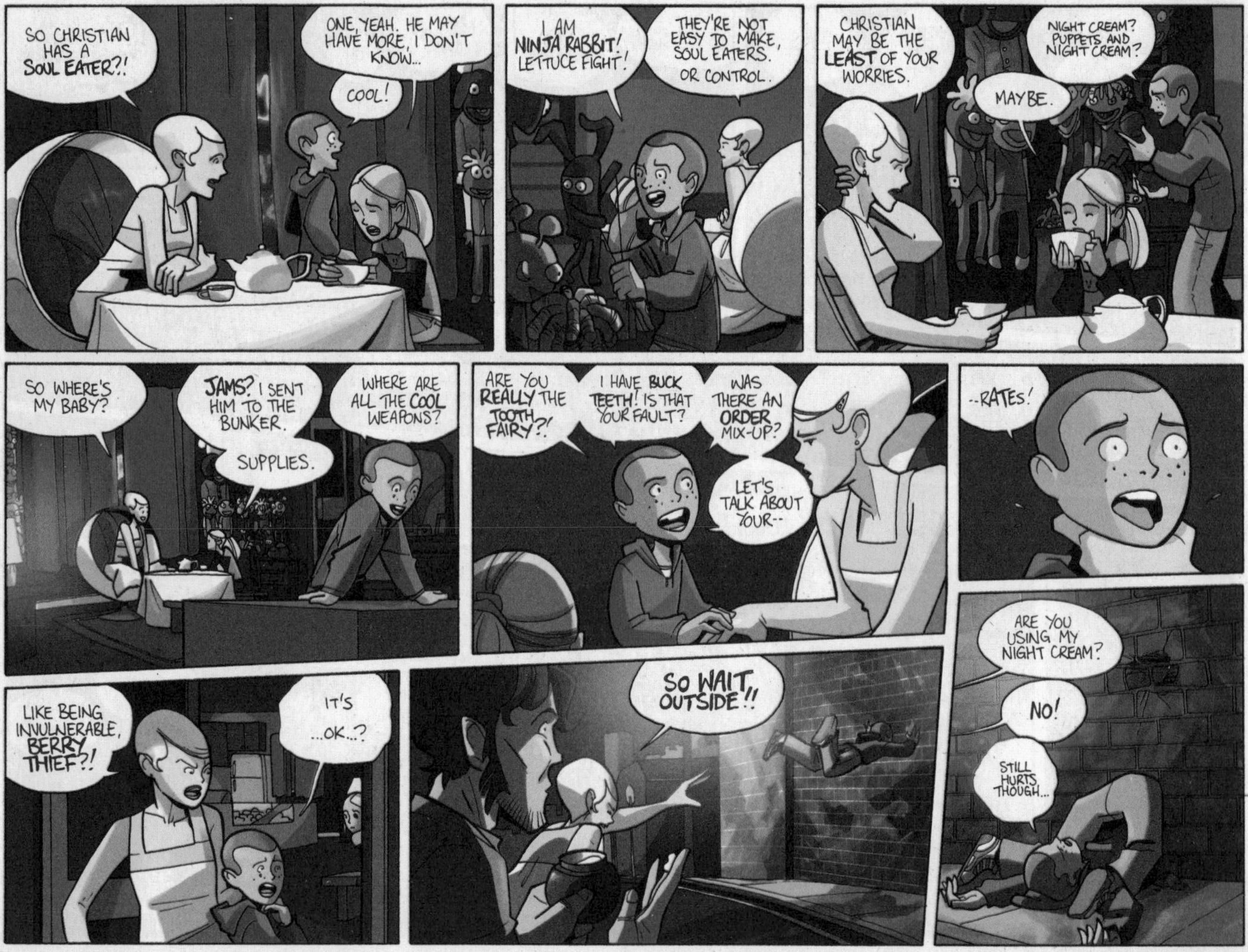

SO CHRISTIAN HAS A SOUL EATER?!
ONE, YEAH. HE MAY HAVE MORE, I DON'T KNOW...
COOL!
I AM NINJA RABBIT! LETTUCE FIGHT!
THEY'RE NOT EASY TO MAKE, SOUL EATERS.
OR CONTROL.
CHRISTIAN MAY BE THE LEAST OF YOUR WORRIES.
NIGHT CREAM? PUPPETS AND NIGHT CREAM?
MAYBE.
SO WHERE'S MY BABY?
JAMS? I SENT HIM TO THE BUNKER.
SUPPLIES.
WHERE ARE ALL THE COOL WEAPONS?
ARE YOU REALLY THE TOOTH FAIRY?!
I HAVE BUCK TEETH! IS THAT YOUR FAULT?
WAS THERE AN ORDER MIX-UP?
LET'S TALK ABOUT YOUR--
--RATES!
LIKE BEING INVULNERABLE, BERRY THIEF?!
IT'S ...OK..?
SO WAIT OUTSIDE!!
ARE YOU USING MY NIGHT CREAM?
NO!
STILL HURTS THOUGH...

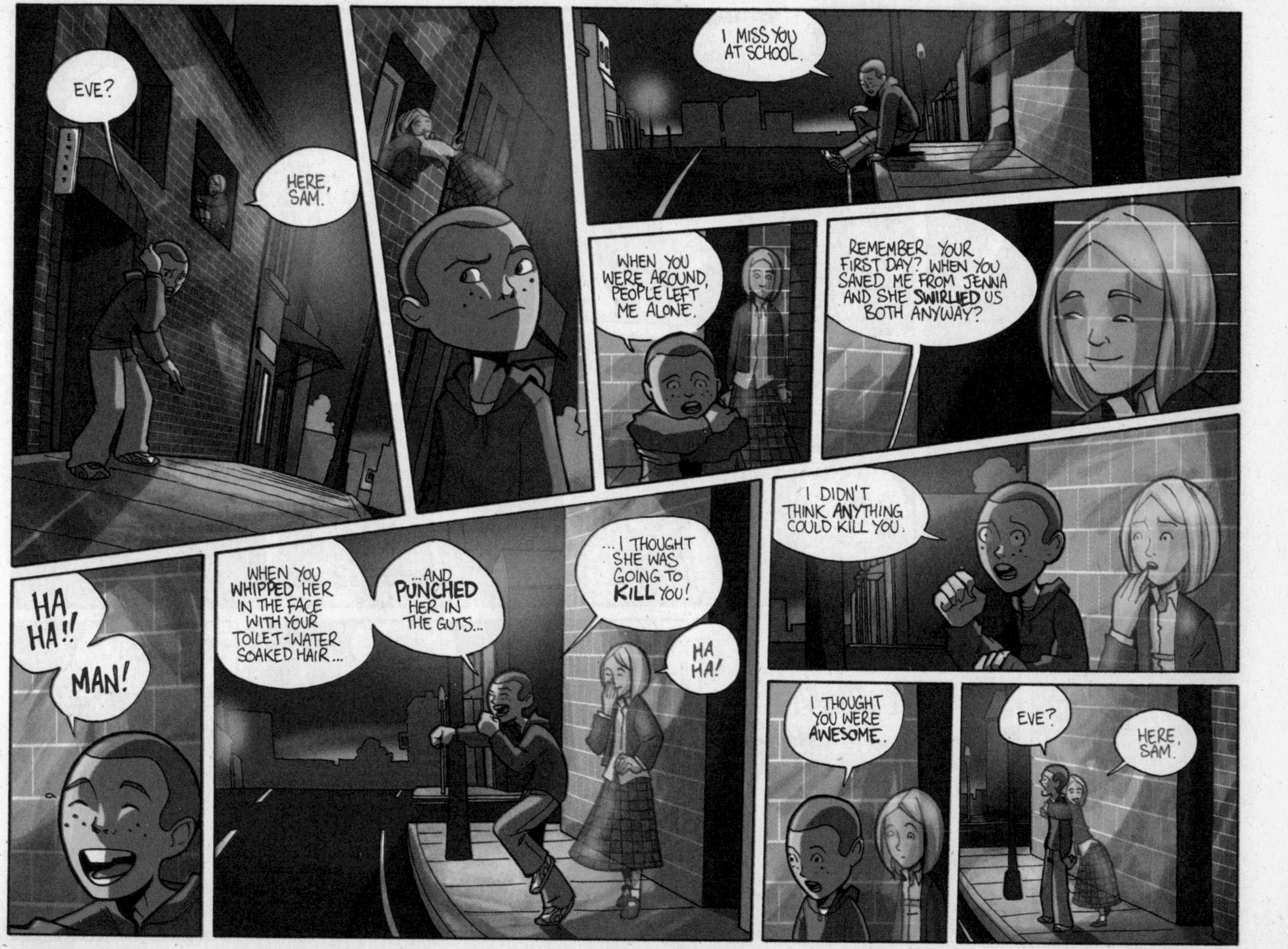
EVE?
HERE, SAM.
I MISS YOU AT SCHOOL.
WHEN YOU WERE AROUND, PEOPLE LEFT ME ALONE.
REMEMBER YOUR FIRST DAY? WHEN YOU SAVED ME FROM JENNA AND SHE SWIRLIED US BOTH ANYWAY?
HA HA!!
MAN!
WHEN YOU WHIPPED HER IN THE FACE WITH YOUR TOILET-WATER SOAKED HAIR...
...AND PUNCHED HER IN THE GUTS...
...I THOUGHT SHE WAS GOING TO KILL YOU!
HA HA!
I DIDN'T THINK ANYTHING COULD KILL YOU.
I THOUGHT YOU WERE AWESOME.
EVE?
HERE, SAM.

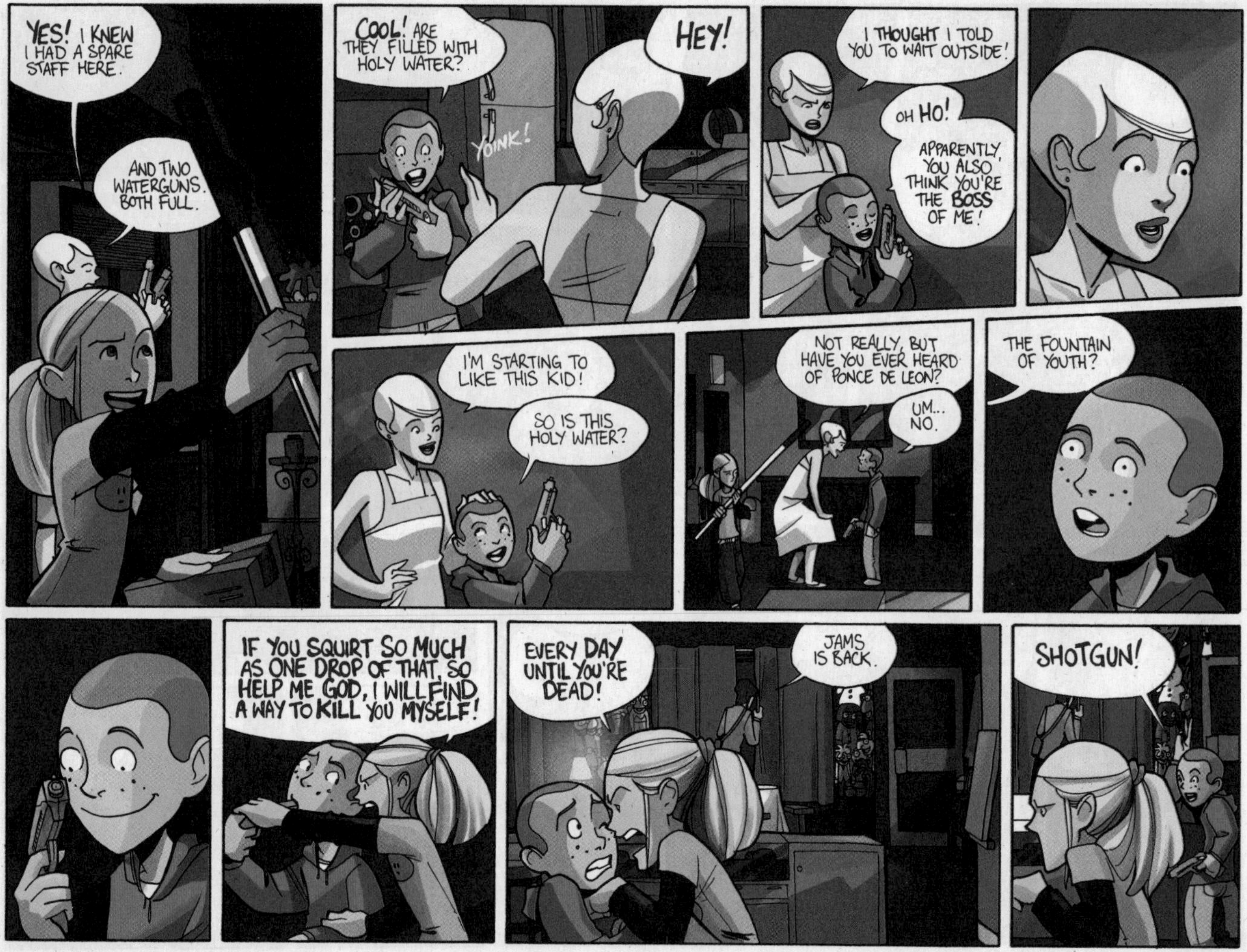

YES! I KNEW I HAD A SPARE STAFF HERE.
AND TWO WATERGUNS. BOTH FULL.
COOL! ARE THEY FILLED WITH HOLY WATER?
YOINK!
HEY!
I THOUGHT I TOLD YOU TO WAIT OUTSIDE!
OH HO!
APPARENTLY, YOU ALSO THINK YOU'RE THE BOSS OF ME!
I'M STARTING TO LIKE THIS KID!
SO IS THIS HOLY WATER?
NOT REALLY, BUT HAVE YOU EVER HEARD OF PONCE DE LEON?
UM... NO.
THE FOUNTAIN OF YOUTH?
IF YOU SQUIRT SO MUCH AS ONE DROP OF THAT, SO HELP ME GOD, I WILL FIND A WAY TO KILL YOU MYSELF!
EVERY DAY UNTIL YOU'RE DEAD!
JAMS IS BACK.
SHOTGUN!

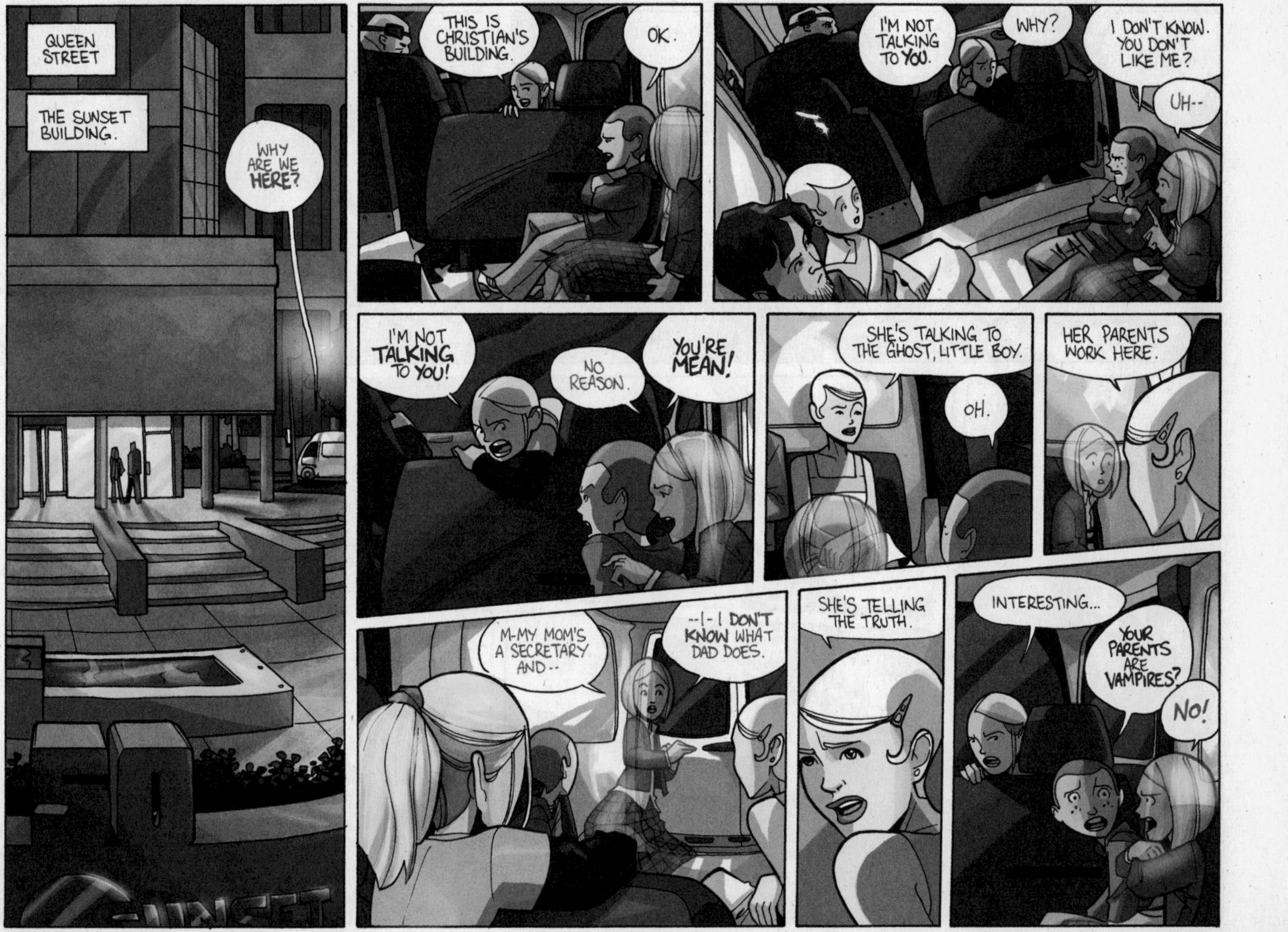
QUEEN STREET
THE SUNSET BUILDING.
WHY ARE WE HERE?
THIS IS CHRISTIAN'S BUILDING.
OK.
I'M NOT TALKING TO YOU.
WHY?
I DON'T KNOW. YOU DON'T LIKE ME?
UH--
I'M NOT TALKING TO YOU!
NO REASON.
YOU'RE MEAN!
SHE'S TALKING TO THE GHOST, LITTLE BOY.
OH.
HER PARENTS WORK HERE.
M-MY MOM'S A SECRETARY AND--
--I-I DON'T KNOW WHAT DAD DOES.
SHE'S TELLING THE TRUTH.
INTERESTING...
YOUR PARENTS ARE VAMPIRES?
NO!

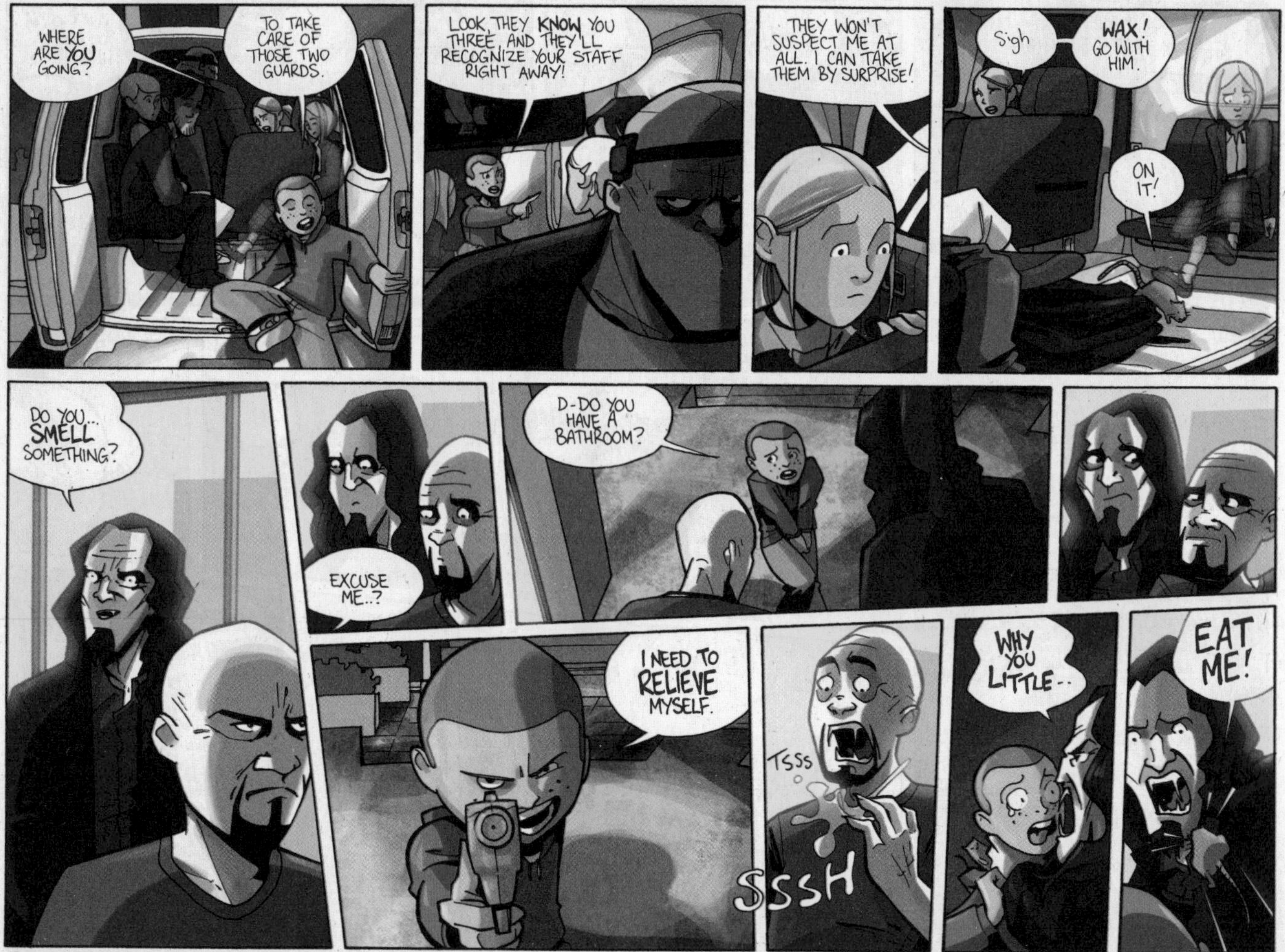
WHERE ARE YOU GOING?
TO TAKE CARE OF THOSE TWO GUARDS.
LOOK, THEY KNOW YOU THREE, AND THEY'LL RECOGNIZE YOUR STAFF RIGHT AWAY!
THEY WON'T SUSPECT ME AT ALL. I CAN TAKE THEM BY SURPRISE!
Sigh
WAX! GO WITH HIM.
ON IT!
DO YOU... SMELL SOMETHING?
EXCUSE ME..?
D-DO YOU HAVE A BATHROOM?
I NEED TO RELIEVE MYSELF.
TSSS
SSSH
WHY YOU LITTLE..
EAT ME!

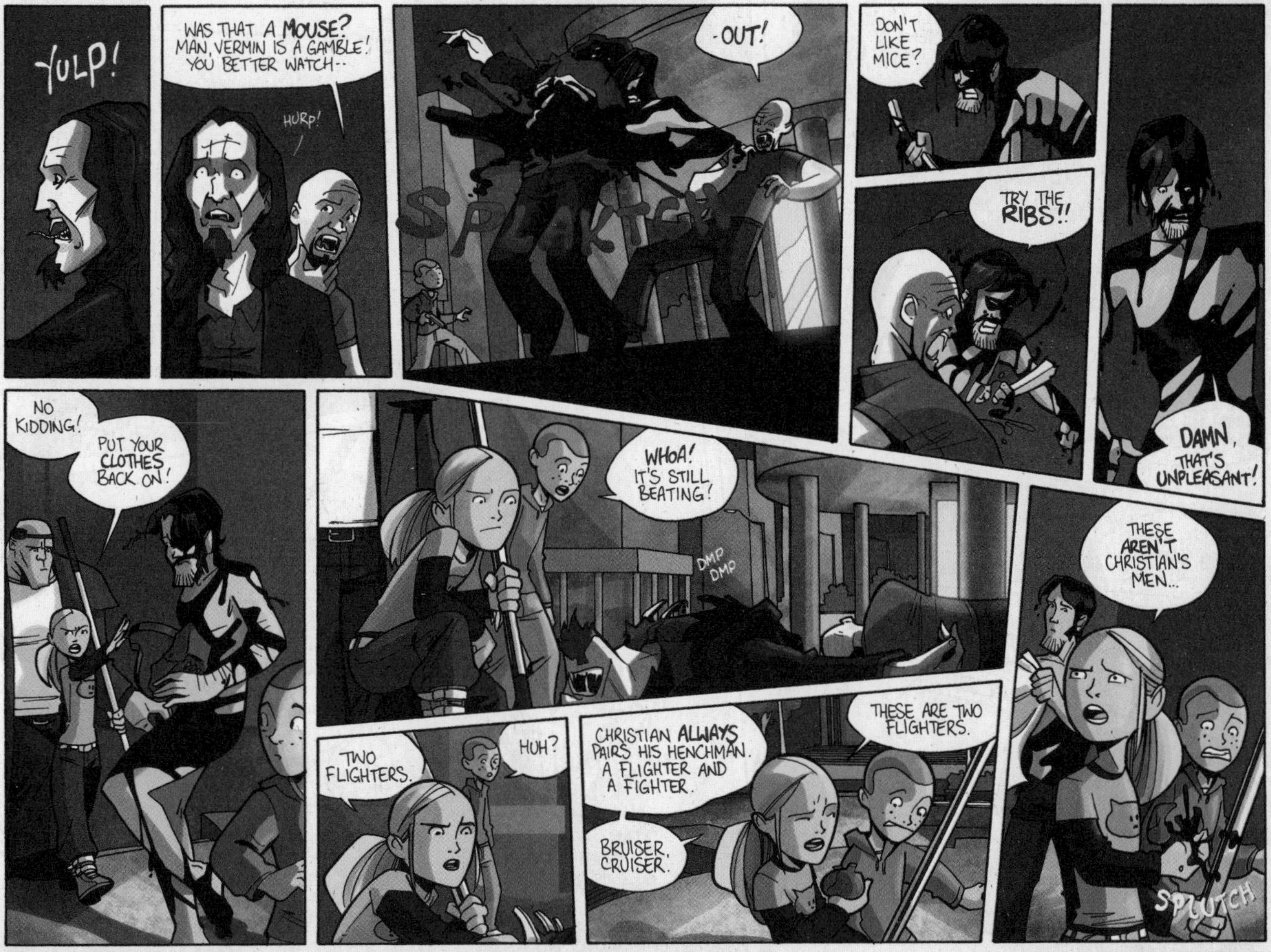
YULP!
WAS THAT A MOUSE? MAN, VERMIN IS A GAMBLE! YOU BETTER WATCH--
HURP!
-OUT!
SPLAKTCH
DON'T LIKE MICE?
TRY THE RIBS!!
DAMN, THAT'S UNPLEASANT!
NO KIDDING!
PUT YOUR CLOTHES BACK ON!
WHOA! IT'S STILL BEATING!
DMP DMP
THESE AREN'T CHRISTIAN'S MEN...
TWO FLIGHTERS.
HUH?
CHRISTIAN ALWAYS PAIRS HIS HENCHMAN. A FLIGHTER AND A FIGHTER.
BRUISER, CRUISER.
THESE ARE TWO FLIGHTERS.
SPLUTCH

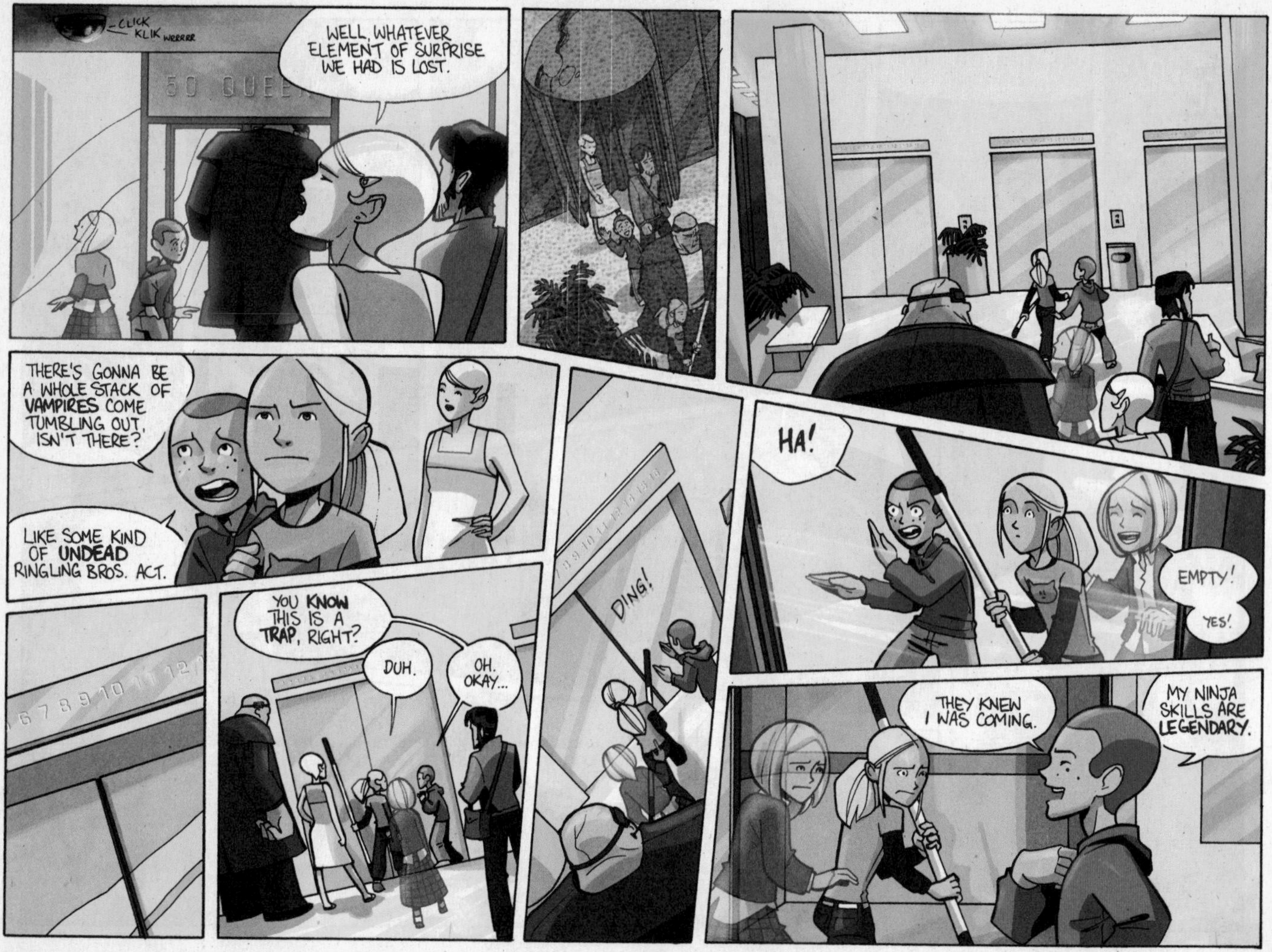
CLICK
KLIK
WRRRRR
50 QUEEN
WELL, WHATEVER ELEMENT OF SURPRISE WE HAD IS LOST.
THERE'S GONNA BE A WHOLE STACK OF VAMPIRES COME TUMBLING OUT, ISN'T THERE?
LIKE SOME KIND OF UNDEAD RINGLING BROS. ACT.
YOU KNOW THIS IS A TRAP, RIGHT?
DUH.
OH. OKAY...
DING!
HA!
EMPTY!
YES!
THEY KNEW I WAS COMING.
MY NINJA SKILLS ARE LEGENDARY.

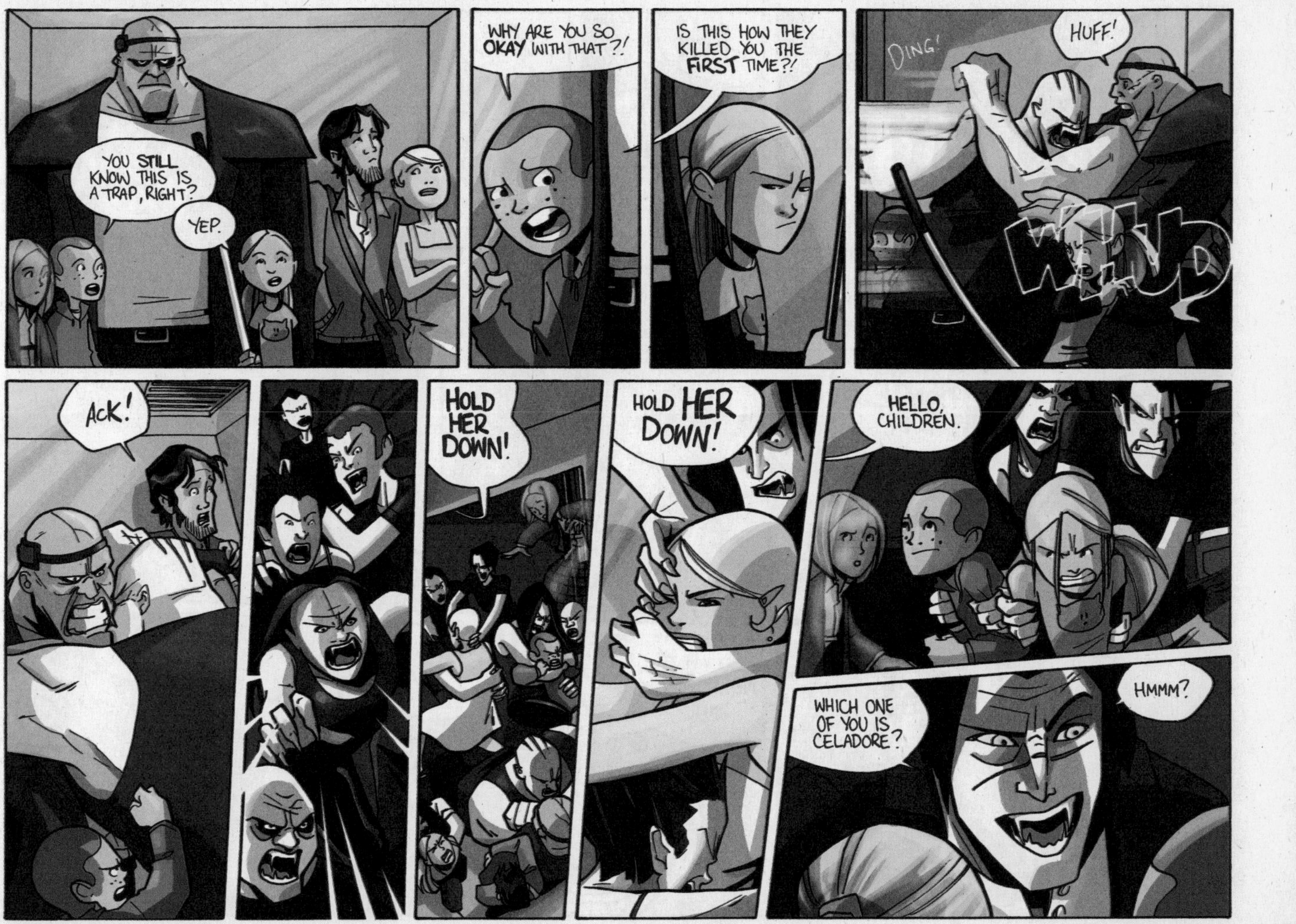
YOU STILL KNOW THIS IS A TRAP, RIGHT?
YEP.
WHY ARE YOU SO OKAY WITH THAT?!
IS THIS HOW THEY KILLED YOU THE FIRST TIME?!
DING!
HUFF!
WHUD
ACK!
HOLD HER DOWN!
HOLD HER DOWN!
HELLO, CHILDREN.
WHICH ONE OF YOU IS CELADORE?
HMMM?

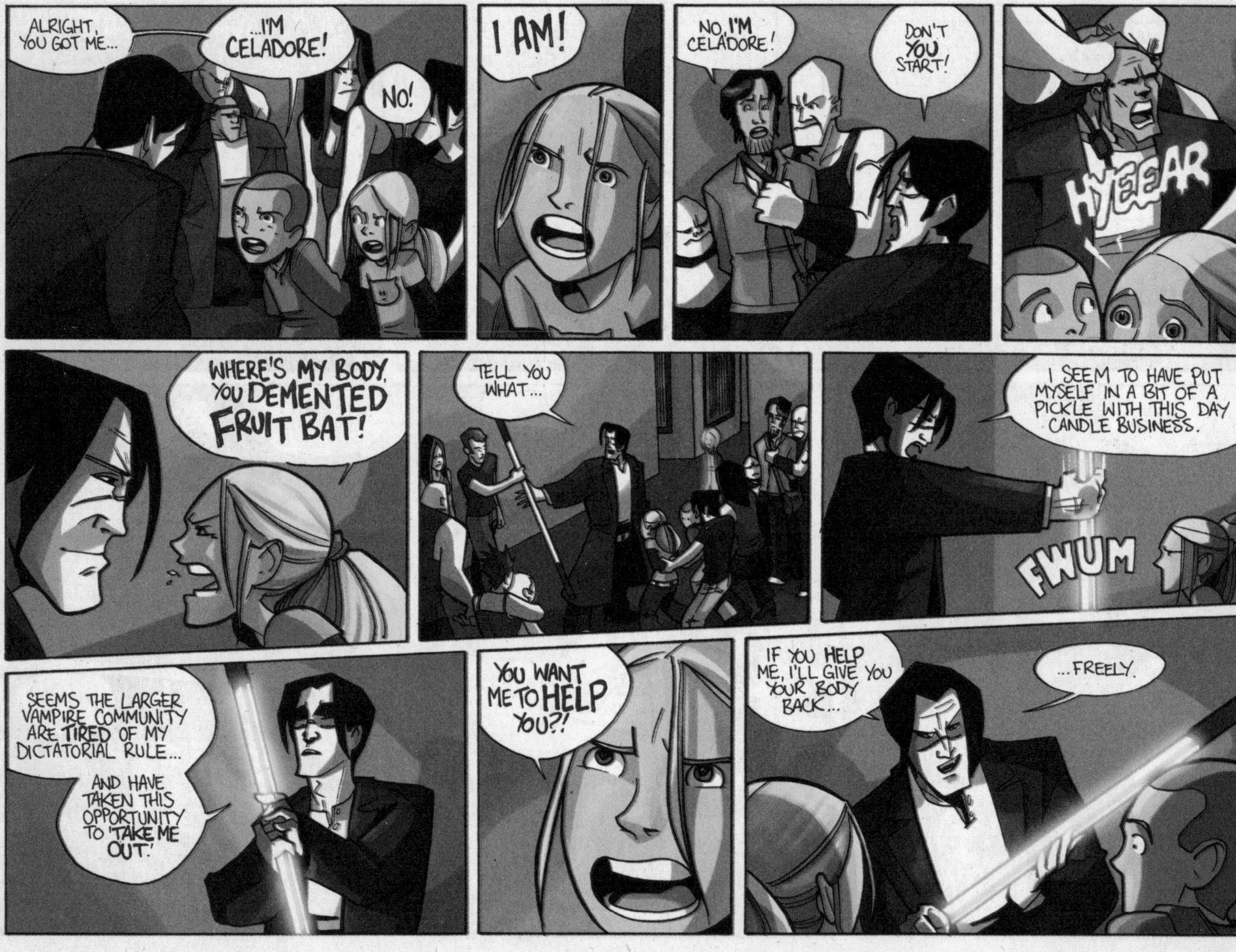
ALRIGHT, YOU GOT ME...
...I'M CELADORE!
NO!
I AM!
NO, I'M CELADORE!
DON'T YOU START!
HYEEAR
WHERE'S MY BODY, YOU DEMENTED FRUIT BAT!
TELL YOU WHAT...
I SEEM TO HAVE PUT MYSELF IN A BIT OF A PICKLE WITH THIS DAY CANDLE BUSINESS.
FWUM
SEEMS THE LARGER VAMPIRE COMMUNITY ARE TIRED OF MY DICTATORIAL RULE...
AND HAVE TAKEN THIS OPPORTUNITY TO 'TAKE ME OUT.'
YOU WANT ME TO HELP YOU?!
IF YOU HELP ME, I'LL GIVE YOU YOUR BODY BACK...
...FREELY.

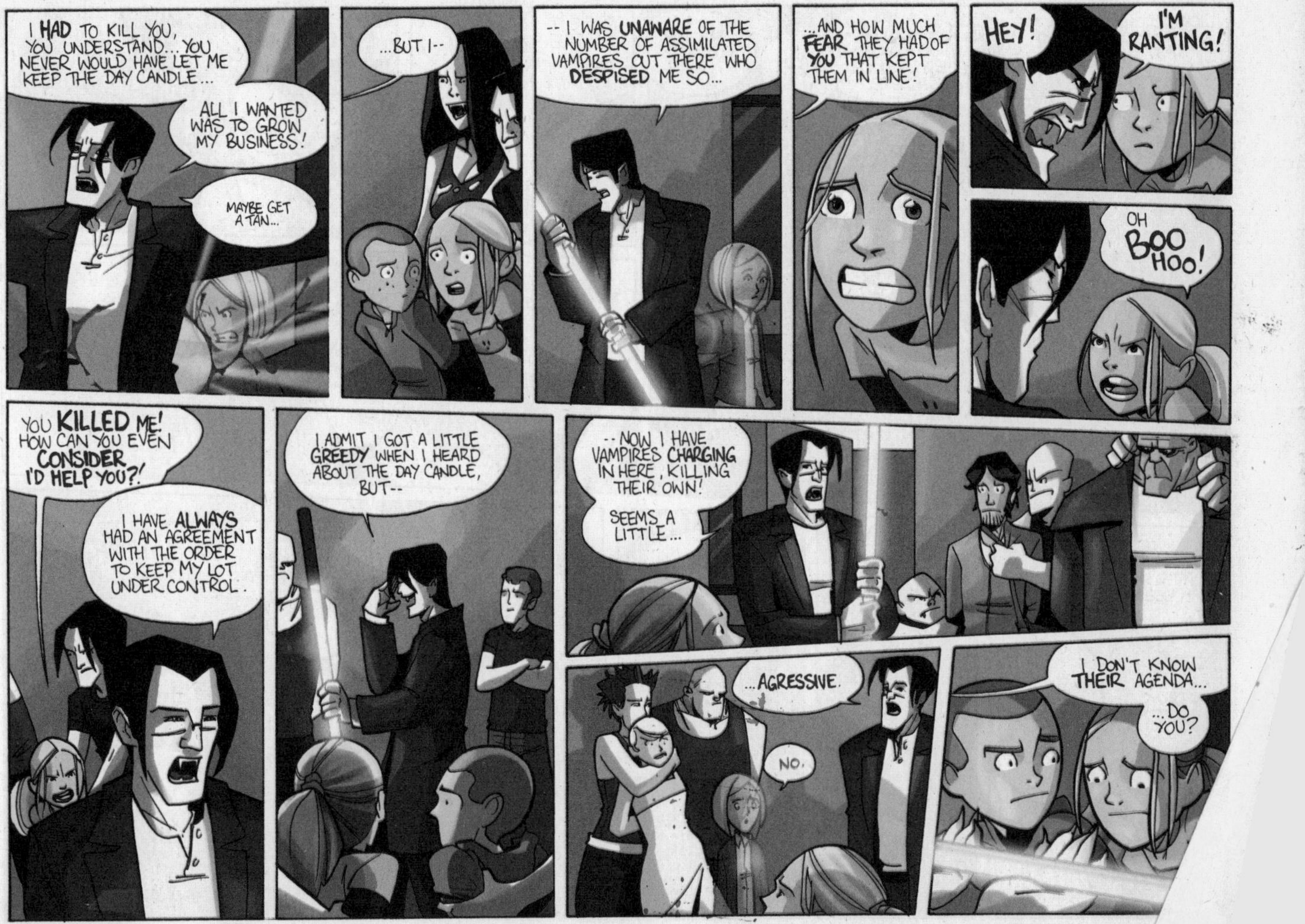

I HAD TO KILL YOU, YOU UNDERSTAND... YOU NEVER WOULD HAVE LET ME KEEP THE DAY CANDLE...
ALL I WANTED WAS TO GROW MY BUSINESS!
MAYBE GET A TAN...
...BUT I--
-- I WAS UNAWARE OF THE NUMBER OF ASSIMILATED VAMPIRES OUT THERE WHO DESPISED ME SO...
...AND HOW MUCH FEAR THEY HAD OF YOU THAT KEPT THEM IN LINE!
HEY!
I'M RANTING!
OH BOO HOO!
YOU KILLED ME! HOW CAN YOU EVEN CONSIDER I'D HELP YOU?!
I HAVE ALWAYS HAD AN AGREEMENT WITH THE ORDER TO KEEP MY LOT UNDER CONTROL.
I ADMIT I GOT A LITTLE GREEDY WHEN I HEARD ABOUT THE DAY CANDLE, BUT--
-- NOW I HAVE VAMPIRES CHARGING IN HERE, KILLING THEIR OWN!
SEEMS A LITTLE...
...AGRESSIVE.
NO.
I DON'T KNOW THEIR AGENDA...
...DO YOU?

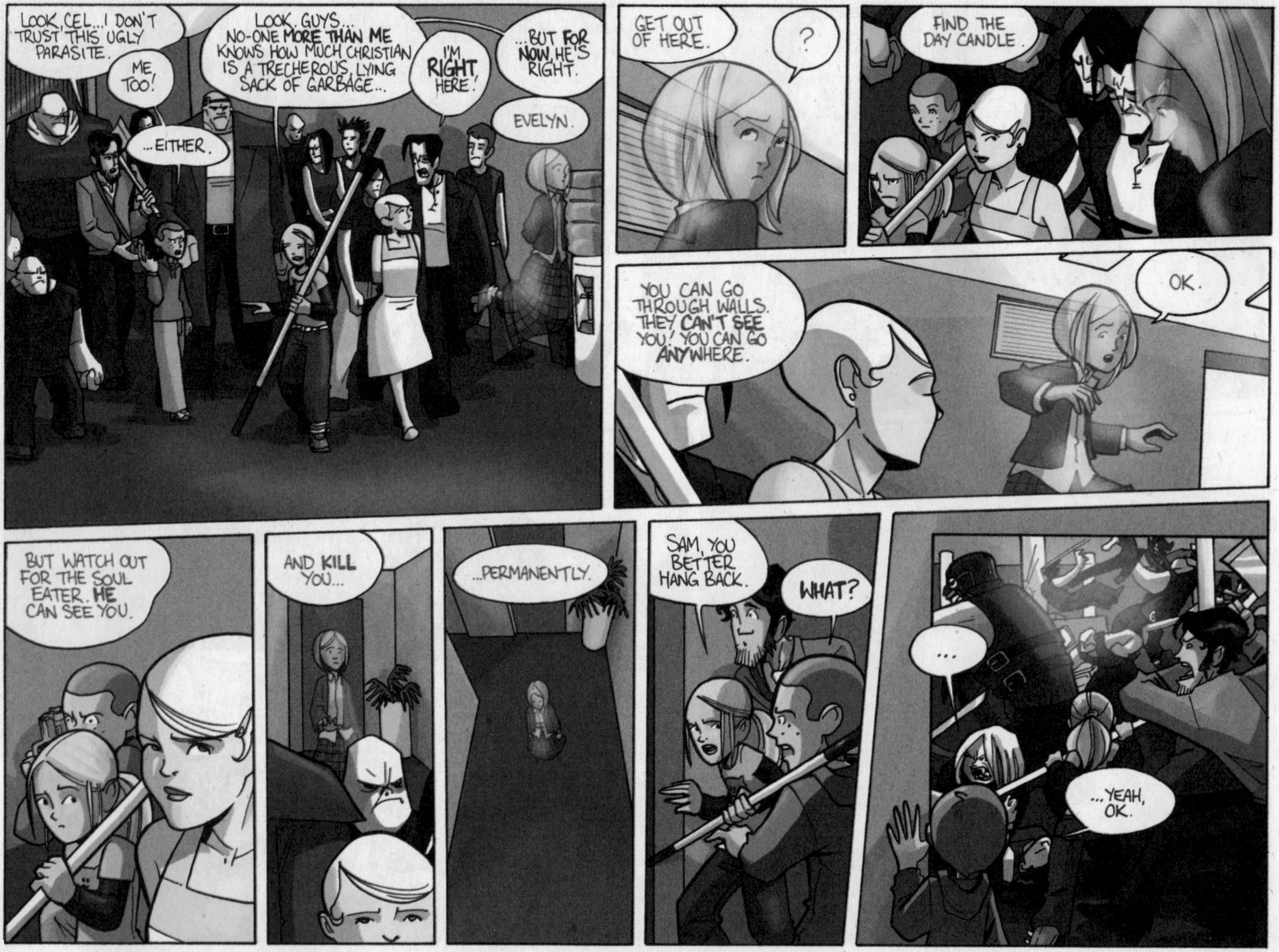
LOOK, CEL... I DON'T TRUST THIS UGLY PARASITE.
ME TOO!
...EITHER.
LOOK, GUYS... NO-ONE MORE THAN ME KNOWS HOW MUCH CHRISTIAN IS A TRECHEROUS, LYING SACK OF GARBAGE...
I'M RIGHT HERE!
...BUT FOR NOW, HE'S RIGHT.
EVELYN.
GET OUT OF HERE.
?
FIND THE DAY CANDLE.
YOU CAN GO THROUGH WALLS. THEY CAN'T SEE YOU! YOU CAN GO ANYWHERE.
OK.
BUT WATCH OUT FOR THE SOUL EATER. HE CAN SEE YOU.
AND KILL YOU...
...PERMANENTLY.
SAM, YOU BETTER HANG BACK.
WHAT?
...
...YEAH, OK.

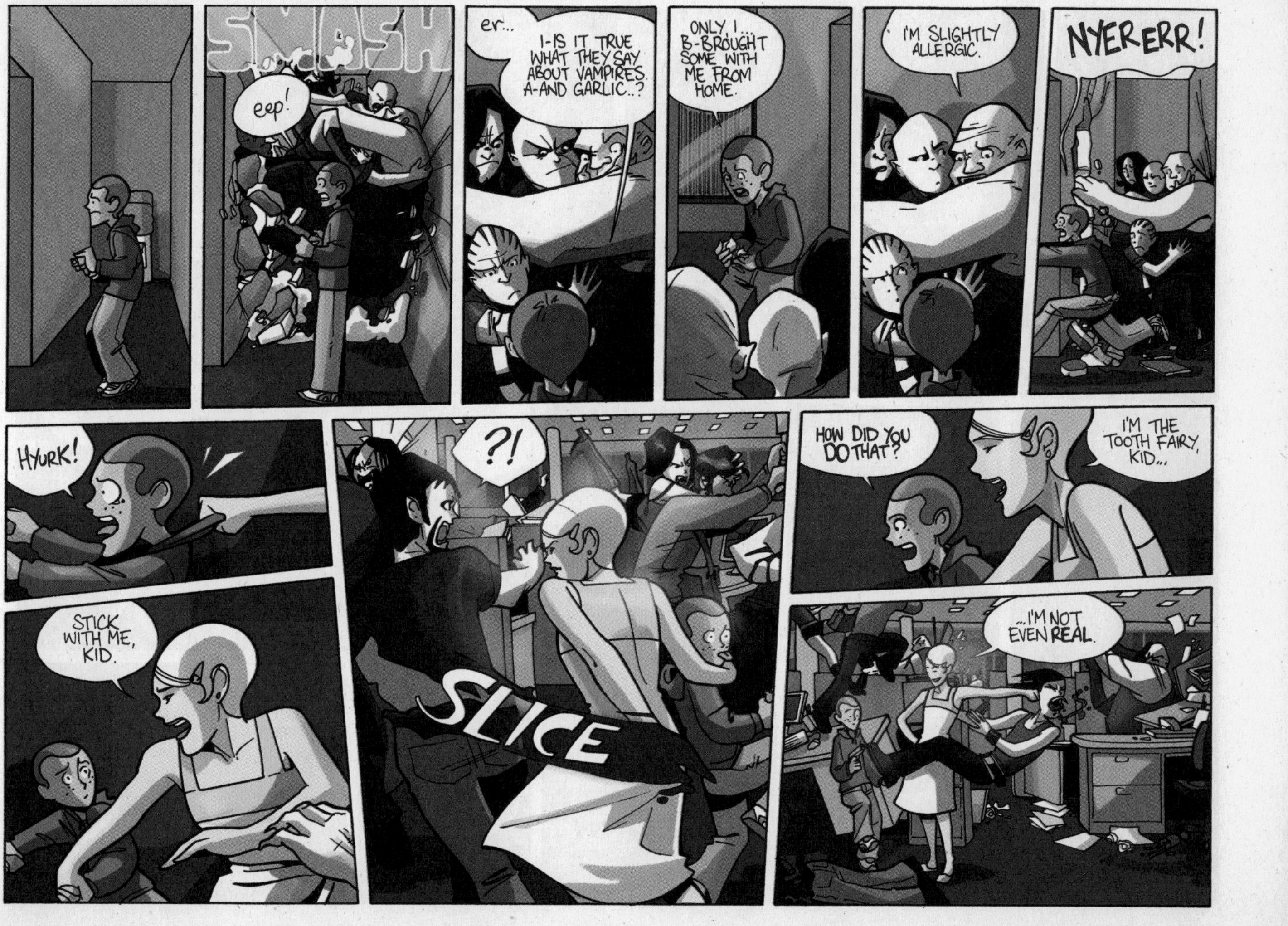
SMASH
eep!
er...
I-IS IT TRUE WHAT THEY SAY ABOUT VAMPIRES. A-AND GARLIC..?
ONLY I... B-BROUGHT SOME WITH ME FROM HOME.
I'M SLIGHTLY ALLERGIC.
NYERERR!
HYURK!
?!
SLICE
HOW DID YOU DO THAT?
I'M THE TOOTH FAIRY, KID...
STICK WITH ME, KID.
...I'M NOT EVEN REAL.

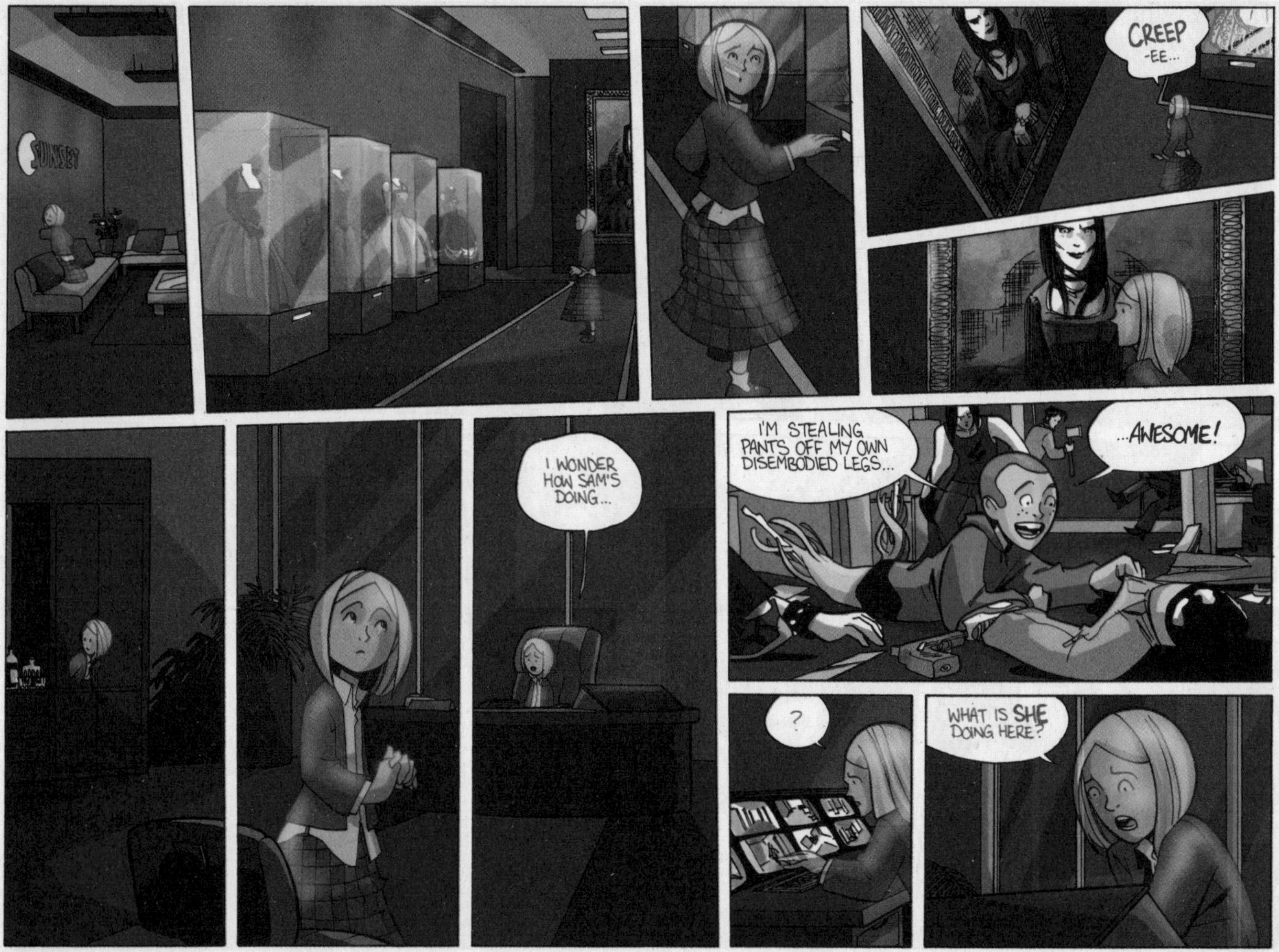
SUNSET
CREEP -EE...
I WONDER HOW SAM'S DOING...
I'M STEALING PANTS OFF MY OWN DISEMBODIED LEGS...
...AWESOME!
?
WHAT IS SHE DOING HERE?

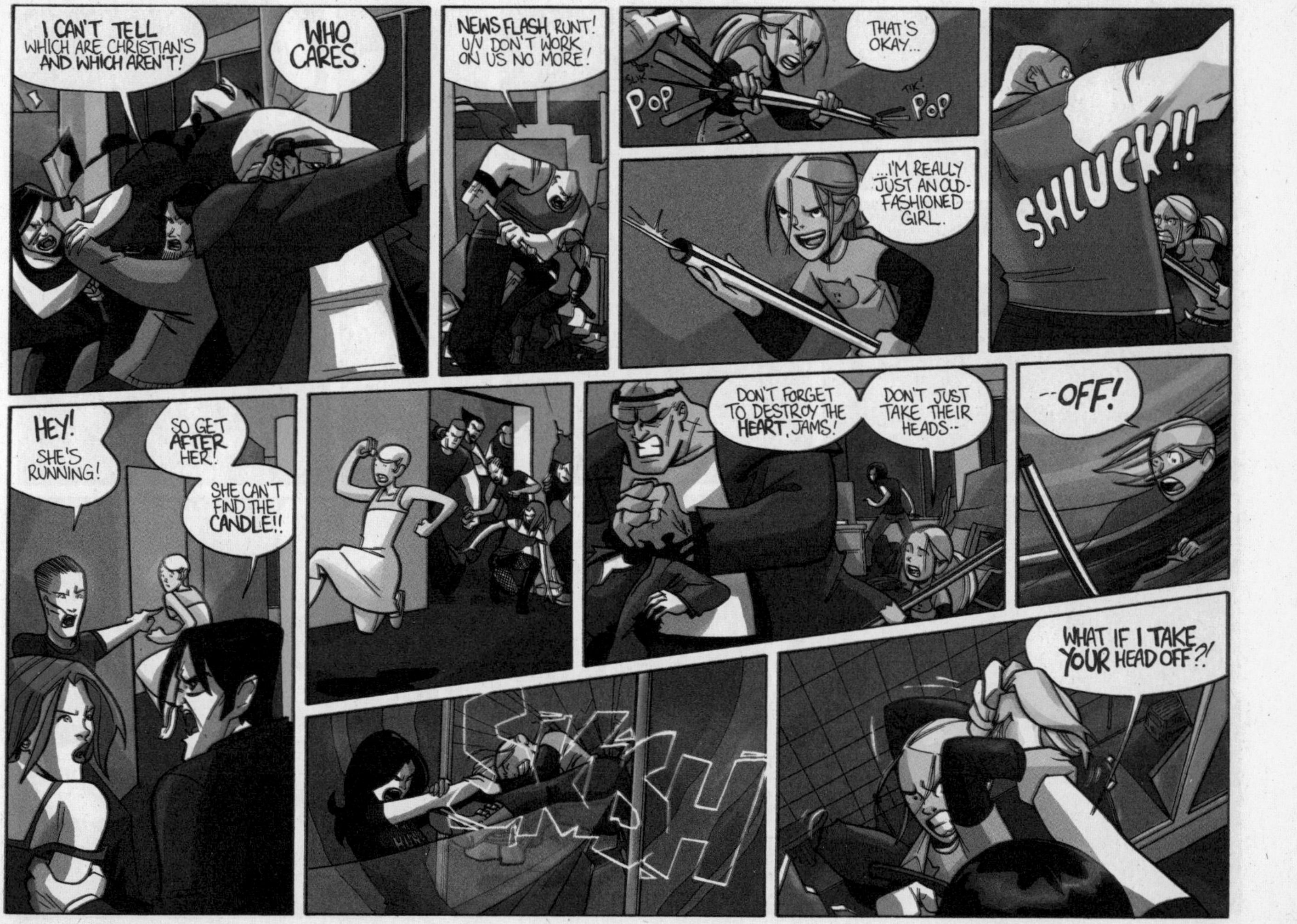

I CAN'T TELL WHICH ARE CHRISTIAN'S AND WHICH AREN'T!
WHO CARES.
NEWS FLASH, RUNT! U/V DON'T WORK ON US NO MORE!
THAT'S OKAY...
POP
POP
...I'M REALLY JUST AN OLD-FASHIONED GIRL.
SHLUCK!!
HEY! SHE'S RUNNING!
SO GET AFTER HER!
SHE CAN'T FIND THE CANDLE!!
DON'T FORGET TO DESTROY THE HEART, JAMS!
DON'T JUST TAKE THEIR HEADS--
--OFF!
WHAT IF I TAKE YOUR HEAD OFF?!

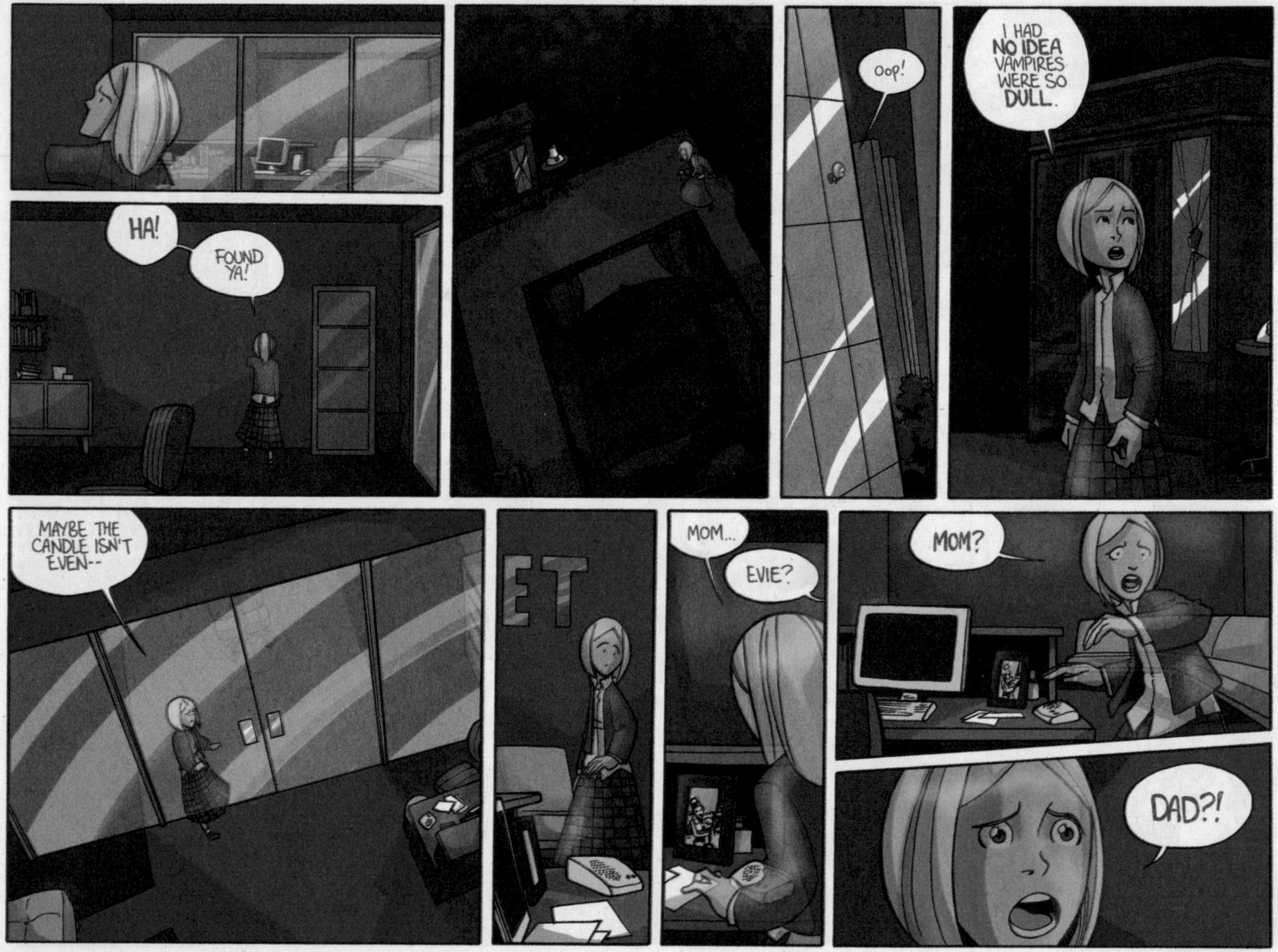
HA!
FOUND YA!
Oop!
I HAD NO IDEA VAMPIRES WERE SO DULL.
MAYBE THE CANDLE ISN'T EVEN--
ET
MOM...
EVIE?
MOM?
DAD?!

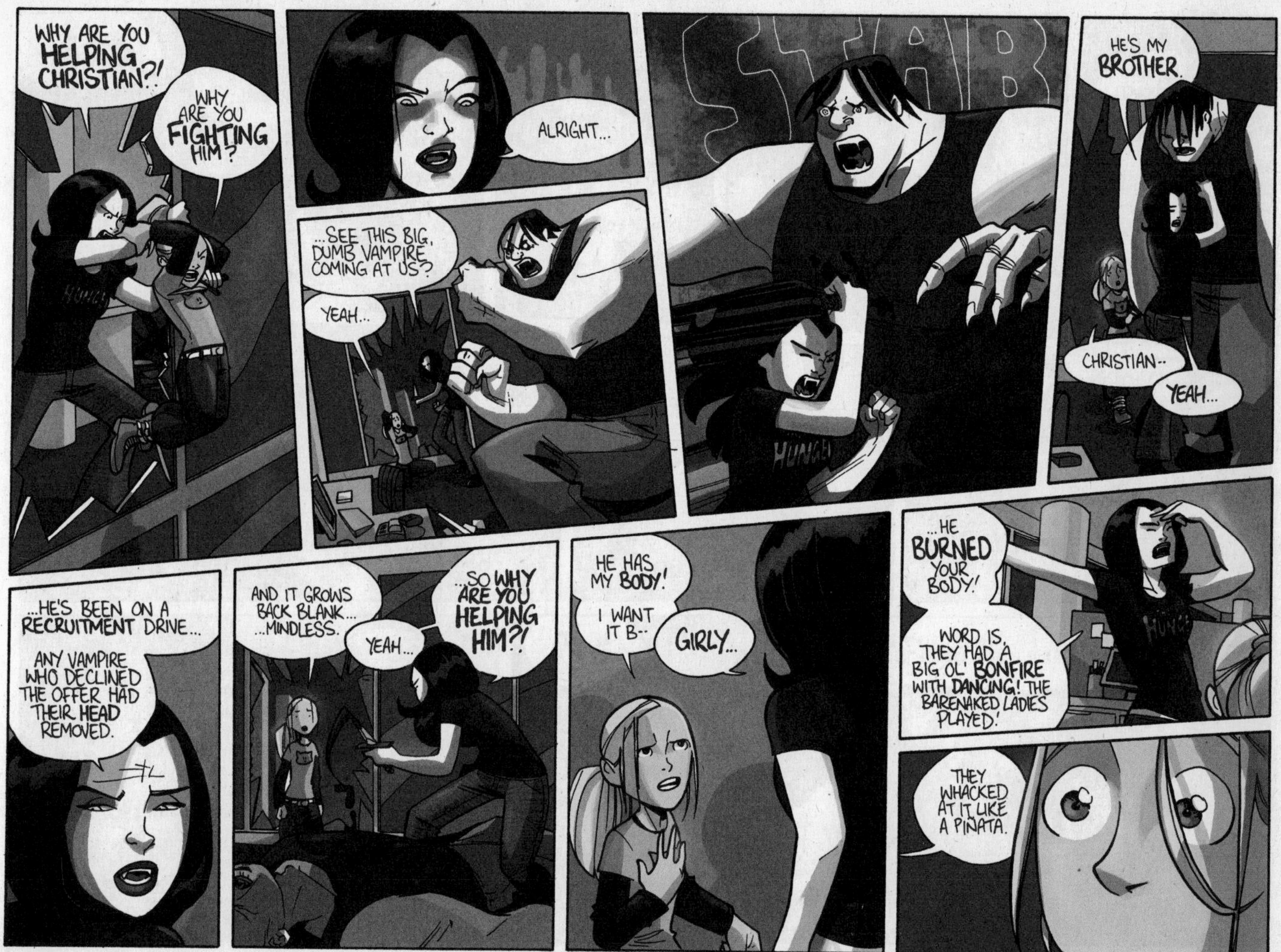
WHY ARE YOU HELPING CHRISTIAN?!
WHY ARE YOU FIGHTING HIM?
ALRIGHT...
...SEE THIS BIG, DUMB VAMPIRE COMING AT US?
YEAH...
STAB
HE'S MY BROTHER.
CHRISTIAN..
YEAH...
...HE'S BEEN ON A RECRUITMENT DRIVE...
ANY VAMPIRE WHO DECLINED THE OFFER HAD THEIR HEAD REMOVED.
AND IT GROWS BACK BLANK... ...MINDLESS.
YEAH...
...SO WHY ARE YOU HELPING HIM?!
HE HAS MY BODY!
I WANT IT B--
GIRLY...
...HE BURNED YOUR BODY!
WORD IS, THEY HAD A BIG OL' BONFIRE WITH DANCING! THE BARENAKED LADIES PLAYED!
THEY WHACKED AT IT LIKE A PIÑATA.

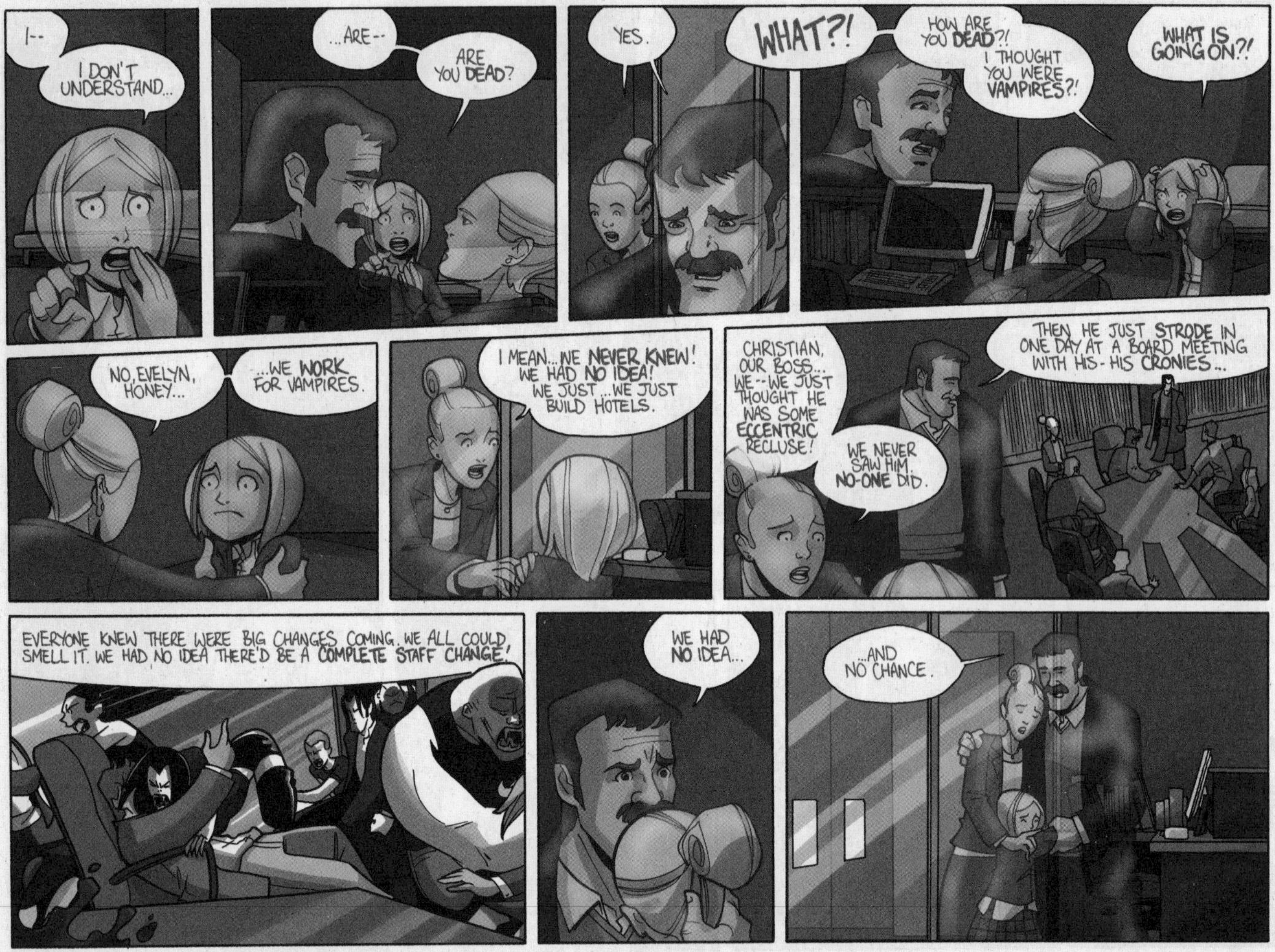
I--
I DON'T UNDERSTAND...
...ARE--
ARE YOU DEAD?
YES.
WHAT?!
HOW ARE YOU DEAD?!
I THOUGHT YOU WERE VAMPIRES?!
WHAT IS GOING ON?!
NO, EVELYN, HONEY...
...WE WORK FOR VAMPIRES.
I MEAN...WE NEVER KNEW! WE HAD NO IDEA!
WE JUST...WE JUST BUILD HOTELS.
CHRISTIAN, OUR BOSS... WE--WE JUST THOUGHT HE WAS SOME ECCENTRIC RECLUSE!
WE NEVER SAW HIM. NO-ONE DID.
THEN HE JUST STRODE IN ONE DAY AT A BOARD MEETING WITH HIS- HIS CRONIES...
EVERYONE KNEW THERE WERE BIG CHANGES COMING. WE ALL COULD SMELL IT. WE HAD NO IDEA THERE'D BE A COMPLETE STAFF CHANGE!
WE HAD NO IDEA...
...AND NO CHANCE.

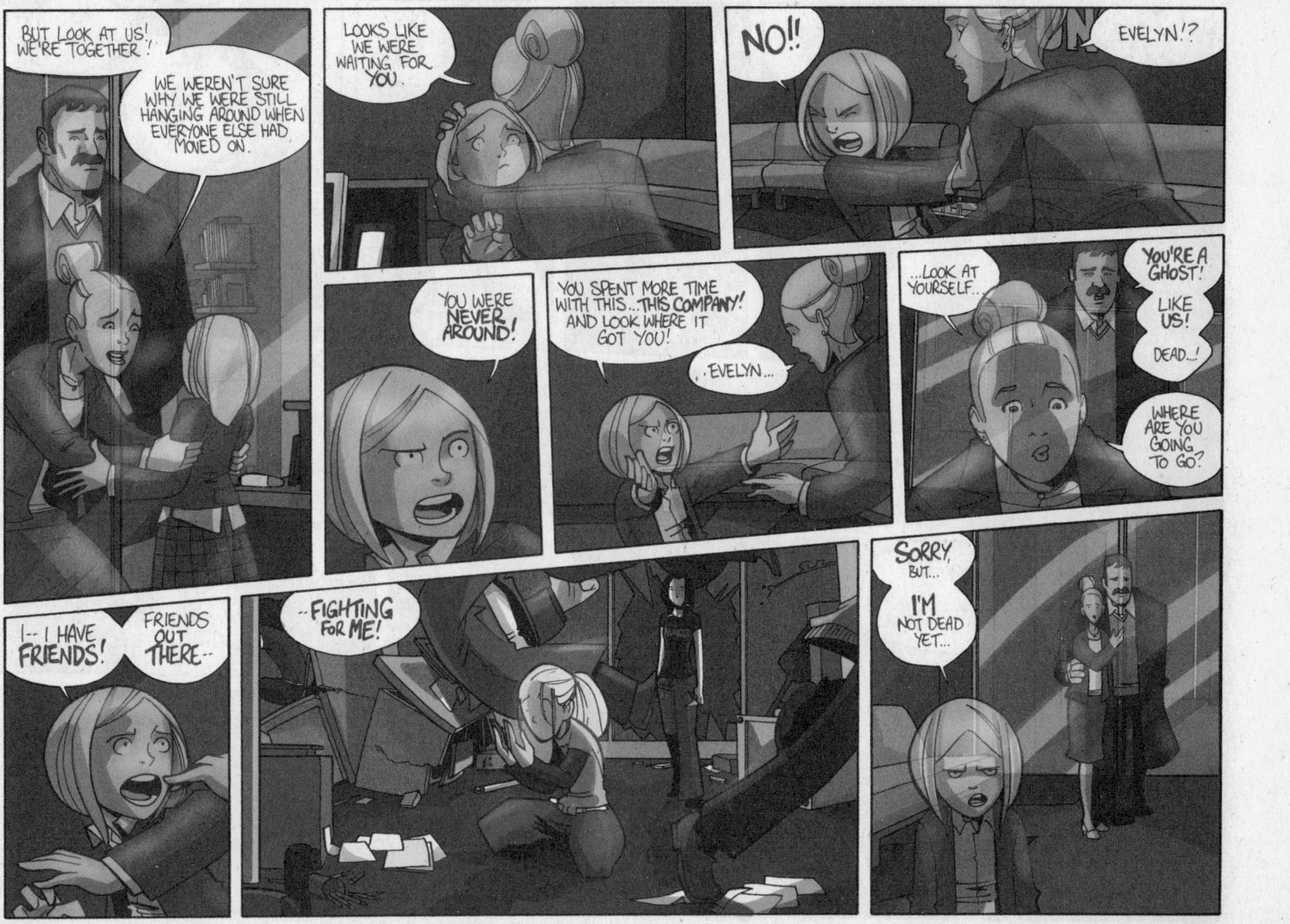
BUT LOOK AT US! WE'RE TOGETHER!
WE WEREN'T SURE WHY WE WERE STILL HANGING AROUND WHEN EVERYONE ELSE HAD MOVED ON.
LOOKS LIKE WE WERE WAITING FOR YOU.
NO!!
EVELYN!?
YOU WERE NEVER AROUND!
YOU SPENT MORE TIME WITH THIS... THIS COMPANY! AND LOOK WHERE IT GOT YOU!
..EVELYN...
...LOOK AT YOURSELF...
YOU'RE A GHOST!
LIKE US!
DEAD...!
WHERE ARE YOU GOING TO GO?
I-- I HAVE FRIENDS!
FRIENDS OUT THERE--
--FIGHTING FOR ME!
SORRY, BUT...
I'M NOT DEAD YET...

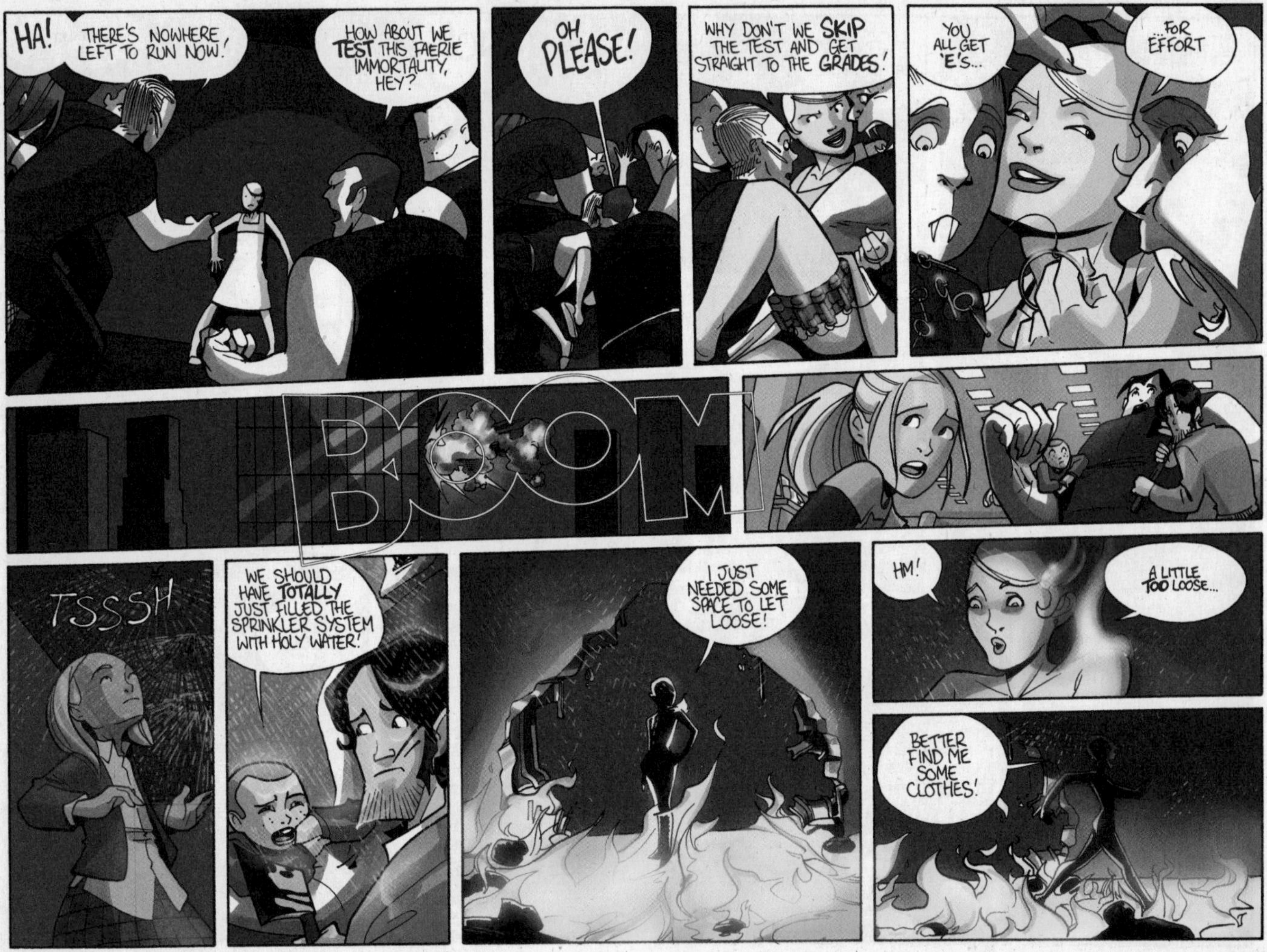
HA!
THERE'S NOWHERE LEFT TO RUN NOW!
HOW ABOUT WE TEST THIS FAERIE IMMORTALITY, HEY?
OH, PLEASE!
WHY DON'T WE SKIP THE TEST AND GET STRAIGHT TO THE GRADES!
YOU ALL GET 'E'S...
...FOR EFFORT
BOOM
TSSSH
WE SHOULD HAVE TOTALLY JUST FILLED THE SPRINKLER SYSTEM WITH HOLY WATER!
I JUST NEEDED SOME SPACE TO LET LOOSE!
HM!
A LITTLE TOO LOOSE...
BETTER FIND ME SOME CLOTHES!

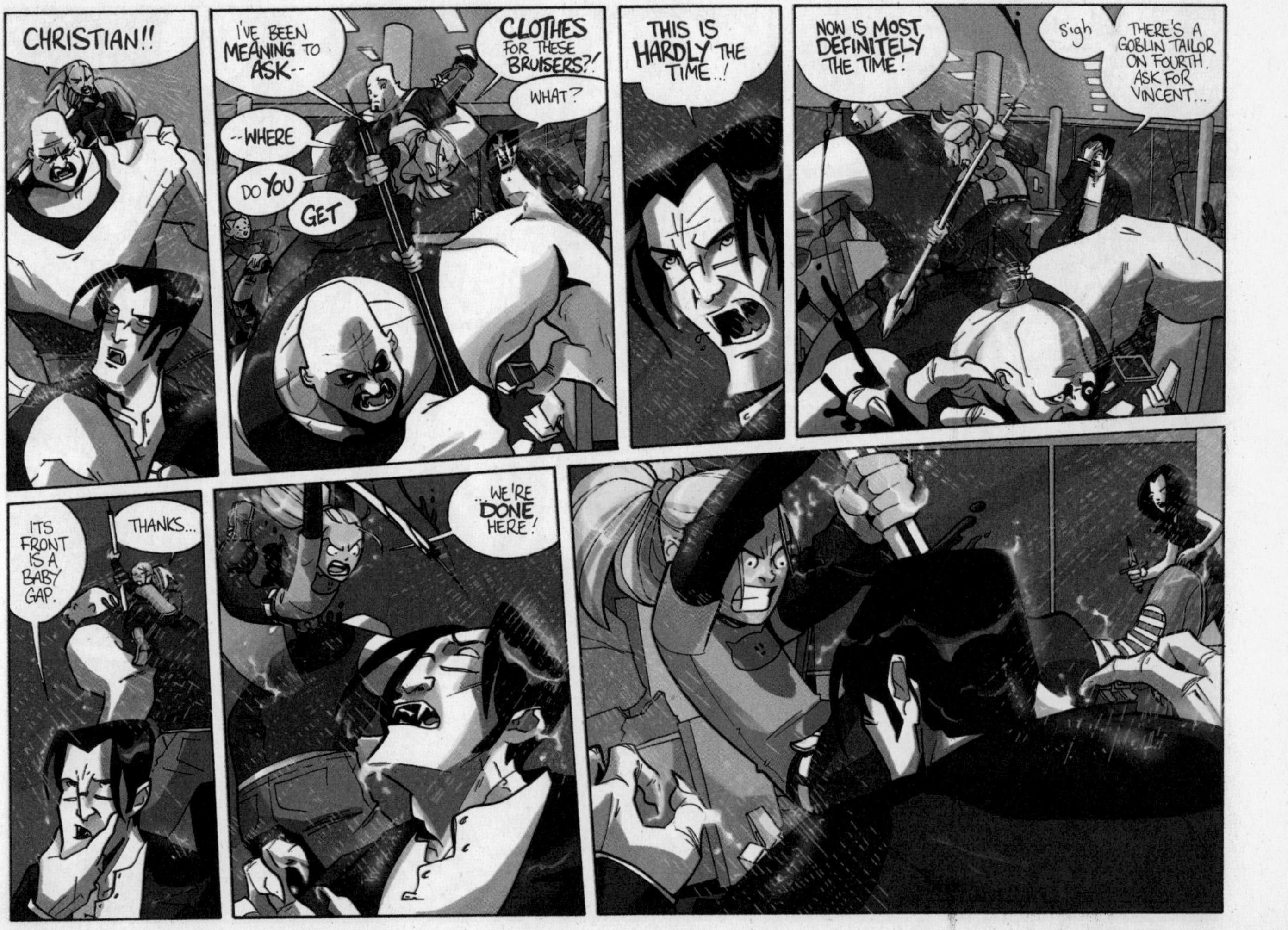
CHRISTIAN!!
I'VE BEEN MEANING TO ASK--
--WHERE
DO YOU
GET
CLOTHES FOR THESE BRUISERS?!
WHAT?
THIS IS HARDLY THE TIME..!
NOW IS MOST DEFINITELY THE TIME!
sigh
THERE'S A GOBLIN TAILOR ON FOURTH. ASK FOR VINCENT...
ITS FRONT IS A BABY GAP.
THANKS...
...WE'RE DONE HERE!

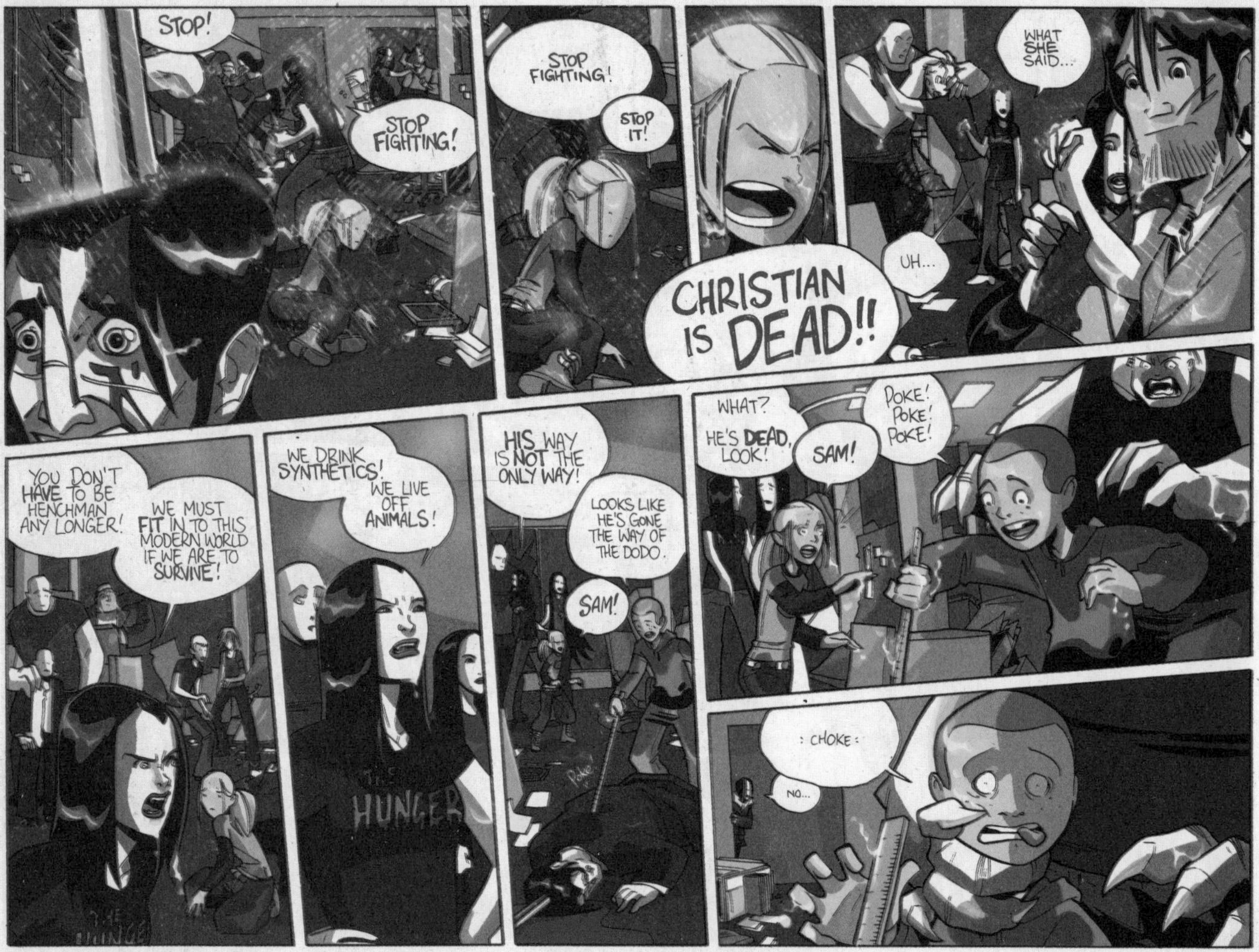
STOP!
STOP FIGHTING!
STOP FIGHTING!
STOP IT!
CHRISTIAN IS DEAD!!
WHAT SHE SAID...
UH...
YOU DON'T HAVE TO BE HENCHMAN ANY LONGER!
WE MUST FIT IN TO THIS MODERN WORLD IF WE ARE TO SURVIVE!
WE DRINK SYNTHETICS!
WE LIVE OFF ANIMALS!
THE HUNGER
HIS WAY IS NOT THE ONLY WAY!
LOOKS LIKE HE'S GONE THE WAY OF THE DODO.
SAM!
POKE
WHAT?
HE'S DEAD, LOOK!
SAM!
POKE! POKE! POKE!
: CHOKE :
NO...

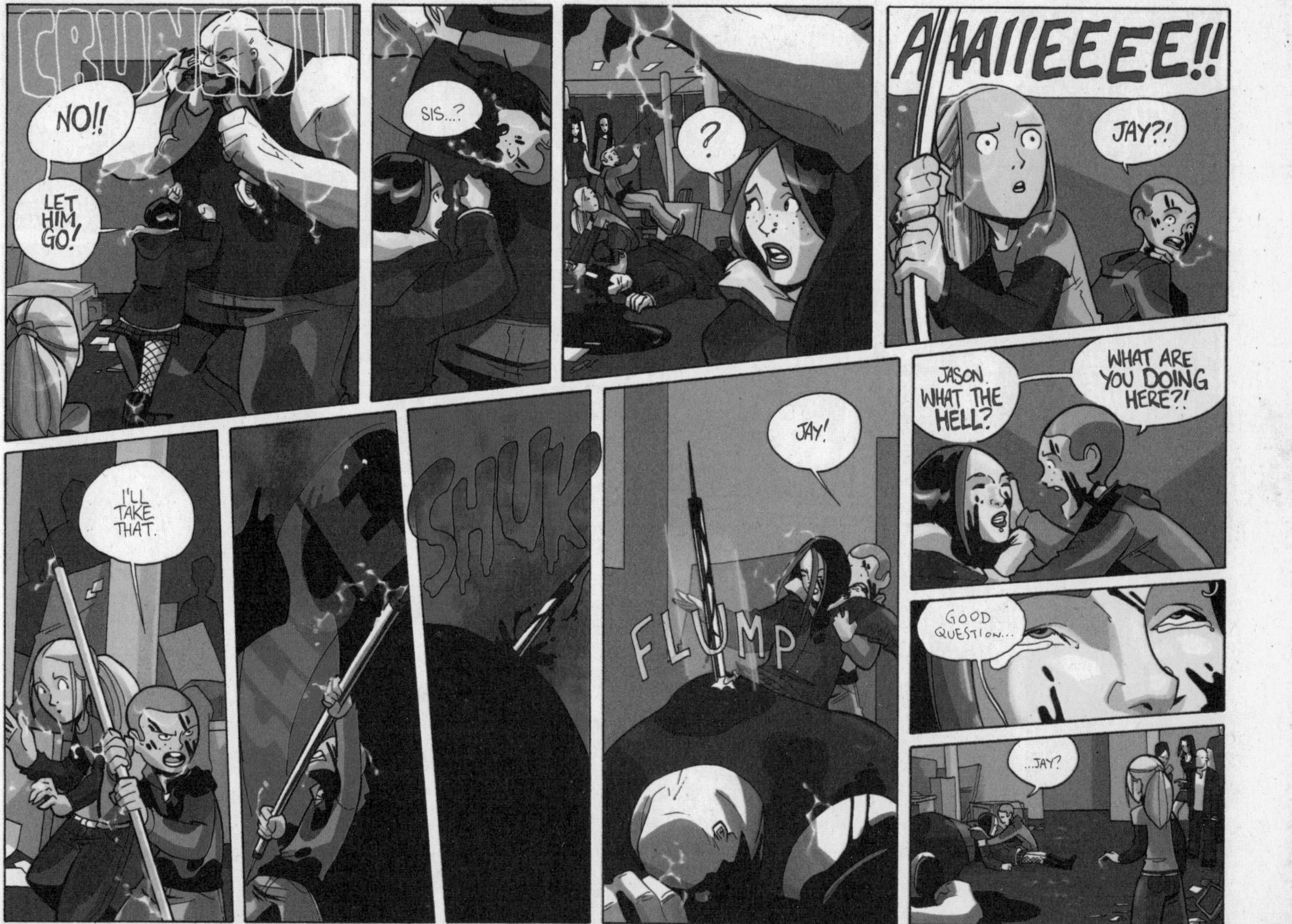

CRUNCH!!
NO!!
LET HIM GO!
SIS...?
?
AAAIIEEEE!!
JAY?!
JASON WHAT THE HELL?
WHAT ARE YOU DOING HERE?!
I'LL TAKE THAT.
SHUK
JAY!
FLUMP
GOOD QUESTION...
...JAY?

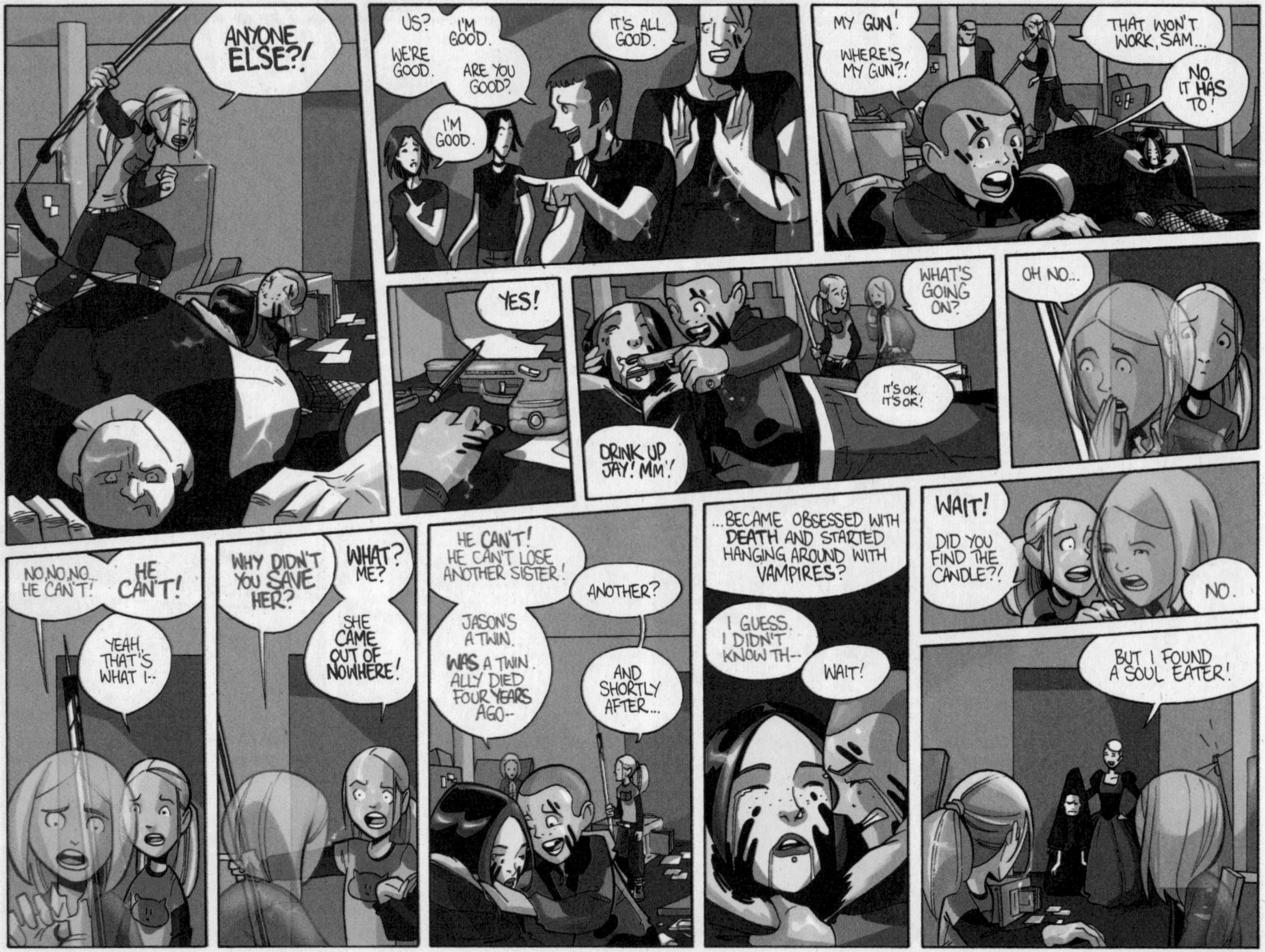
ANYONE ELSE?!
US?
I'M GOOD.
WE'RE GOOD.
ARE YOU GOOD?
I'M GOOD.
IT'S ALL GOOD.
MY GUN!
WHERE'S MY GUN?!
THAT WON'T WORK, SAM...
NO. IT HAS TO!
YES!
WHAT'S GOING ON?
IT'S OK. IT'S OK!
DRINK UP JAY! MM'!
OH NO...
NO,NO,NO... HE CAN'T!
HE CAN'T!
YEAH, THAT'S WHAT I--
WHY DIDN'T YOU SAVE HER?
WHAT? ME?
SHE CAME OUT OF NOWHERE!
HE CAN'T! HE CAN'T LOSE ANOTHER SISTER!
ANOTHER?
JASON'S A TWIN.
WAS A TWIN. ALLY DIED FOUR YEARS AGO--
AND SHORTLY AFTER...
...BECAME OBSESSED WITH DEATH AND STARTED HANGING AROUND WITH VAMPIRES?
I GUESS. I DIDN'T KNOW TH--
WAIT!
WAIT!
DID YOU FIND THE CANDLE?!
NO.
BUT I FOUND A SOUL EATER!

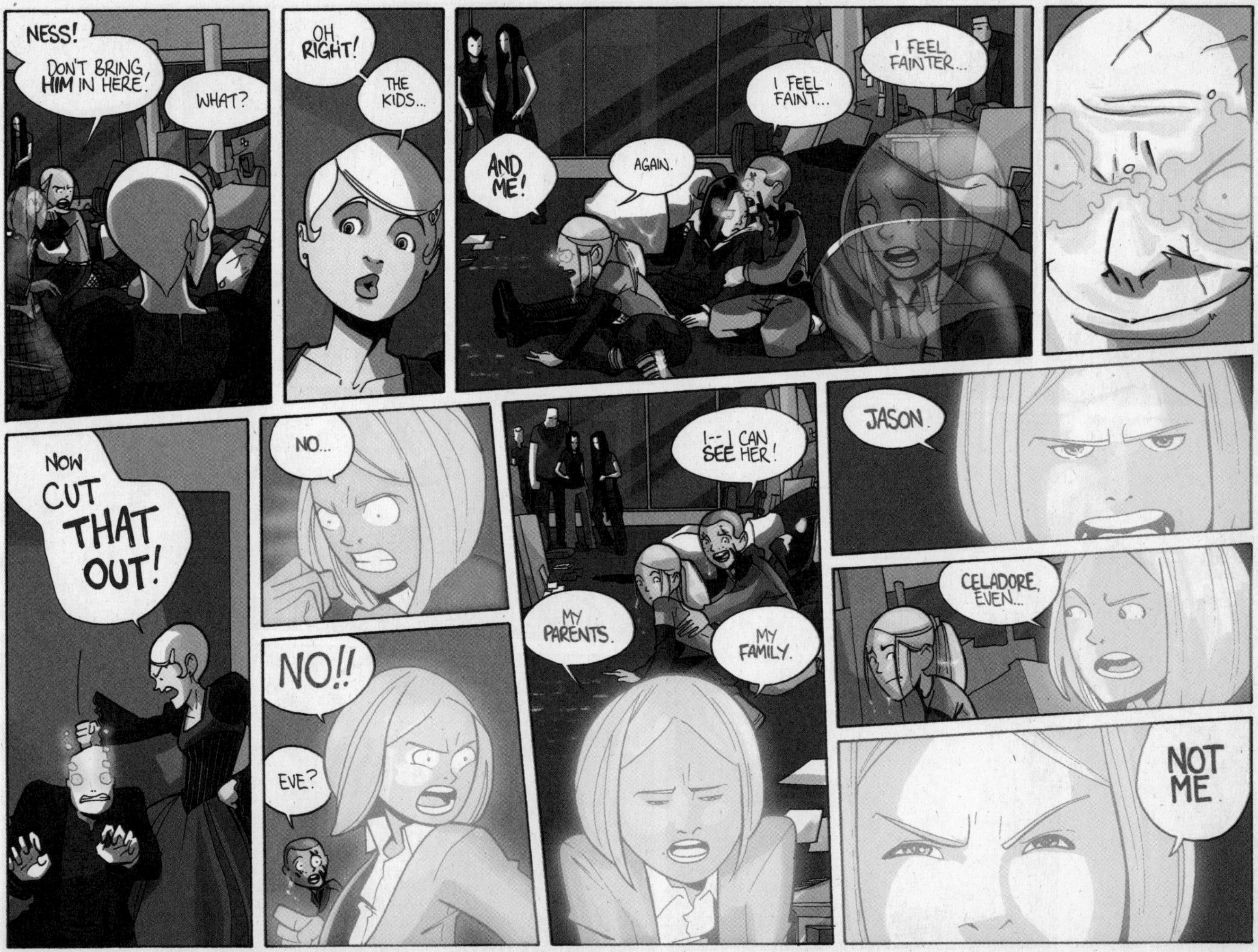
NESS!
DON'T BRING HIM IN HERE!
WHAT?
OH RIGHT!
THE KIDS...
AND ME!
AGAIN.
I FEEL FAINT...
I FEEL FAINTER...
NOW CUT THAT OUT!
NO...
NO!!
EVE?
I-- I CAN SEE HER!
MY PARENTS.
MY FAMILY.
JASON.
CELADORE, EVEN...
NOT ME.

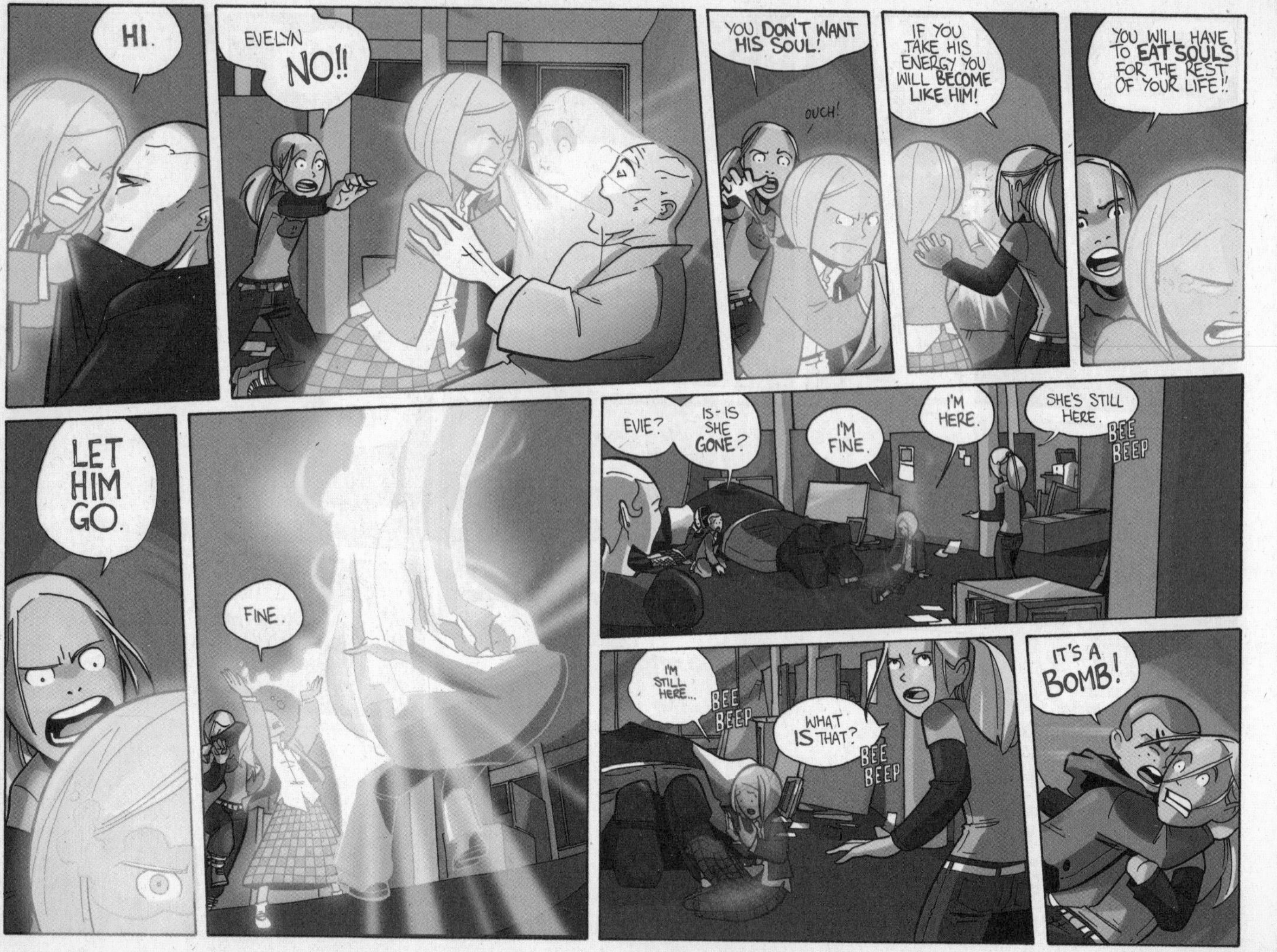
HI.
EVELYN NO!!
YOU DON'T WANT HIS SOUL!
OUCH!
IF YOU TAKE HIS ENERGY YOU WILL BECOME LIKE HIM!
YOU WILL HAVE TO EAT SOULS FOR THE REST OF YOUR LIFE!!
LET HIM GO.
FINE.
EVIE?
IS-IS SHE GONE?
I'M FINE.
I'M HERE.
SHE'S STILL HERE.
BEE BEEP
I'M STILL HERE...
BEE BEEP
WHAT IS THAT?
BEE BEEP
IT'S A BOMB!

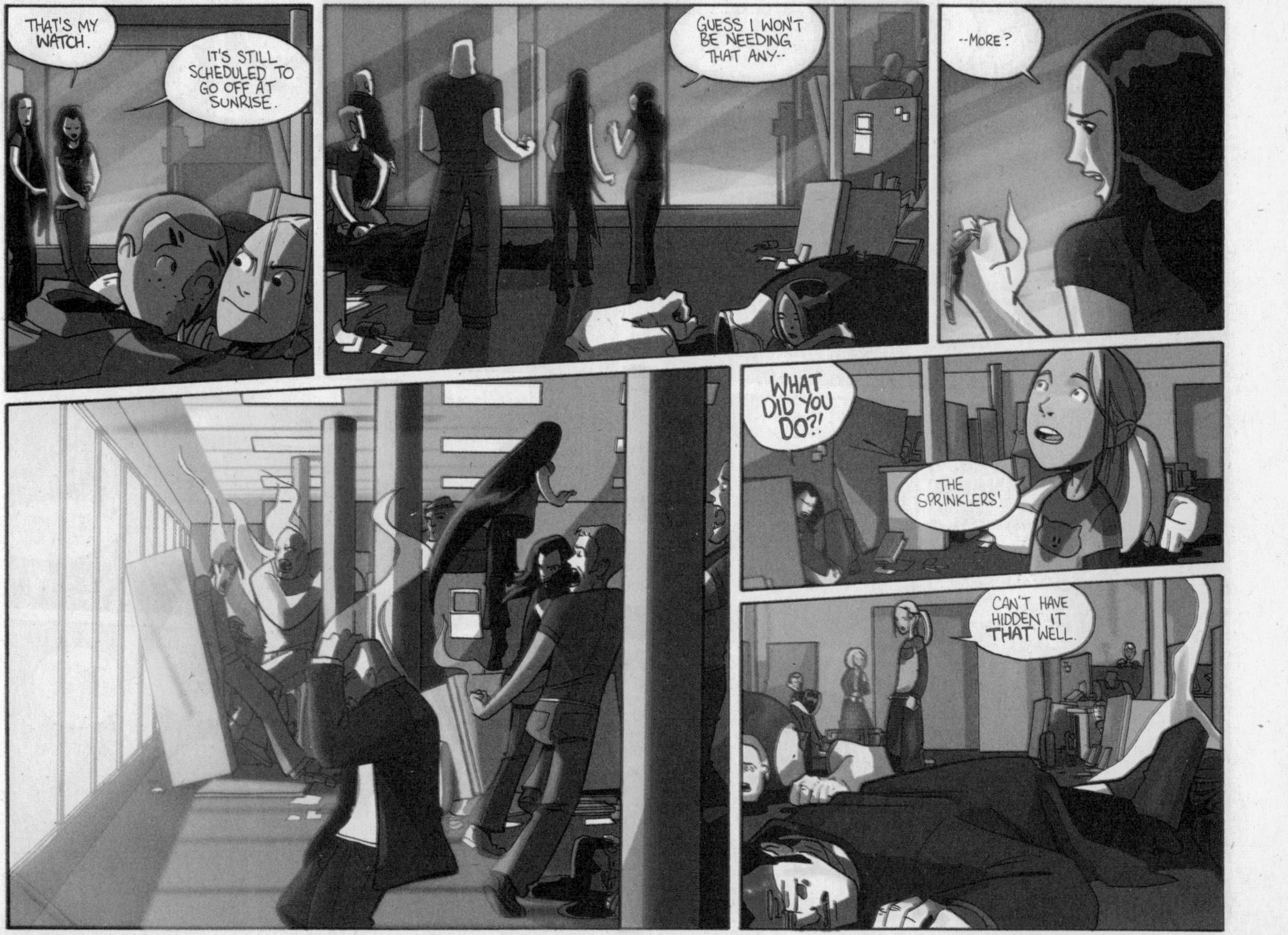
THAT'S MY WATCH.
IT'S STILL SCHEDULED TO GO OFF AT SUNRISE.
GUESS I WON'T BE NEEDING THAT ANY--
--MORE?
WHAT DID YOU DO?!
THE SPRINKLERS!
CAN'T HAVE HIDDEN IT THAT WELL.

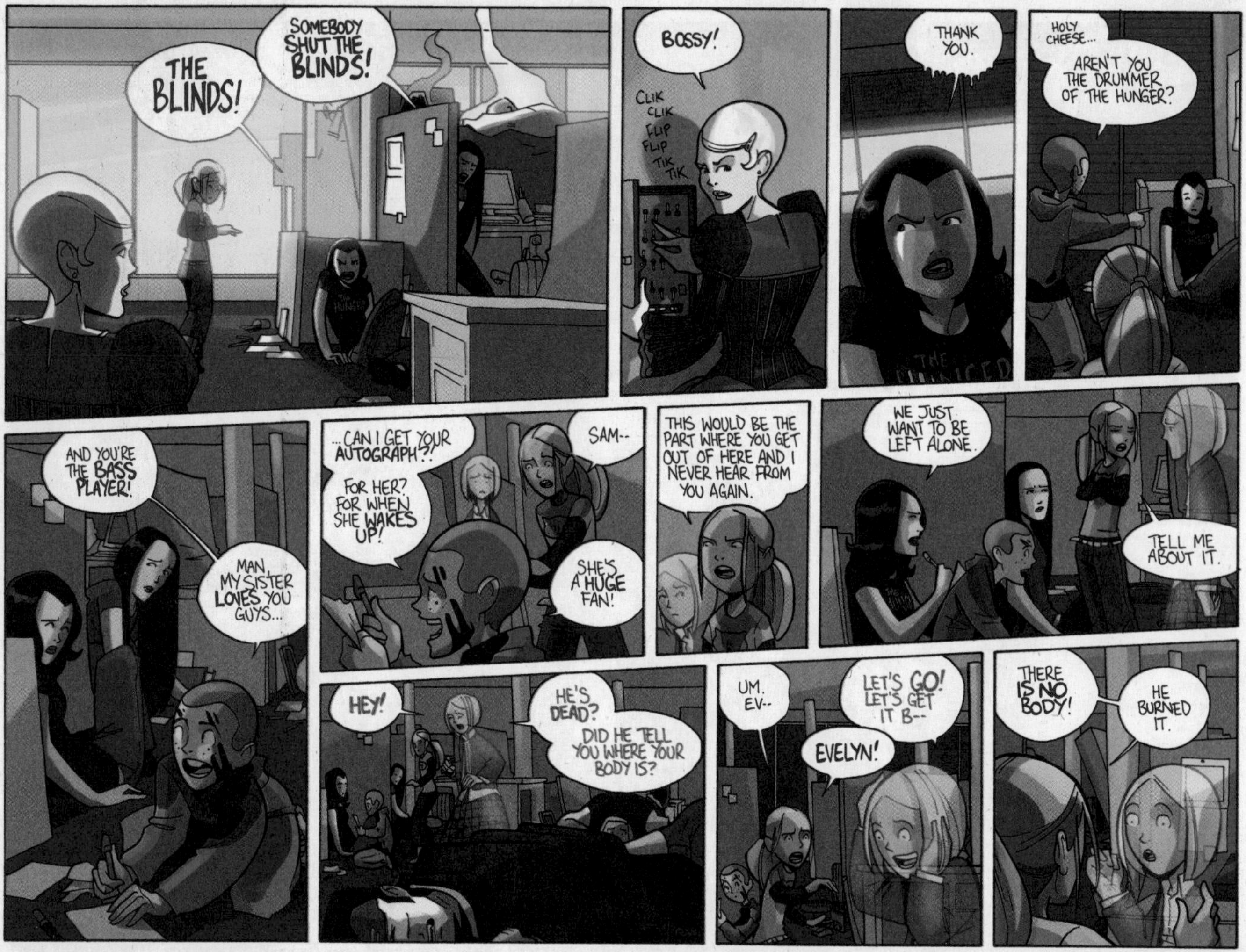
THE BLINDS!
SOMEBODY SHUT THE BLINDS!
BOSSY!
CLIK CLIK FLIP FLIP TIK TIK
THANK YOU.
HOLY CHEESE...
AREN'T YOU THE DRUMMER OF THE HUNGER?
AND YOU'RE THE BASS PLAYER!
MAN, MY SISTER LOVES YOU GUYS...
...CAN I GET YOUR AUTOGRAPH?!
FOR HER? FOR WHEN SHE WAKES UP!
SAM--
SHE'S A HUGE FAN!
THIS WOULD BE THE PART WHERE YOU GET OUT OF HERE AND I NEVER HEAR FROM YOU AGAIN.
WE JUST WANT TO BE LEFT ALONE.
TELL ME ABOUT IT.
HEY!
HE'S DEAD?
DID HE TELL YOU WHERE YOUR BODY IS?
UM. EV--
LET'S GO! LET'S GET IT B--
EVELYN!
THERE IS NO BODY!
HE BURNED IT.

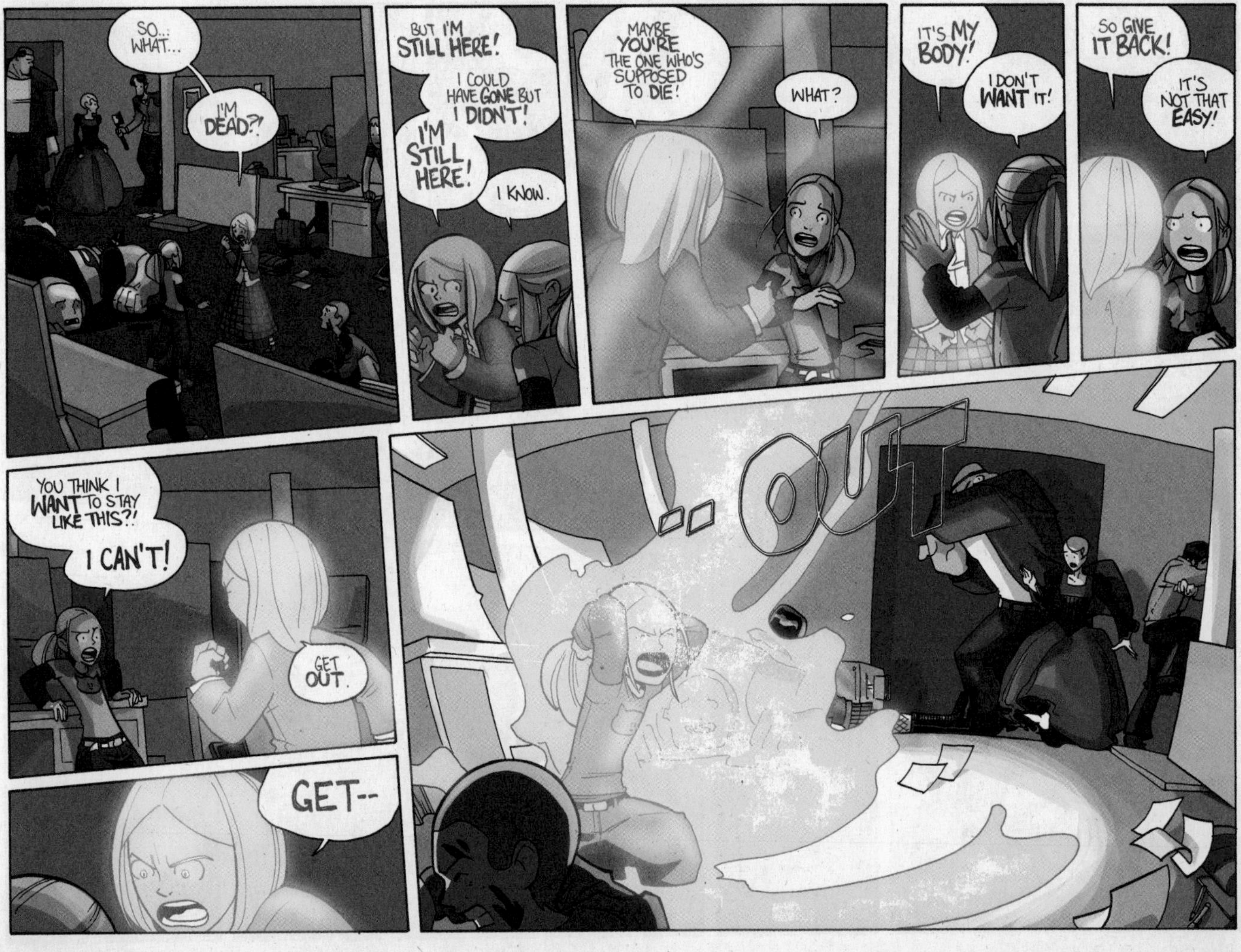
SO... WHAT...
I'M DEAD?!
BUT I'M STILL HERE!
I COULD HAVE GONE BUT I DIDN'T!
I'M STILL HERE!
I KNOW.
MAYBE YOU'RE THE ONE WHO'S SUPPOSED TO DIE!
WHAT?
IT'S MY BODY!
I DON'T WANT IT!
SO GIVE IT BACK!
IT'S NOT THAT EASY!
YOU THINK I WANT TO STAY LIKE THIS?!
I CAN'T!
GET OUT.
GET--
..OUT

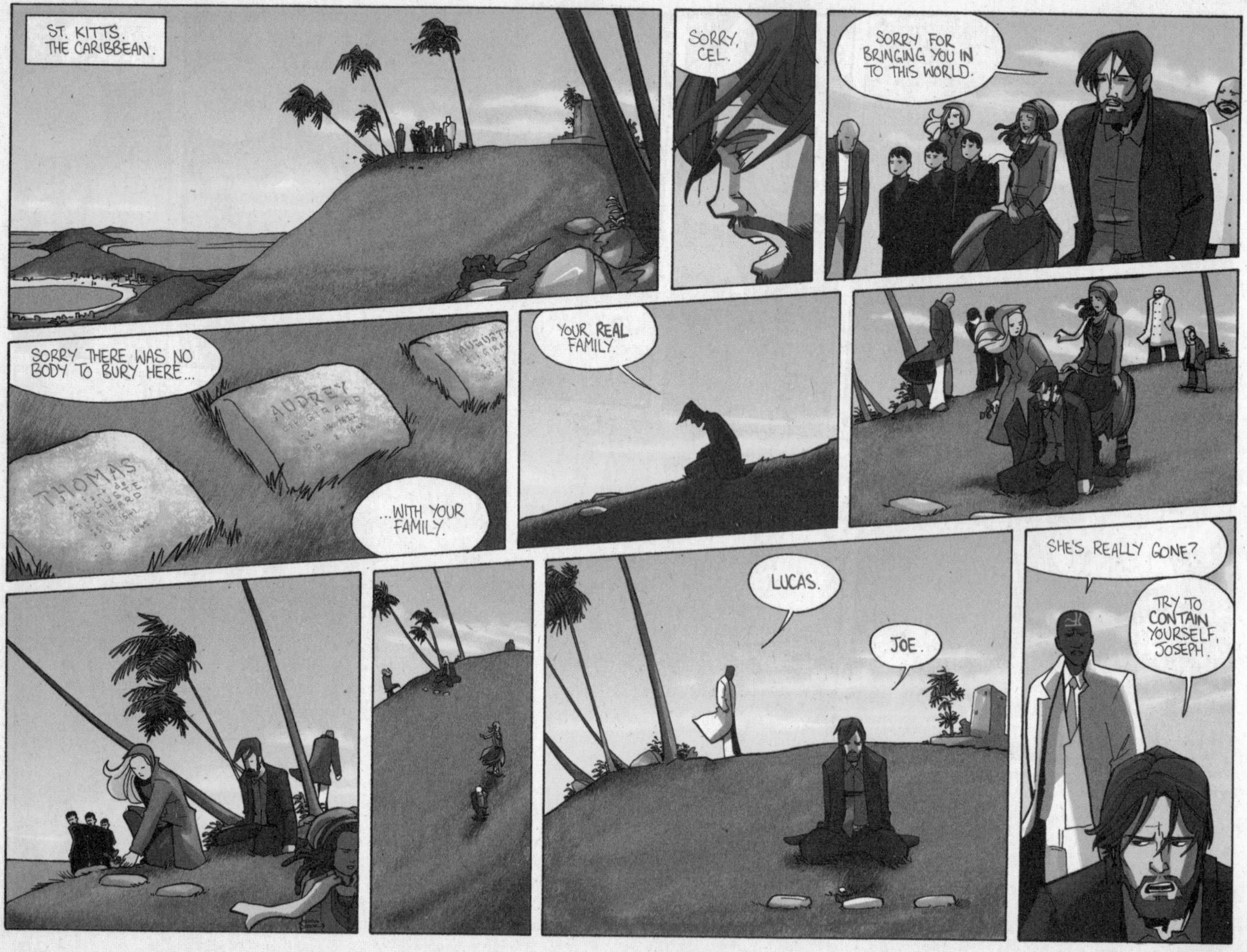
ST. KITTS. THE CARIBBEAN.
SORRY, CEL.
SORRY FOR BRINGING YOU IN TO THIS WORLD.
SORRY THERE WAS NO BODY TO BURY HERE...
AUDREY
THOMAS
...WITH YOUR FAMILY.
YOUR REAL FAMILY.
LUCAS.
JOE.
SHE'S REALLY GONE?
TRY TO CONTAIN YOURSELF, JOSEPH.

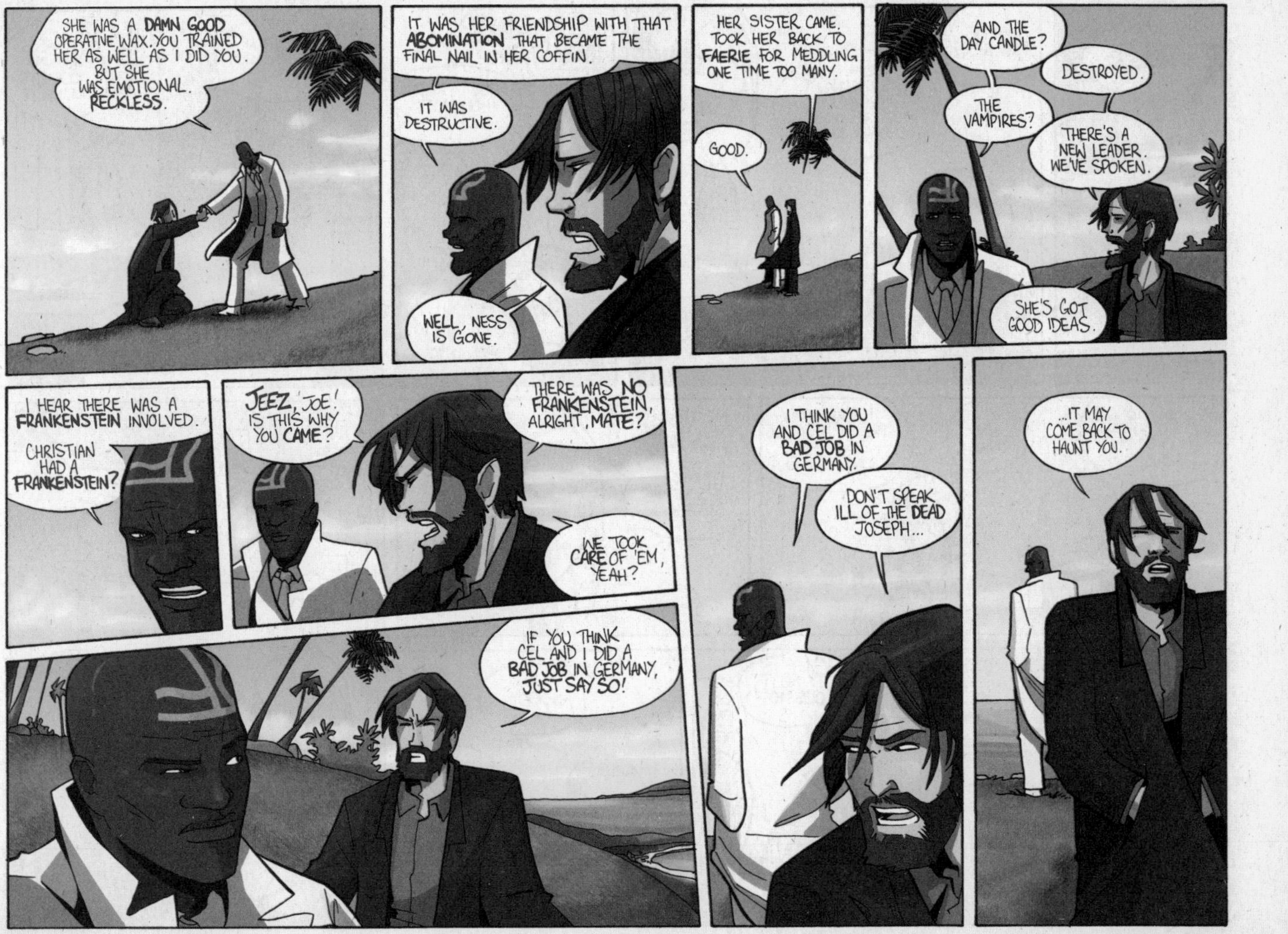
SHE WAS A DAMN GOOD OPERATIVE, WAX. YOU TRAINED HER AS WELL AS I DID YOU. BUT SHE WAS EMOTIONAL. RECKLESS.
IT WAS HER FRIENDSHIP WITH THAT ABOMINATION THAT BECAME THE FINAL NAIL IN HER COFFIN.
IT WAS DESTRUCTIVE.
WELL, NESS IS GONE.
HER SISTER CAME. TOOK HER BACK TO FAERIE FOR MEDDLING ONE TIME TOO MANY.
GOOD.
AND THE DAY CANDLE?
DESTROYED.
THE VAMPIRES?
THERE'S A NEW LEADER. WE'VE SPOKEN.
SHE'S GOT GOOD IDEAS.
I HEAR THERE WAS A FRANKENSTEIN INVOLVED.
CHRISTIAN HAD A FRANKENSTEIN?
JEEZ, JOE! IS THIS WHY YOU CAME?
THERE WAS NO FRANKENSTEIN, ALRIGHT, MATE?
WE TOOK CARE OF 'EM, YEAH?
IF YOU THINK CEL AND I DID A BAD JOB IN GERMANY, JUST SAY SO!
I THINK YOU AND CEL DID A BAD JOB IN GERMANY.
DON'T SPEAK ILL OF THE DEAD JOSEPH...
...IT MAY COME BACK TO HAUNT YOU.

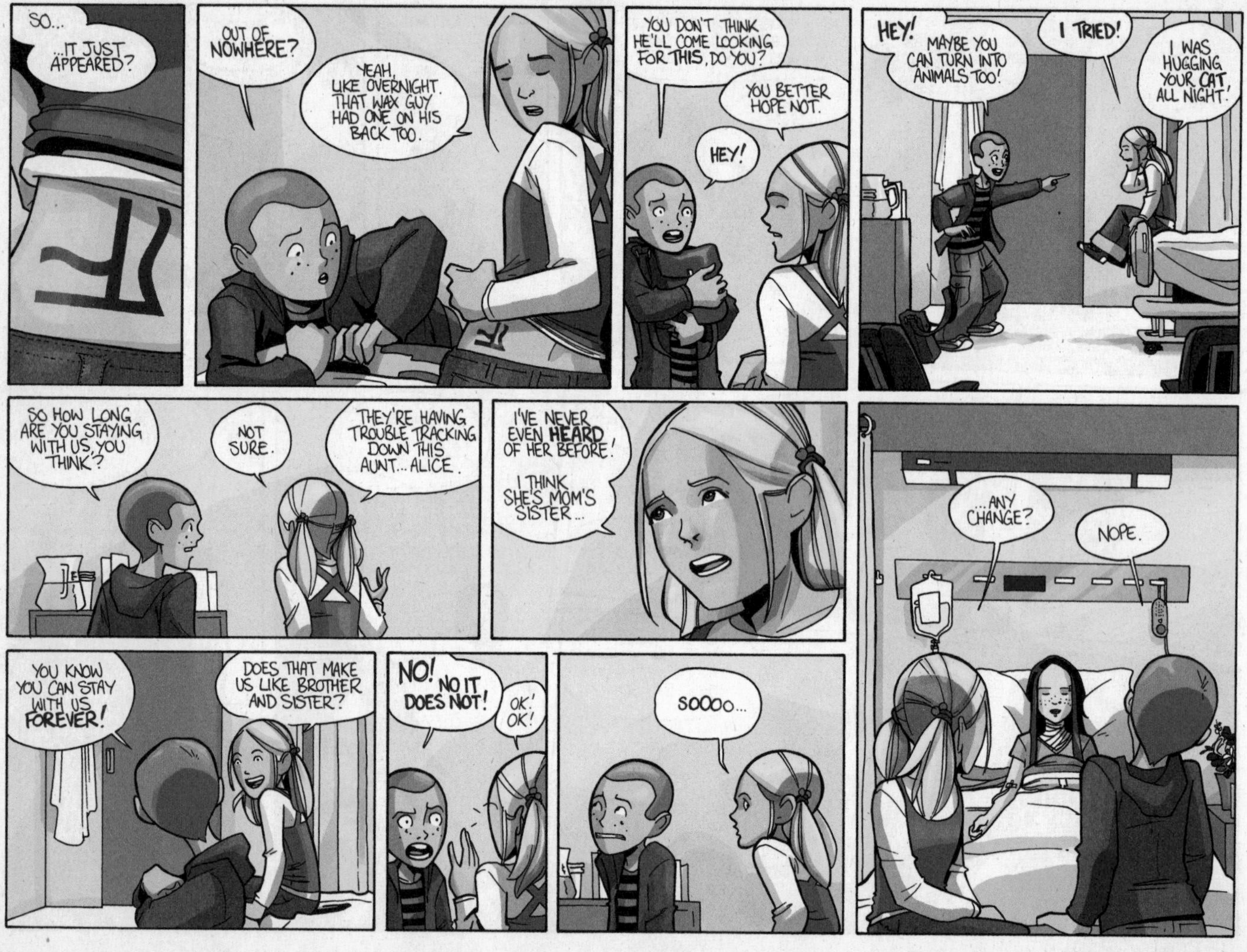

SO...
...IT JUST APPEARED?
OUT OF NOWHERE?
YEAH, LIKE OVERNIGHT. THAT WAX GUY HAD ONE ON HIS BACK TOO.
YOU DON'T THINK HE'LL COME LOOKING FOR THIS, DO YOU?
YOU BETTER HOPE NOT.
HEY!
HEY!
MAYBE YOU CAN TURN INTO ANIMALS TOO!
I TRIED!
I WAS HUGGING YOUR CAT ALL NIGHT!
SO HOW LONG ARE YOU STAYING WITH US, YOU THINK?
NOT SURE.
THEY'RE HAVING TROUBLE TRACKING DOWN THIS AUNT... ALICE.
I'VE NEVER EVEN HEARD OF HER BEFORE!
I THINK SHE'S MOM'S SISTER...
...ANY CHANGE?
NOPE.
YOU KNOW YOU CAN STAY WITH US FOREVER!
DOES THAT MAKE US LIKE BROTHER AND SISTER?
NO! NO IT DOES NOT!
OK! OK!
SOOOO...

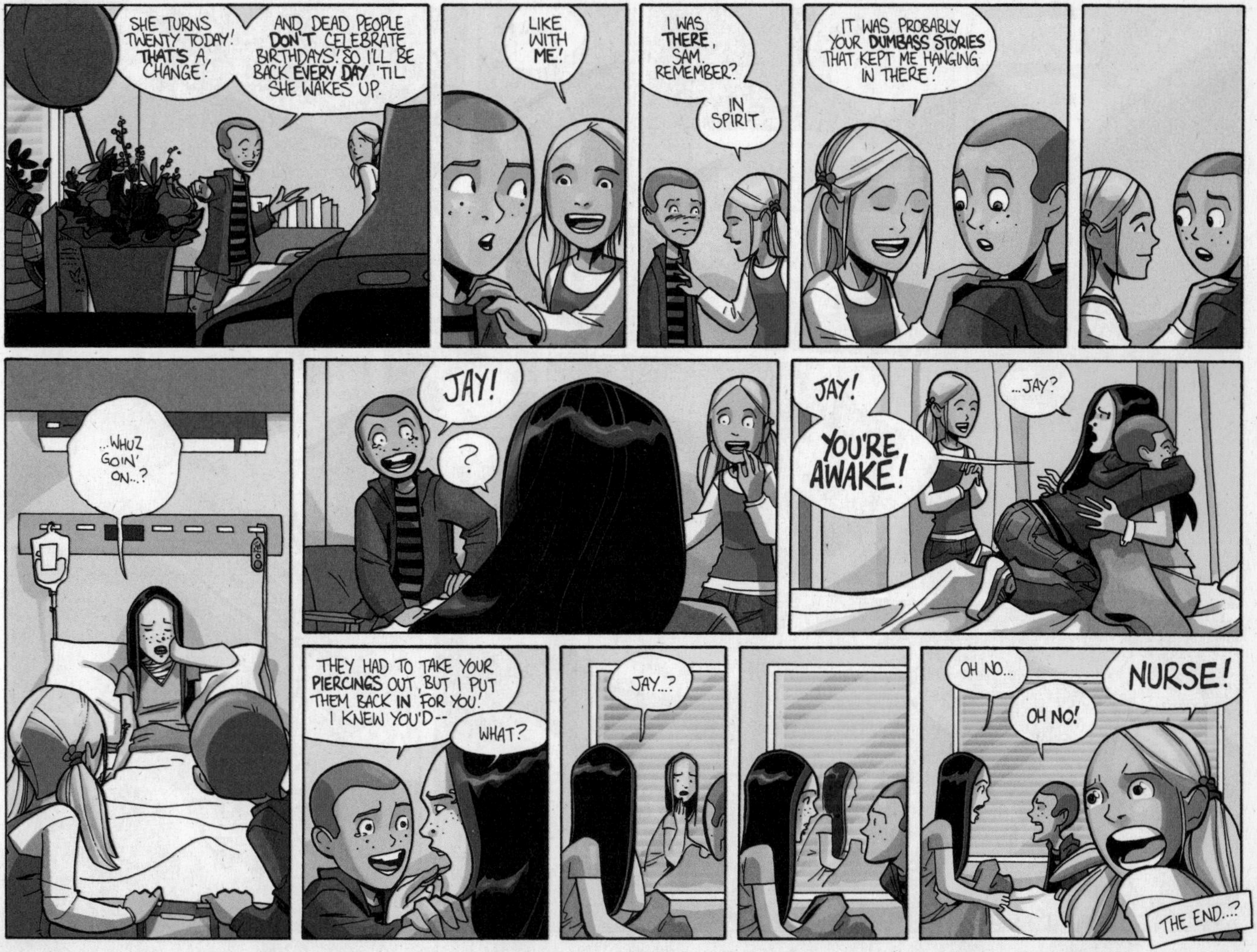
SHE TURNS TWENTY TODAY! THAT'S A CHANGE!
AND DEAD PEOPLE DON'T CELEBRATE BIRTHDAYS! SO I'LL BE BACK EVERY DAY 'TIL SHE WAKES UP.
LIKE WITH ME!
I WAS THERE, SAM. REMEMBER?
IN SPIRIT.
IT WAS PROBABLY YOUR DUMBASS STORIES THAT KEPT ME HANGING IN THERE!
...WHU'Z GOIN' ON...?
JAY!
?
JAY!
YOU'RE AWAKE!
...JAY?
THEY HAD TO TAKE YOUR PIERCINGS OUT, BUT I PUT THEM BACK IN FOR YOU! I KNEW YOU'D--
WHAT?
JAY...?
OH NO...
OH NO!
NURSE!
THE END...?

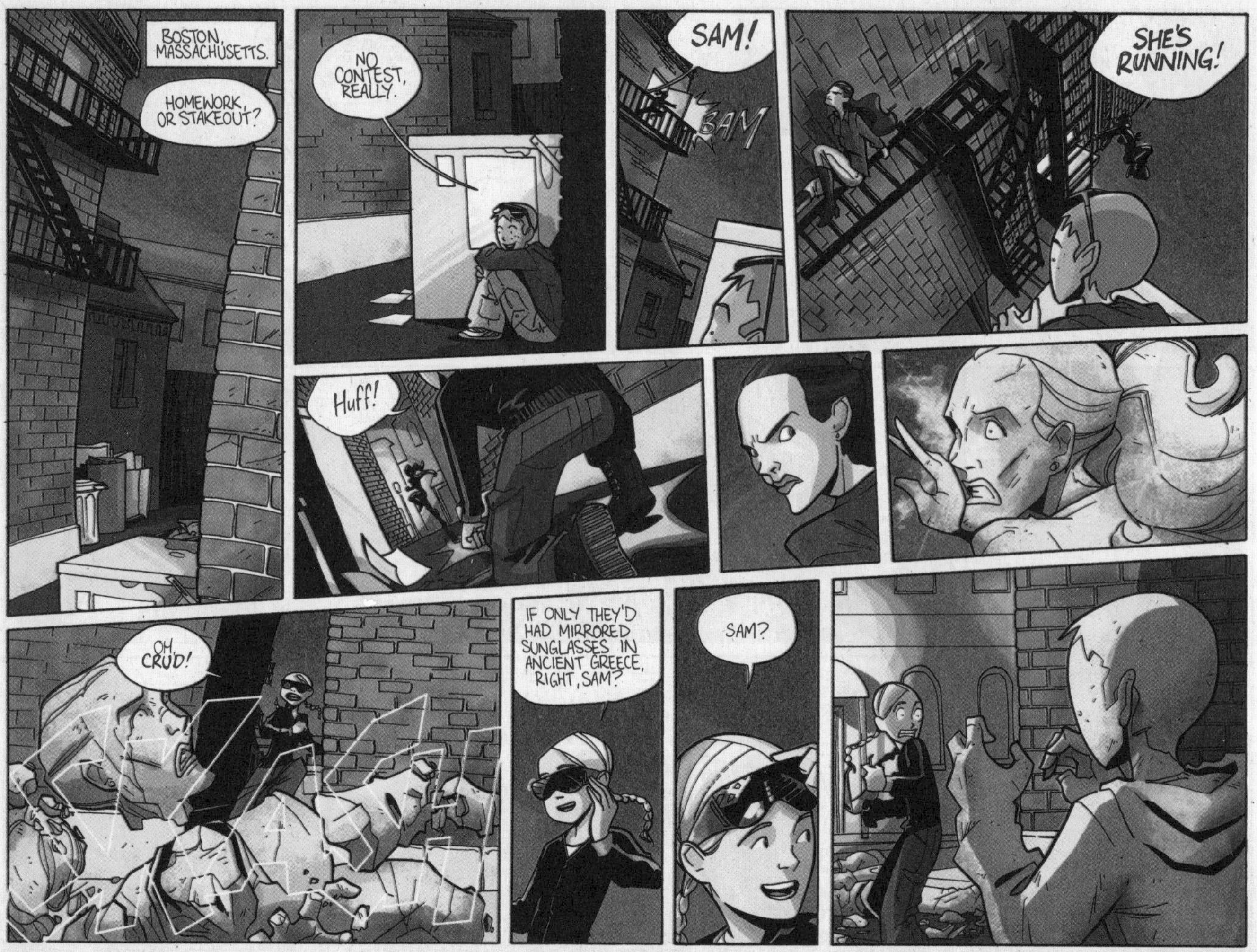
BOSTON, MASSACHUSETTS.
HOMEWORK, OR STAKEOUT?
NO CONTEST, REALLY.
SAM!
BAM
SHE'S RUNNING!
Huff!
OH, CRUD!
IF ONLY THEY'D HAD MIRRORED SUNGLASSES IN ANCIENT GREECE, RIGHT, SAM?
SAM?

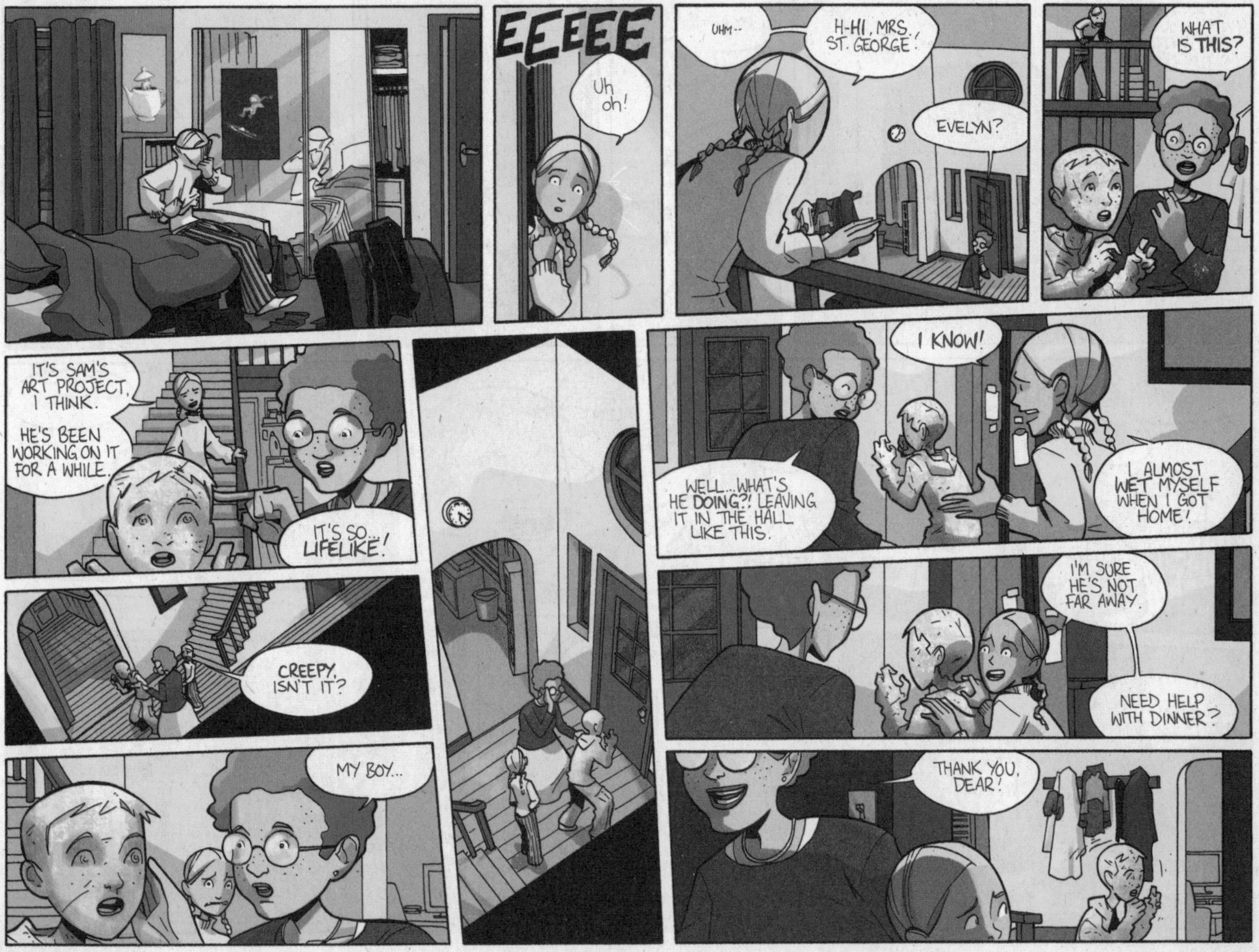
EEEEE
Uh oh!
UHM--
H-HI, MRS. ST. GEORGE!
EVELYN?
WHAT IS THIS?
IT'S SAM'S ART PROJECT, I THINK.
HE'S BEEN WORKING ON IT FOR A WHILE.
IT'S SO... LIFELIKE!
CREEPY, ISN'T IT?
MY BOY...
I KNOW!
WELL...WHAT'S HE DOING?! LEAVING IT IN THE HALL LIKE THIS.
I ALMOST WET MYSELF WHEN I GOT HOME!
I'M SURE HE'S NOT FAR AWAY.
NEED HELP WITH DINNER?
THANK YOU, DEAR!

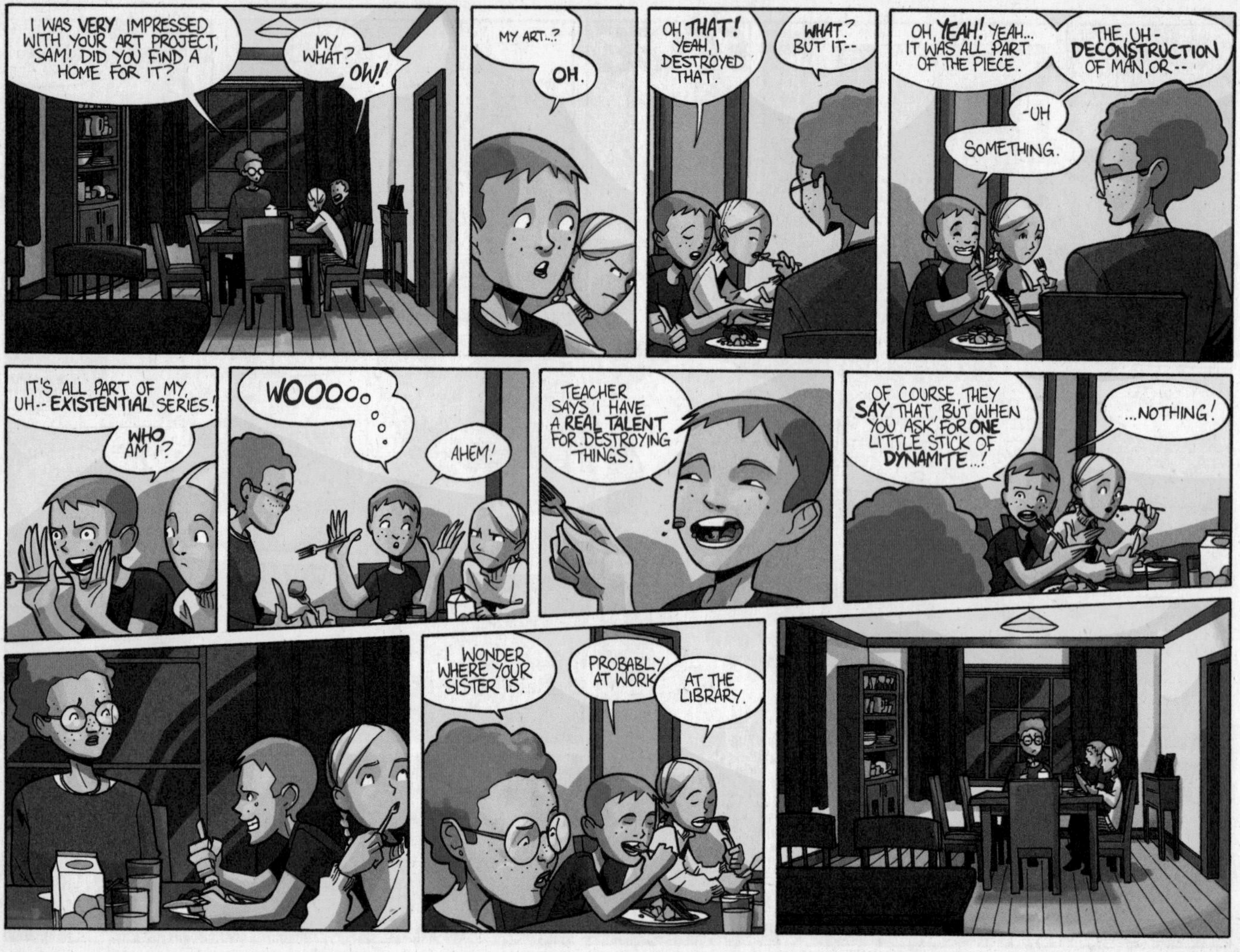
I WAS VERY IMPRESSED WITH YOUR ART PROJECT, SAM! DID YOU FIND A HOME FOR IT?
MY WHAT?
OW!
MY ART...?
OH.
OH, THAT! YEAH, I DESTROYED THAT.
WHAT? BUT IT--
OH, YEAH! YEAH... IT WAS ALL PART OF THE PIECE.
THE, UH- DECONSTRUCTION OF MAN, OR --
-UH
SOMETHING.
IT'S ALL PART OF MY, UH-- EXISTENTIAL SERIES!
WHO AM I?
WOOOOo
AHEM!
TEACHER SAYS I HAVE A REAL TALENT FOR DESTROYING THINGS.
OF COURSE, THEY SAY THAT, BUT WHEN YOU ASK FOR ONE LITTLE STICK OF DYNAMITE...!
...NOTHING!
I WONDER WHERE YOUR SISTER IS.
PROBABLY AT WORK
AT THE LIBRARY.

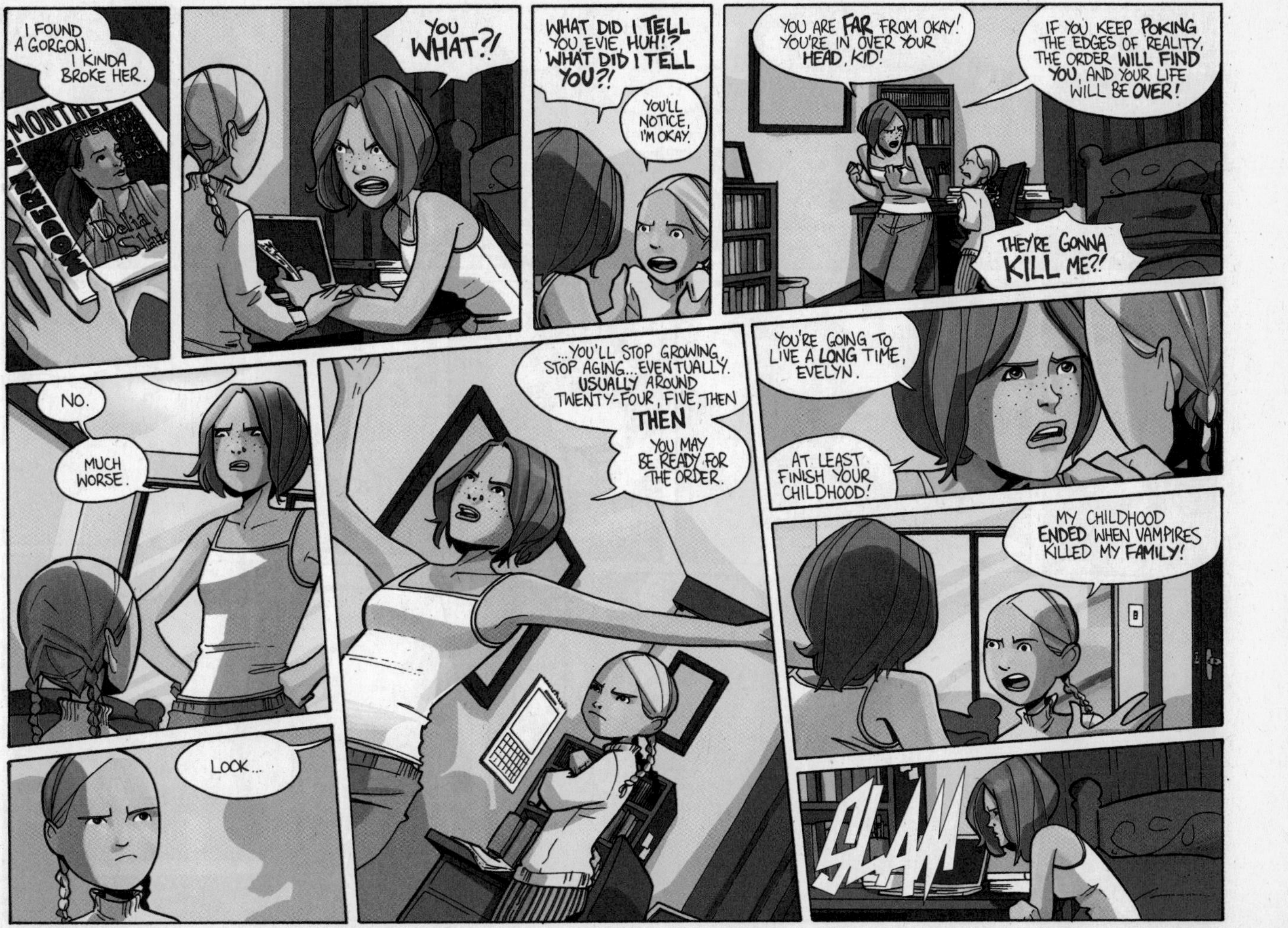
I FOUND A GORGON. I KINDA BROKE HER.
MODERN MONTHLY
YOU WHAT?!
WHAT DID I TELL YOU, EVIE, HUH!? WHAT DID I TELL YOU?!
YOU'LL NOTICE, I'M OKAY.
YOU ARE FAR FROM OKAY! YOU'RE IN OVER YOUR HEAD, KID!
IF YOU KEEP POKING THE EDGES OF REALITY, THE ORDER WILL FIND YOU, AND YOUR LIFE WILL BE OVER!
THEY'RE GONNA KILL ME?!
NO.
MUCH WORSE.
LOOK...
...YOU'LL STOP GROWING, STOP AGING... EVENTUALLY. USUALLY AROUND TWENTY-FOUR, FIVE, THEN
THEN
YOU MAY BE READY FOR THE ORDER.
YOU'RE GOING TO LIVE A LONG TIME, EVELYN.
AT LEAST FINISH YOUR CHILDHOOD!
MY CHILDHOOD ENDED WHEN VAMPIRES KILLED MY FAMILY!
SLAM

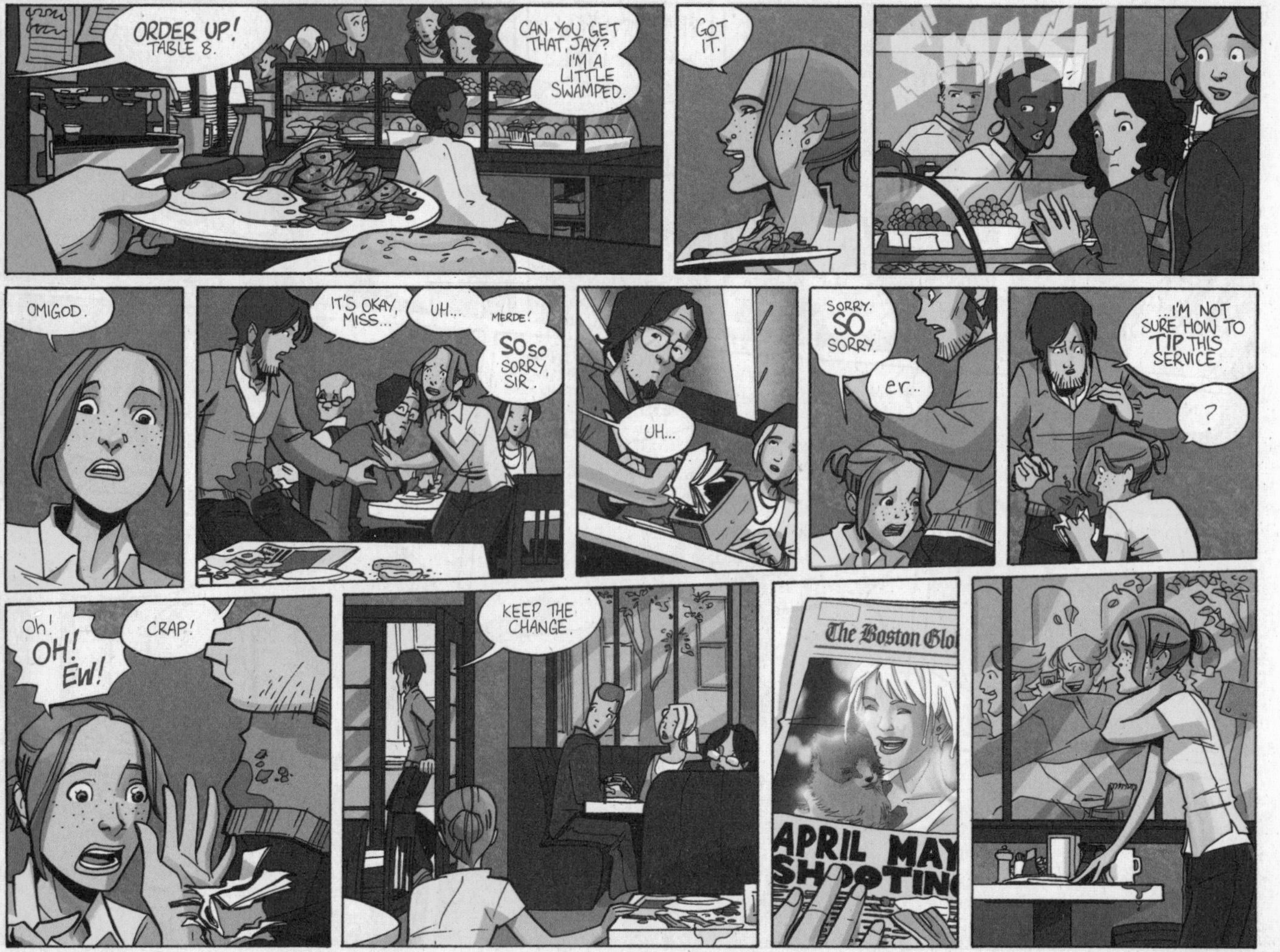
ORDER UP! TABLE 8.
CAN YOU GET THAT, JAY? I'M A LITTLE SWAMPED.
GOT IT.
SMASH
OMIGOD.
IT'S OKAY, MISS...
UH...
MERDE!
SO so SORRY, SIR.
UH...
SORRY. SO SORRY.
er...
...I'M NOT SURE HOW TO TIP THIS SERVICE.
?
Oh! OH! EW!
CRAP!
KEEP THE CHANGE.
The Boston Glo
APRIL MAY
SHOOTIN

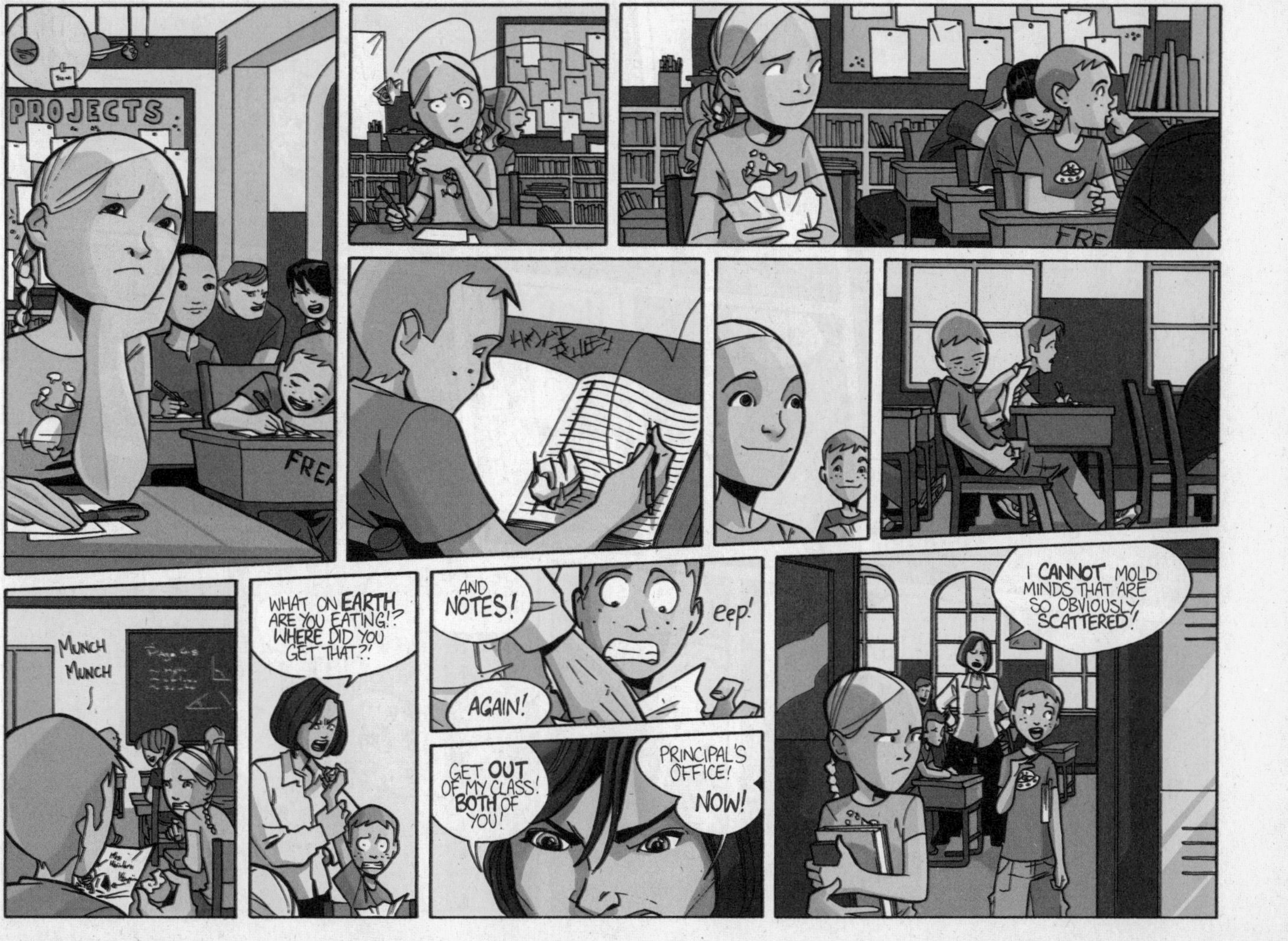
PROJECTS
FREA
HOYT RULES!
FRE
MUNCH MUNCH
WHAT ON EARTH ARE YOU EATING!? WHERE DID YOU GET THAT?!
AND NOTES!
eep!
AGAIN!
GET OUT OF MY CLASS! BOTH OF YOU!
PRINCIPAL'S OFFICE!
NOW!
I CANNOT MOLD MINDS THAT ARE SO OBVIOUSLY SCATTERED!

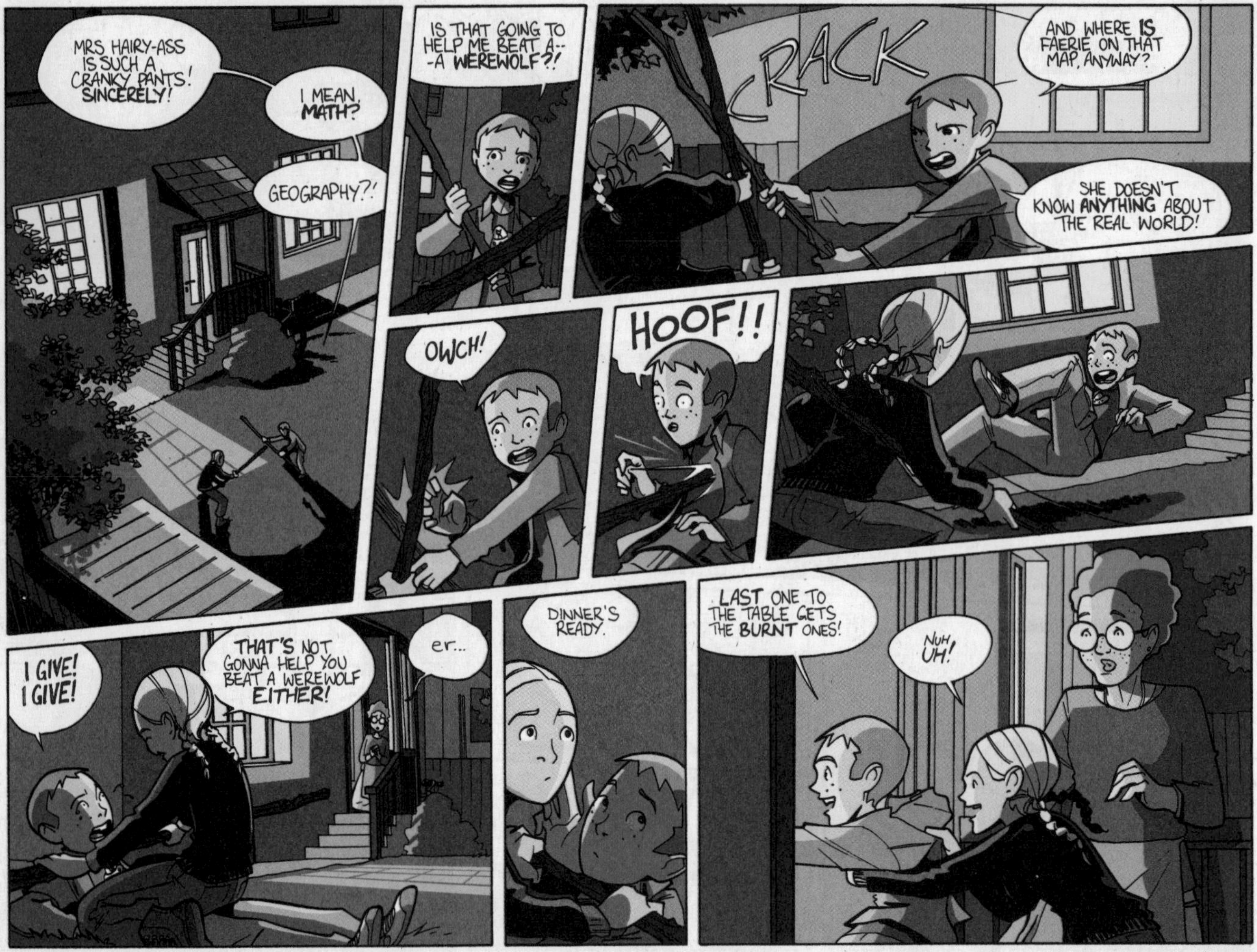
MRS HAIRY-ASS IS SUCH A CRANKY PANTS! SINCERELY!
I MEAN, MATH?
GEOGRAPHY?!
IS THAT GOING TO HELP ME BEAT A-- -A WEREWOLF?!
CRACK
AND WHERE IS FAERIE ON THAT MAP, ANYWAY?
SHE DOESN'T KNOW ANYTHING ABOUT THE REAL WORLD!
OWCH!
HOOF!!
I GIVE! I GIVE!
THAT'S NOT GONNA HELP YOU BEAT A WEREWOLF EITHER!
er...
DINNER'S READY.
LAST ONE TO THE TABLE GETS THE BURNT ONES!
NUH UH!

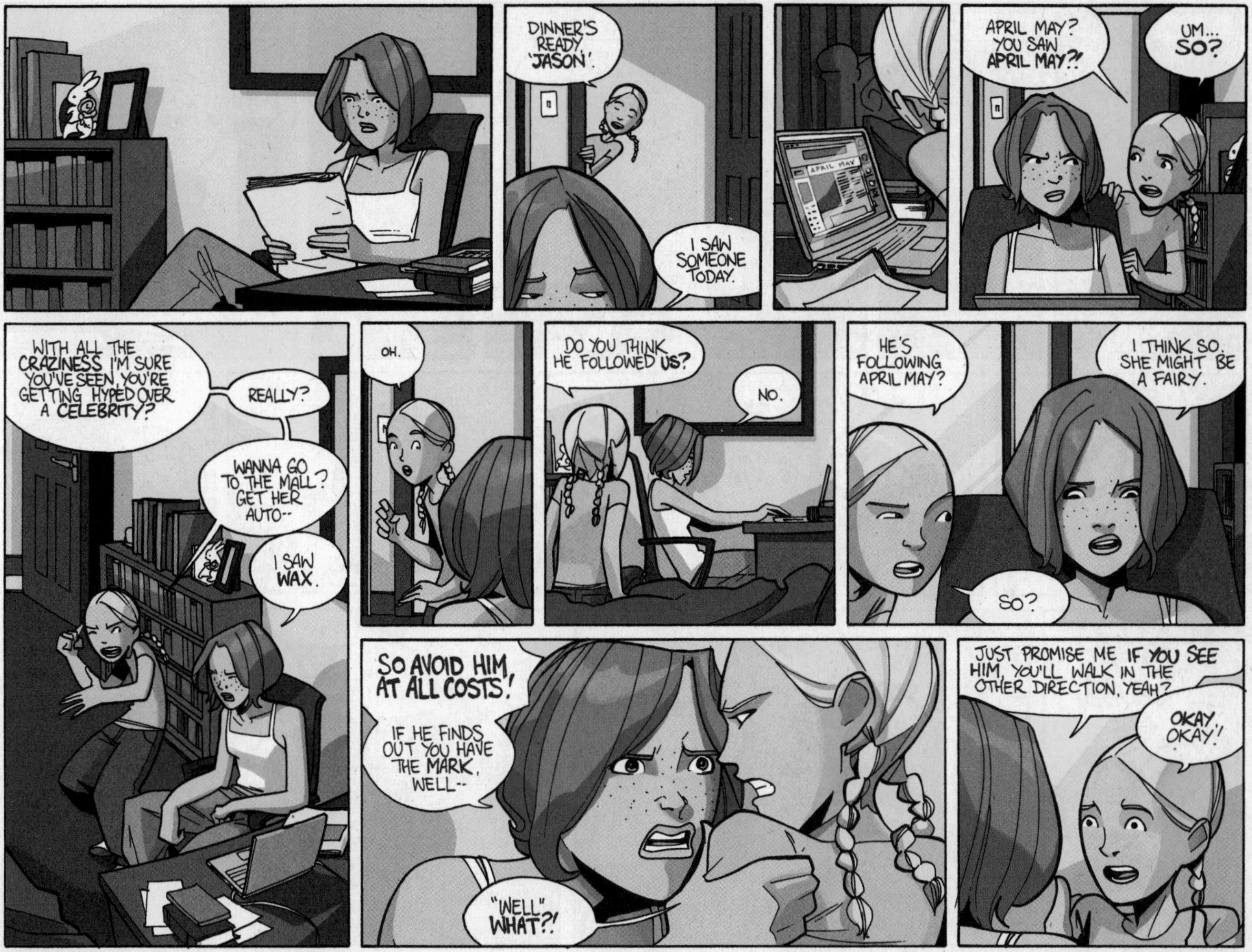

DINNER'S READY 'JASON'.
I SAW SOMEONE TODAY.
APRIL MAY
APRIL MAY? YOU SAW APRIL MAY?!
UM... SO?
WITH ALL THE CRAZINESS I'M SURE YOU'VE SEEN, YOU'RE GETTING HYPED OVER A CELEBRITY?
REALLY?
WANNA GO TO THE MALL? GET HER AUTO--
I SAW WAX.
OH.
DO YOU THINK HE FOLLOWED US?
NO.
HE'S FOLLOWING APRIL MAY?
I THINK SO. SHE MIGHT BE A FAIRY.
SO?
SO AVOID HIM, AT ALL COSTS!
IF HE FINDS OUT YOU HAVE THE MARK, WELL--
"WELL" WHAT?!
JUST PROMISE ME IF YOU SEE HIM, YOU'LL WALK IN THE OTHER DIRECTION, YEAH?
OKAY, OKAY!

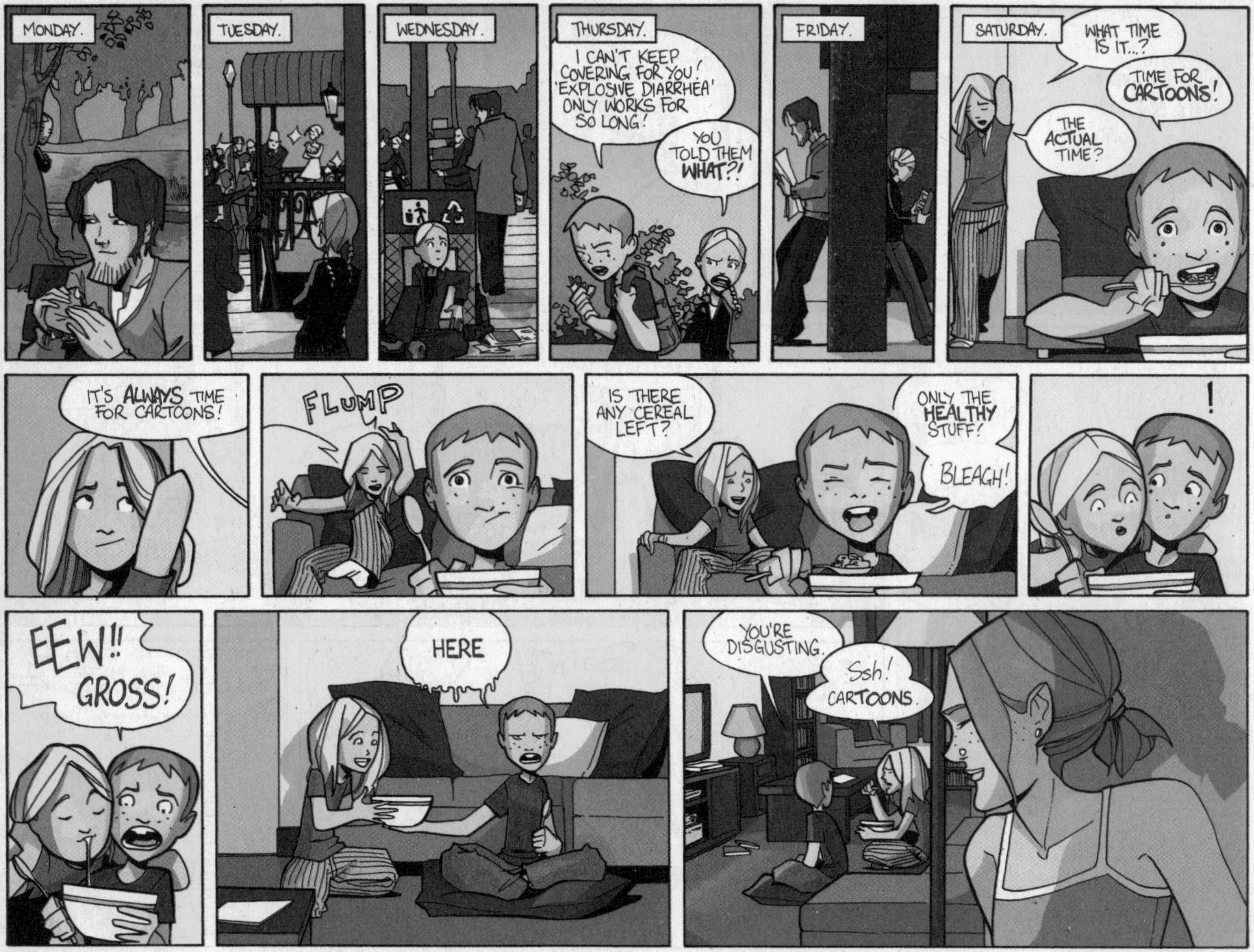
MONDAY.
TUESDAY.
WEDNESDAY.
THURSDAY.
I CAN'T KEEP COVERING FOR YOU! 'EXPLOSIVE DIARRHEA' ONLY WORKS FOR SO LONG!
YOU TOLD THEM WHAT?!
FRIDAY.
SATURDAY.
WHAT TIME IS IT...?
TIME FOR CARTOONS!
THE ACTUAL TIME?
IT'S ALWAYS TIME FOR CARTOONS!
FLUMP
IS THERE ANY CEREAL LEFT?
ONLY THE HEALTHY STUFF!
BLEAGH!
!
EEW!! GROSS!
HERE
YOU'RE DISGUSTING.
Ssh! CARTOONS.

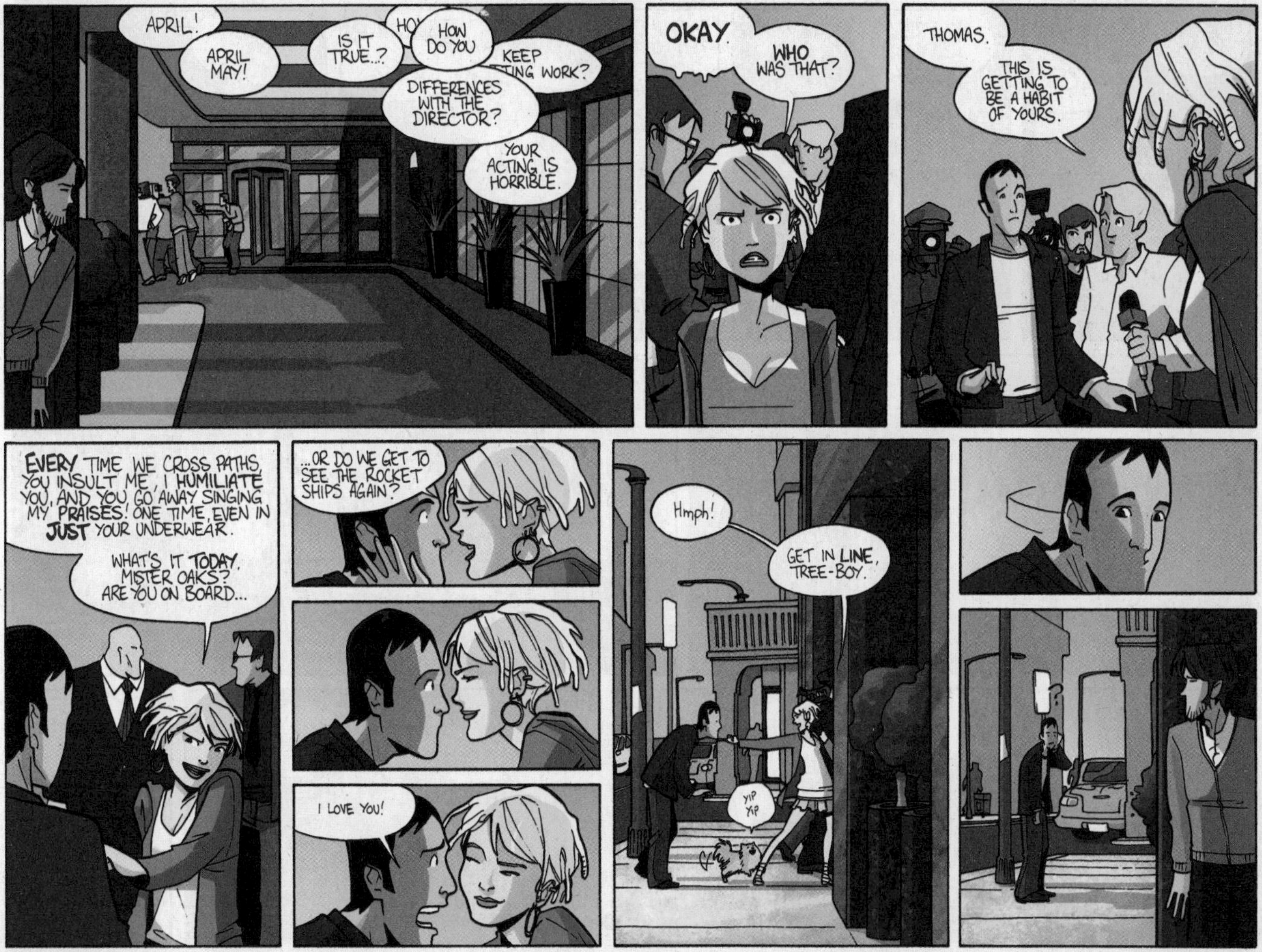
APRIL!
APRIL MAY!
IS IT TRUE...?
HOW DO YOU
KEEP
TING WORK?
DIFFERENCES WITH THE DIRECTOR?
YOUR ACTING IS HORRIBLE.
OKAY.
WHO WAS THAT?
THOMAS.
THIS IS GETTING TO BE A HABIT OF YOURS.
EVERY TIME WE CROSS PATHS, YOU INSULT ME, I HUMILIATE YOU, AND YOU GO AWAY SINGING MY PRAISES! ONE TIME, EVEN IN JUST YOUR UNDERWEAR.
WHAT'S IT TODAY, MISTER OAKS? ARE YOU ON BOARD...
...OR DO WE GET TO SEE THE ROCKET SHIPS AGAIN?
I LOVE YOU!
Hmph!
GET IN LINE, TREE-BOY.
YIP YIP

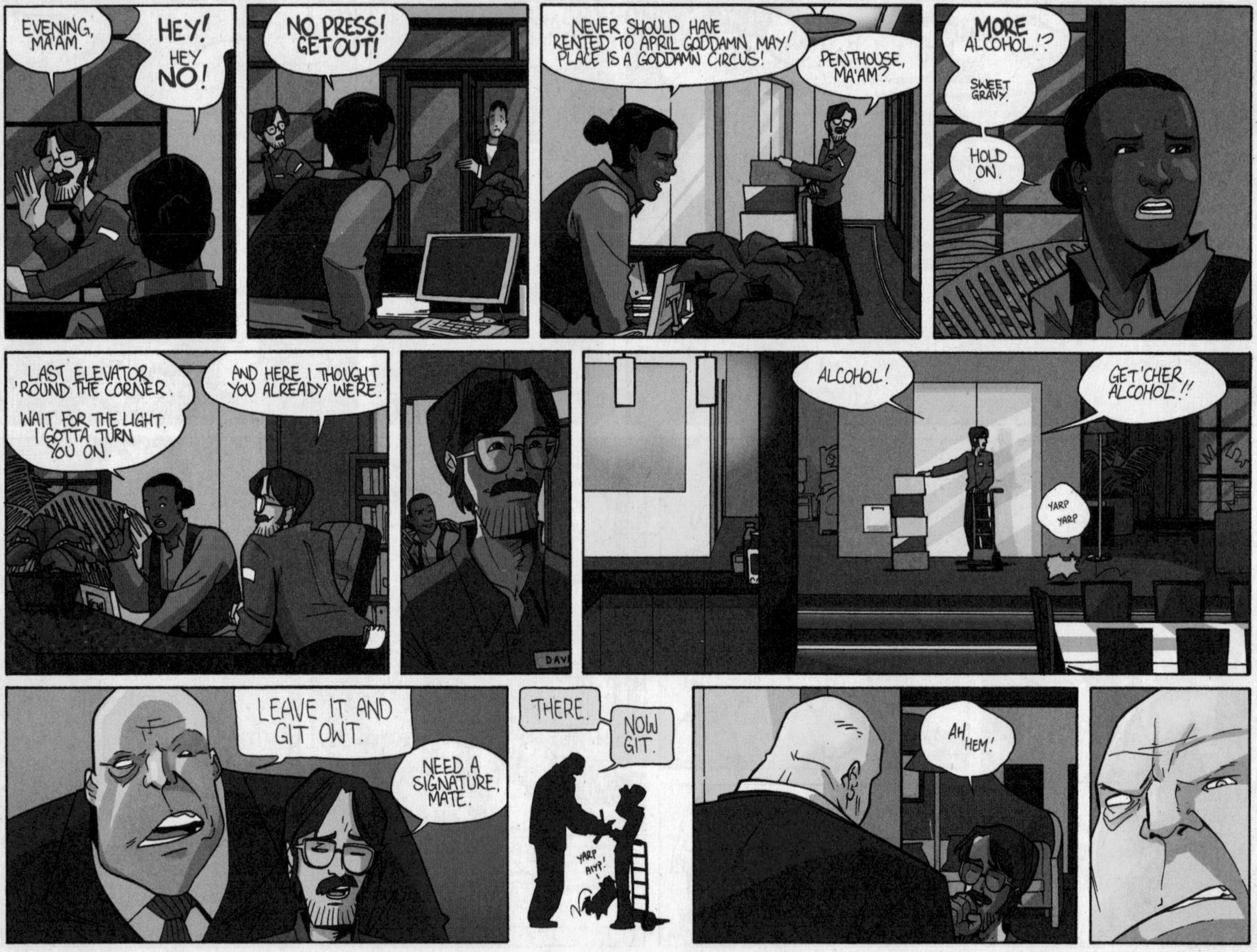
EVENING, MA'AM.
HEY! HEY NO!
NO PRESS! GET OUT!
NEVER SHOULD HAVE RENTED TO APRIL GODDAMN MAY! PLACE IS A GODDAMN CIRCUS!
PENTHOUSE, MA'AM?
MORE ALCOHOL!?
SWEET GRAVY.
HOLD ON.
LAST ELEVATOR 'ROUND THE CORNER.
WAIT FOR THE LIGHT. I GOTTA TURN YOU ON.
AND HERE I THOUGHT YOU ALREADY WERE.
DAV
ALCOHOL!
GET'CHER ALCOHOL!!
YARP YARP
LEAVE IT AND GIT OWT.
NEED A SIGNATURE, MATE.
THERE.
NOW GIT.
YARP AWP!
AH HEM!

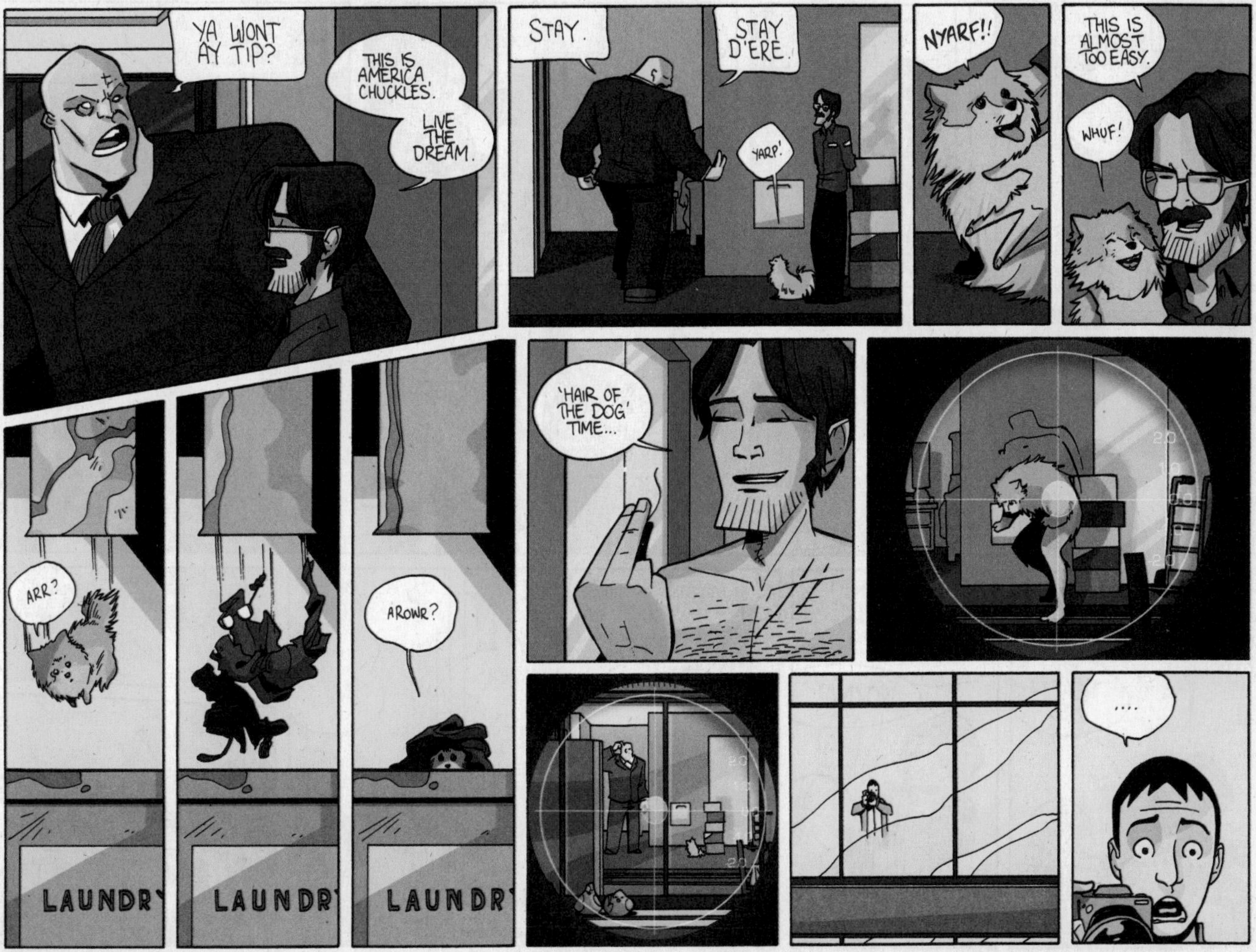
YA WONT AY TIP?
THIS IS AMERICA, CHUCKLES'.
LIVE THE DREAM.
STAY.
STAY D'ERE.
YARP!
NYARF!!
THIS IS ALMOST TOO EASY.
WHUF!
ARR?
AROWR?
LAUNDRY
LAUNDRY
LAUNDRY
'HAIR OF THE DOG' TIME...
....

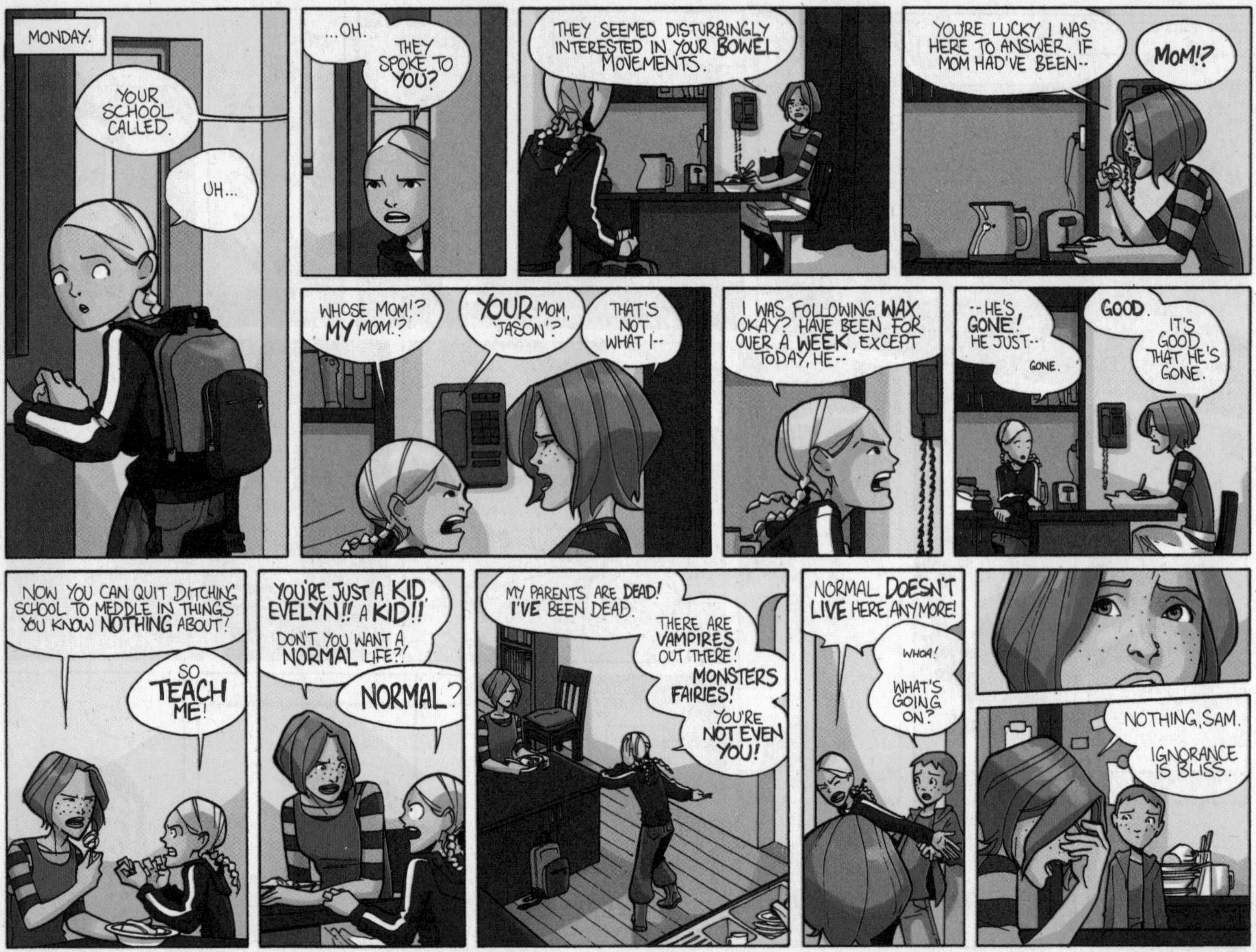
MONDAY.
YOUR SCHOOL CALLED.
UH...
...OH.
THEY SPOKE TO YOU?
THEY SEEMED DISTURBINGLY INTERESTED IN YOUR BOWEL MOVEMENTS.
YOU'RE LUCKY I WAS HERE TO ANSWER. IF MOM HAD'VE BEEN--
MOM!?
WHOSE MOM!? MY MOM!?
YOUR MOM, 'JASON'?
THAT'S NOT WHAT I--
I WAS FOLLOWING WAX, OKAY? HAVE BEEN FOR OVER A WEEK, EXCEPT TODAY, HE--
--HE'S GONE! HE JUST--
GONE.
GOOD.
IT'S GOOD THAT HE'S GONE.
NOW YOU CAN QUIT DITCHING SCHOOL TO MEDDLE IN THINGS YOU KNOW NOTHING ABOUT!
SO TEACH ME!
YOU'RE JUST A KID, EVELYN!! A KID!!
DON'T YOU WANT A NORMAL LIFE?!
NORMAL?
MY PARENTS ARE DEAD! I'VE BEEN DEAD.
THERE ARE VAMPIRES OUT THERE!
MONSTERS FAIRIES!
YOU'RE NOT EVEN YOU!
NORMAL DOESN'T LIVE HERE ANYMORE!
WHOA!
WHAT'S GOING ON?
NOTHING, SAM.
IGNORANCE IS BLISS.

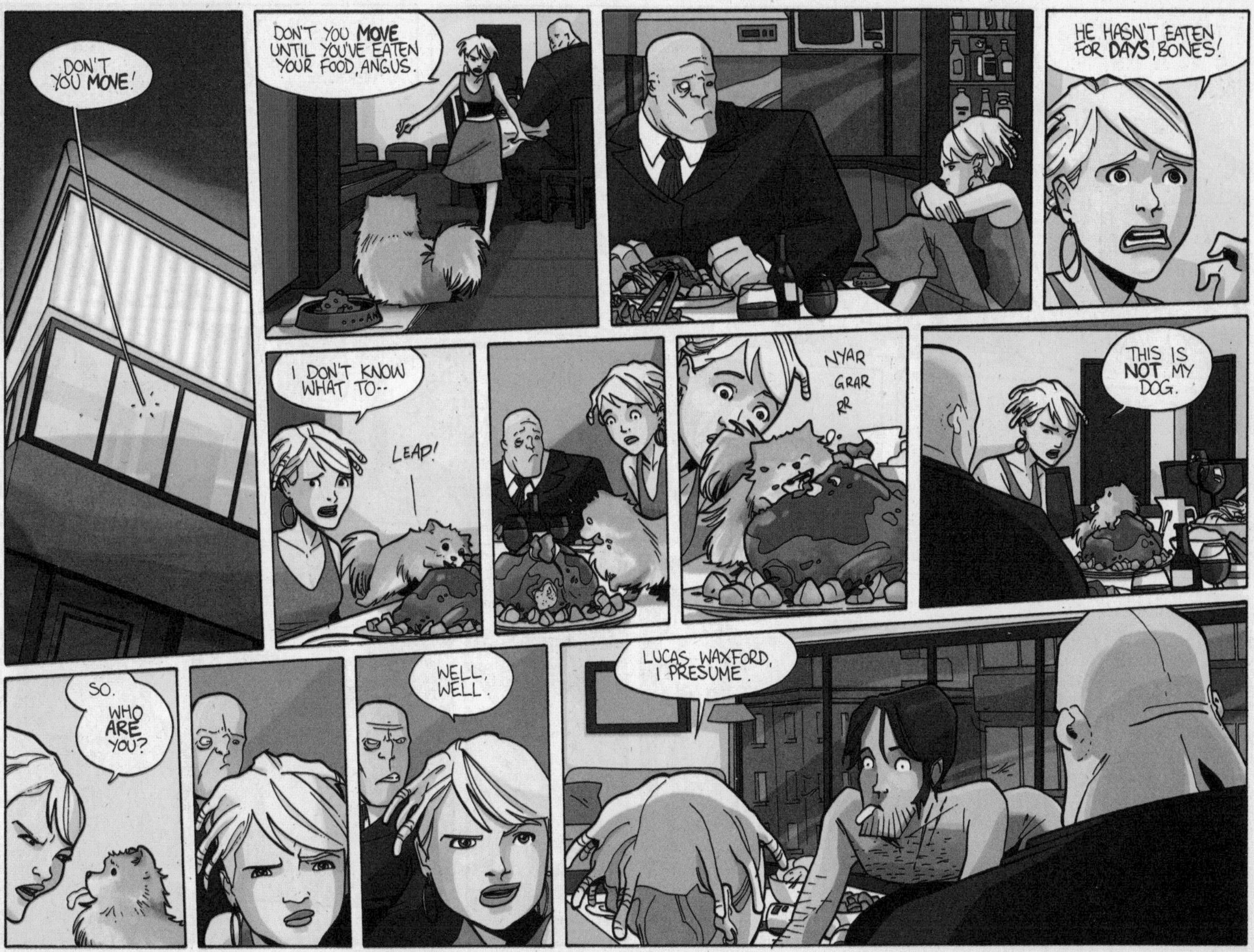
DON'T YOU MOVE!
DON'T YOU MOVE UNTIL YOU'VE EATEN YOUR FOOD, ANGUS.
HE HASN'T EATEN FOR DAYS, BONES!
I DON'T KNOW WHAT TO--
LEAP!
NYAR
GRAR
RR
THIS IS NOT MY DOG.
SO.
WHO ARE YOU?
WELL, WELL.
LUCAS WAXFORD, I PRESUME.

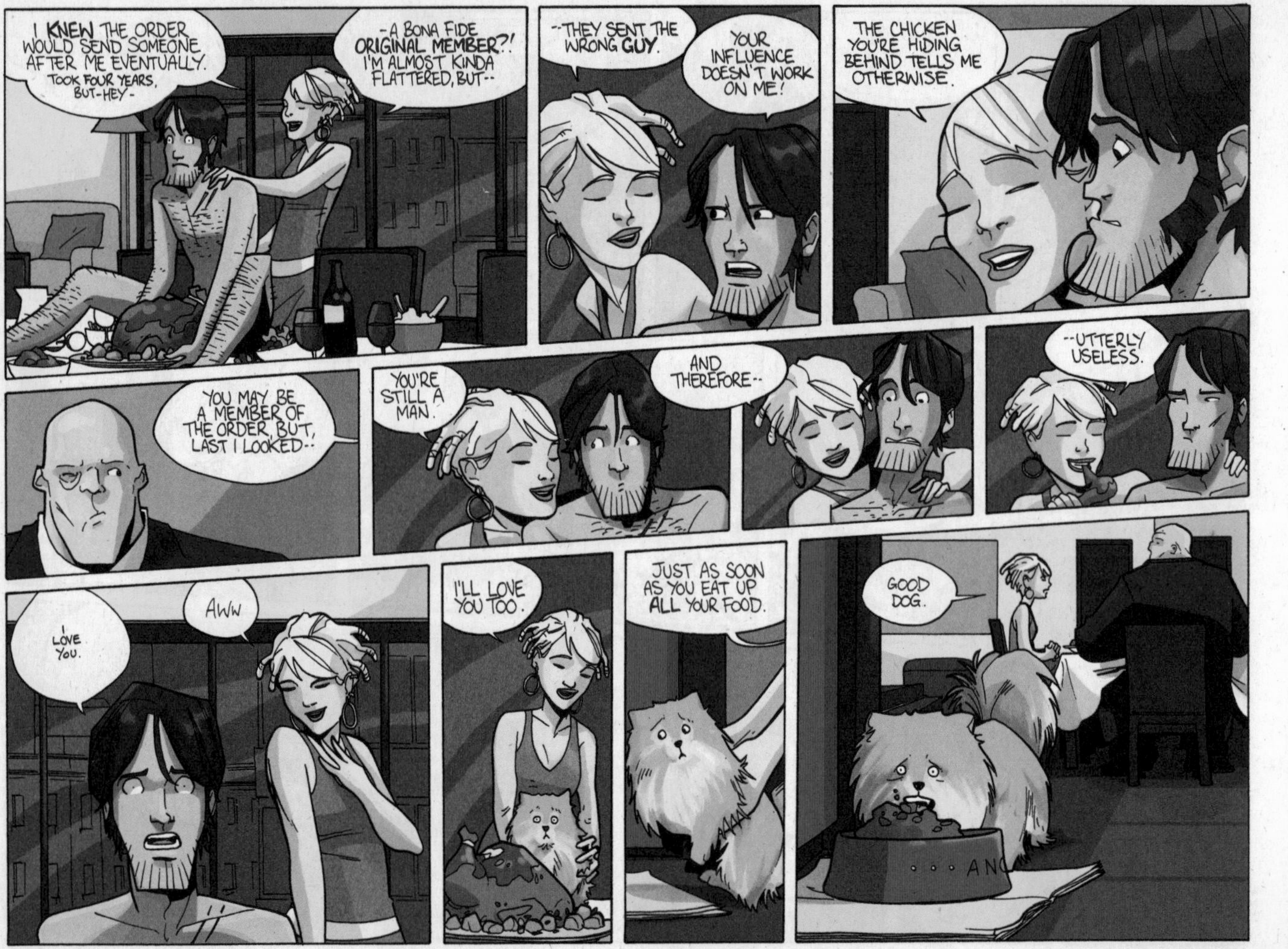
I KNEW THE ORDER WOULD SEND SOMEONE AFTER ME EVENTUALLY. TOOK FOUR YEARS, BUT-HEY-
-A BONA FIDE ORIGINAL MEMBER?! I'M ALMOST KINDA FLATTERED, BUT--
--THEY SENT THE WRONG GUY.
YOUR INFLUENCE DOESN'T WORK ON ME!
THE CHICKEN YOU'RE HIDING BEHIND TELLS ME OTHERWISE.
YOU MAY BE A MEMBER OF THE ORDER, BUT, LAST I LOOKED--
YOU'RE STILL A MAN.
AND THEREFORE--
--UTTERLY USELESS.
I LOVE YOU.
AWW
I'LL LOVE YOU TOO.
JUST AS SOON AS YOU EAT UP ALL YOUR FOOD.
GOOD DOG.

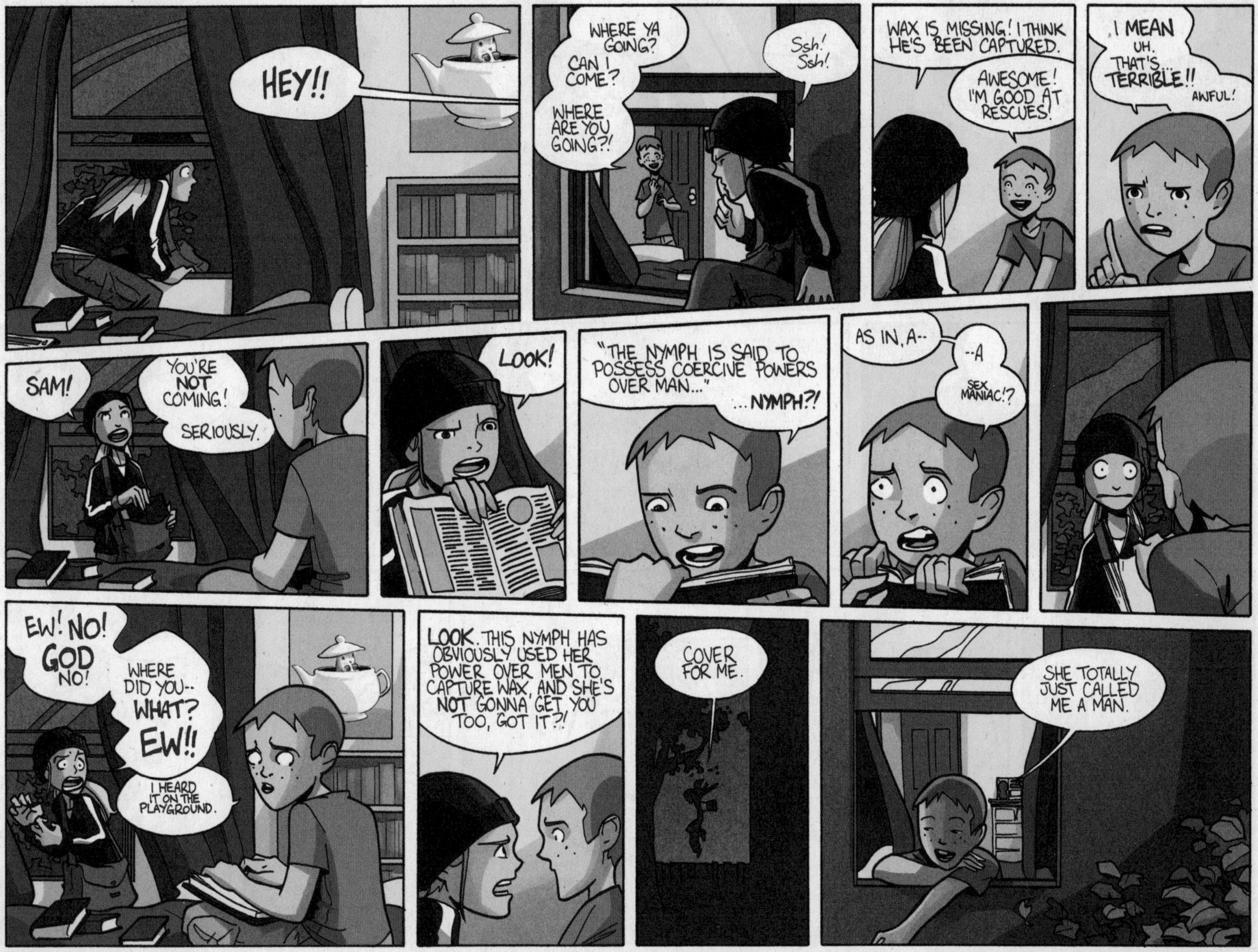
HEY!!
WHERE YA GOING? CAN I COME?
WHERE ARE YOU GOING?!
Ssh! Ssh!
WAX IS MISSING! I THINK HE'S BEEN CAPTURED.
AWESOME! I'M GOOD AT RESCUES!
I MEAN UH. THAT'S... TERRIBLE!!
AWFUL!
SAM!
YOU'RE NOT COMING!
SERIOUSLY.
LOOK!
"THE NYMPH IS SAID TO POSSESS COERCIVE POWERS OVER MAN..."
...NYMPH?!
AS IN, A--
--A SEX MANIAC!?
EW! NO! GOD NO!
WHERE DID YOU-- WHAT? EW!!
I HEARD IT ON THE PLAYGROUND.
LOOK. THIS NYMPH HAS OBVIOUSLY USED HER POWER OVER MEN TO CAPTURE WAX, AND SHE'S NOT GONNA GET YOU TOO, GOT IT?!
COVER FOR ME.
SHE TOTALLY JUST CALLED ME A MAN.

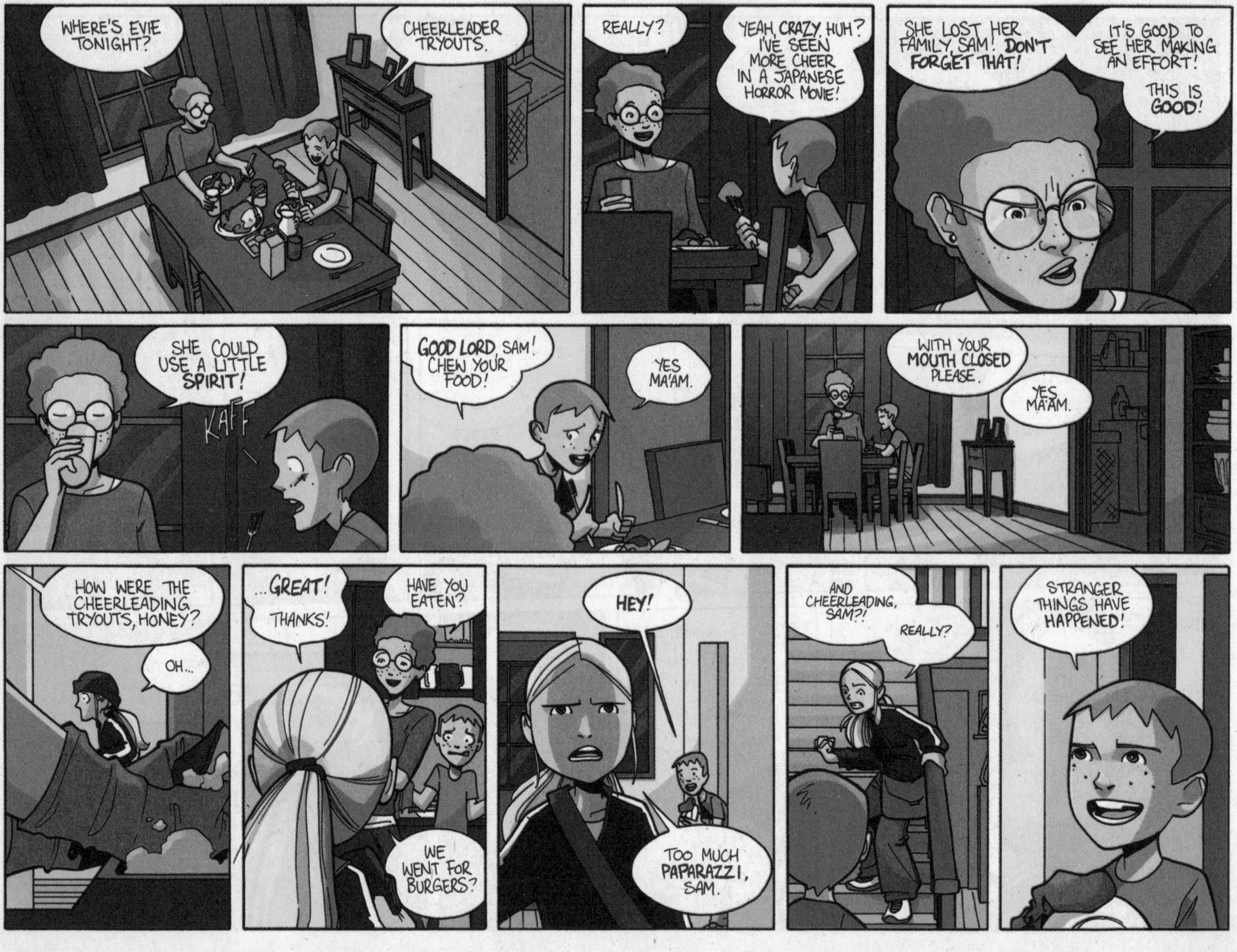
WHERE'S EVIE TONIGHT?
CHEERLEADER TRYOUTS.
REALLY?
YEAH, CRAZY, HUH? I'VE SEEN MORE CHEER IN A JAPANESE HORROR MOVIE!
SHE LOST HER FAMILY, SAM! DON'T FORGET THAT!
IT'S GOOD TO SEE HER MAKING AN EFFORT!
THIS IS GOOD!
SHE COULD USE A LITTLE SPIRIT!
KAFF
GOOD LORD, SAM! CHEW YOUR FOOD!
YES MA'AM.
WITH YOUR MOUTH CLOSED PLEASE.
YES MA'AM.
HOW WERE THE CHEERLEADING TRYOUTS, HONEY?
OH...
...GREAT!
THANKS!
HAVE YOU EATEN?
WE WENT FOR BURGERS?
HEY!
TOO MUCH PAPARAZZI, SAM.
AND CHEERLEADING, SAM?!
REALLY?
STRANGER THINGS HAVE HAPPENED!

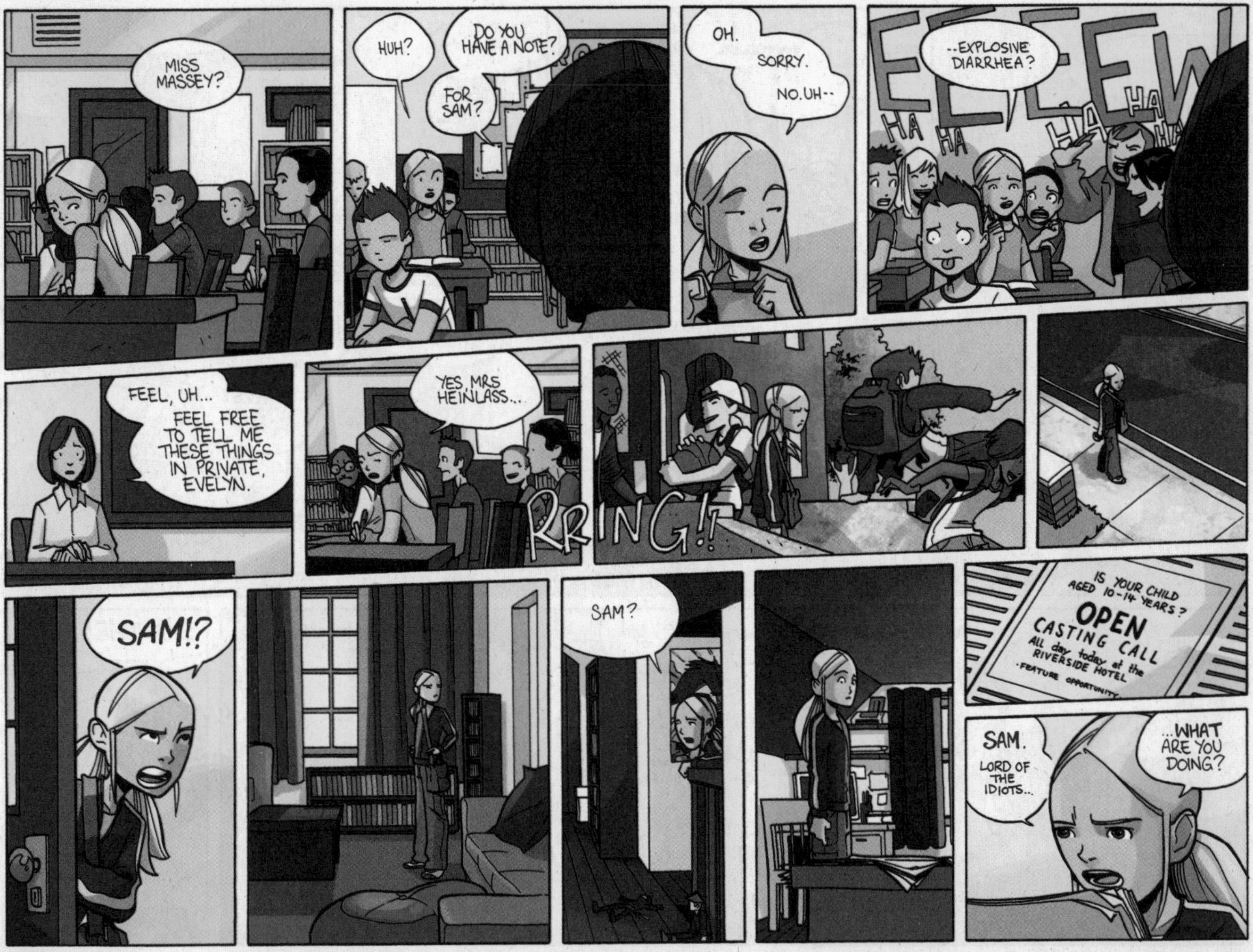
MISS MASSEY?
HUH?
DO YOU HAVE A NOTE?
FOR SAM?
OH.
SORRY.
NO. UH--
--EXPLOSIVE DIARRHEA?
EEEEW!
HA HA
HA HA
HA HA
FEEL, UH...
FEEL FREE TO TELL ME THESE THINGS IN PRIVATE, EVELYN.
YES, MRS HEINLASS...
RRING!!
SAM!?
SAM?
IS YOUR CHILD AGED 10-14 YEARS?
OPEN CASTING CALL
All day today at the RIVERSIDE HOTEL
-FEATURE OPPORTUNITY
SAM.
LORD OF THE IDIOTS...
...WHAT ARE YOU DOING?

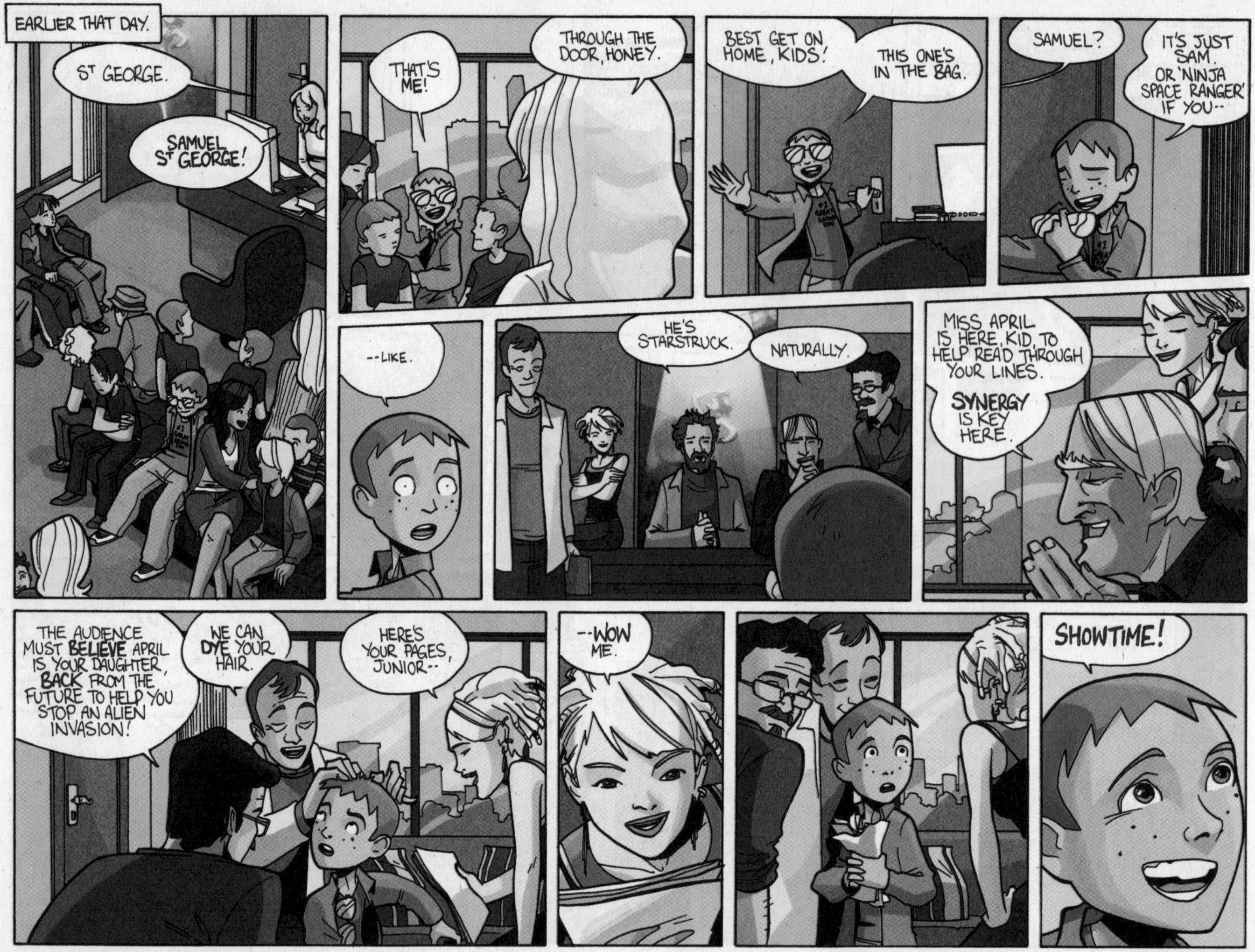
EARLIER THAT DAY.
ST GEORGE.
SAMUEL ST GEORGE!
THAT'S ME!
THROUGH THE DOOR, HONEY.
BEST GET ON HOME, KIDS!
THIS ONE'S IN THE BAG.
SAMUEL?
IT'S JUST SAM. OR 'NINJA SPACE RANGER' IF YOU--
--LIKE.
HE'S STARSTRUCK.
NATURALLY.
MISS APRIL IS HERE, KID, TO HELP READ THROUGH YOUR LINES.
SYNERGY IS KEY HERE.
THE AUDIENCE MUST BELIEVE APRIL IS YOUR DAUGHTER, BACK FROM THE FUTURE TO HELP YOU STOP AN ALIEN INVASION!
WE CAN DYE YOUR HAIR.
HERE'S YOUR PAGES, JUNIOR--
--WOW ME.
SHOWTIME!

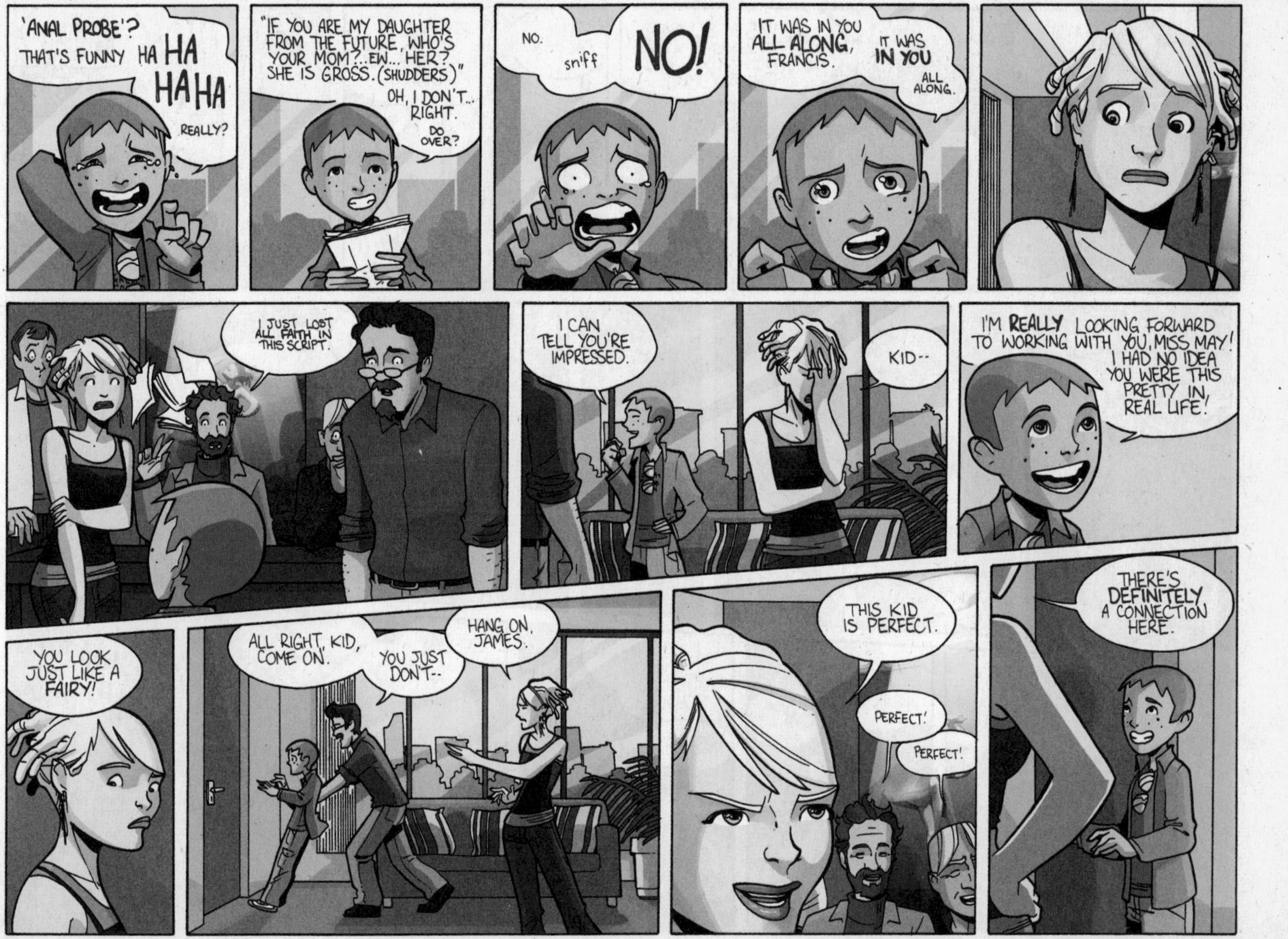
'ANAL PROBE'? THAT'S FUNNY HA HA HA HA
REALLY?
"IF YOU ARE MY DAUGHTER FROM THE FUTURE, WHO'S YOUR MOM?...EW... HER? SHE IS GROSS. (SHUDDERS)"
OH, I DON'T... RIGHT.
DO OVER?
NO.
sniff
NO!
IT WAS IN YOU ALL ALONG, FRANCIS.
IT WAS IN YOU ALL ALONG.
I JUST LOST ALL FAITH IN THIS SCRIPT.
I CAN TELL YOU'RE IMPRESSED.
KID--
I'M REALLY LOOKING FORWARD TO WORKING WITH YOU, MISS MAY! I HAD NO IDEA YOU WERE THIS PRETTY IN REAL LIFE!
YOU LOOK JUST LIKE A FAIRY!
ALL RIGHT, KID, COME ON.
YOU JUST DON'T--
HANG ON, JAMES.
THIS KID IS PERFECT.
PERFECT!
PERFECT!
THERE'S DEFINITELY A CONNECTION HERE.

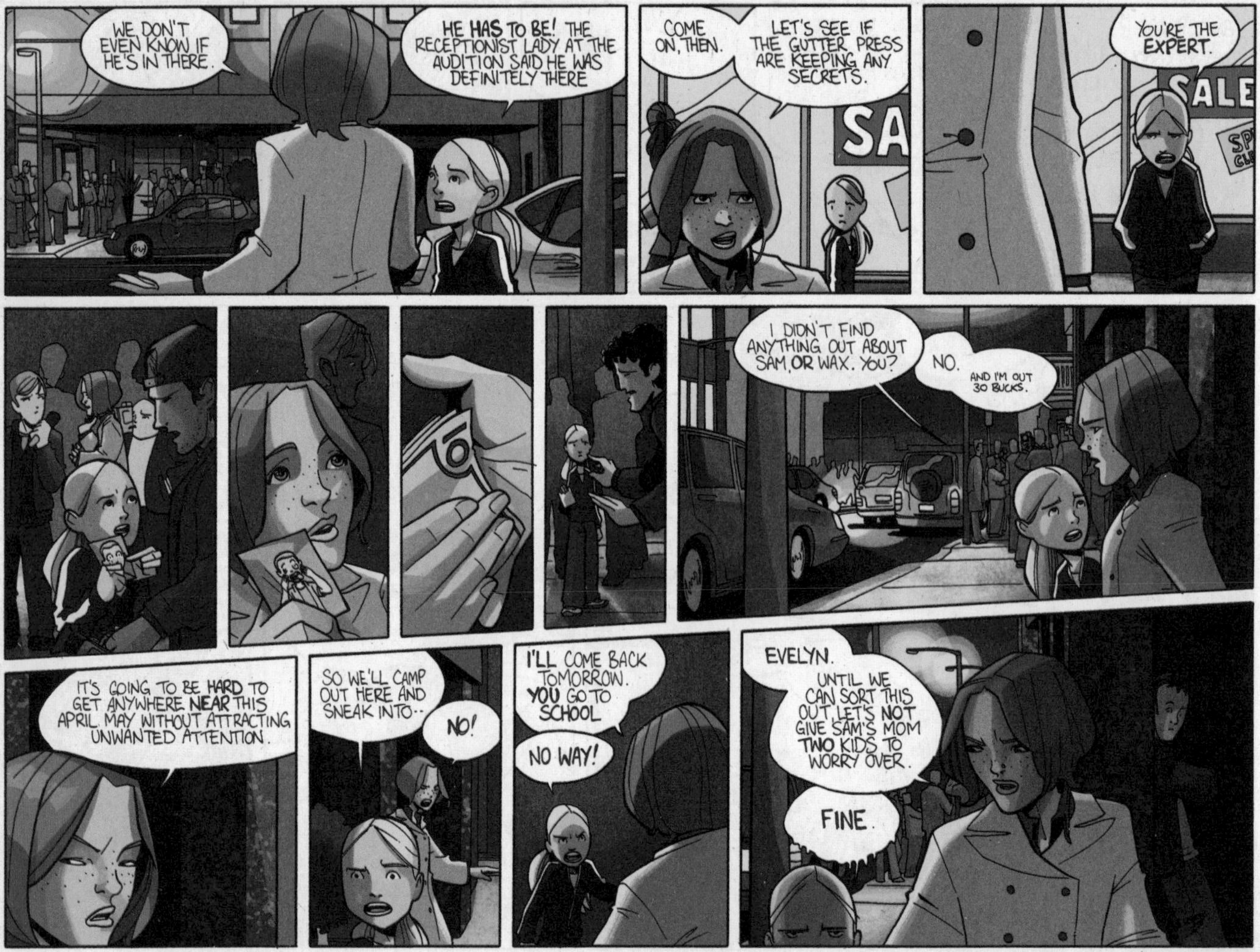
WE DON'T EVEN KNOW IF HE'S IN THERE.
HE HAS TO BE! THE RECEPTIONIST LADY AT THE AUDITION SAID HE WAS DEFINITELY THERE
COME ON, THEN.
LET'S SEE IF THE GUTTER PRESS ARE KEEPING ANY SECRETS.
YOU'RE THE EXPERT.
SALE
I DIDN'T FIND ANYTHING OUT ABOUT SAM, OR WAX. YOU?
NO.
AND I'M OUT 30 BUCKS.
IT'S GOING TO BE HARD TO GET ANYWHERE NEAR THIS APRIL MAY WITHOUT ATTRACTING UNWANTED ATTENTION.
SO WE'LL CAMP OUT HERE AND SNEAK INTO...
NO!
I'LL COME BACK TOMORROW. YOU GO TO SCHOOL
NO WAY!
EVELYN.
UNTIL WE CAN SORT THIS OUT, LET'S NOT GIVE SAM'S MOM TWO KIDS TO WORRY OVER.
FINE.

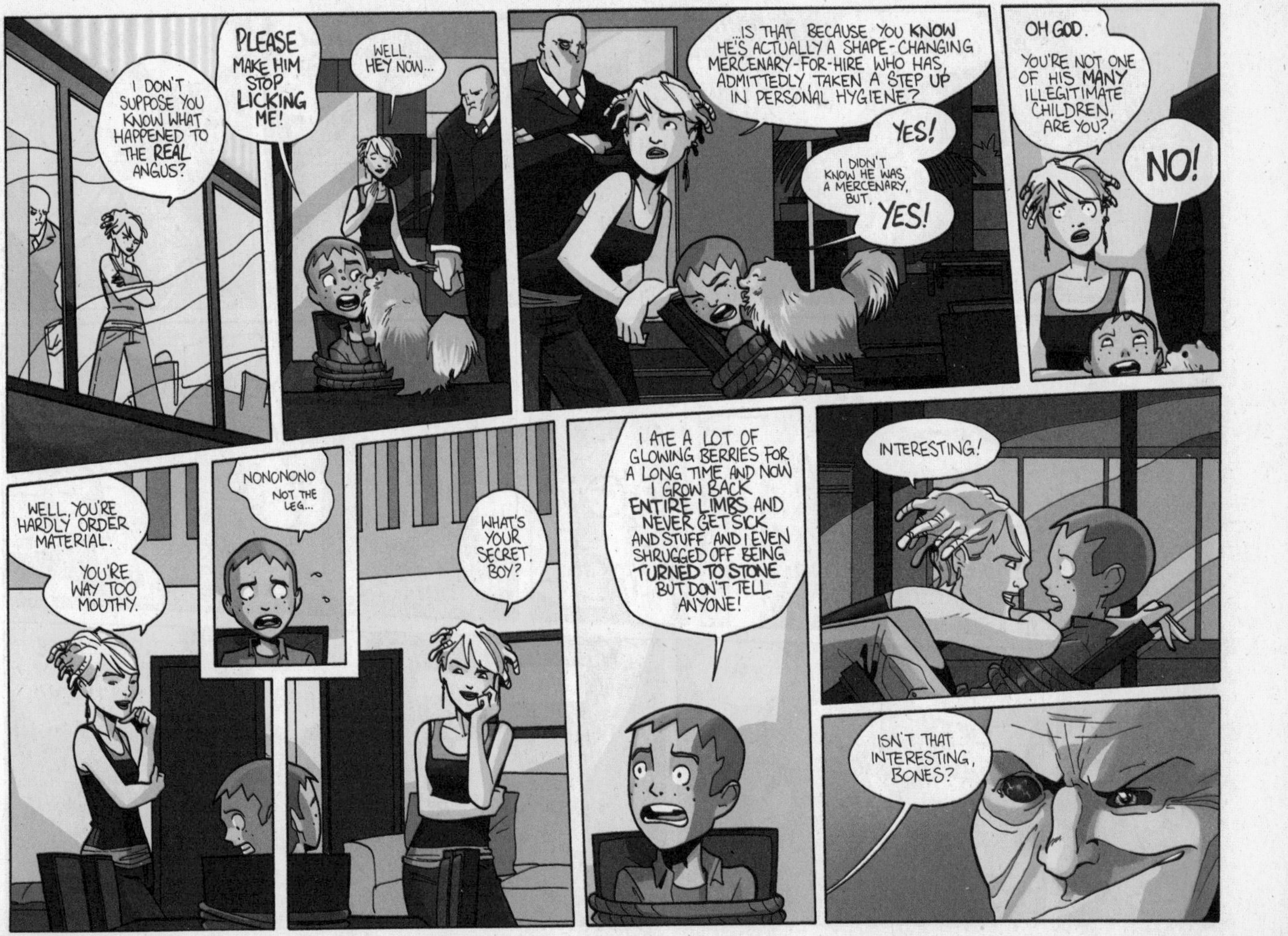
I DON'T SUPPOSE YOU KNOW WHAT HAPPENED TO THE REAL ANGUS?
PLEASE MAKE HIM STOP LICKING ME!
WELL, HEY NOW...
...IS THAT BECAUSE YOU KNOW HE'S ACTUALLY A SHAPE-CHANGING MERCENARY-FOR-HIRE WHO HAS, ADMITTEDLY, TAKEN A STEP UP IN PERSONAL HYGIENE?
YES!
I DIDN'T KNOW HE WAS A MERCENARY, BUT, YES!
OH GOD.
YOU'RE NOT ONE OF HIS MANY ILLEGITIMATE CHILDREN, ARE YOU?
NO!
WELL, YOU'RE HARDLY ORDER MATERIAL.
YOU'RE WAY TOO MOUTHY.
NONONONO
NOT THE LEG...
WHAT'S YOUR SECRET, BOY?
I ATE A LOT OF GLOWING BERRIES FOR A LONG TIME AND NOW I GROW BACK ENTIRE LIMBS AND NEVER GET SICK AND STUFF AND I EVEN SHRUGGED OFF BEING TURNED TO STONE BUT DON'T TELL ANYONE!
INTERESTING!
ISN'T THAT INTERESTING, BONES?

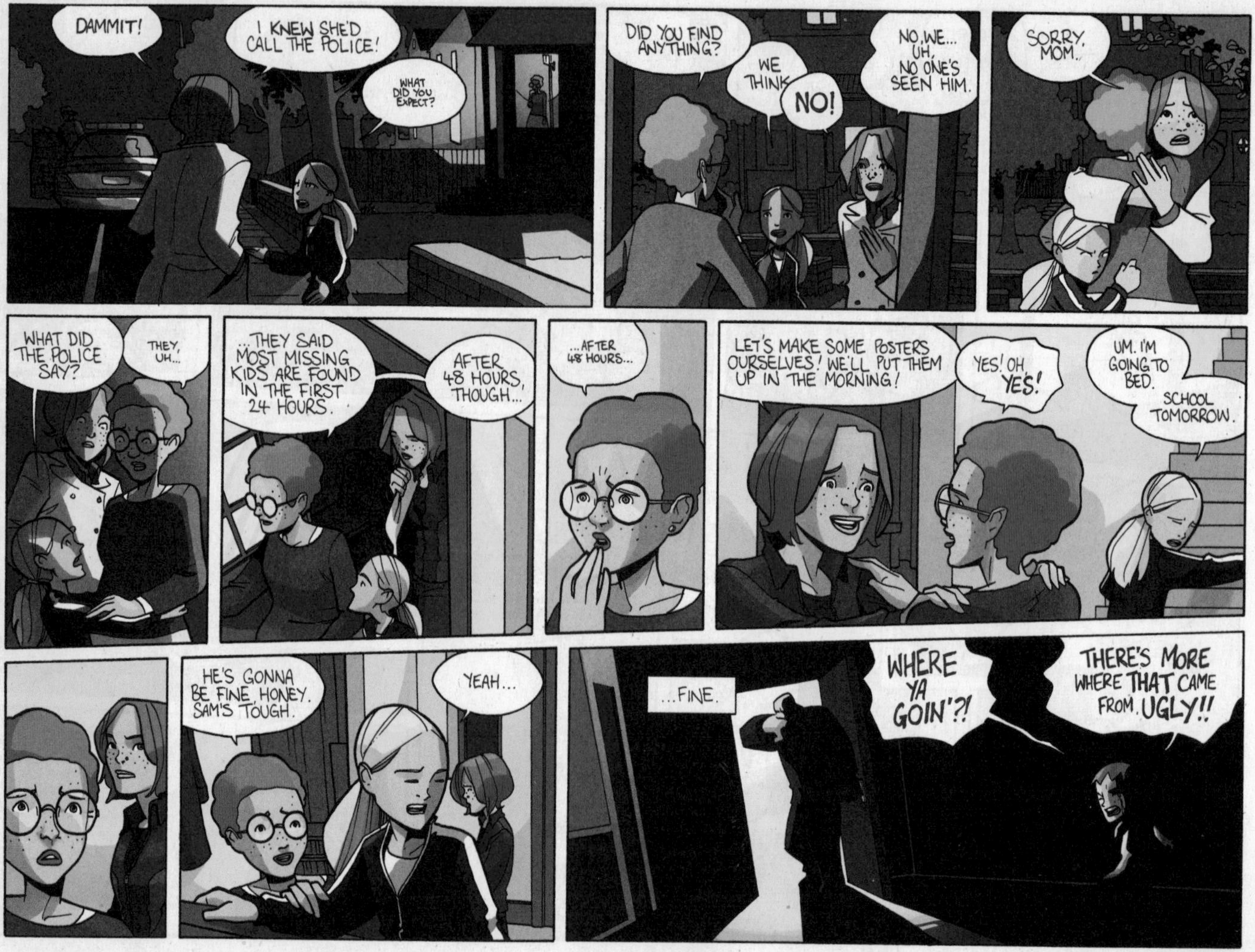
DAMMIT!
I KNEW SHE'D CALL THE POLICE!
WHAT DID YOU EXPECT?
DID YOU FIND ANYTHING?
WE THINK
NO!
NO, WE... UH, NO ONE'S SEEN HIM.
SORRY, MOM...
WHAT DID THE POLICE SAY?
THEY, UH...
...THEY SAID MOST MISSING KIDS ARE FOUND IN THE FIRST 24 HOURS.
AFTER 48 HOURS, THOUGH...
...AFTER 48 HOURS...
LET'S MAKE SOME POSTERS OURSELVES! WE'LL PUT THEM UP IN THE MORNING!
YES! OH YES!
UM. I'M GOING TO BED.
SCHOOL TOMORROW.
HE'S GONNA BE FINE, HONEY. SAM'S TOUGH.
YEAH...
...FINE.
WHERE YA GOIN'?!
THERE'S MORE WHERE THAT CAME FROM, UGLY!!

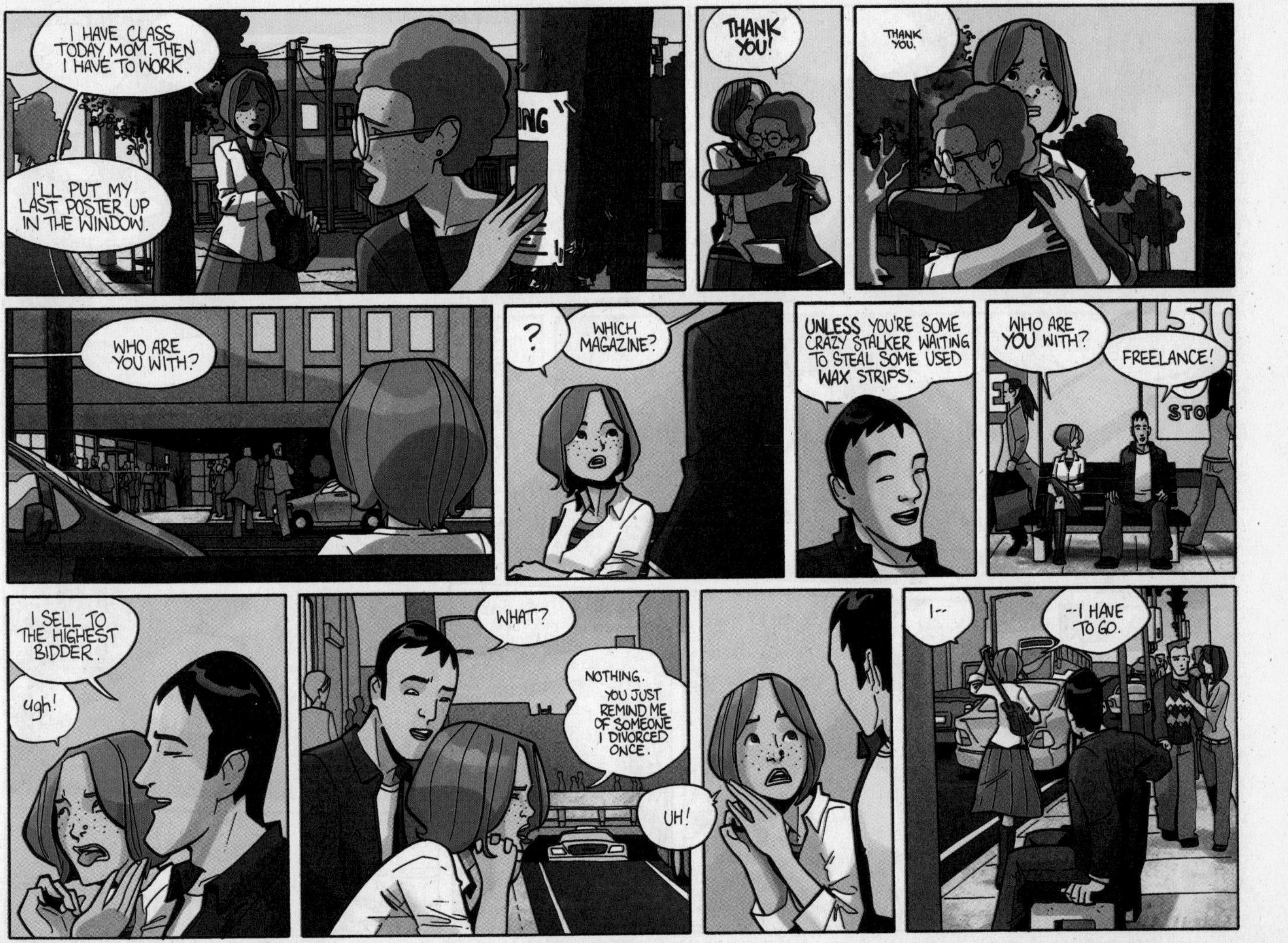
I HAVE CLASS TODAY, MOM. THEN I HAVE TO WORK.
I'LL PUT MY LAST POSTER UP IN THE WINDOW.
THANK YOU!
THANK YOU.
WHO ARE YOU WITH?
?
WHICH MAGAZINE?
UNLESS YOU'RE SOME CRAZY STALKER WAITING TO STEAL SOME USED WAX STRIPS.
WHO ARE YOU WITH?
FREELANCE!
I SELL TO THE HIGHEST BIDDER.
ugh!
WHAT?
NOTHING. YOU JUST REMIND ME OF SOMEONE I DIVORCED ONCE.
UH!
I--
--I HAVE TO GO.

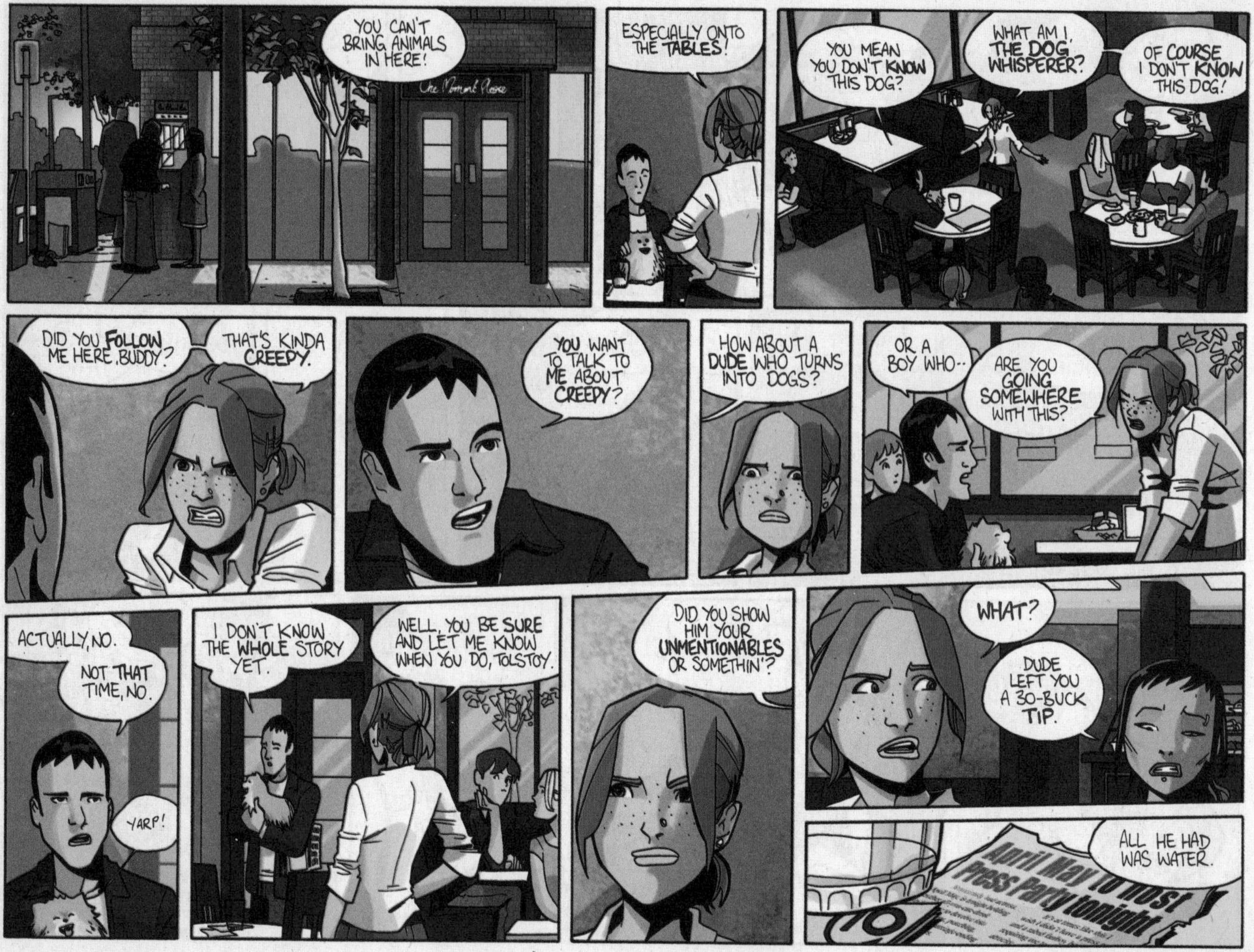
YOU CAN'T BRING ANIMALS IN HERE!
One Moment Please
ESPECIALLY ONTO THE TABLES!
YOU MEAN YOU DON'T KNOW THIS DOG?
WHAT AM I, THE DOG WHISPERER?
OF COURSE I DON'T KNOW THIS DOG!
DID YOU FOLLOW ME HERE, BUDDY?
THAT'S KINDA CREEPY.
YOU WANT TO TALK TO ME ABOUT CREEPY?
HOW ABOUT A DUDE WHO TURNS INTO DOGS?
OR A BOY WHO--
ARE YOU GOING SOMEWHERE WITH THIS?
ACTUALLY, NO.
NOT THAT TIME, NO.
YARP!
I DON'T KNOW THE WHOLE STORY YET.
WELL, YOU BE SURE AND LET ME KNOW WHEN YOU DO, TOLSTOY.
DID YOU SHOW HIM YOUR UNMENTIONABLES OR SOMETHIN'?
WHAT?
DUDE LEFT YOU A 30-BUCK TIP.
ALL HE HAD WAS WATER.
April May to host Press Party tonight

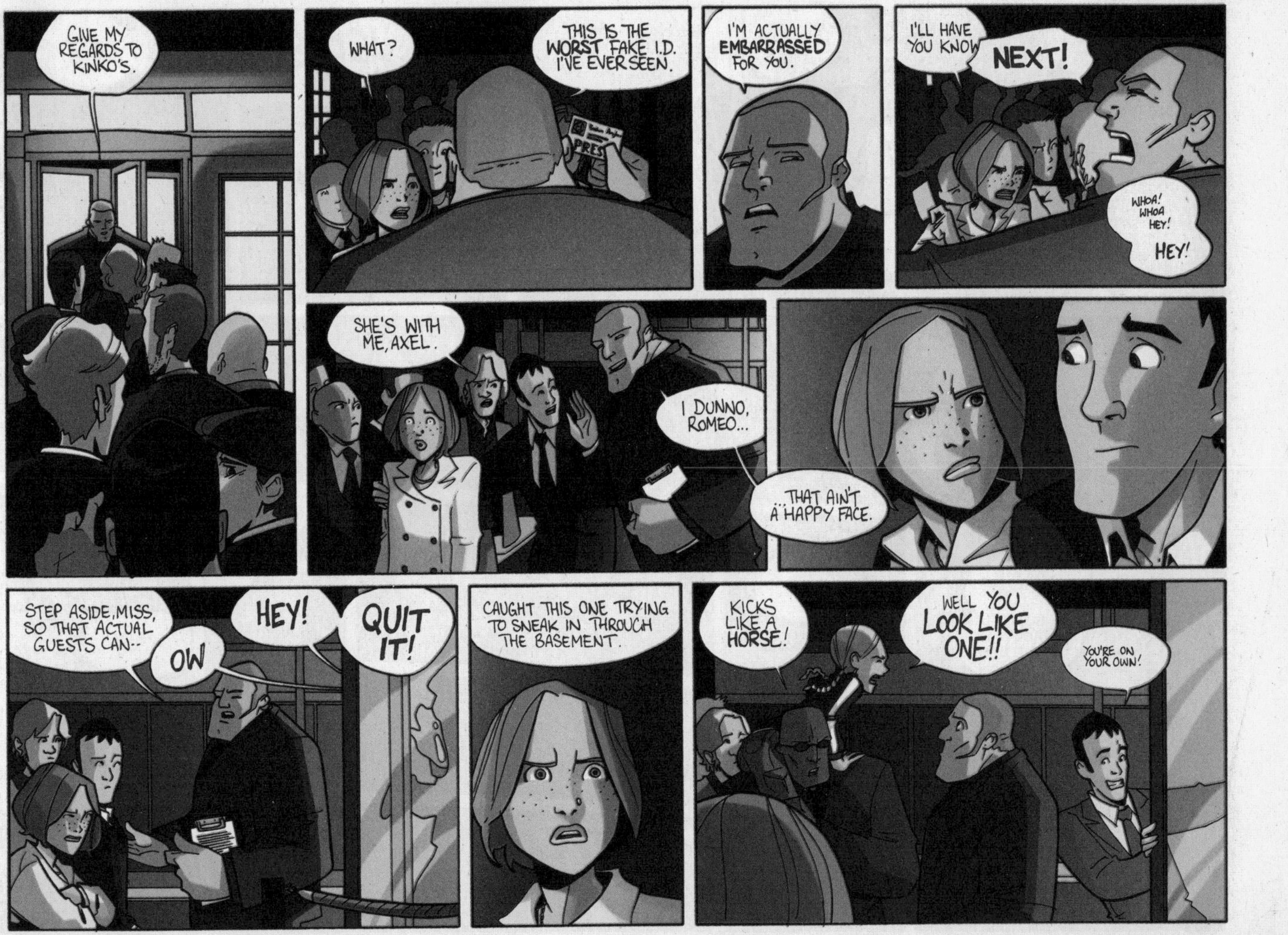

GIVE MY REGARDS TO KINKO'S.
WHAT?
THIS IS THE WORST FAKE I.D. I'VE EVER SEEN.
I'M ACTUALLY EMBARRASSED FOR YOU.
I'LL HAVE YOU KNOW
NEXT!
WHOA! WHOA HEY!
HEY!
SHE'S WITH ME, AXEL.
I DUNNO, ROMEO...
...THAT AIN'T A HAPPY FACE.
STEP ASIDE, MISS, SO THAT ACTUAL GUESTS CAN--
OW
HEY!
QUIT IT!
CAUGHT THIS ONE TRYING TO SNEAK IN THROUGH THE BASEMENT.
KICKS LIKE A HORSE!
WELL YOU LOOK LIKE ONE!!
YOU'RE ON YOUR OWN!

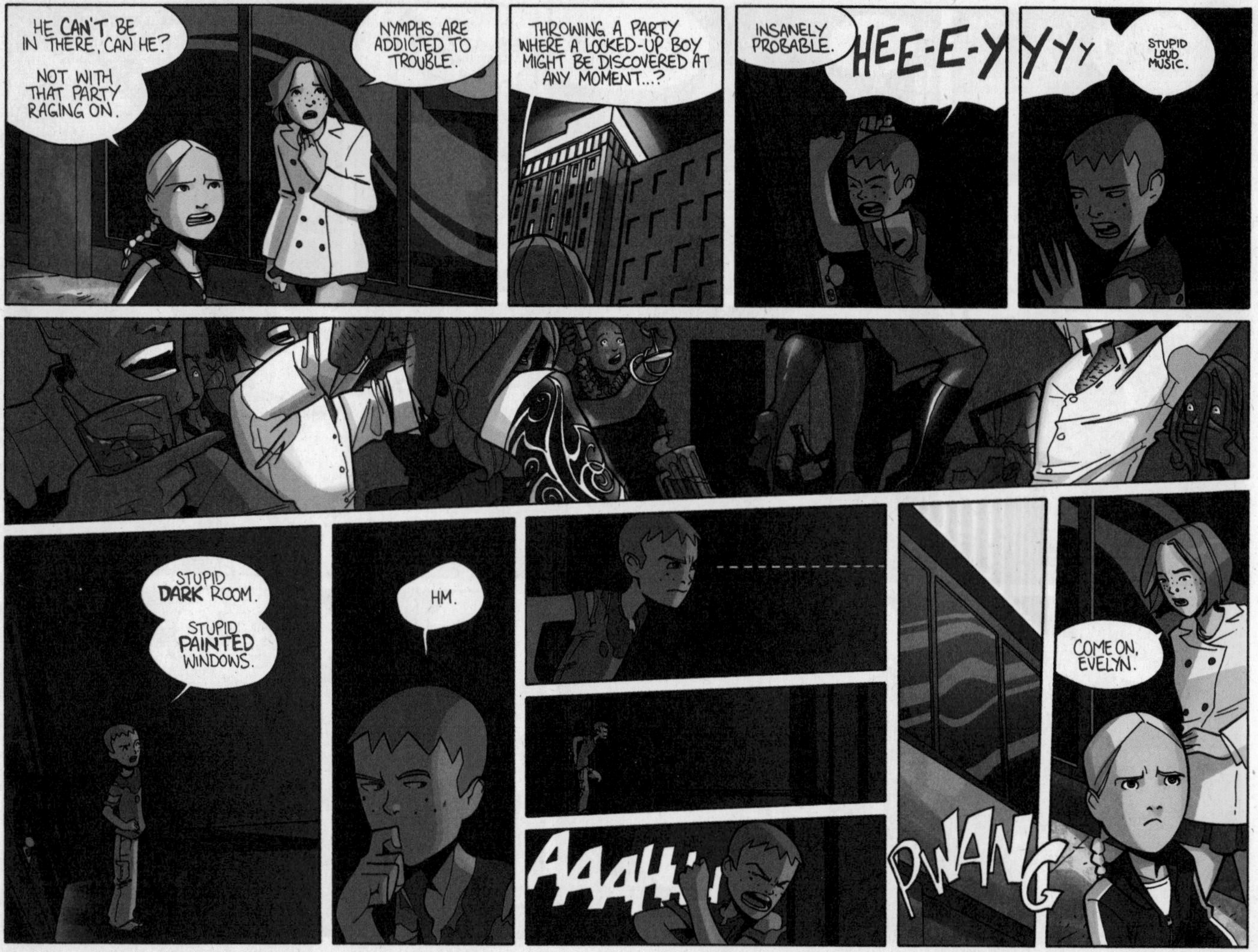
HE CAN'T BE IN THERE, CAN HE?
NOT WITH THAT PARTY RAGING ON.
NYMPHS ARE ADDICTED TO TROUBLE.
THROWING A PARTY WHERE A LOCKED-UP BOY MIGHT BE DISCOVERED AT ANY MOMENT...?
INSANELY PROBABLE.
HEE-E-YYYY
STUPID LOUD MUSIC.
STUPID DARK ROOM.
STUPID PAINTED WINDOWS.
HM.
AAAH
PWANG
COME ON, EVELYN.

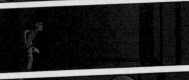

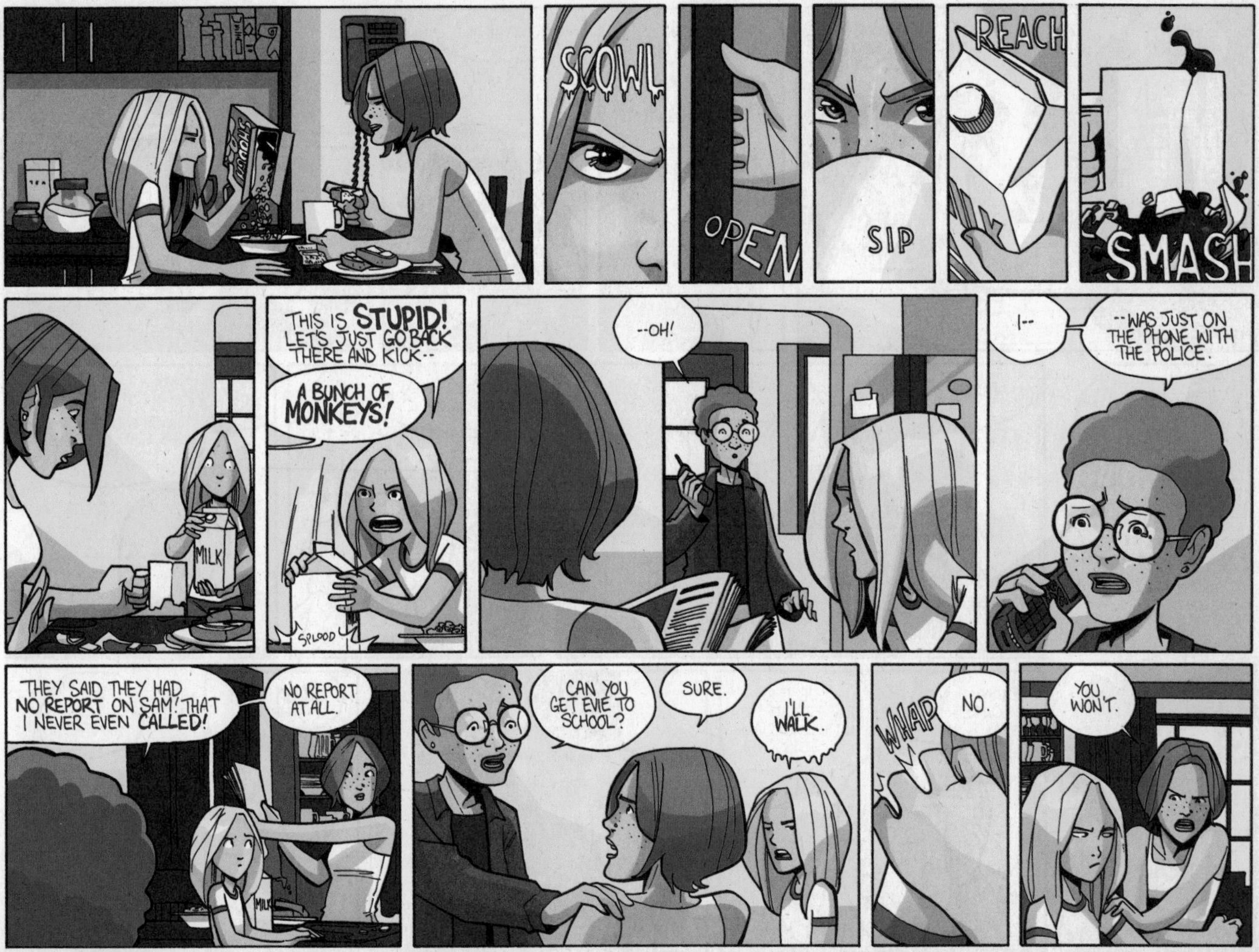
SCOWL
OPEN
SIP
REACH
SMASH
MILK
THIS IS STUPID! LET'S JUST GO BACK THERE AND KICK--
A BUNCH OF MONKEYS!
SPLOOD
--OH!
I--
--WAS JUST ON THE PHONE WITH THE POLICE.
THEY SAID THEY HAD NO REPORT ON SAM! THAT I NEVER EVEN CALLED!
NO REPORT AT ALL.
MILK
CAN YOU GET EVIE TO SCHOOL?
SURE.
I'LL WALK.
WHAP
NO.
YOU WON'T.

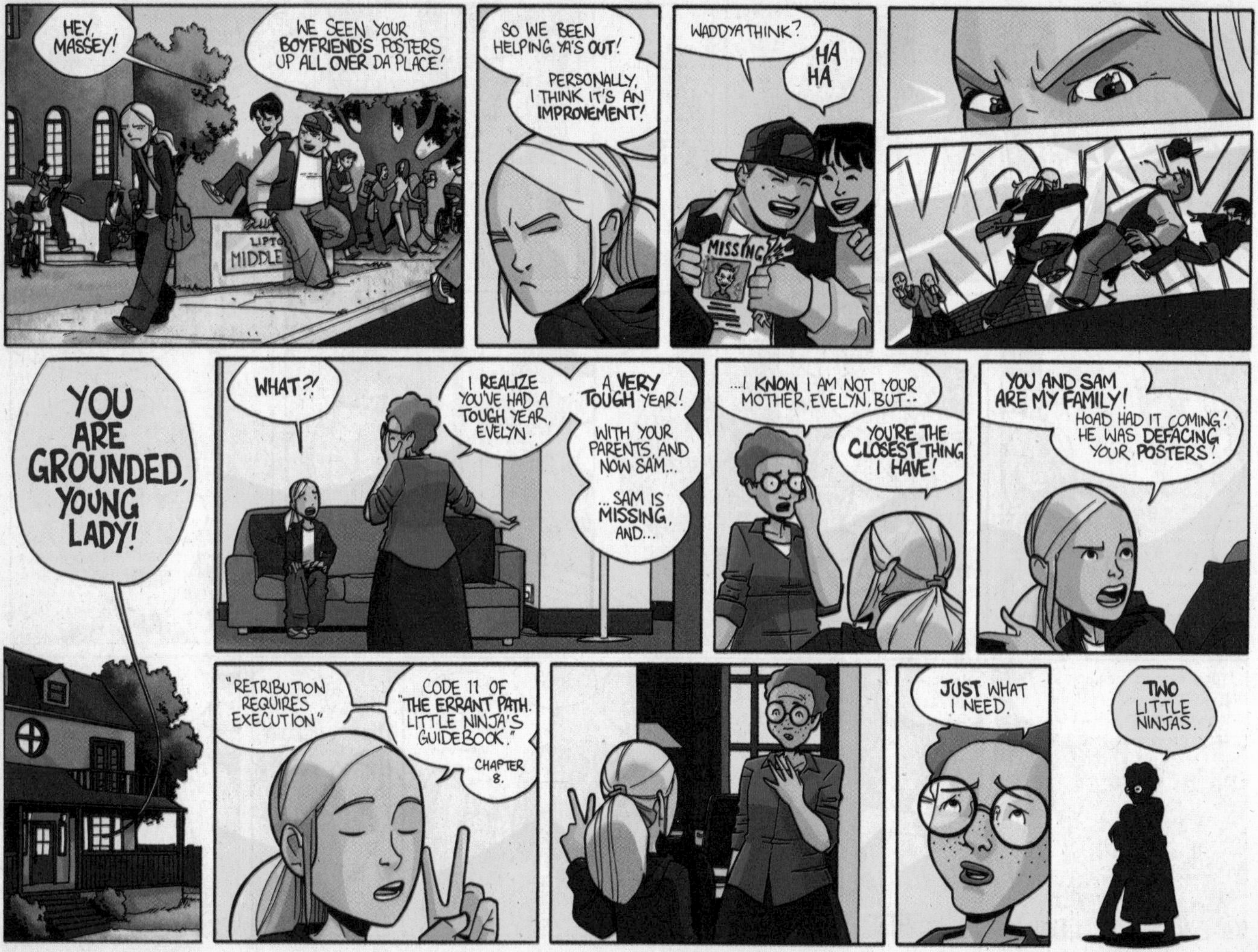
HEY, MASSEY!
WE SEEN YOUR BOYFRIEND'S POSTERS UP ALL OVER DA PLACE!
LIPTO
MIDDLE S
SO WE BEEN HELPING YA'S OUT!
PERSONALLY, I THINK IT'S AN IMPROVEMENT!
WADDYATHINK?
HA HA
MISSING
YOU ARE GROUNDED, YOUNG LADY!
WHAT?!
I REALIZE YOU'VE HAD A TOUGH YEAR, EVELYN.
A VERY TOUGH YEAR!
WITH YOUR PARENTS, AND NOW SAM...
...SAM IS MISSING, AND...
...I KNOW I AM NOT YOUR MOTHER, EVELYN, BUT--
YOU'RE THE CLOSEST THING I HAVE!
YOU AND SAM ARE MY FAMILY!
HOAD HAD IT COMING! HE WAS DEFACING YOUR POSTERS!
"RETRIBUTION REQUIRES EXECUTION"
CODE 11 OF "THE ERRANT PATH. LITTLE NINJA'S GUIDEBOOK."
CHAPTER 8.
JUST WHAT I NEED.
TWO LITTLE NINJAS.

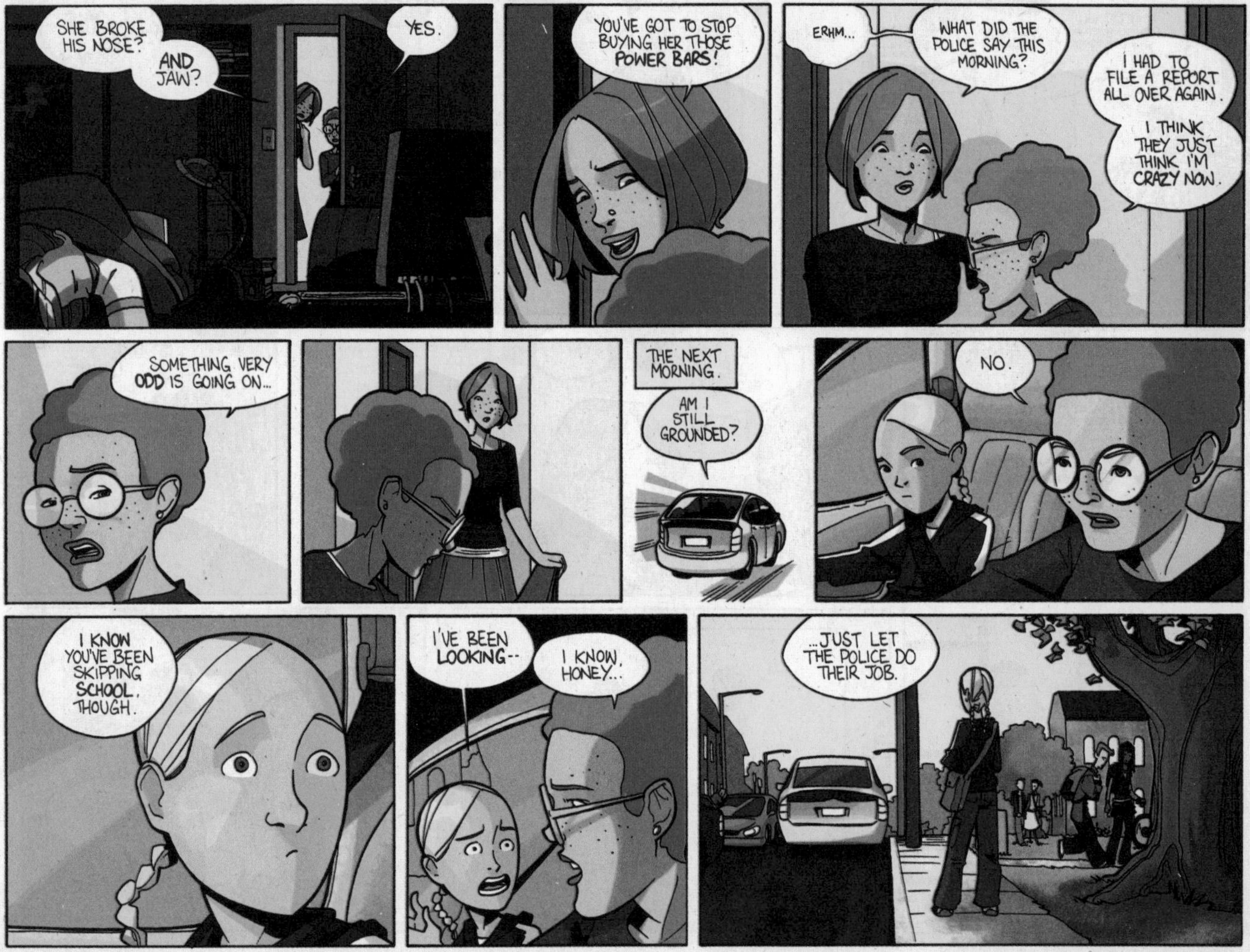
SHE BROKE HIS NOSE?
AND JAW?
YES.
YOU'VE GOT TO STOP BUYING HER THOSE POWER BARS!
ERHM...
WHAT DID THE POLICE SAY THIS MORNING?
I HAD TO FILE A REPORT ALL OVER AGAIN.
I THINK THEY JUST THINK I'M CRAZY NOW.
SOMETHING VERY ODD IS GOING ON...
THE NEXT MORNING.
AM I STILL GROUNDED?
NO.
I KNOW YOU'VE BEEN SKIPPING SCHOOL, THOUGH.
I'VE BEEN LOOKING--
I KNOW, HONEY...
...JUST LET THE POLICE DO THEIR JOB.

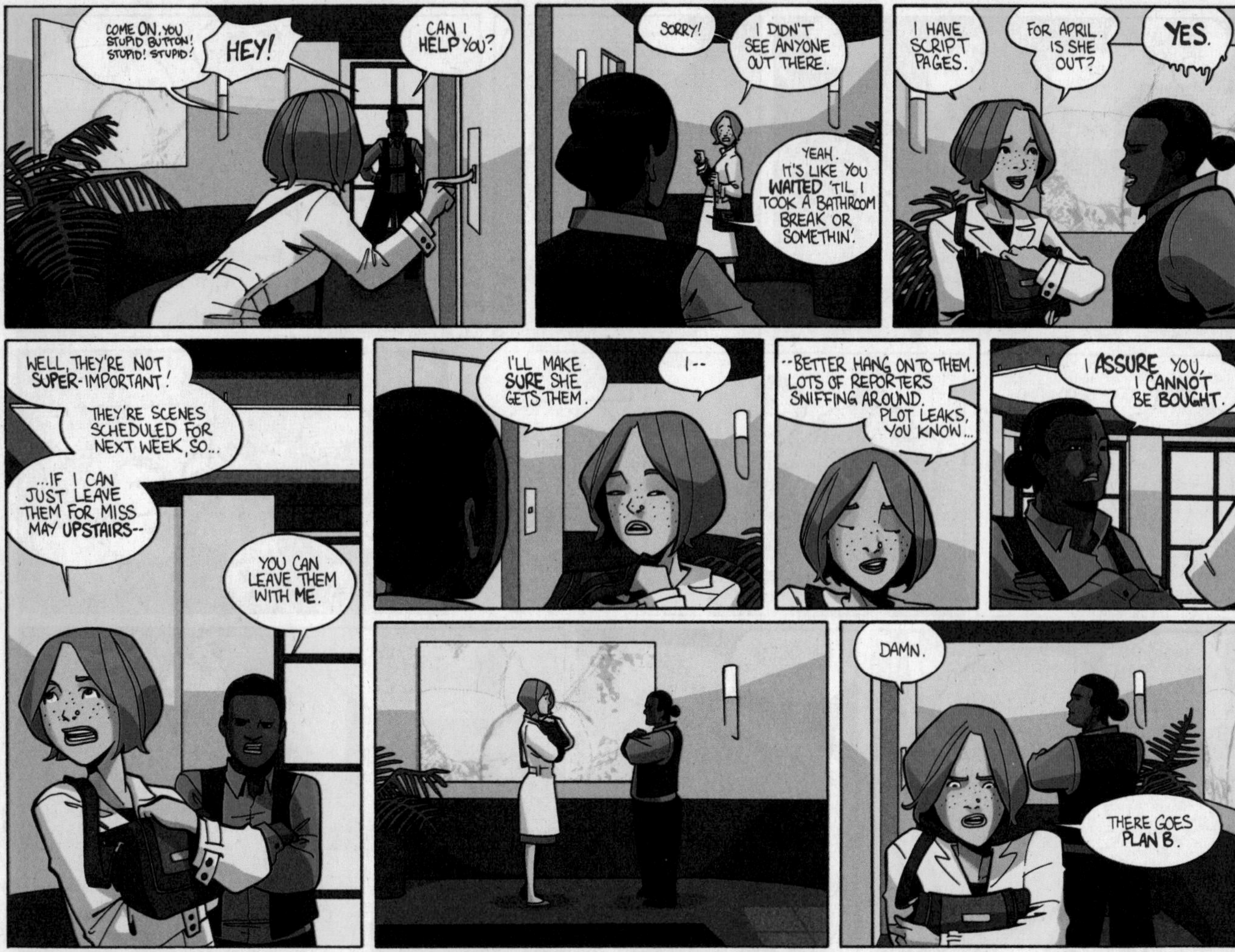
COME ON, YOU STUPID BUTTON! STUPID! STUPID!
HEY!
CAN I HELP YOU?
SORRY!
I DIDN'T SEE ANYONE OUT THERE.
YEAH. IT'S LIKE YOU WAITED 'TIL I TOOK A BATHROOM BREAK OR SOMETHIN'.
I HAVE SCRIPT PAGES.
FOR APRIL. IS SHE OUT?
YES.
WELL, THEY'RE NOT SUPER-IMPORTANT!
THEY'RE SCENES SCHEDULED FOR NEXT WEEK, SO...
...IF I CAN JUST LEAVE THEM FOR MISS MAY UPSTAIRS--
YOU CAN LEAVE THEM WITH ME.
I'LL MAKE SURE SHE GETS THEM.
I--
--BETTER HANG ON TO THEM. LOTS OF REPORTERS SNIFFING AROUND.
PLOT LEAKS, YOU KNOW...
I ASSURE YOU, I CANNOT BE BOUGHT.
DAMN.
THERE GOES PLAN B.

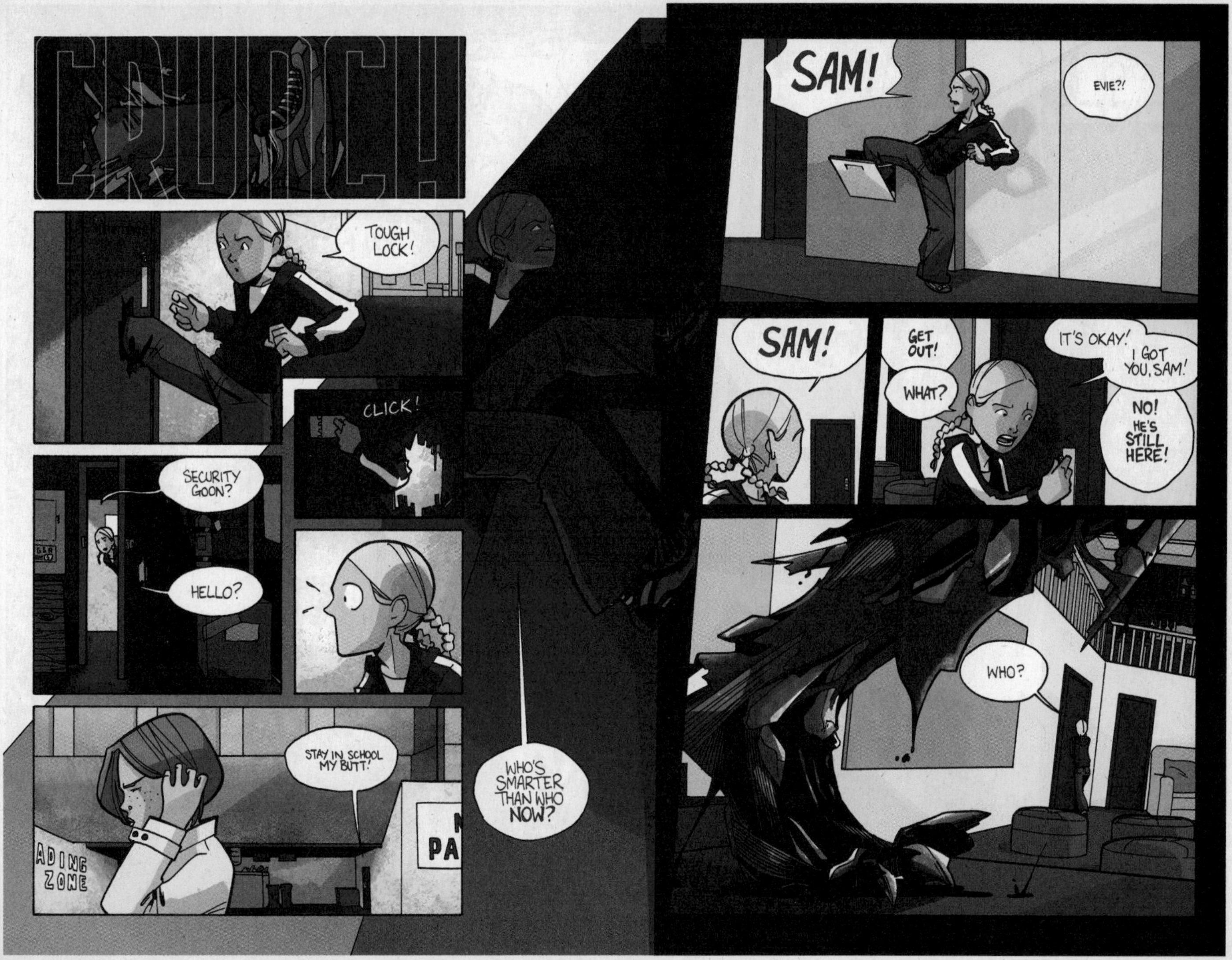
CRUNCH
TOUGH LOCK!
CLICK!
SECURITY GOON?
HELLO?
STAY IN SCHOOL MY BUTT!
ADING ZONE
WHO'S SMARTER THAN WHO NOW?
SAM!
EVIE?!
SAM!
GET OUT!
WHAT?
IT'S OKAY!
I GOT YOU, SAM!
NO! HE'S STILL HERE!
WHO?

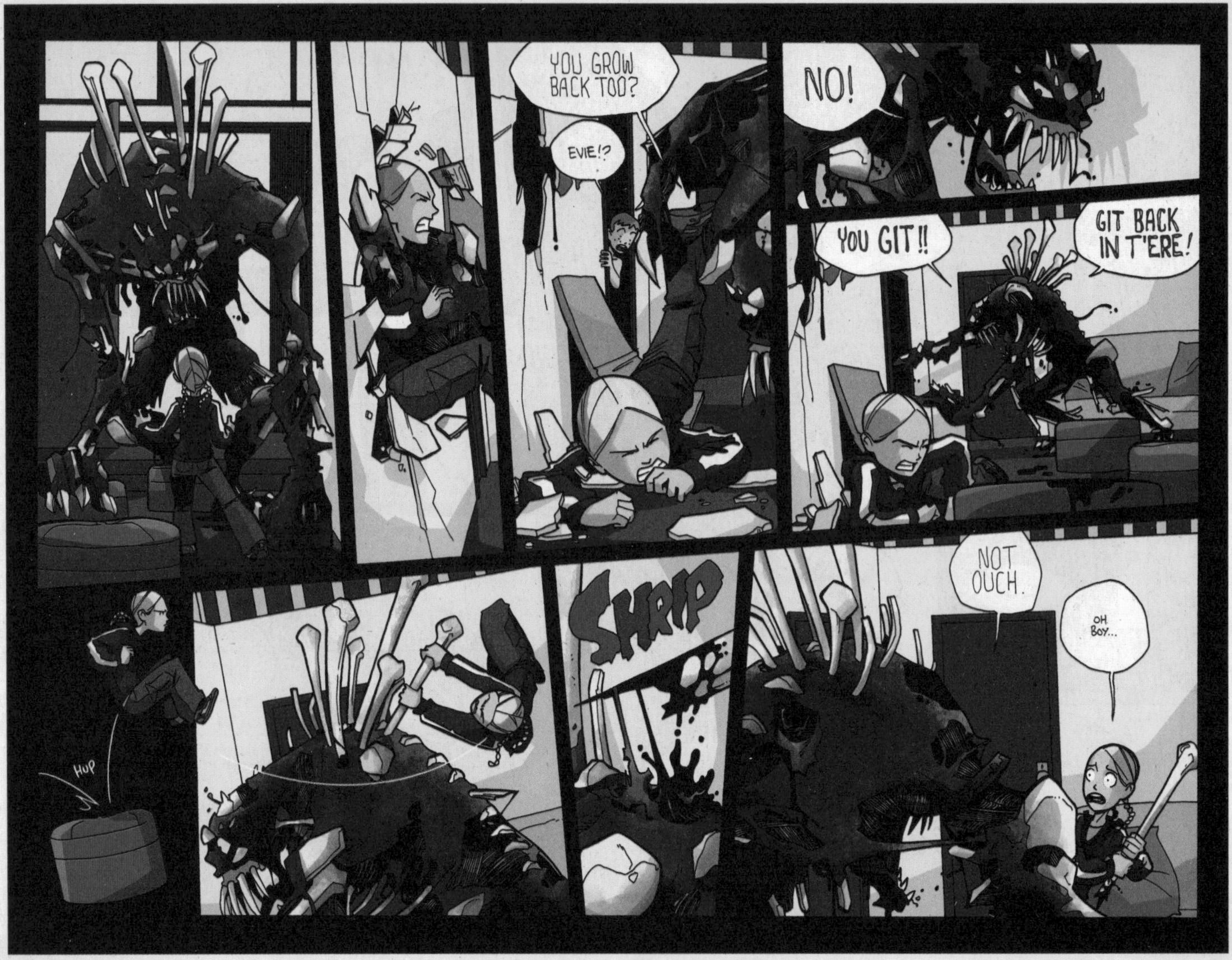
YOU GROW BACK TOO?
EVIE!?
NO!
YOU GIT!!
GIT BACK IN T'ERE!
HUP
SHRIP
NOT OUCH.
OH BOY...

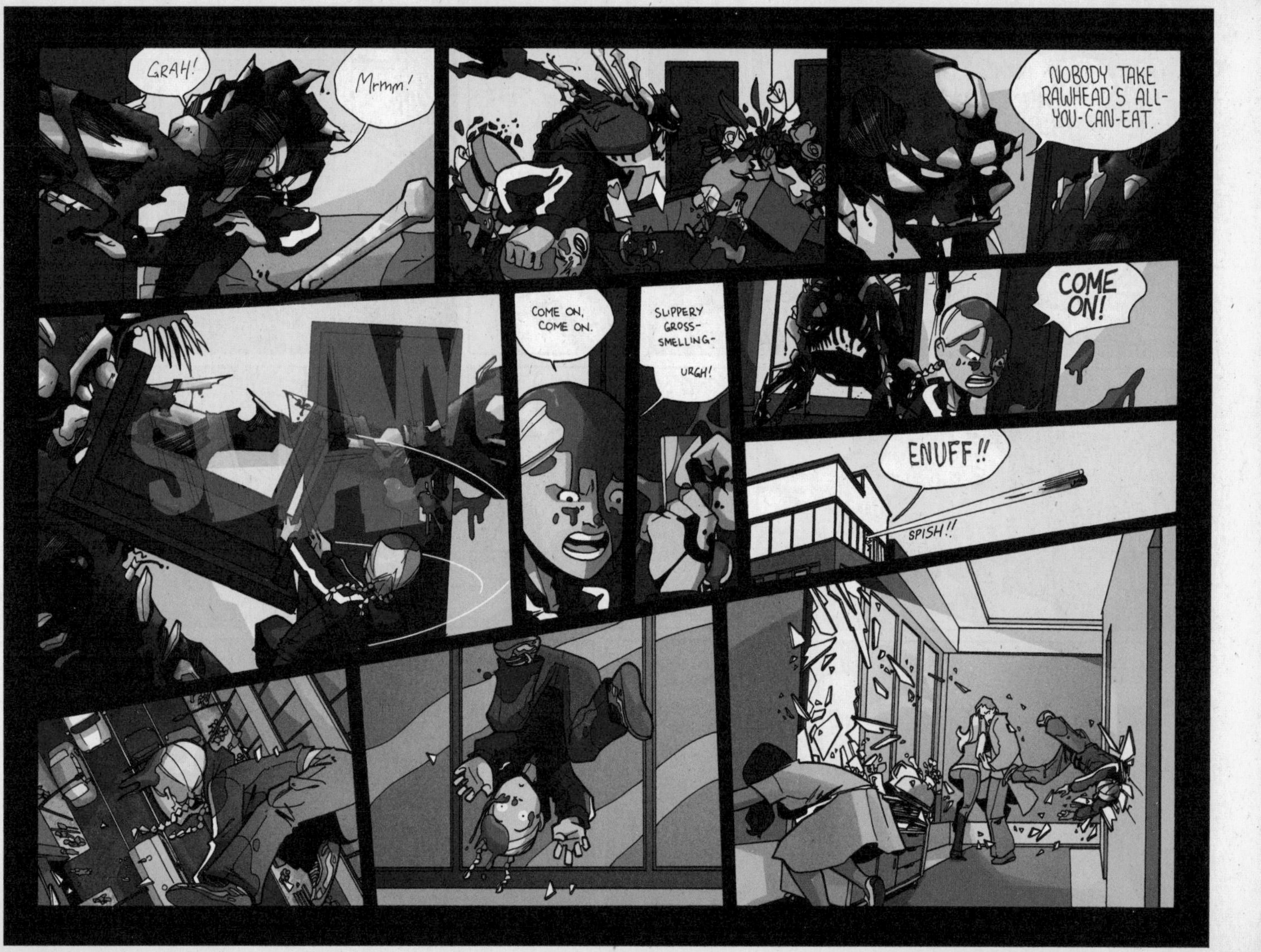
GRAH!
Mrmm!
NOBODY TAKE RAWHEAD'S ALL-YOU-CAN-EAT.
SLAM
COME ON, COME ON.
SLIPPERY GROSS-SMELLING-
URGH!
COME ON!
ENUFF!!
SPISH!!

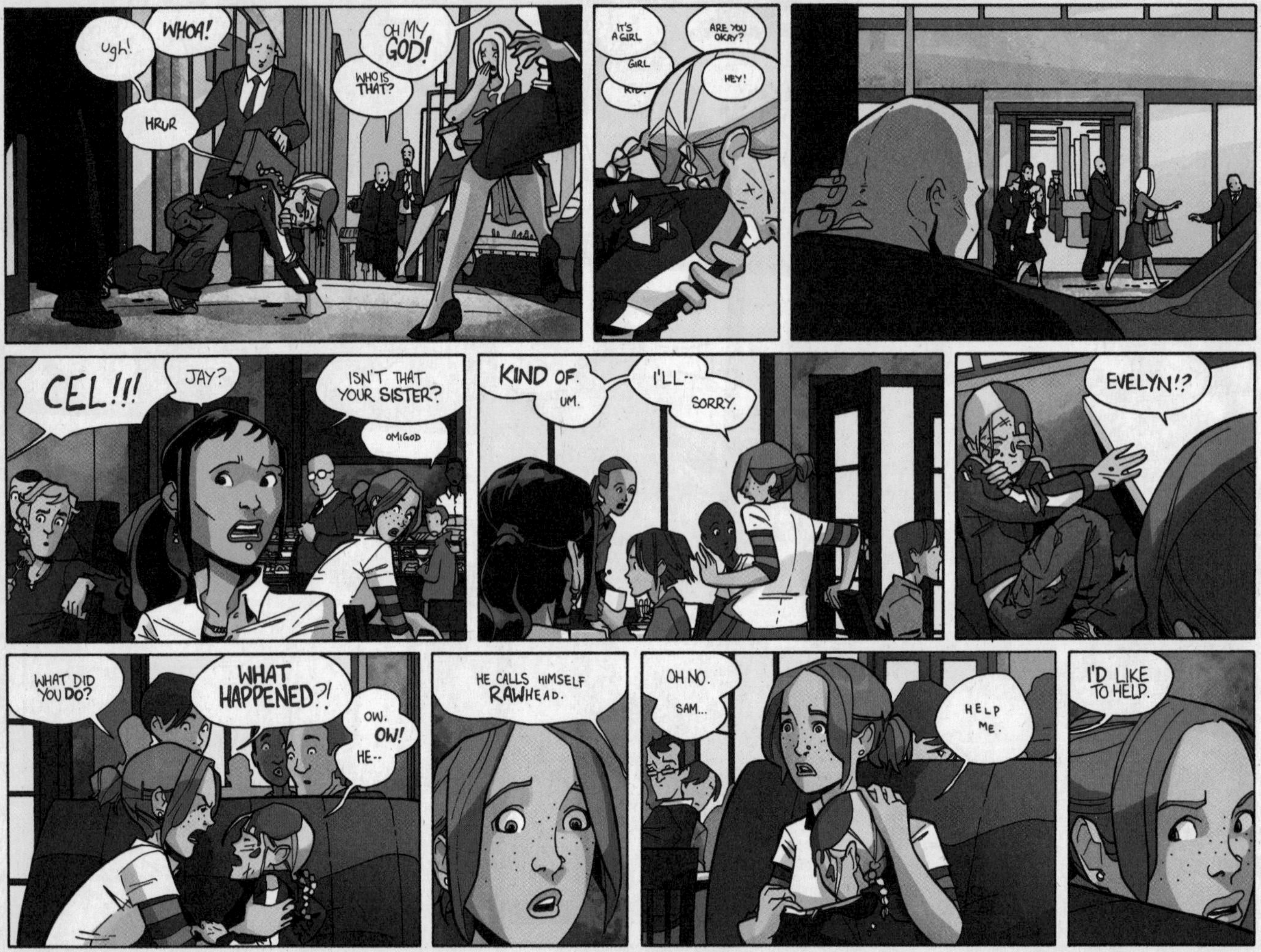
ugh!
WHOA!
HRUR
OH MY GOD!
WHO IS THAT?
IT'S A GIRL
GIRL
ARE YOU OKAY?
HEY!
CEL!!!
JAY?
ISN'T THAT YOUR SISTER?
OMIGOD
KIND OF.
UM.
I'LL--
SORRY.
EVELYN!?
WHAT DID YOU DO?
WHAT HAPPENED?!
OW. OW!
HE--
HE CALLS HIMSELF RAWHEAD.
OH NO.
SAM...
HELP ME.
I'D LIKE TO HELP.

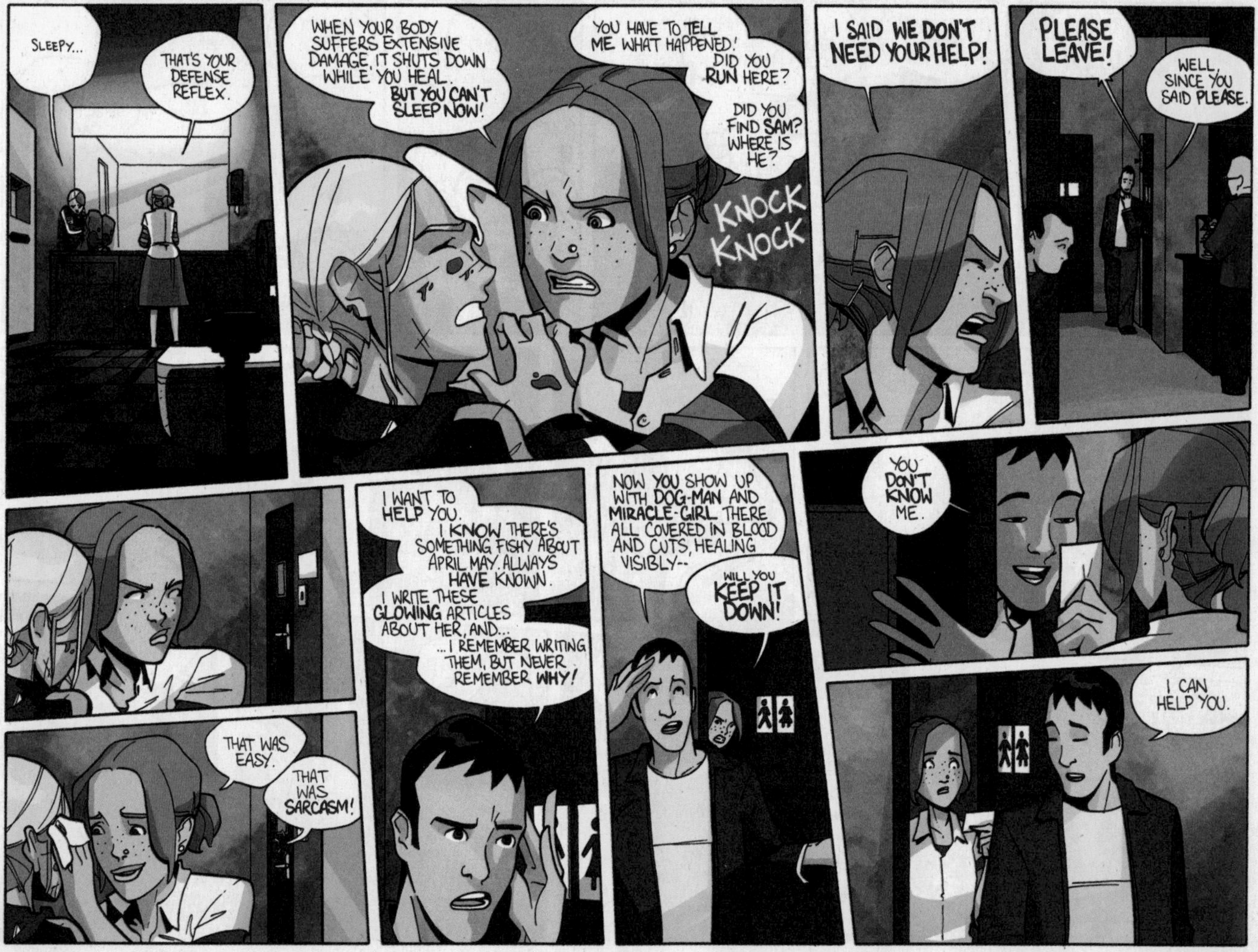

SLEEPY...
THAT'S YOUR DEFENSE REFLEX.
WHEN YOUR BODY SUFFERS EXTENSIVE DAMAGE, IT SHUTS DOWN WHILE YOU HEAL. BUT YOU CAN'T SLEEP NOW!
YOU HAVE TO TELL ME WHAT HAPPENED! DID YOU RUN HERE?
DID YOU FIND SAM? WHERE IS HE?
KNOCK KNOCK
I SAID WE DON'T NEED YOUR HELP!
PLEASE LEAVE!
WELL, SINCE YOU SAID PLEASE.
THAT WAS EASY.
THAT WAS SARCASM!
I WANT TO HELP YOU.
I KNOW THERE'S SOMETHING FISHY ABOUT APRIL MAY. ALWAYS HAVE KNOWN.
I WRITE THESE GLOWING ARTICLES ABOUT HER, AND...
...I REMEMBER WRITING THEM, BUT NEVER REMEMBER WHY!
NOW YOU SHOW UP WITH DOG-MAN AND MIRACLE-GIRL THERE ALL COVERED IN BLOOD AND CUTS, HEALING VISIBLY--
WILL YOU KEEP IT DOWN!
YOU DON'T KNOW ME.
I CAN HELP YOU.

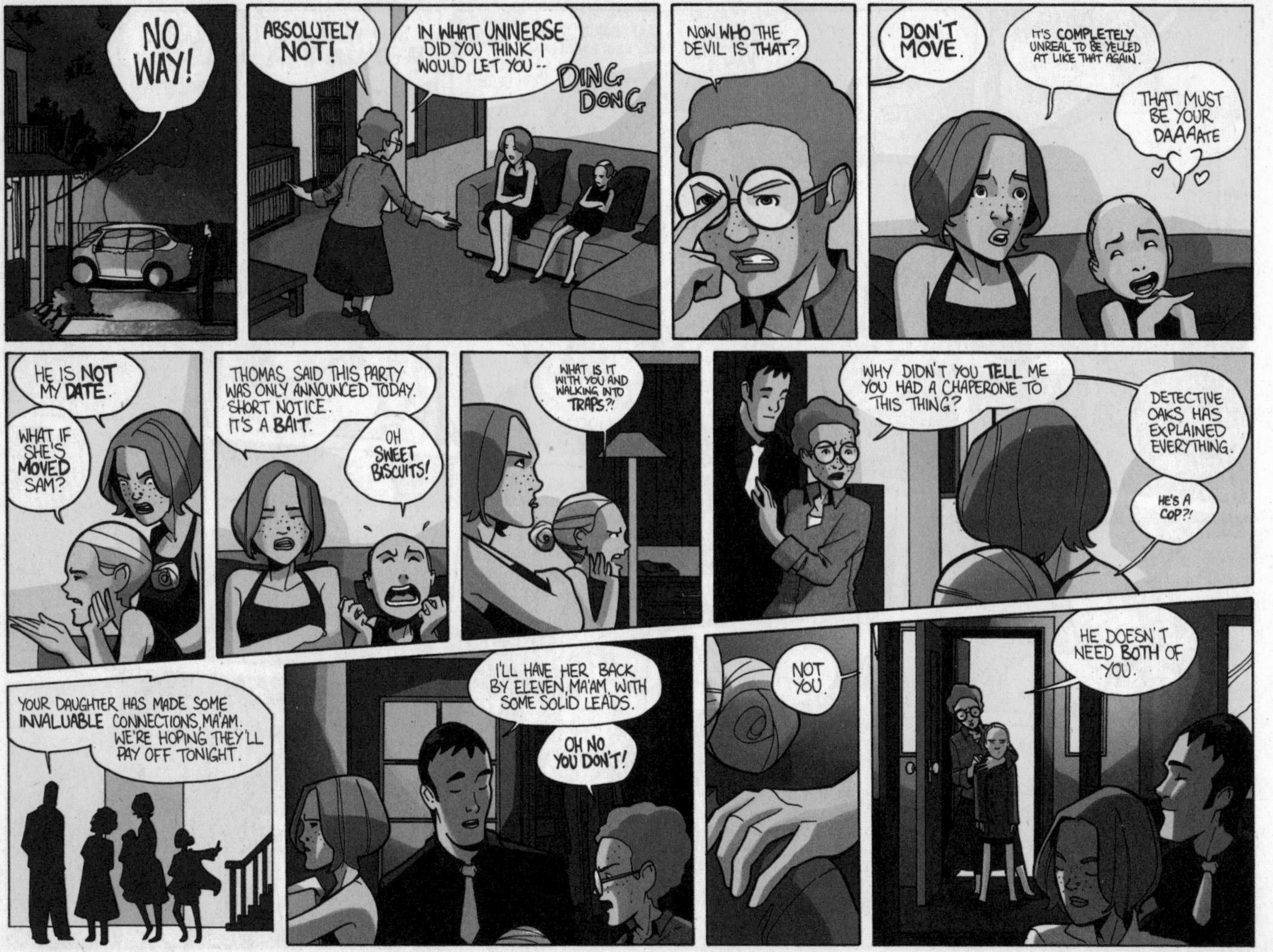
NO WAY!
ABSOLUTELY NOT!
IN WHAT UNIVERSE DID YOU THINK I WOULD LET YOU --
DING DONG
NOW WHO THE DEVIL IS THAT?
DON'T MOVE.
IT'S COMPLETELY UNREAL TO BE YELLED AT LIKE THAT AGAIN.
THAT MUST BE YOUR DAAAATE
HE IS NOT MY DATE.
WHAT IF SHE'S MOVED SAM?
THOMAS SAID THIS PARTY WAS ONLY ANNOUNCED TODAY. SHORT NOTICE. IT'S A BAIT.
OH SWEET BISCUITS!
WHAT IS IT WITH YOU AND WALKING INTO TRAPS?!
WHY DIDN'T YOU TELL ME YOU HAD A CHAPERONE TO THIS THING?
DETECTIVE OAKS HAS EXPLAINED EVERYTHING.
HE'S A COP?!
YOUR DAUGHTER HAS MADE SOME INVALUABLE CONNECTIONS, MA'AM. WE'RE HOPING THEY'LL PAY OFF TONIGHT.
I'LL HAVE HER BACK BY ELEVEN, MA'AM, WITH SOME SOLID LEADS.
OH NO YOU DON'T!
NOT YOU.
HE DOESN'T NEED BOTH OF YOU.

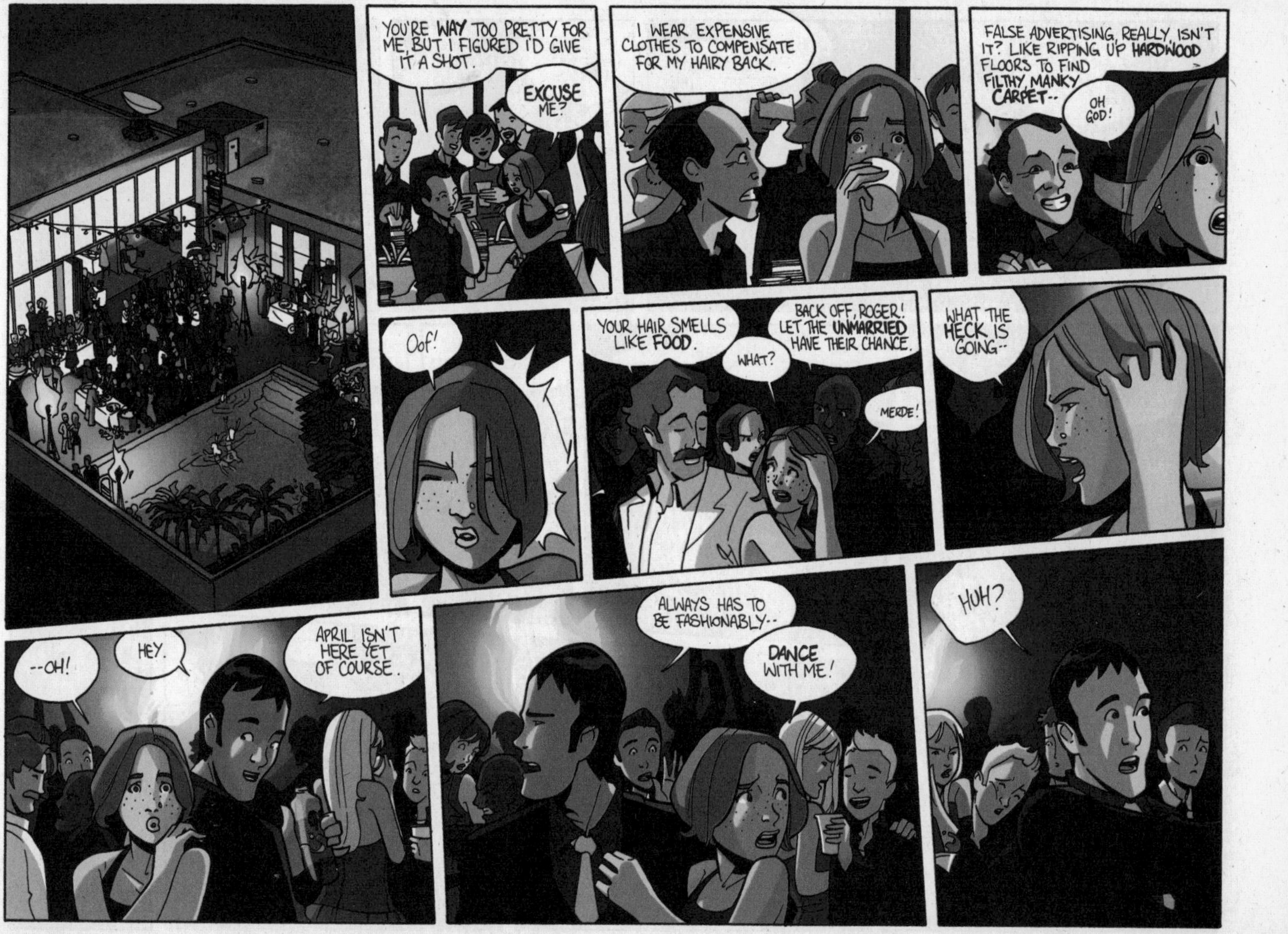

YOU'RE WAY TOO PRETTY FOR ME, BUT I FIGURED I'D GIVE IT A SHOT.
EXCUSE ME?
I WEAR EXPENSIVE CLOTHES TO COMPENSATE FOR MY HAIRY BACK.
FALSE ADVERTISING, REALLY, ISN'T IT? LIKE RIPPING UP HARDWOOD FLOORS TO FIND FILTHY, MANKY CARPET--
OH GOD!
Oof!
YOUR HAIR SMELLS LIKE FOOD.
WHAT?
BACK OFF, ROGER! LET THE UNMARRIED HAVE THEIR CHANCE.
MERDE!
WHAT THE HECK IS GOING--
--OH!
HEY.
APRIL ISN'T HERE YET OF COURSE.
ALWAYS HAS TO BE FASHIONABLY--
DANCE WITH ME!
HUH?

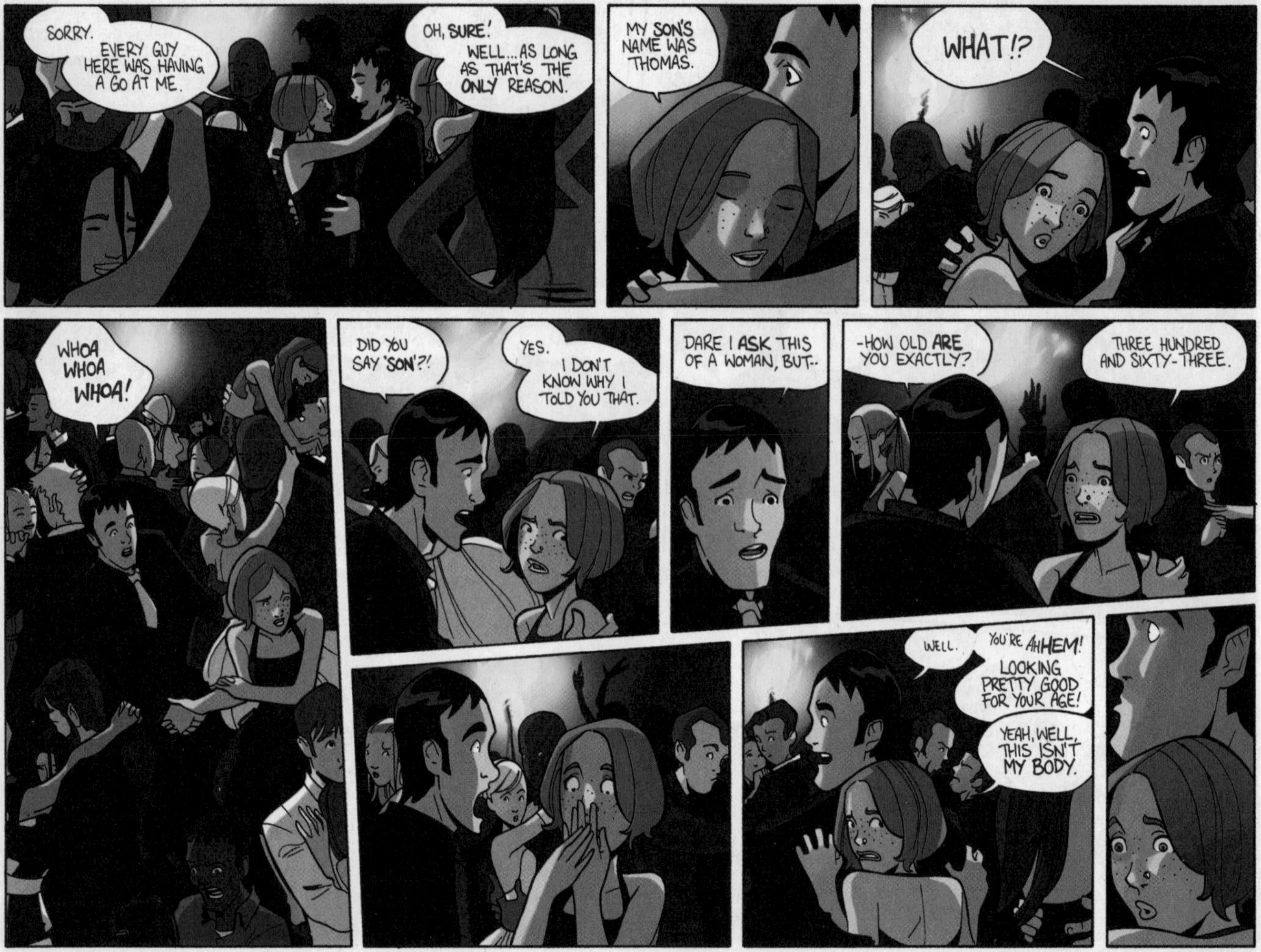
SORRY.
EVERY GUY HERE WAS HAVING A GO AT ME.
OH, SURE!
WELL... AS LONG AS THAT'S THE ONLY REASON.
MY SON'S NAME WAS THOMAS.
WHAT!?
WHOA WHOA WHOA!
DID YOU SAY 'SON'?!
YES.
I DON'T KNOW WHY I TOLD YOU THAT.
DARE I ASK THIS OF A WOMAN, BUT-
-HOW OLD ARE YOU EXACTLY?
THREE HUNDRED AND SIXTY-THREE.
WELL.
YOU'RE AHHEM! LOOKING PRETTY GOOD FOR YOUR AGE!
YEAH, WELL, THIS ISN'T MY BODY.

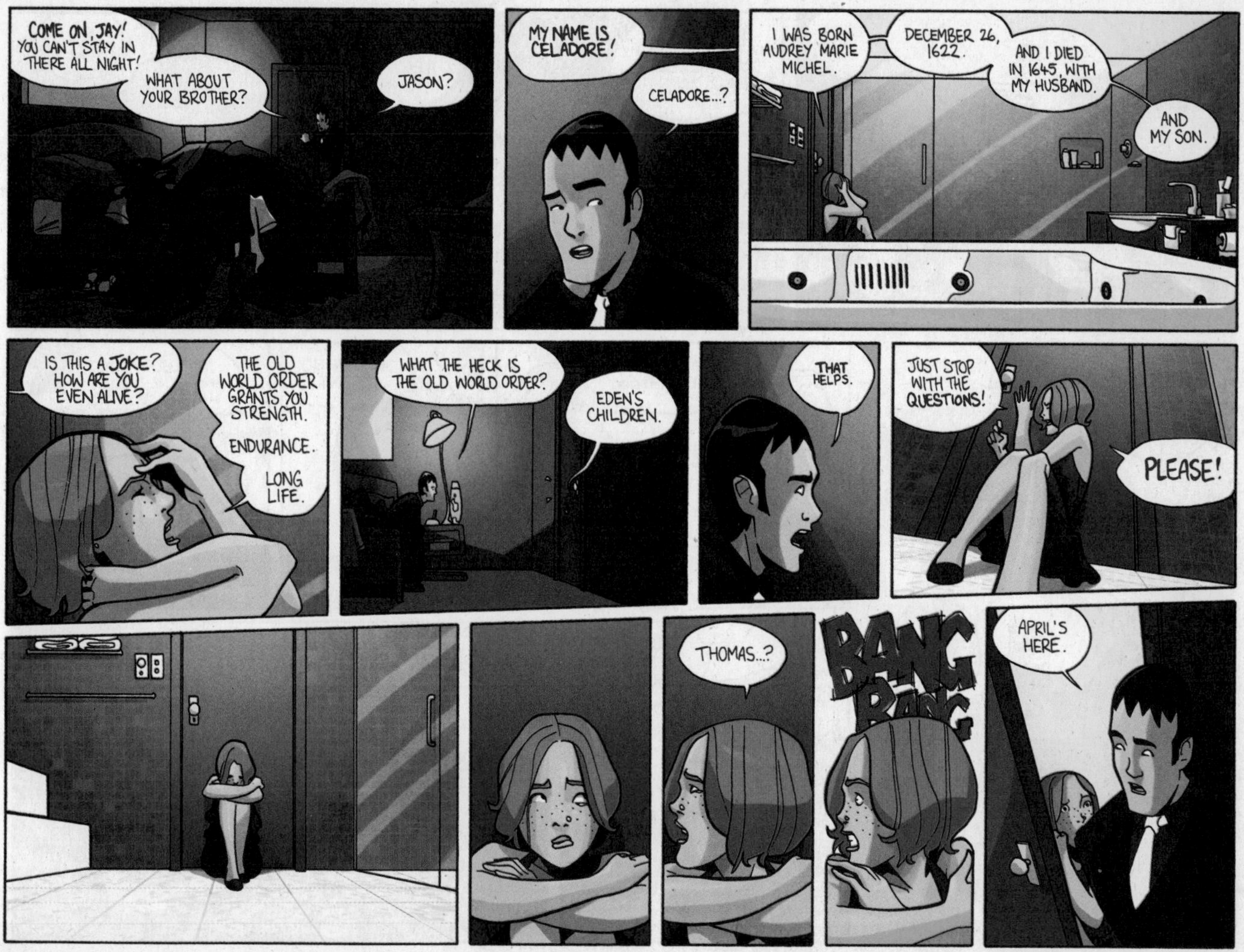
COME ON, JAY! YOU CAN'T STAY IN THERE ALL NIGHT!
WHAT ABOUT YOUR BROTHER?
JASON?
MY NAME IS, CELADORE!
CELADORE...?
I WAS BORN AUDREY MARIE MICHEL.
DECEMBER 26, 1622.
AND I DIED IN 1645, WITH MY HUSBAND.
AND MY SON.
IS THIS A JOKE? HOW ARE YOU EVEN ALIVE?
THE OLD WORLD ORDER GRANTS YOU STRENGTH.
ENDURANCE.
LONG LIFE.
WHAT THE HECK IS THE OLD WORLD ORDER?
EDEN'S CHILDREN.
THAT HELPS.
JUST STOP WITH THE QUESTIONS!
PLEASE!
THOMAS...?
BANG BANG
APRIL'S HERE.

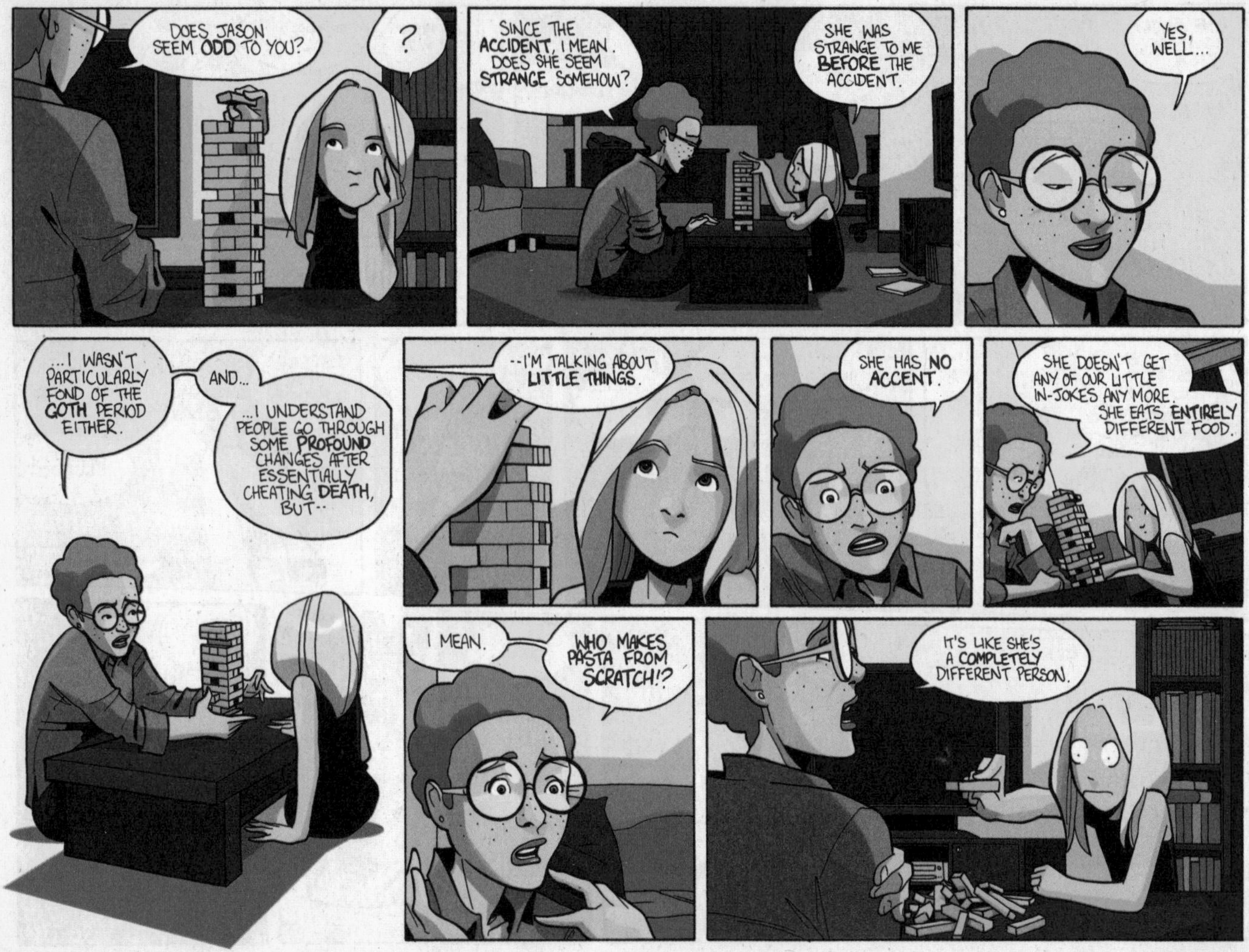
DOES JASON SEEM ODD TO YOU?
?
SINCE THE ACCIDENT, I MEAN. DOES SHE SEEM STRANGE SOMEHOW?
SHE WAS STRANGE TO ME BEFORE THE ACCIDENT.
YES, WELL...
...I WASN'T PARTICULARLY FOND OF THE GOTH PERIOD EITHER.
AND...
...I UNDERSTAND PEOPLE GO THROUGH SOME PROFOUND CHANGES AFTER ESSENTIALLY CHEATING DEATH, BUT--
--I'M TALKING ABOUT LITTLE THINGS.
SHE HAS NO ACCENT.
SHE DOESN'T GET ANY OF OUR LITTLE IN-JOKES ANY MORE.
SHE EATS ENTIRELY DIFFERENT FOOD.
I MEAN.
WHO MAKES PASTA FROM SCRATCH!?
IT'S LIKE SHE'S A COMPLETELY DIFFERENT PERSON.

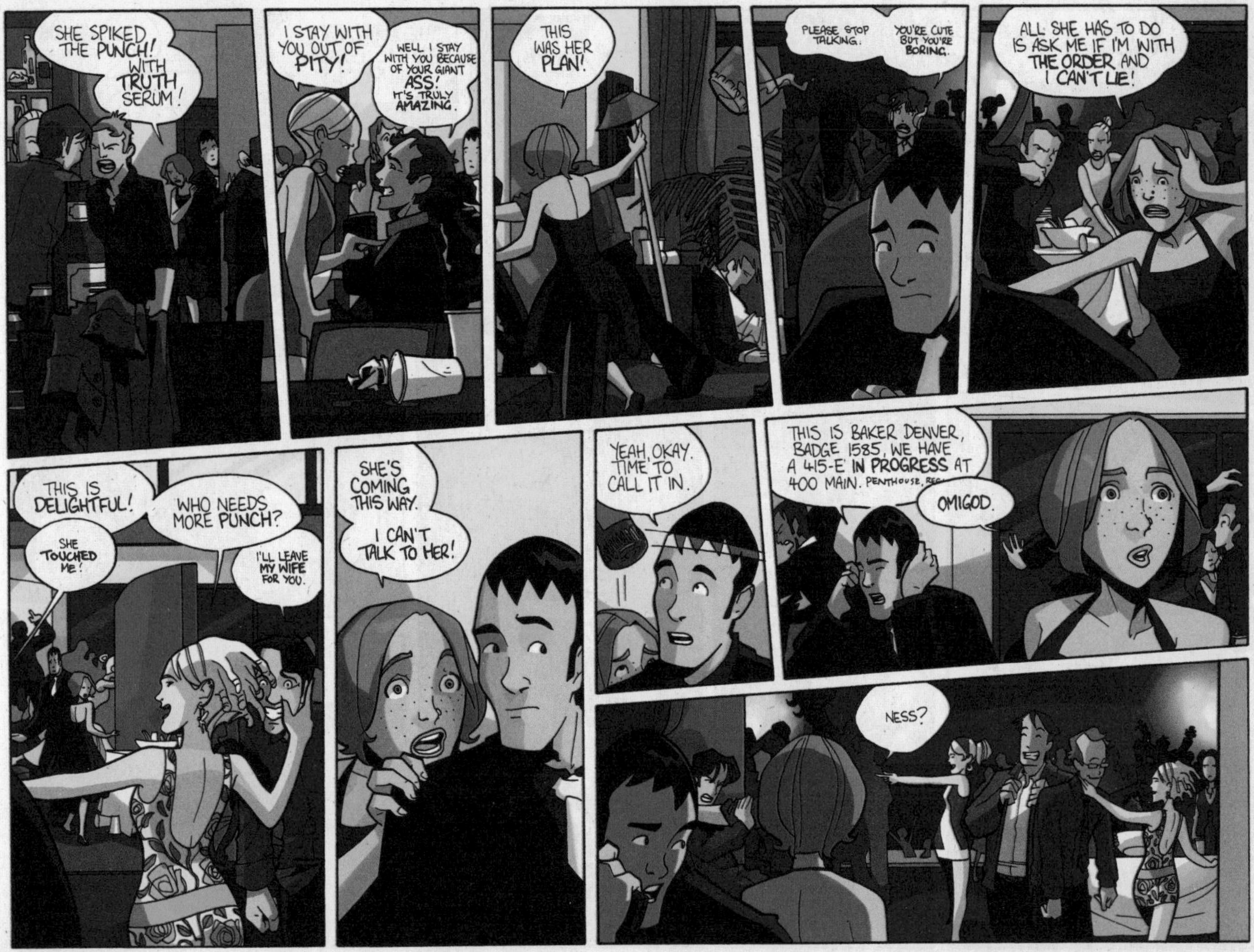
SHE SPIKED THE PUNCH!
WITH TRUTH SERUM!
I STAY WITH YOU OUT OF PITY!
WELL I STAY WITH YOU BECAUSE OF YOUR GIANT ASS! IT'S TRULY AMAZING.
THIS WAS HER PLAN!
PLEASE STOP TALKING.
YOU'RE CUTE BUT YOU'RE BORING.
ALL SHE HAS TO DO IS ASK ME IF I'M WITH THE ORDER AND I CAN'T LIE!
THIS IS DELIGHTFUL!
SHE TOUCHED ME!
WHO NEEDS MORE PUNCH?
I'LL LEAVE MY WIFE FOR YOU.
SHE'S COMING THIS WAY.
I CAN'T TALK TO HER!
YEAH, OKAY. TIME TO CALL IT IN.
THIS IS BAKER DENVER, BADGE 1585, WE HAVE A 415-E IN PROGRESS AT 400 MAIN. PENTHOUSE,
OMIGOD.
NESS?

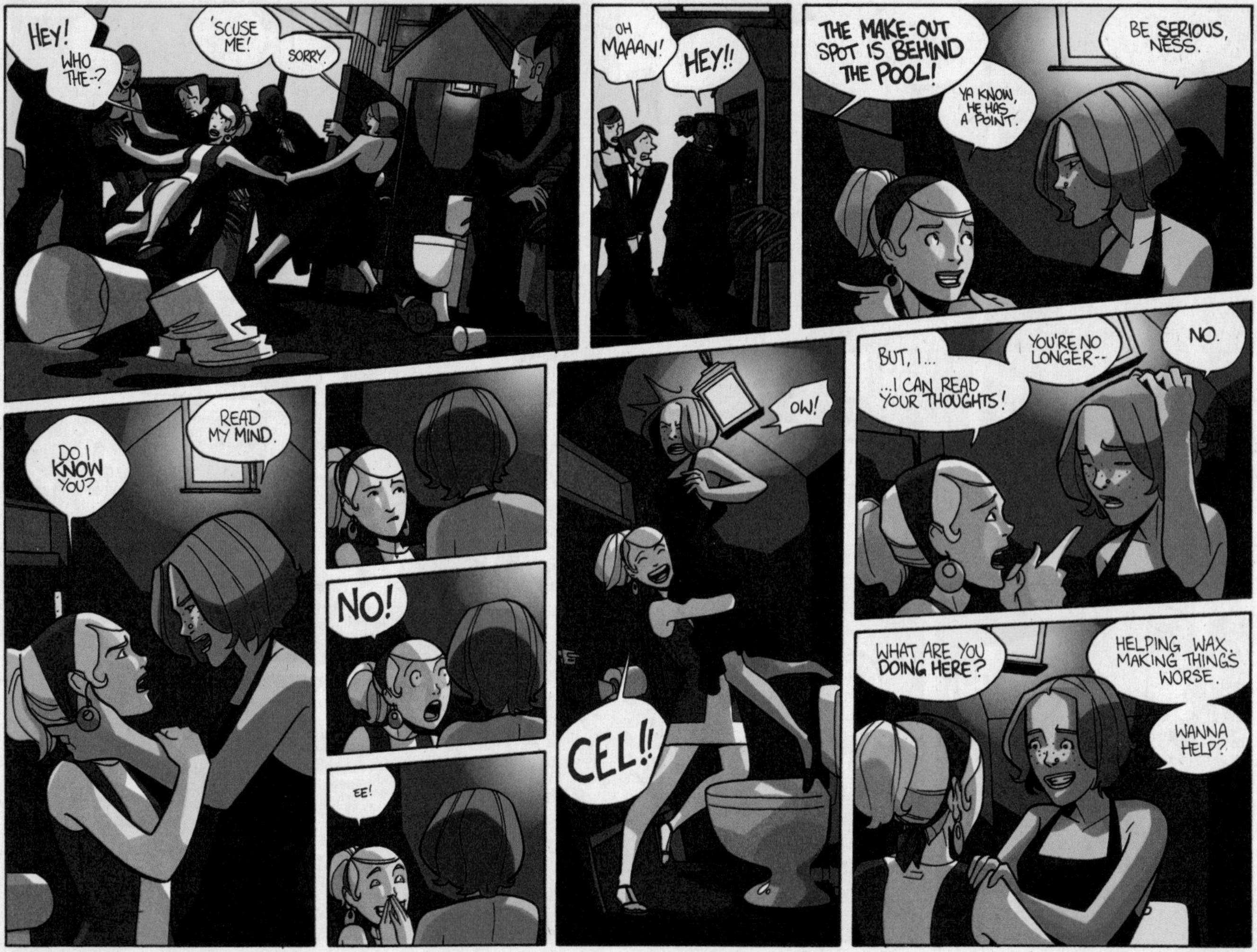
HEY! WHO THE--?
'SCUSE ME!
SORRY.
OH MAAAN!
HEY!!
THE MAKE-OUT SPOT IS BEHIND THE POOL!
YA KNOW, HE HAS A POINT.
BE SERIOUS, NESS.
DO I KNOW YOU?
READ MY MIND.
NO!
EE!
OW!
CEL!!
BUT, I...
...I CAN READ YOUR THOUGHTS!
YOU'RE NO LONGER--
NO.
WHAT ARE YOU DOING HERE?
HELPING WAX. MAKING THINGS WORSE.
WANNA HELP?

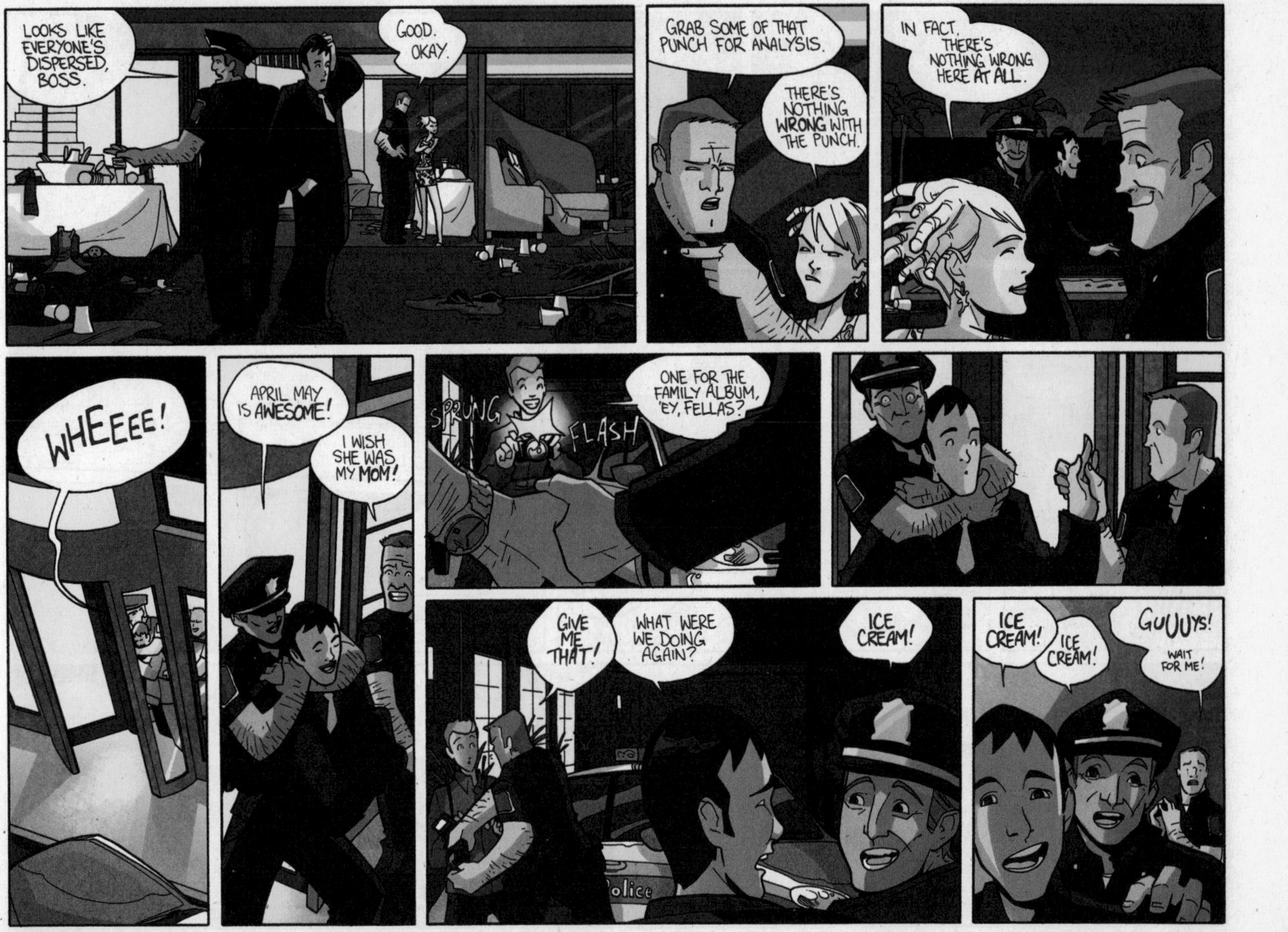
LOOKS LIKE EVERYONE'S DISPERSED, BOSS.
GOOD. OKAY.
GRAB SOME OF THAT PUNCH FOR ANALYSIS.
THERE'S NOTHING WRONG WITH THE PUNCH.
IN FACT, THERE'S NOTHING WRONG HERE AT ALL.
WHEEEE!
APRIL MAY IS AWESOME!
I WISH SHE WAS MY MOM!
SPRUNG
FLASH
ONE FOR THE FAMILY ALBUM, 'EY, FELLAS?
GIVE ME THAT!
WHAT WERE WE DOING AGAIN?
ICE CREAM!
Police
ICE CREAM!
ICE CREAM!
GUUUYS!
WAIT FOR ME!

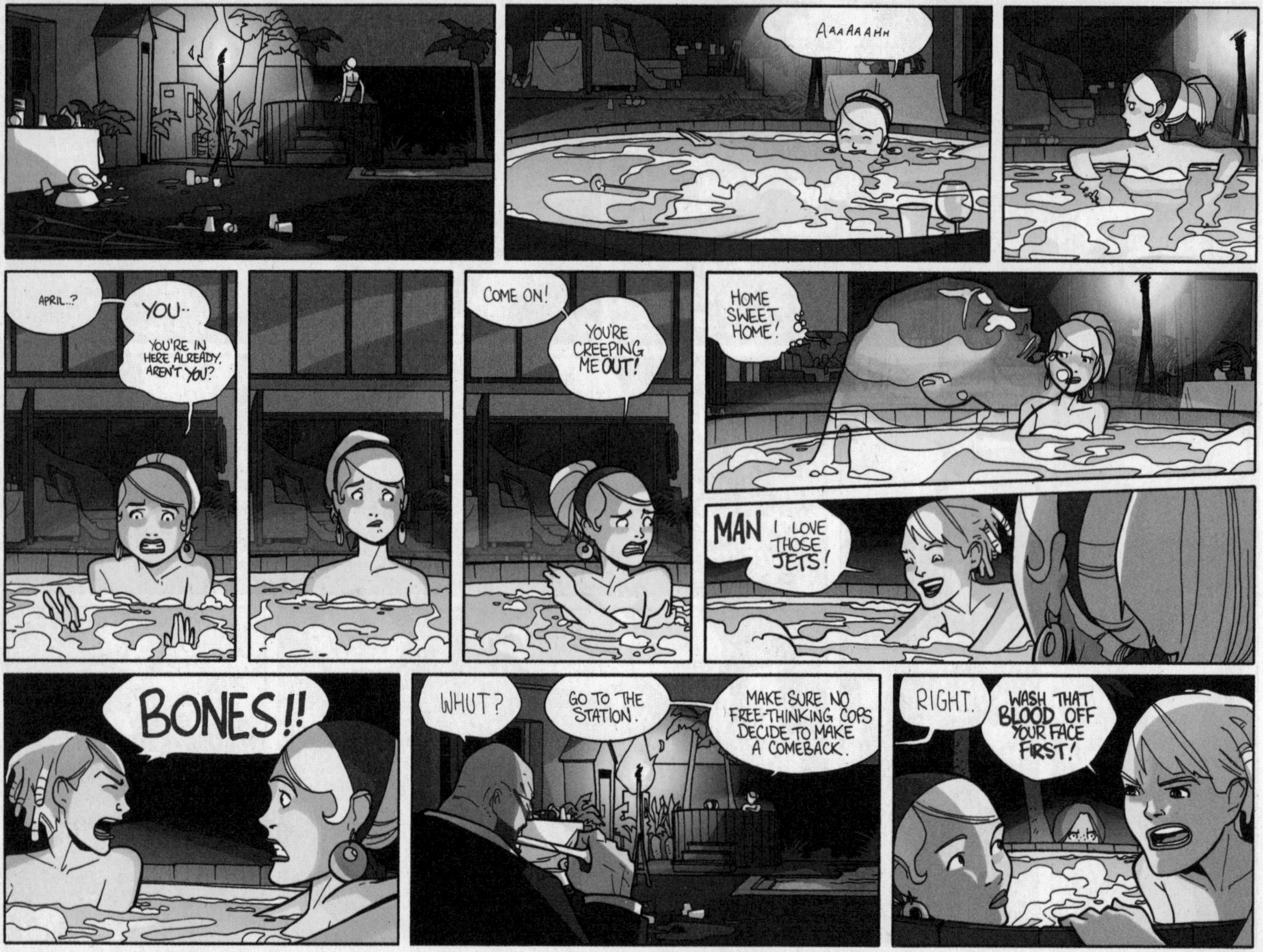
AAAAAAHH
APRIL..?
YOU..
YOU'RE IN HERE ALREADY, AREN'T YOU?
COME ON!
YOU'RE CREEPING ME OUT!
HOME SWEET HOME!
MAN I LOVE THOSE JETS!
BONES!!
WHUT?
GO TO THE STATION.
MAKE SURE NO FREE-THINKING COPS DECIDE TO MAKE A COMEBACK.
RIGHT.
WASH THAT BLOOD OFF YOUR FACE FIRST!

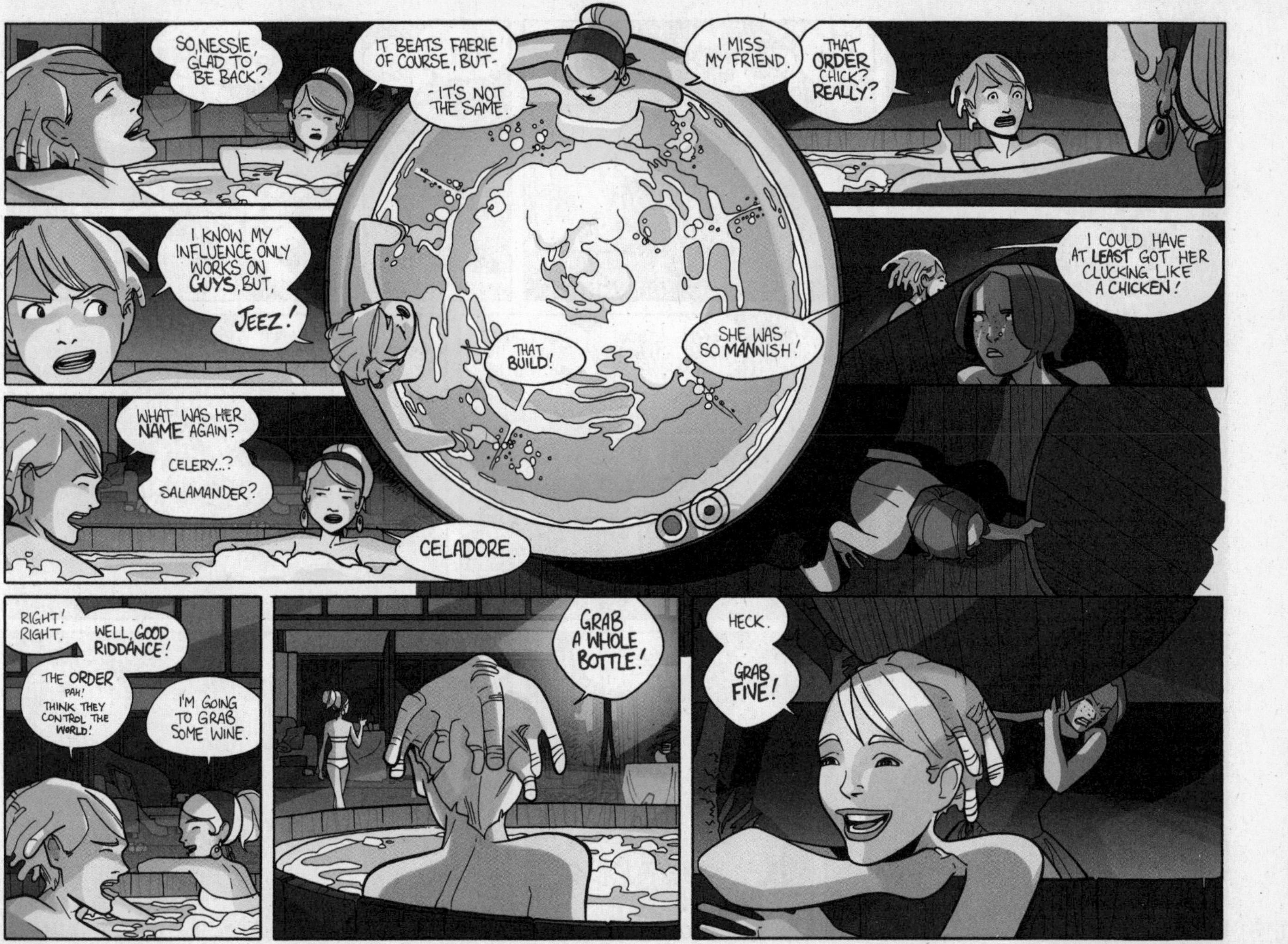
SO, NESSIE, GLAD TO BE BACK?
IT BEATS FAERIE OF COURSE, BUT-
- IT'S NOT THE SAME.
I MISS MY FRIEND.
THAT ORDER CHICK? REALLY?
I KNOW MY INFLUENCE ONLY WORKS ON GUYS, BUT,
JEEZ!
THAT BUILD!
SHE WAS SO MANNISH!
I COULD HAVE AT LEAST GOT HER CLUCKING LIKE A CHICKEN!
WHAT WAS HER NAME AGAIN?
CELERY..?
SALAMANDER?
CELADORE.
RIGHT! RIGHT.
WELL, GOOD RIDDANCE!
THE ORDER PAH! THINK THEY CONTROL THE WORLD!
I'M GOING TO GRAB SOME WINE.
GRAB A WHOLE BOTTLE!
HECK.
GRAB FIVE!

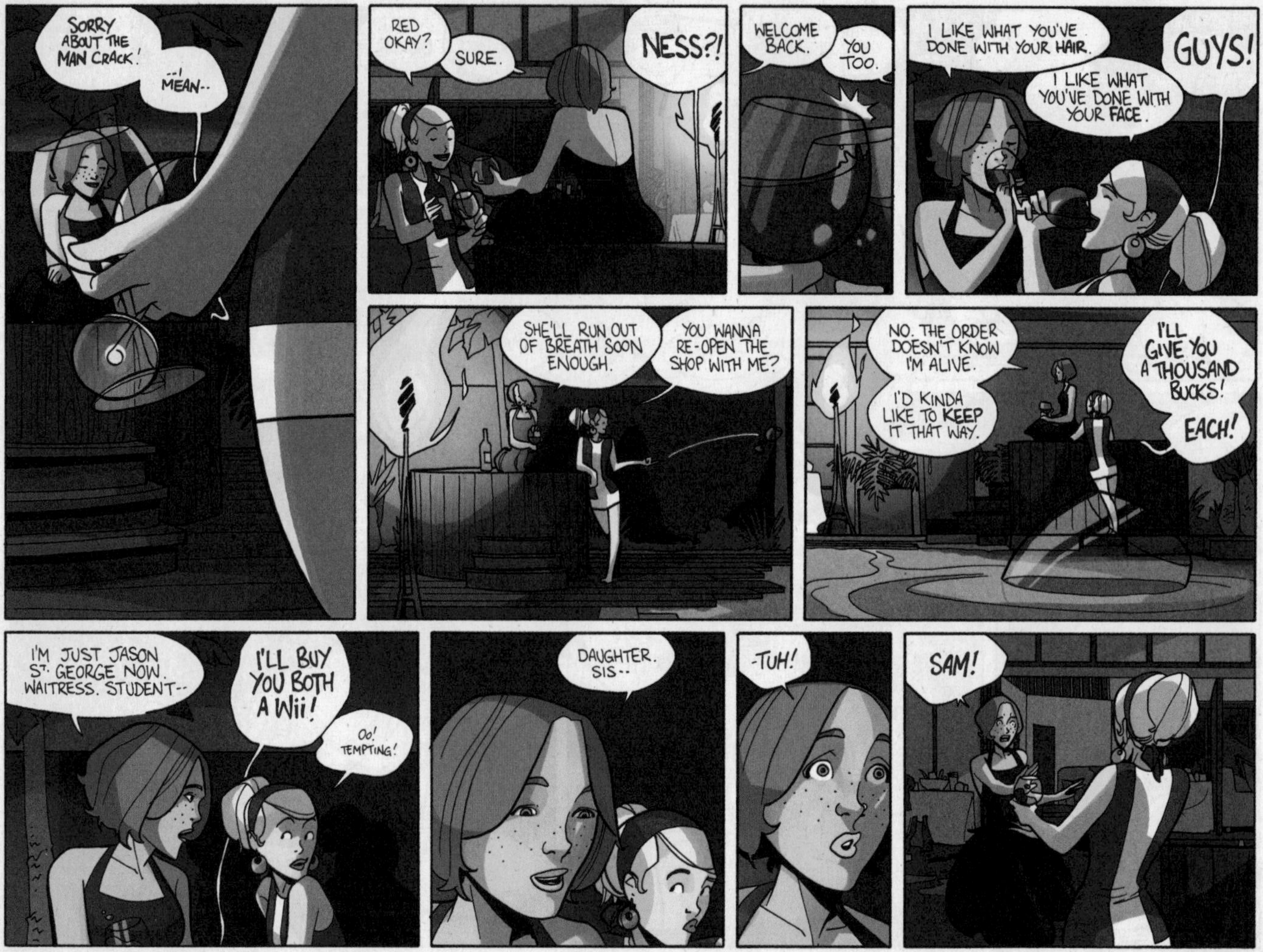
SORRY ABOUT THE MAN CRACK!
--I MEAN--
RED OKAY?
SURE.
NESS?!
WELCOME BACK.
YOU TOO.
I LIKE WHAT YOU'VE DONE WITH YOUR HAIR.
I LIKE WHAT YOU'VE DONE WITH YOUR FACE.
GUYS!
SHE'LL RUN OUT OF BREATH SOON ENOUGH.
YOU WANNA RE-OPEN THE SHOP WITH ME?
NO. THE ORDER DOESN'T KNOW I'M ALIVE.
I'D KINDA LIKE TO KEEP IT THAT WAY.
I'LL GIVE YOU A THOUSAND BUCKS!
EACH!
I'M JUST JASON ST. GEORGE NOW. WAITRESS. STUDENT--
I'LL BUY YOU BOTH A Wii!
OO! TEMPTING!
DAUGHTER. SIS--
-TUH!
SAM!

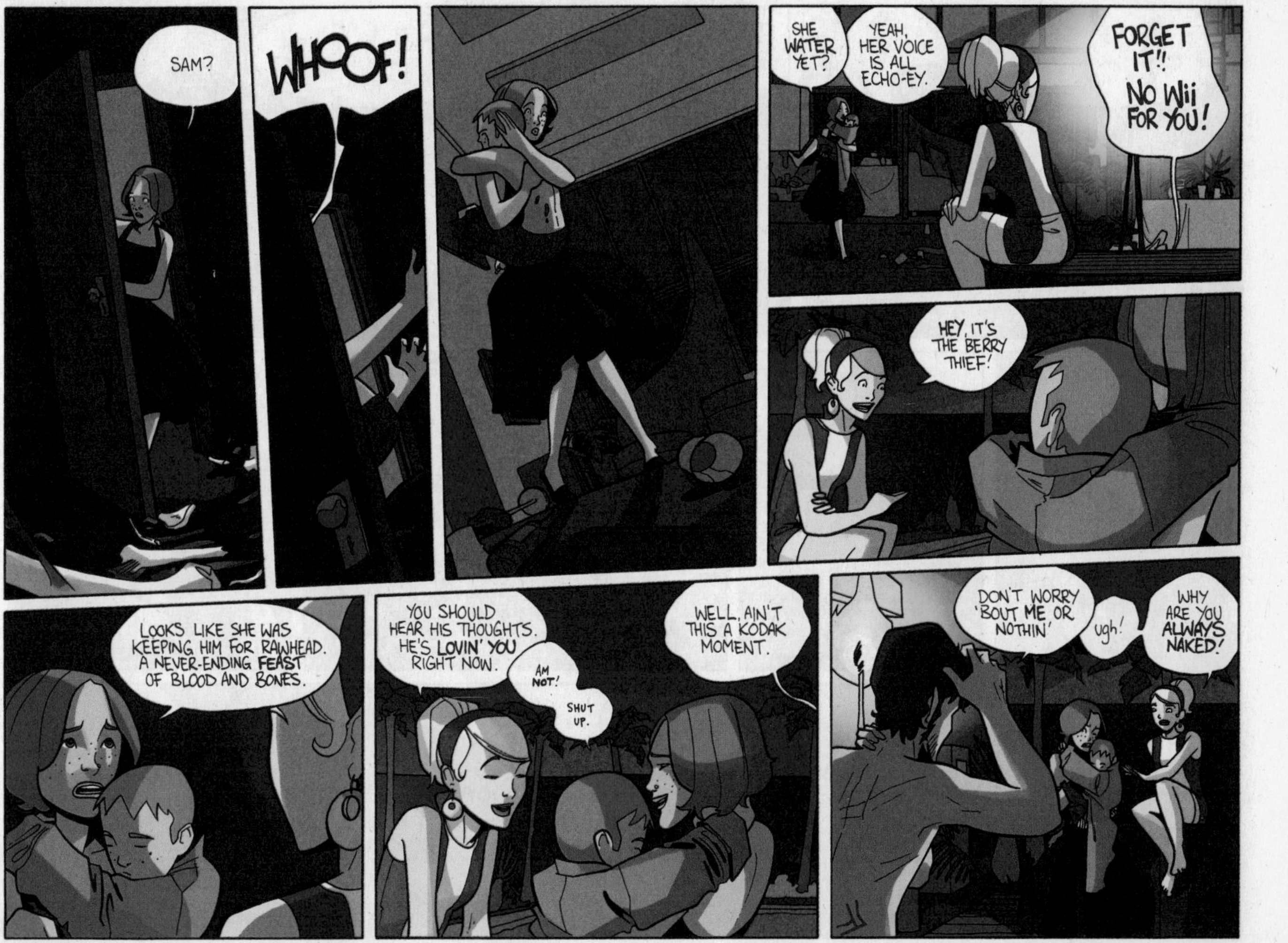
SAM?
WHOOF!
SHE WATER YET?
YEAH, HER VOICE IS ALL ECHO-EY.
FORGET IT!! No Wii FOR YOU!
HEY, IT'S THE BERRY THIEF!
LOOKS LIKE SHE WAS KEEPING HIM FOR RAWHEAD. A NEVER-ENDING FEAST OF BLOOD AND BONES.
YOU SHOULD HEAR HIS THOUGHTS. HE'S LOVIN' YOU RIGHT NOW.
AM NOT!
SHUT UP.
WELL, AIN'T THIS A KODAK MOMENT.
DON'T WORRY 'BOUT ME OR NOTHIN'
ugh!
WHY ARE YOU ALWAYS NAKED!

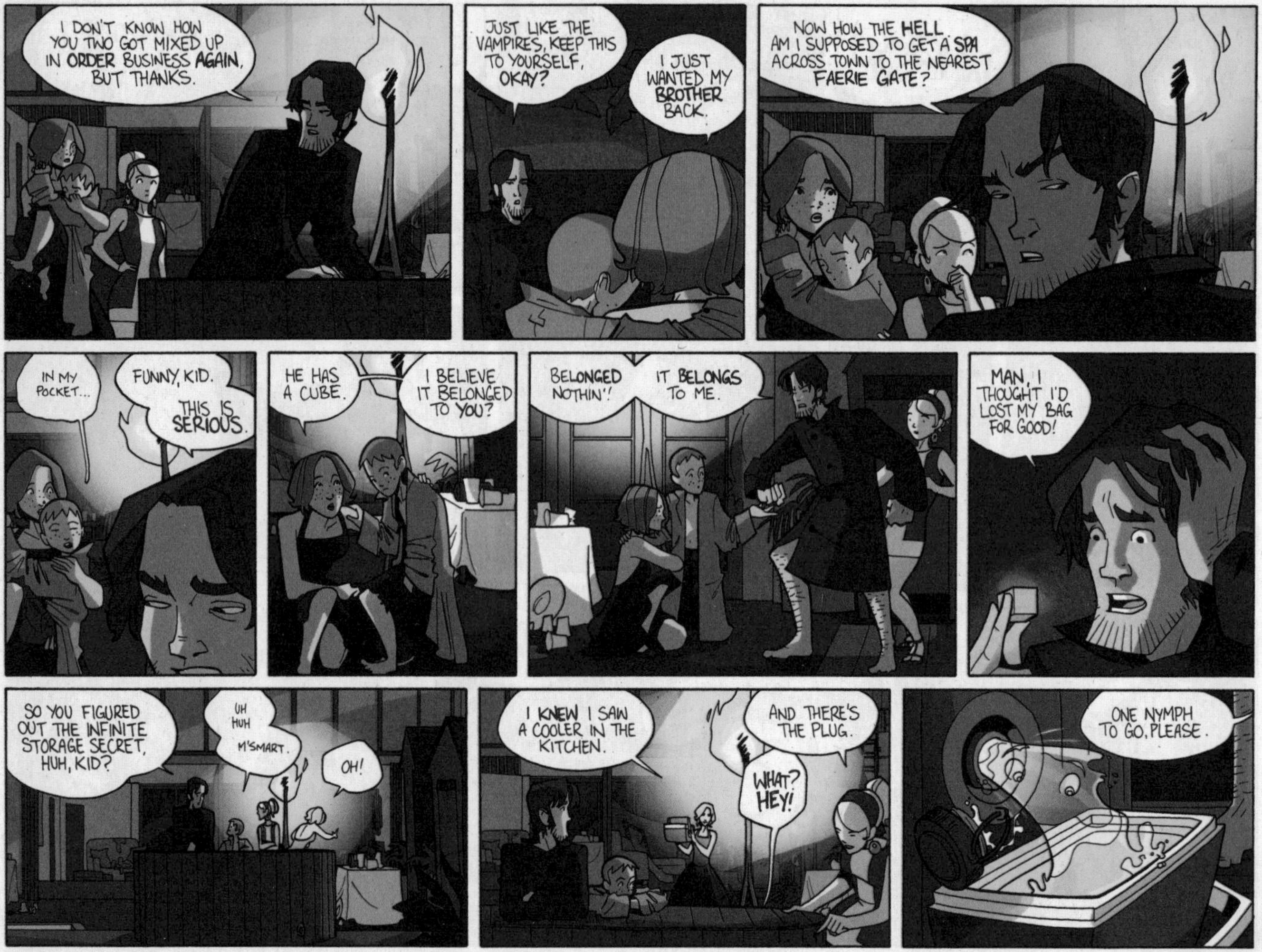
I DON'T KNOW HOW YOU TWO GOT MIXED UP IN **ORDER** BUSINESS **AGAIN**, BUT THANKS.
JUST LIKE THE VAMPIRES, KEEP THIS TO YOURSELF, **OKAY?**
I JUST WANTED MY **BROTHER** BACK.
NOW HOW THE **HELL** AM I SUPPOSED TO GET A **SPA** ACROSS TOWN TO THE NEAREST **FAERIE GATE?**
IN MY POCKET...
FUNNY, KID.
THIS IS **SERIOUS**.
HE HAS A CUBE.
I BELIEVE IT BELONGED TO **YOU?**
BELONGED NOTHIN'!
IT **BELONGS** TO ME.
MAN, I THOUGHT I'D LOST MY BAG FOR GOOD!
SO YOU FIGURED OUT THE INFINITE STORAGE SECRET, HUH, KID?
UH HUH
M'SMART.
OH!
I **KNEW** I SAW A COOLER IN THE KITCHEN.
AND THERE'S THE PLUG.
WHAT? HEY!
ONE NYMPH TO GO, PLEASE.

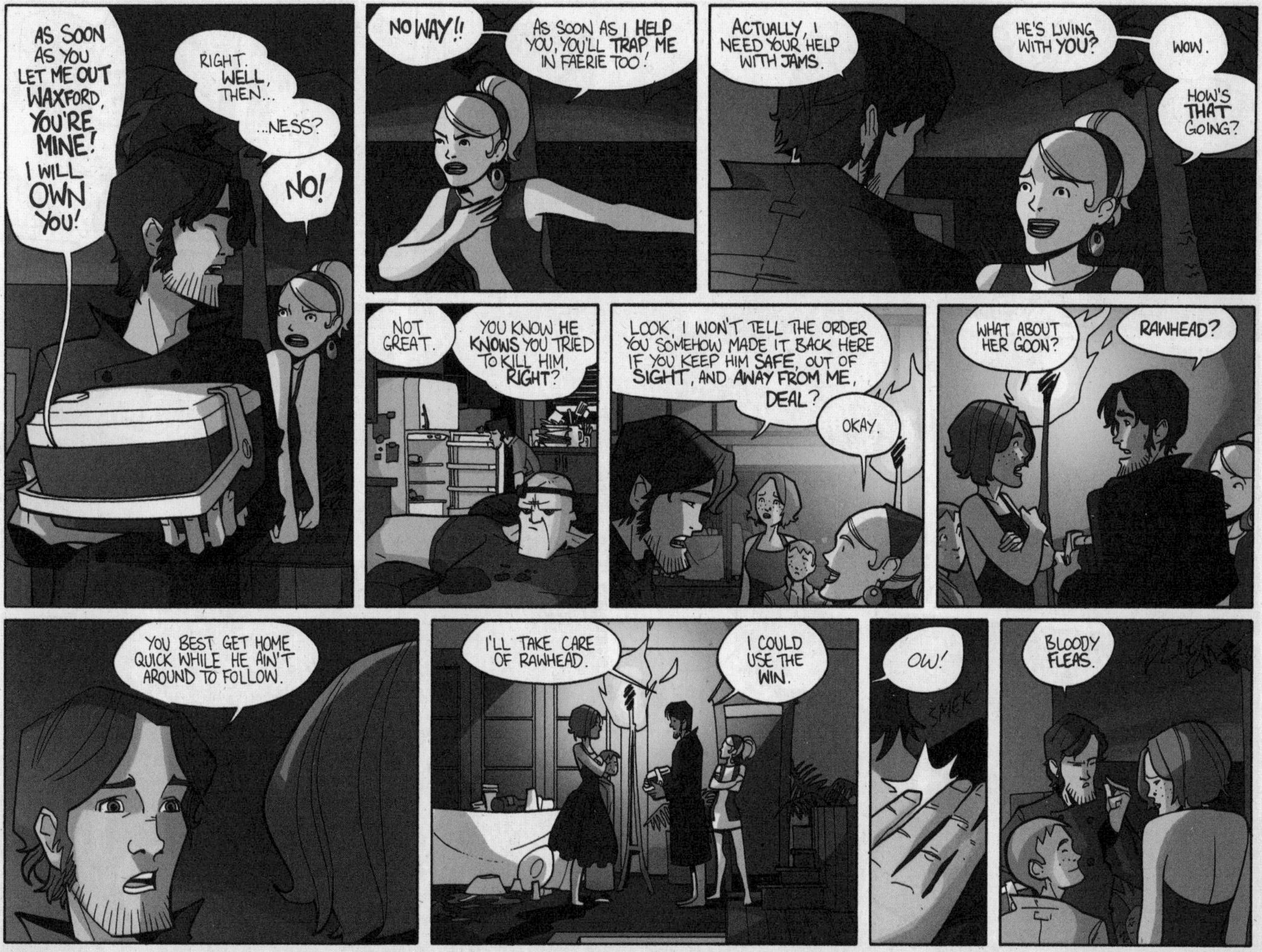

AS SOON AS YOU LET ME OUT WAXFORD, YOU'RE MINE! I WILL OWN YOU!
RIGHT. WELL, THEN...
...NESS?
NO!
NO WAY!!
AS SOON AS I HELP YOU, YOU'LL TRAP ME IN FAERIE TOO!
ACTUALLY, I NEED YOUR HELP WITH JAMS.
HE'S LIVING WITH YOU?
WOW.
HOW'S THAT GOING?
NOT GREAT.
YOU KNOW HE KNOWS YOU TRIED TO KILL HIM, RIGHT?
LOOK, I WON'T TELL THE ORDER YOU SOMEHOW MADE IT BACK HERE IF YOU KEEP HIM SAFE, OUT OF SIGHT, AND AWAY FROM ME. DEAL?
OKAY.
WHAT ABOUT HER GOON?
RAWHEAD?
YOU BEST GET HOME QUICK WHILE HE AIN'T AROUND TO FOLLOW.
I'LL TAKE CARE OF RAWHEAD.
I COULD USE THE WIN.
OW!
SMEK!
BLOODY FLEAS.

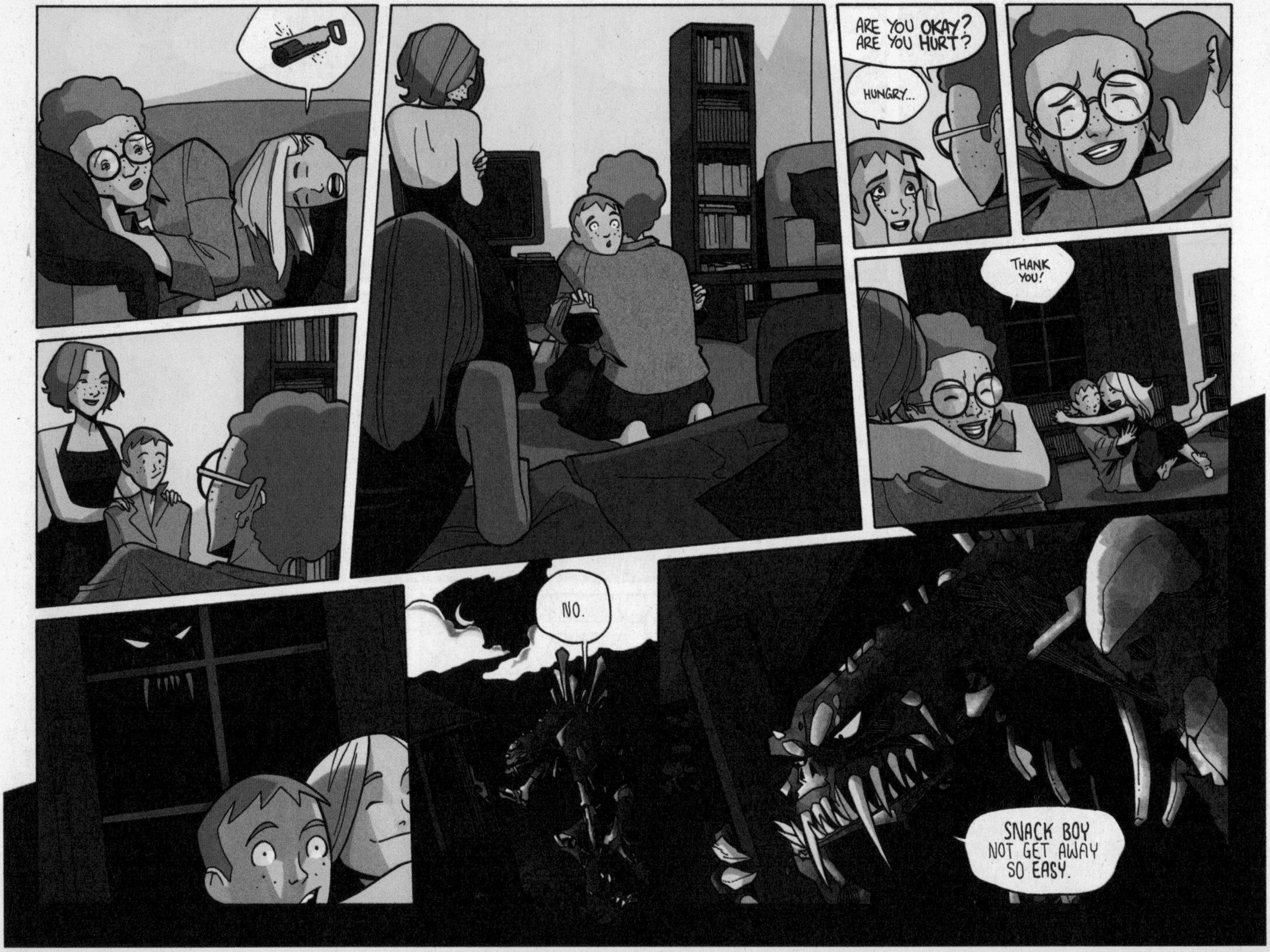
ARE YOU OKAY? ARE YOU HURT?
HUNGRY...
THANK YOU!
NO.
SNACK BOY NOT GET AWAY SO EASY.

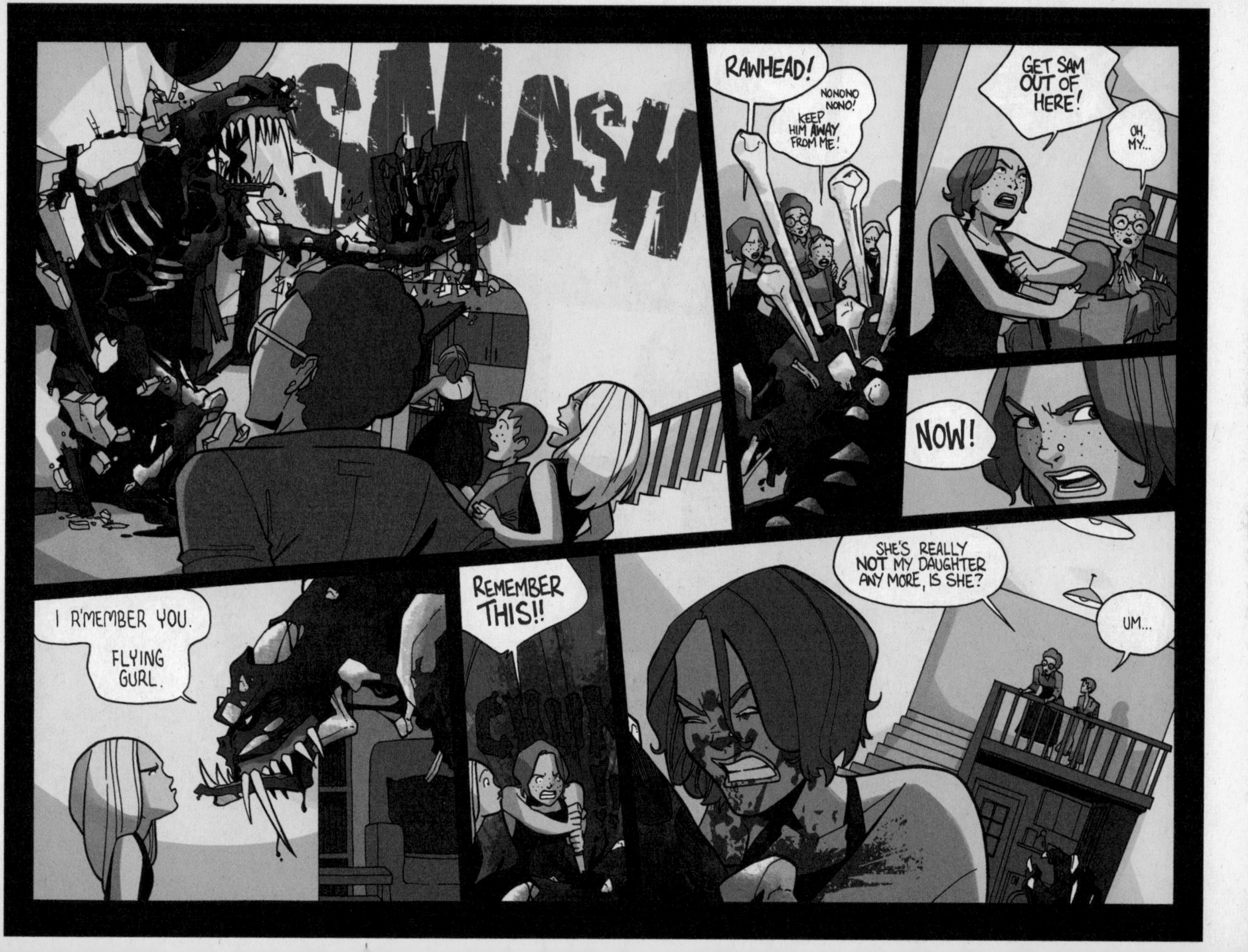
SMASH
RAWHEAD!
NONONO NONO!
KEEP HIM AWAY FROM ME!
GET SAM OUT OF HERE!
OH, MY...
NOW!
I R'MEMBER YOU.
FLYING GURL.
REMEMBER THIS!!
SHE'S REALLY NOT MY DAUGHTER ANY MORE, IS SHE?
UM...

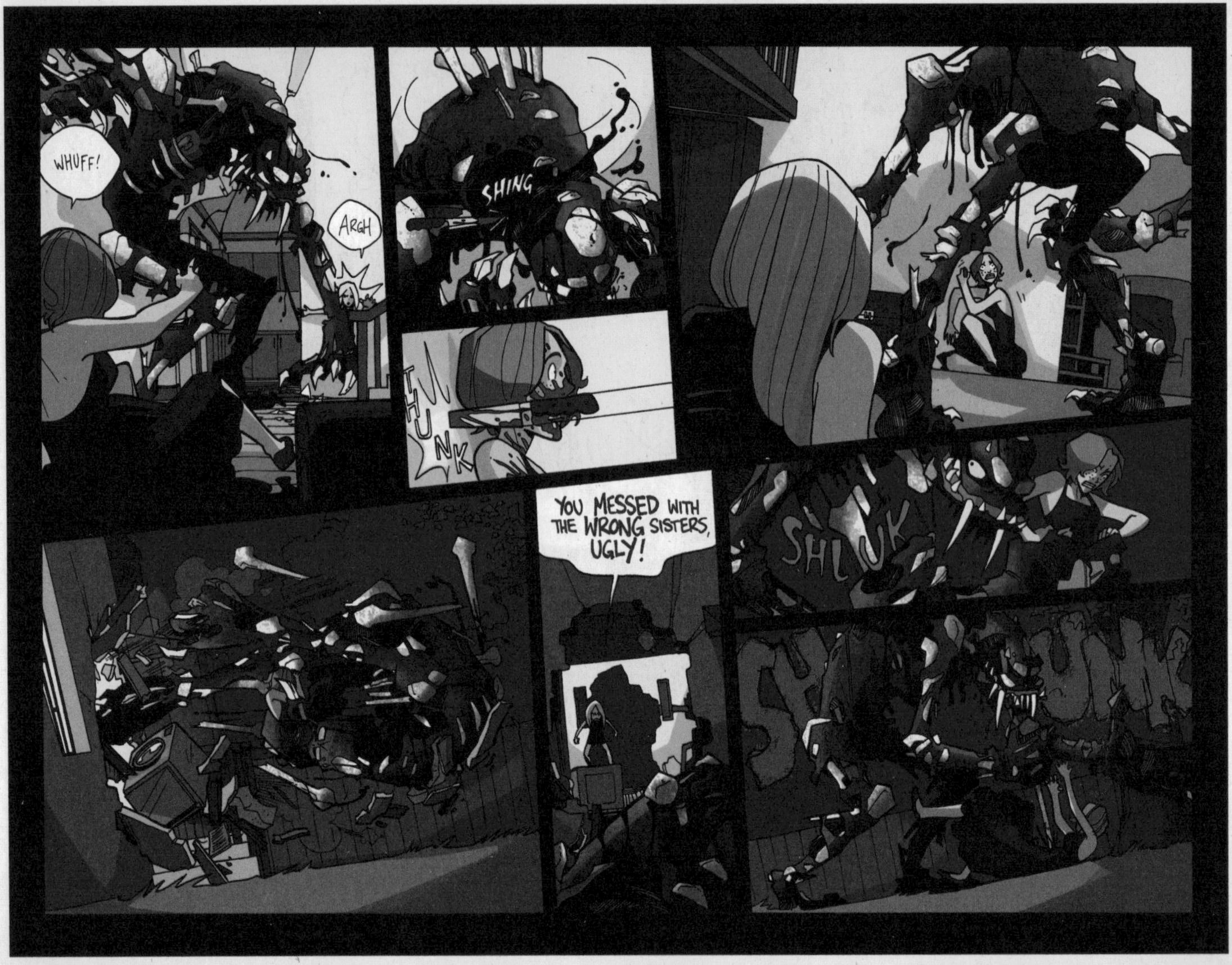
WHUFF!
ARGH
SHING
THUNK
YOU MESSED WITH THE WRONG SISTERS, UGLY!
SHLUK

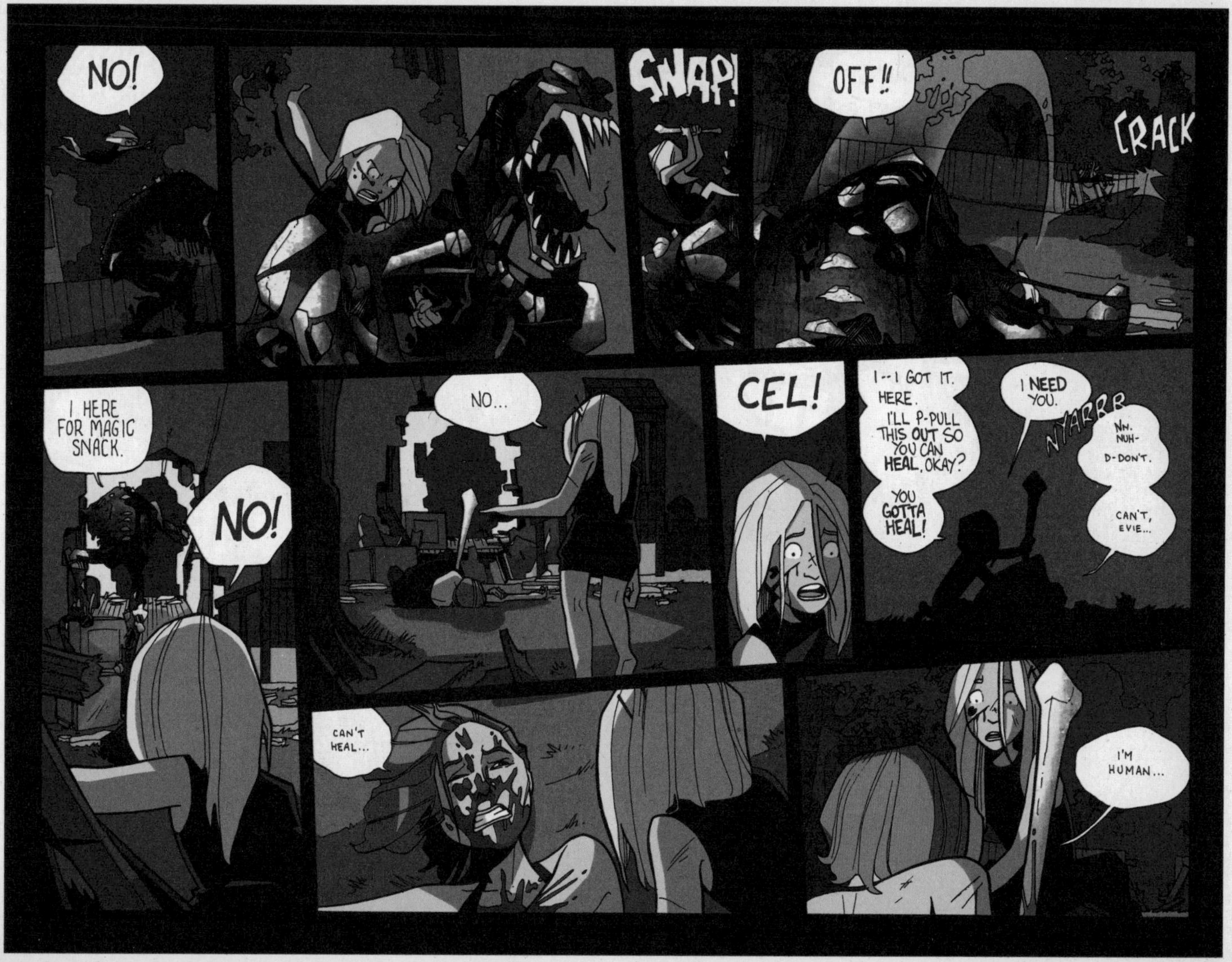
NO!
SNAP!
OFF!!
CRACK
I HERE FOR MAGIC SNACK.
NO!
NO...
CEL!
I-- I GOT IT. HERE.
I'LL P-PULL THIS OUT SO YOU CAN HEAL, OKAY?
YOU GOTTA HEAL!
I NEED YOU.
NYARRR
NN. NUH-
D-DON'T.
CAN'T, EVIE...
CAN'T HEAL...
I'M HUMAN...

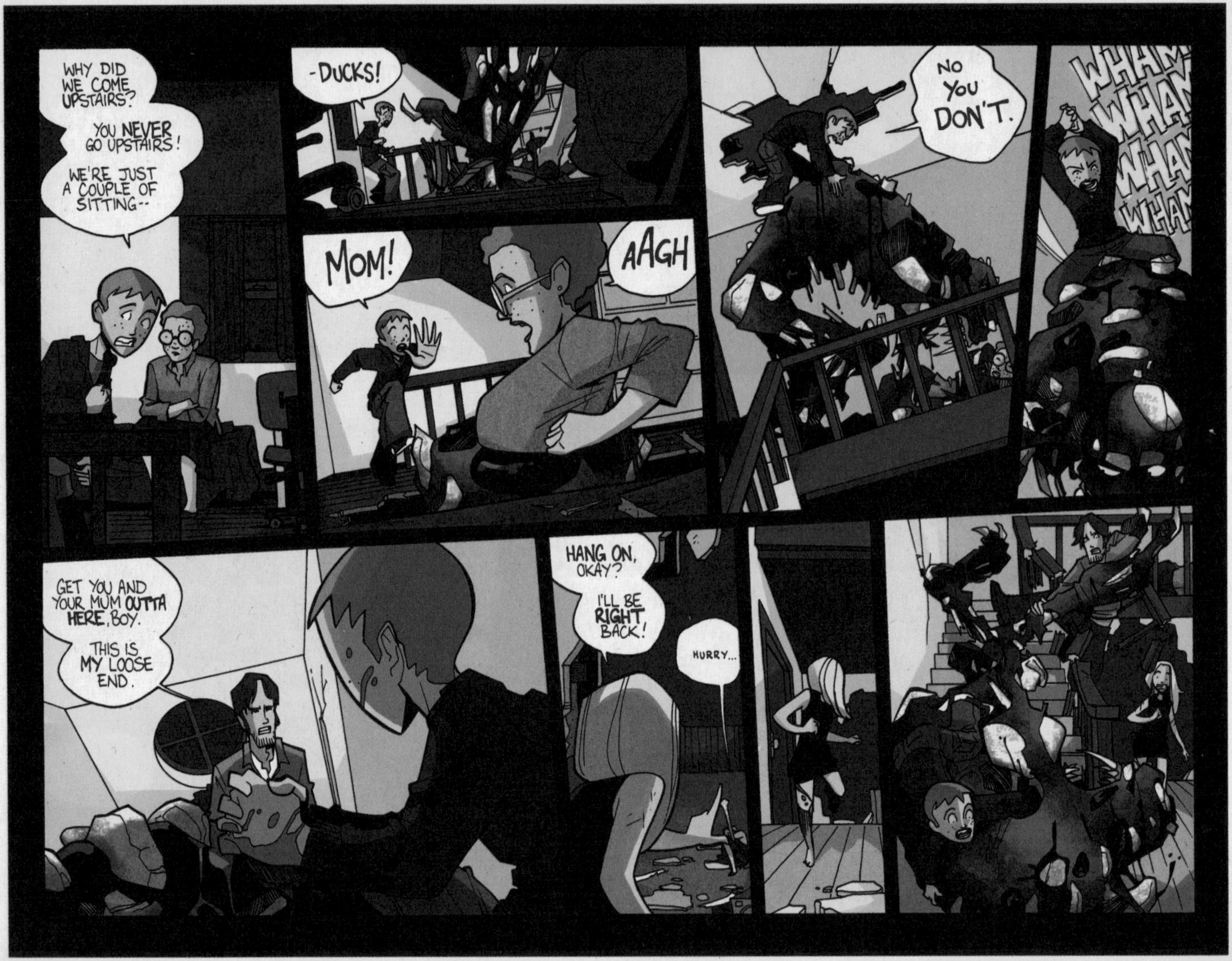

WHY DID WE COME UPSTAIRS?
YOU NEVER GO UPSTAIRS!
WE'RE JUST A COUPLE OF SITTING--
-DUCKS!
MOM!
AAGH
NO YOU DON'T.
WHAM WHAM WHAM WHAM WHAM
GET YOU AND YOUR MUM OUTTA HERE, BOY.
THIS IS MY LOOSE END.
HANG ON, OKAY?
I'LL BE RIGHT BACK!
HURRY...

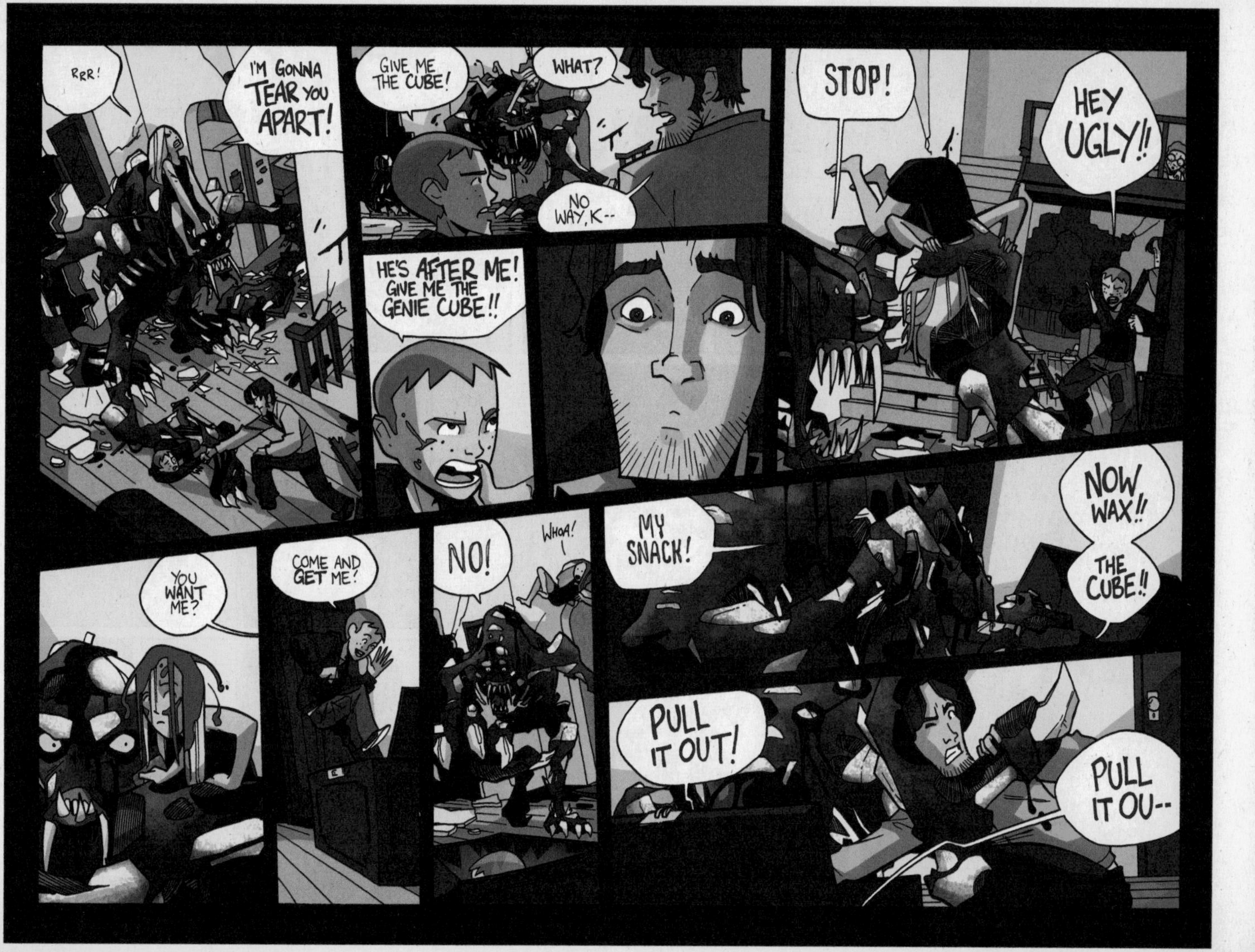
RRR!
I'M GONNA TEAR YOU APART!
GIVE ME THE CUBE!
WHAT?
NO WAY, K--
STOP!
HEY UGLY!!
HE'S AFTER ME! GIVE ME THE GENIE CUBE!!
YOU WANT ME?
COME AND GET ME!
NO!
WHOA!
MY SNACK!
NOW WAX!!
THE CUBE!!
PULL IT OUT!
PULL IT OU--

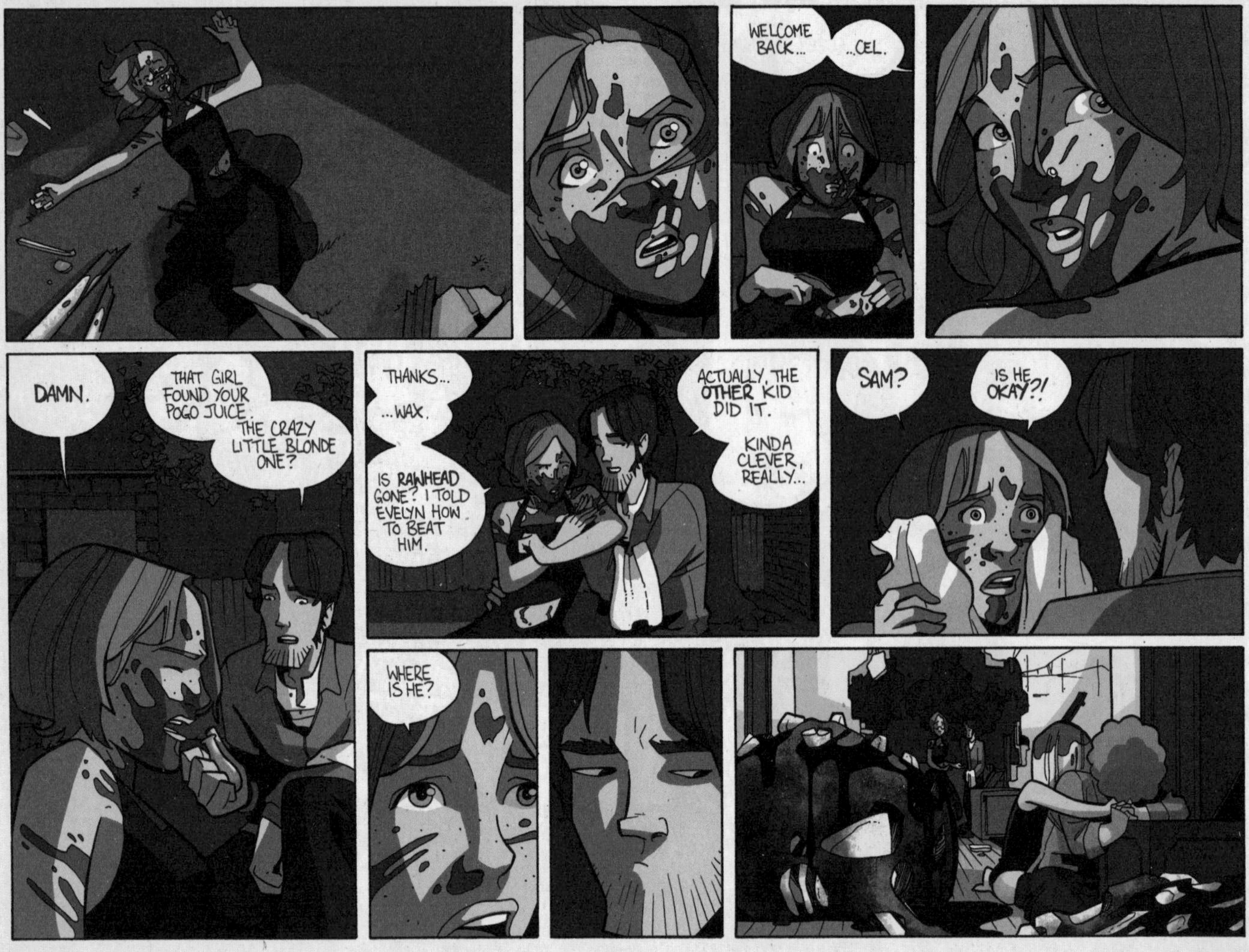

WELCOME BACK...
...CEL.
DAMN.
THAT GIRL FOUND YOUR POGO JUICE.
THE CRAZY LITTLE BLONDE ONE?
THANKS...
...WAX.
IS RAWHEAD GONE? I TOLD EVELYN HOW TO BEAT HIM.
ACTUALLY, THE OTHER KID DID IT.
KINDA CLEVER, REALLY...
SAM?
IS HE OKAY?!
WHERE IS HE?

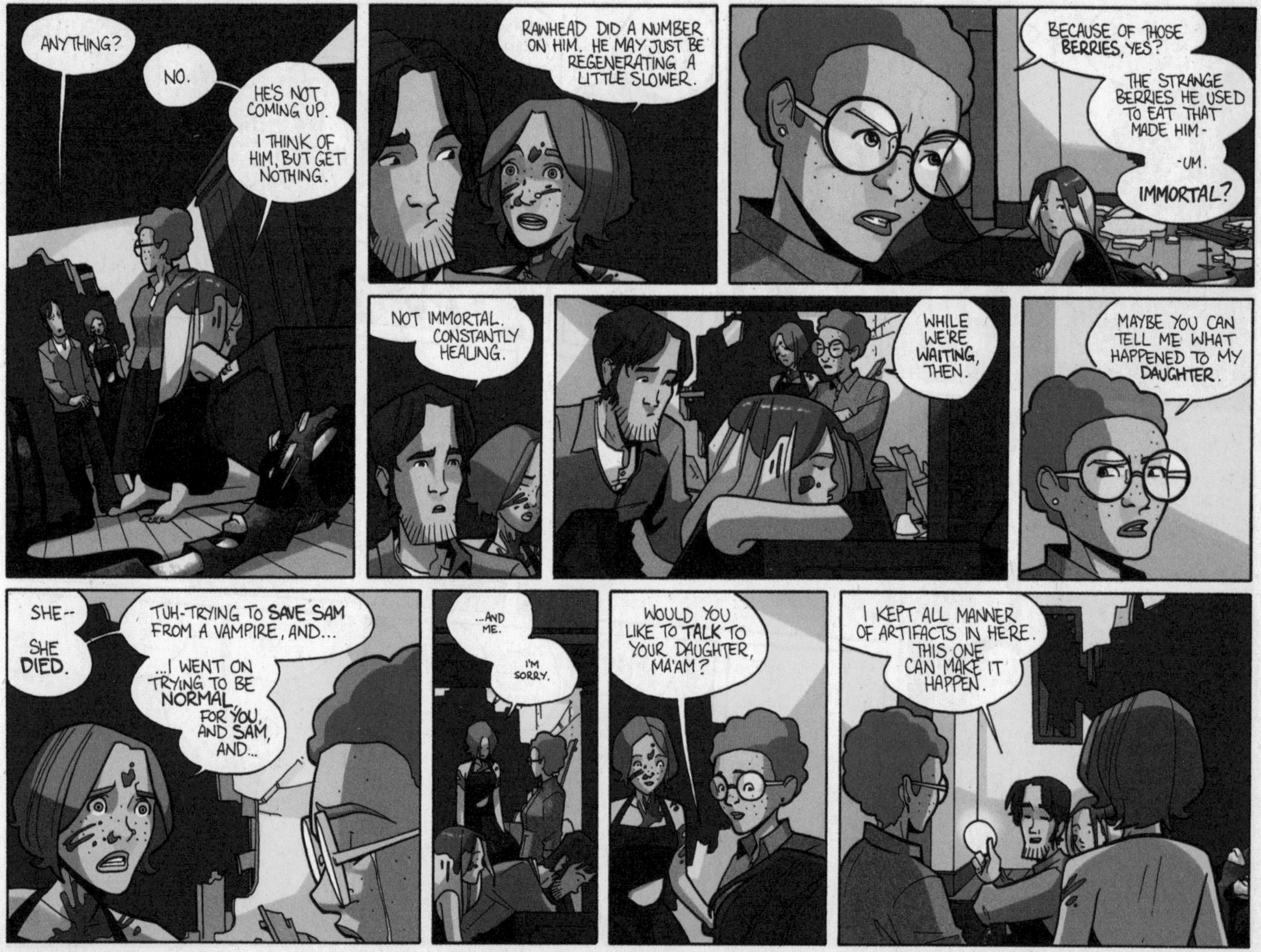
ANYTHING?
NO.
HE'S NOT COMING UP.
I THINK OF HIM, BUT GET NOTHING.
RAWHEAD DID A NUMBER ON HIM. HE MAY JUST BE REGENERATING A LITTLE SLOWER.
BECAUSE OF THOSE BERRIES, YES?
THE STRANGE BERRIES HE USED TO EAT THAT MADE HIM -
-UM.
IMMORTAL?
NOT IMMORTAL. CONSTANTLY HEALING.
WHILE WE'RE WAITING, THEN.
MAYBE YOU CAN TELL ME WHAT HAPPENED TO MY DAUGHTER.
SHE--
SHE DIED.
TUH-TRYING TO SAVE SAM FROM A VAMPIRE, AND...
...I WENT ON TRYING TO BE NORMAL, FOR YOU, AND SAM, AND...
...AND ME.
I'M SORRY.
WOULD YOU LIKE TO TALK TO YOUR DAUGHTER, MA'AM?
I KEPT ALL MANNER OF ARTIFACTS IN HERE. THIS ONE CAN MAKE IT HAPPEN.

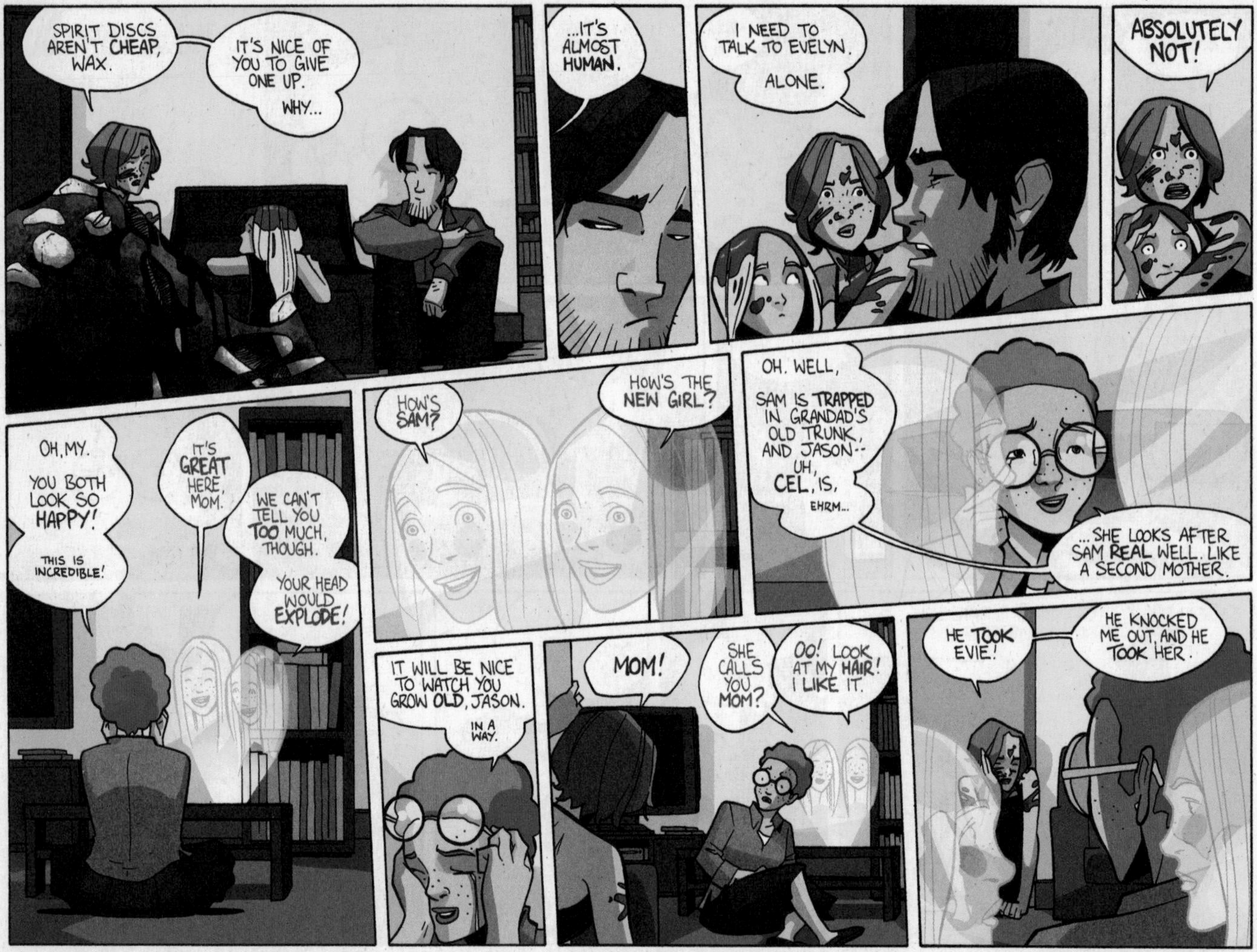
SPIRIT DISCS AREN'T CHEAP, WAX.
IT'S NICE OF YOU TO GIVE ONE UP.
WHY...
...IT'S ALMOST HUMAN.
I NEED TO TALK TO EVELYN.
ALONE.
ABSOLUTELY NOT!
OH, MY.
YOU BOTH LOOK SO HAPPY!
THIS IS INCREDIBLE!
IT'S GREAT HERE, MOM.
WE CAN'T TELL YOU TOO MUCH, THOUGH.
YOUR HEAD WOULD EXPLODE!
HOW'S SAM?
HOW'S THE NEW GIRL?
OH. WELL,
SAM IS TRAPPED IN GRANDAD'S OLD TRUNK, AND JASON-- UH, CEL, IS,
EHRM...
...SHE LOOKS AFTER SAM REAL WELL. LIKE A SECOND MOTHER.
IT WILL BE NICE TO WATCH YOU GROW OLD, JASON.
IN A WAY.
MOM!
SHE CALLS YOU MOM?
OO! LOOK AT MY HAIR! I LIKE IT.
HE TOOK EVIE!
HE KNOCKED ME OUT, AND HE TOOK HER.

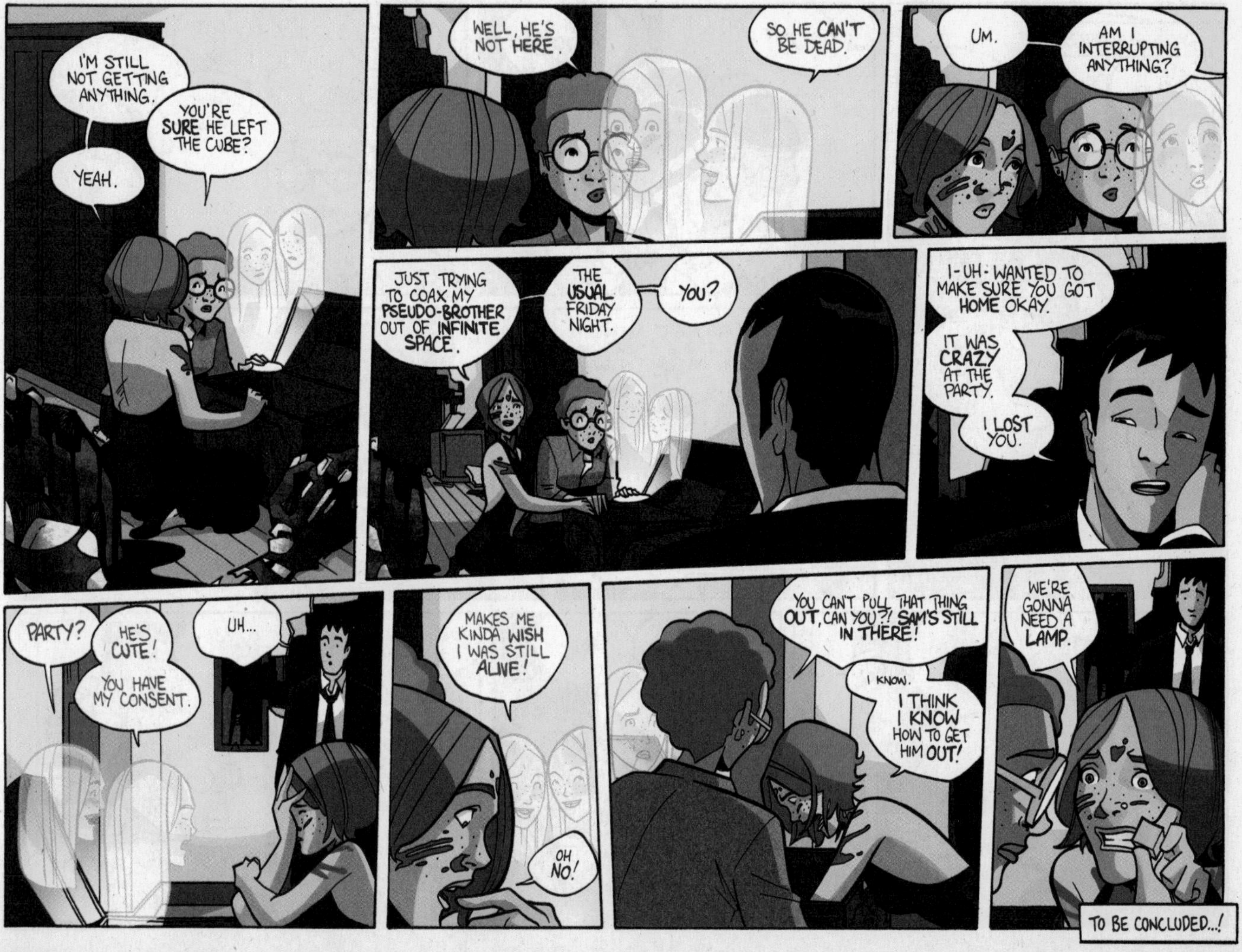

I'M STILL NOT GETTING ANYTHING.
YOU'RE SURE HE LEFT THE CUBE?
YEAH.
WELL, HE'S NOT HERE.
SO HE CAN'T BE DEAD.
UM.
AM I INTERRUPTING ANYTHING?
JUST TRYING TO COAX MY PSEUDO-BROTHER OUT OF INFINITE SPACE.
THE USUAL FRIDAY NIGHT.
YOU?
I-UH- WANTED TO MAKE SURE YOU GOT HOME OKAY.
IT WAS CRAZY AT THE PARTY.
I LOST YOU.
PARTY?
HE'S CUTE!
YOU HAVE MY CONSENT.
UH...
MAKES ME KINDA WISH I WAS STILL ALIVE!
OH NO!
YOU CAN'T PULL THAT THING OUT, CAN YOU?! SAM'S STILL IN THERE!
I KNOW.
I THINK I KNOW HOW TO GET HIM OUT!
WE'RE GONNA NEED A LAMP.
TO BE CONCLUDED...!

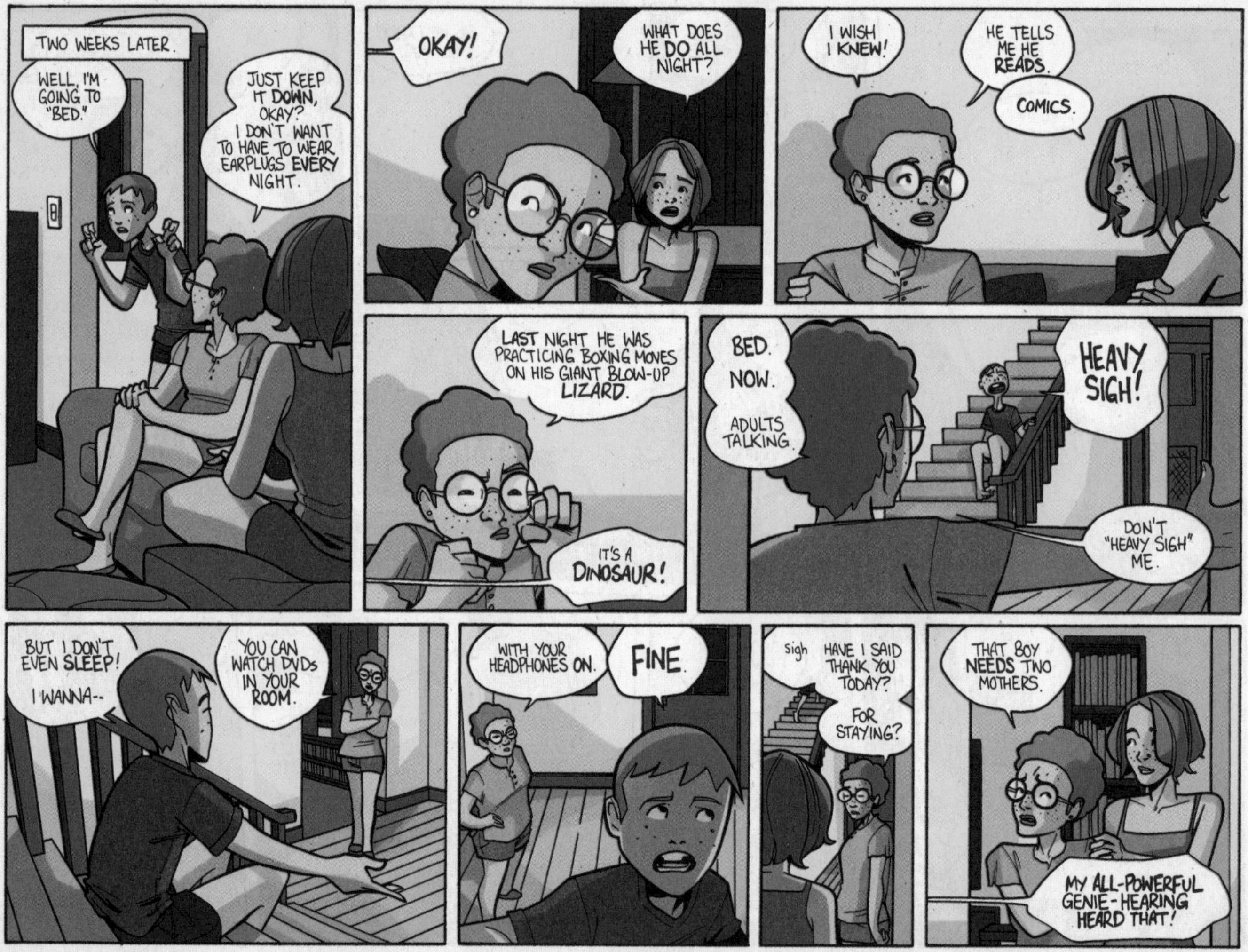
TWO WEEKS LATER.
WELL, I'M GOING TO "BED."
JUST KEEP IT DOWN, OKAY? I DON'T WANT TO HAVE TO WEAR EARPLUGS EVERY NIGHT.
OKAY!
WHAT DOES HE DO ALL NIGHT?
I WISH I KNEW!
HE TELLS ME HE READS.
COMICS.
LAST NIGHT HE WAS PRACTICING BOXING MOVES ON HIS GIANT BLOW-UP LIZARD.
IT'S A DINOSAUR!
BED.
NOW.
ADULTS TALKING.
HEAVY SIGH!
DON'T "HEAVY SIGH" ME.
BUT I DON'T EVEN SLEEP!
I WANNA--
YOU CAN WATCH DVDs IN YOUR ROOM.
WITH YOUR HEADPHONES ON.
FINE.
Sigh
HAVE I SAID THANK YOU TODAY?
FOR STAYING?
THAT BOY NEEDS TWO MOTHERS.
MY ALL-POWERFUL GENIE-HEARING HEARD THAT!

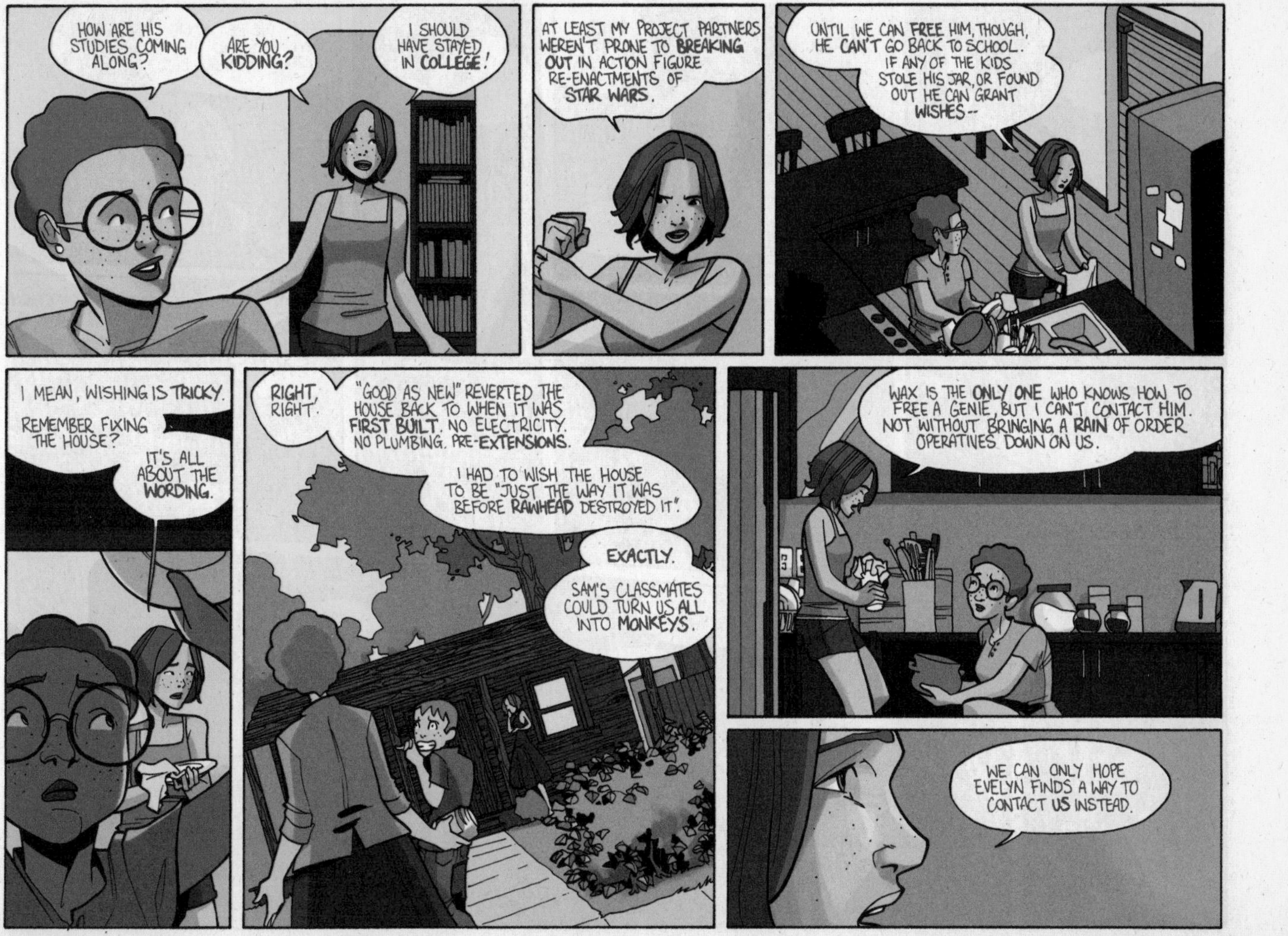
HOW ARE HIS STUDIES COMING ALONG?
ARE YOU KIDDING?
I SHOULD HAVE STAYED IN COLLEGE!
AT LEAST MY PROJECT PARTNERS WEREN'T PRONE TO BREAKING OUT IN ACTION FIGURE RE-ENACTMENTS OF STAR WARS.
UNTIL WE CAN FREE HIM, THOUGH, HE CAN'T GO BACK TO SCHOOL.
IF ANY OF THE KIDS STOLE HIS JAR, OR FOUND OUT HE CAN GRANT WISHES--
I MEAN, WISHING IS TRICKY.
REMEMBER FIXING THE HOUSE?
IT'S ALL ABOUT THE WORDING.
RIGHT, RIGHT.
"GOOD AS NEW" REVERTED THE HOUSE BACK TO WHEN IT WAS FIRST BUILT. NO ELECTRICITY. NO PLUMBING. PRE-EXTENSIONS.
I HAD TO WISH THE HOUSE TO BE "JUST THE WAY IT WAS BEFORE RAWHEAD DESTROYED IT".
EXACTLY.
SAM'S CLASSMATES COULD TURN US ALL INTO MONKEYS.
WAX IS THE ONLY ONE WHO KNOWS HOW TO FREE A GENIE, BUT I CAN'T CONTACT HIM. NOT WITHOUT BRINGING A RAIN OF ORDER OPERATIVES DOWN ON US.
WE CAN ONLY HOPE EVELYN FINDS A WAY TO CONTACT US INSTEAD.

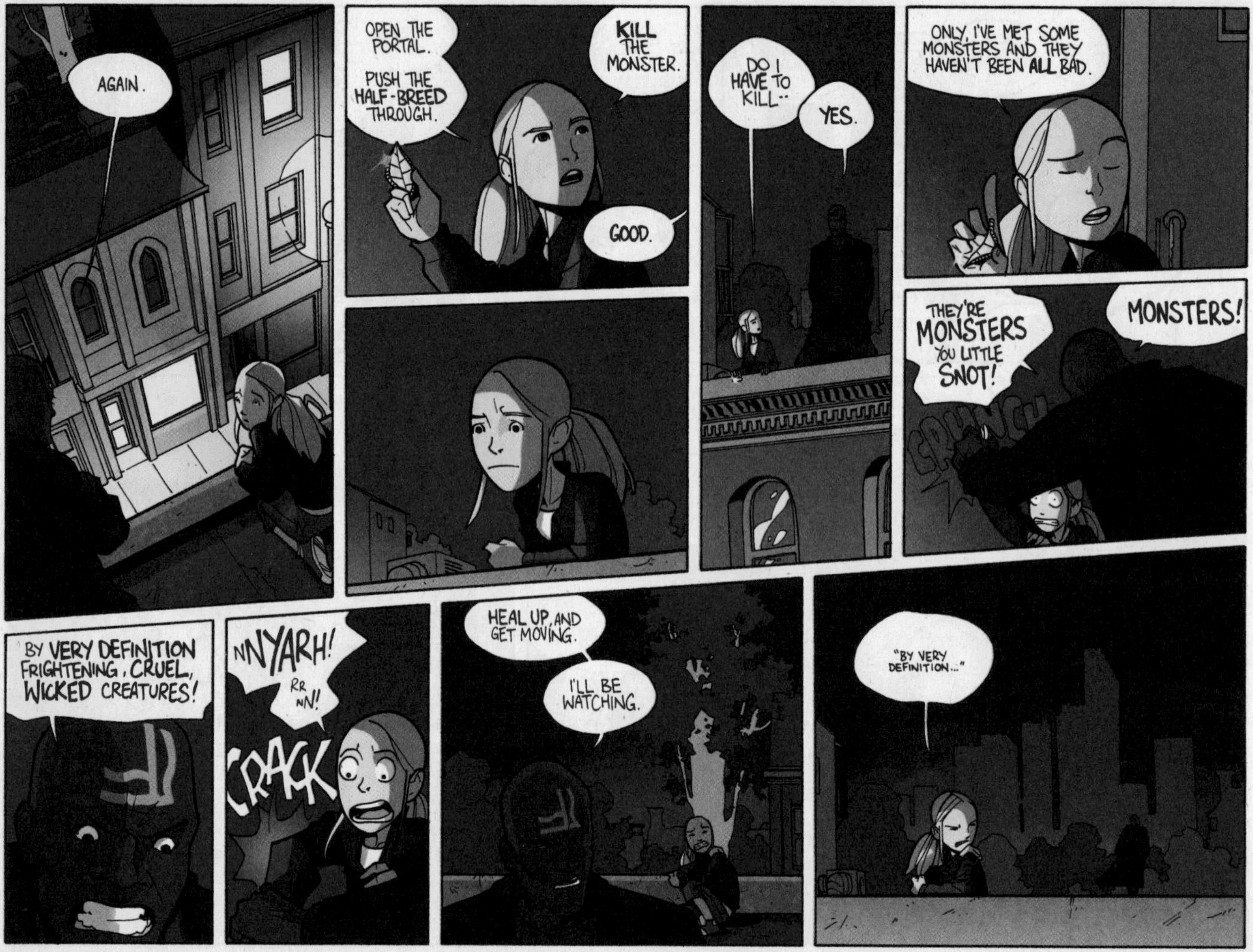
AGAIN.
OPEN THE PORTAL.
PUSH THE HALF-BREED THROUGH.
KILL THE MONSTER.
GOOD.
DO I HAVE TO KILL--
YES.
ONLY, I'VE MET SOME MONSTERS AND THEY HAVEN'T BEEN ALL BAD.
THEY'RE MONSTERS YOU LITTLE SNOT!
MONSTERS!
CRUNCH
BY VERY DEFINITION FRIGHTENING, CRUEL, WICKED CREATURES!
NNYARH!
RR NN!
CRACK
HEAL UP, AND GET MOVING.
I'LL BE WATCHING.
"BY VERY DEFINITION..."

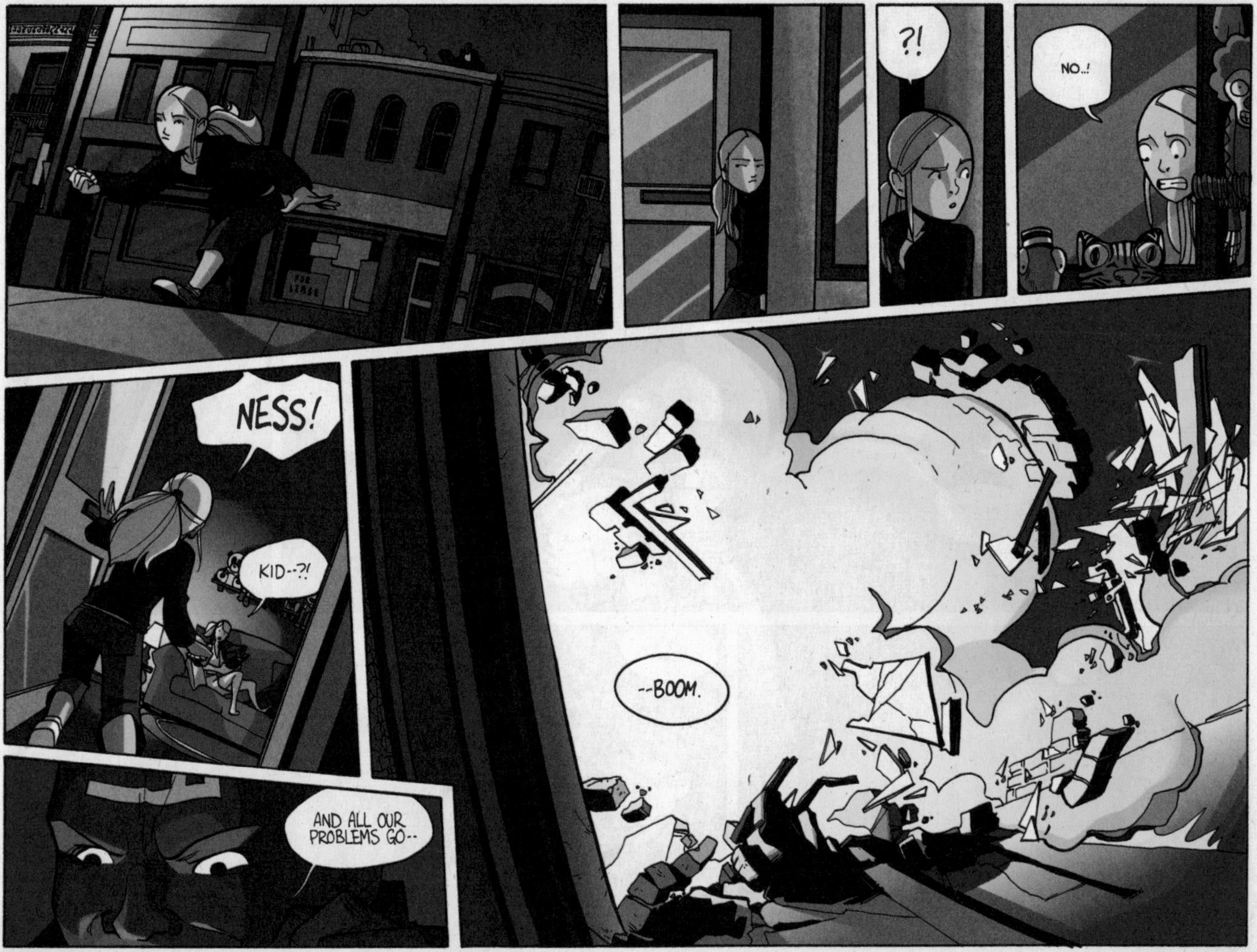
FOR LEASE
?!
NO..!
NESS!
KID--?!
AND ALL OUR PROBLEMS GO--
--BOOM.

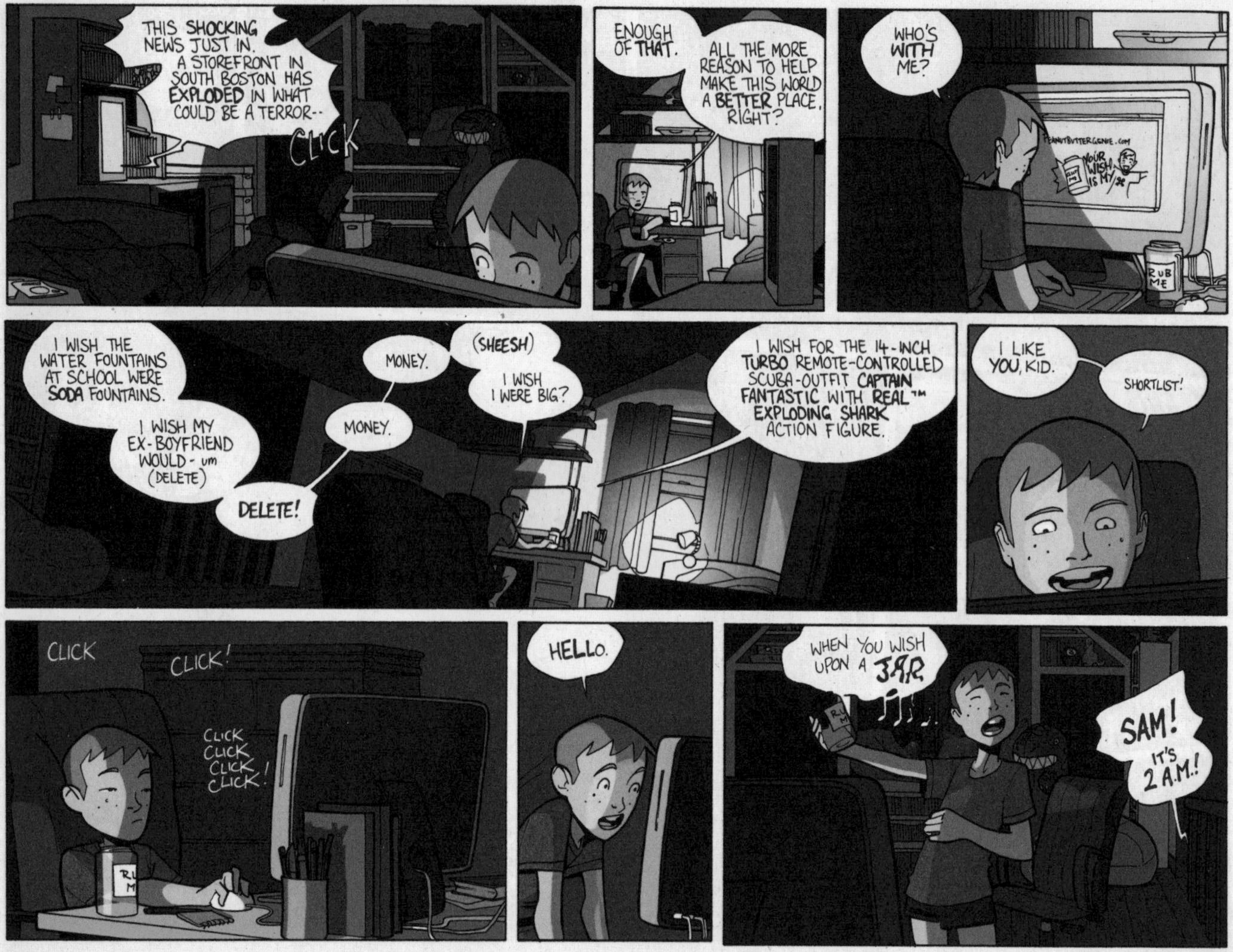
THIS SHOCKING NEWS JUST IN. A STOREFRONT IN SOUTH BOSTON HAS EXPLODED IN WHAT COULD BE A TERROR--
CLICK
ENOUGH OF THAT.
ALL THE MORE REASON TO HELP MAKE THIS WORLD A BETTER PLACE, RIGHT?
WHO'S WITH ME?
PEANUTBUTTERGENIE.COM
YOUR WISH IS MY
RUB ME
I WISH THE WATER FOUNTAINS AT SCHOOL WERE SODA FOUNTAINS.
I WISH MY EX-BOYFRIEND WOULD- um (DELETE)
DELETE!
MONEY.
MONEY.
(SHEESH)
I WISH I WERE BIG?
I WISH FOR THE 14-INCH TURBO REMOTE-CONTROLLED SCUBA-OUTFIT CAPTAIN FANTASTIC WITH REAL™ EXPLODING SHARK ACTION FIGURE.
I LIKE YOU, KID.
SHORTLIST!
CLICK
CLICK!
CLICK CLICK CLICK CLICK!
HELLo.
WHEN YOU WISH UPON A JAR
SAM! IT'S 2 A.M.!

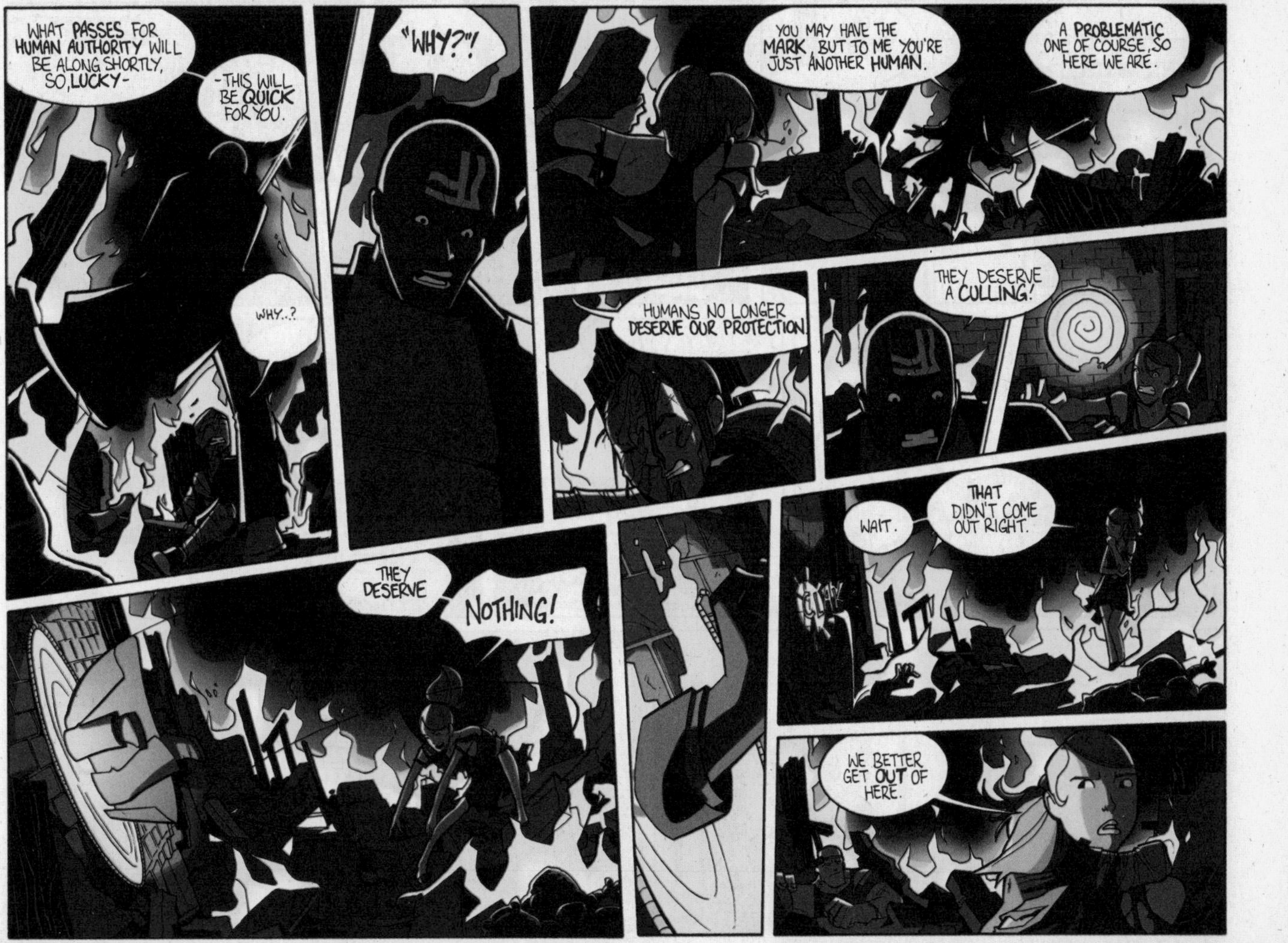
WHAT PASSES FOR HUMAN AUTHORITY WILL BE ALONG SHORTLY, SO, LUCKY-
-THIS WILL BE QUICK FOR YOU.
WHY..?
"WHY?"!
YOU MAY HAVE THE MARK, BUT TO ME YOU'RE JUST ANOTHER HUMAN.
A PROBLEMATIC ONE OF COURSE, SO HERE WE ARE.
HUMANS NO LONGER DESERVE OUR PROTECTION!
THEY DESERVE A CULLING!
THEY DESERVE
NOTHING!
WAIT.
THAT DIDN'T COME OUT RIGHT.
WE BETTER GET OUT OF HERE.

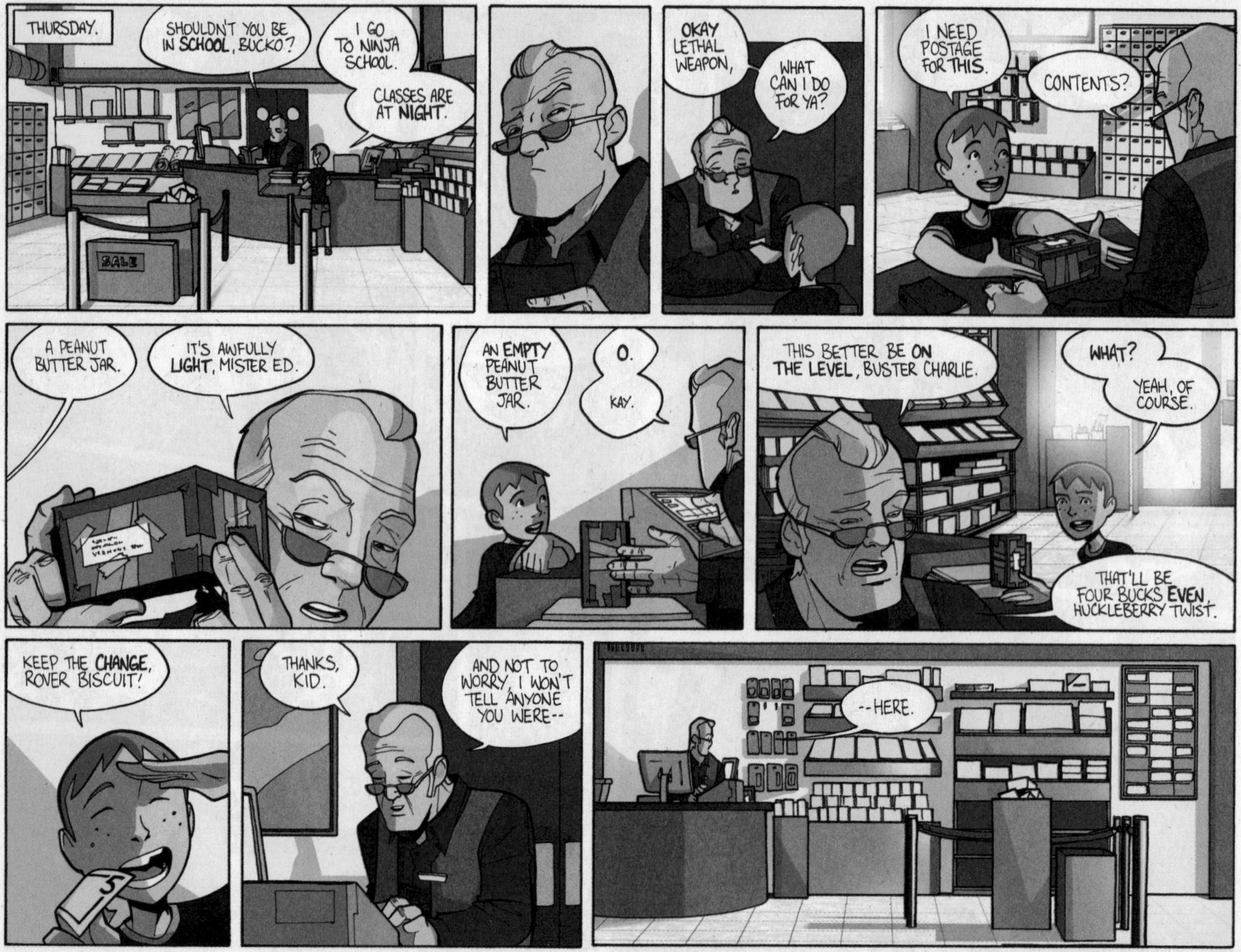
THURSDAY.
SHOULDN'T YOU BE IN SCHOOL, BUCKO?
I GO TO NINJA SCHOOL.
CLASSES ARE AT NIGHT.
SALE
OKAY LETHAL WEAPON,
WHAT CAN I DO FOR YA?
I NEED POSTAGE FOR THIS.
CONTENTS?
A PEANUT BUTTER JAR.
IT'S AWFULLY LIGHT, MISTER ED.
AN EMPTY PEANUT BUTTER JAR.
O.
KAY.
THIS BETTER BE ON THE LEVEL, BUSTER CHARLIE.
WHAT?
YEAH, OF COURSE.
THAT'LL BE FOUR BUCKS EVEN, HUCKLEBERRY TWIST.
KEEP THE CHANGE, ROVER BISCUIT!
5
THANKS, KID.
AND NOT TO WORRY, I WON'T TELL ANYONE YOU WERE--
--HERE.

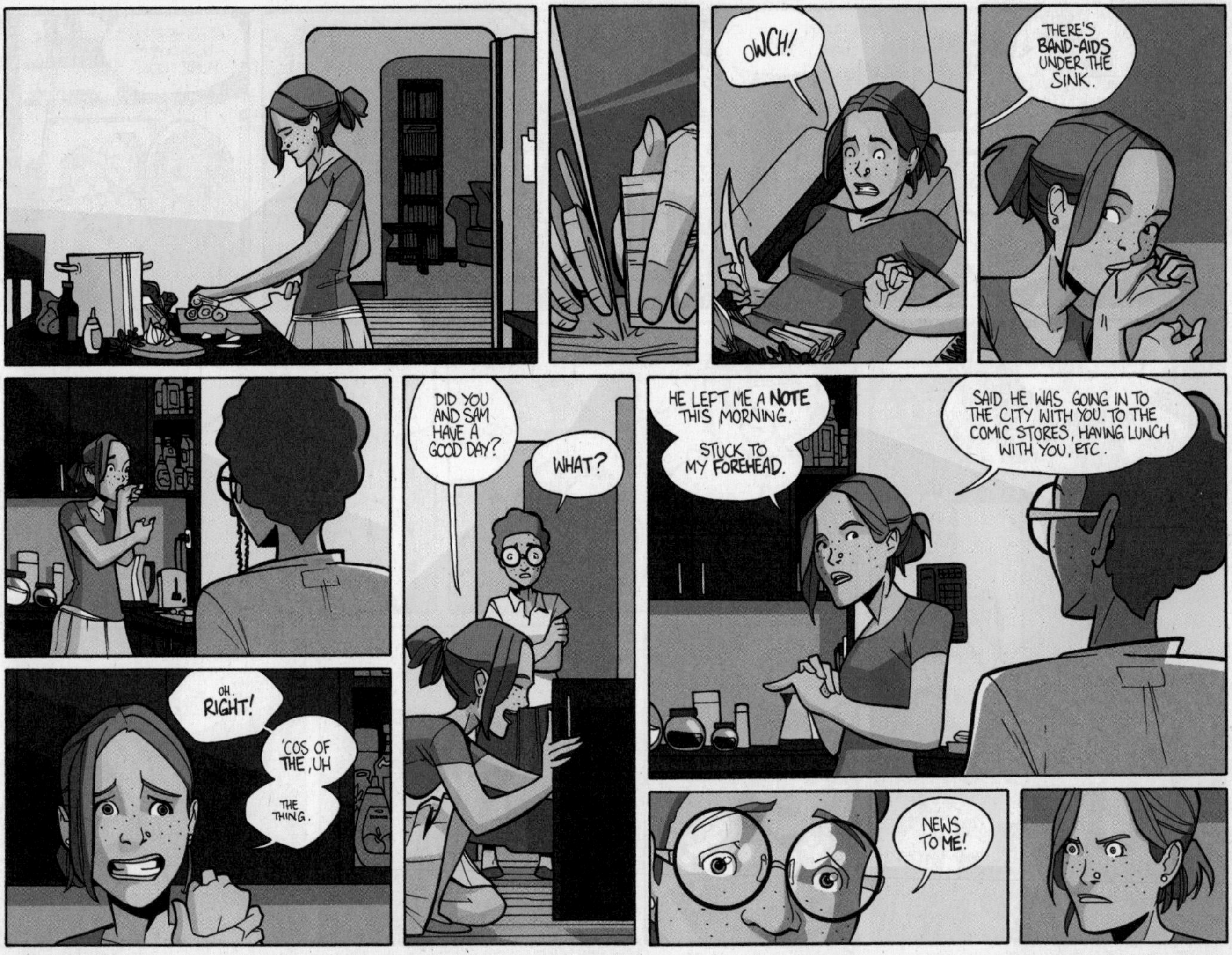
OWCH!
THERE'S BAND-AIDS UNDER THE SINK.
DID YOU AND SAM HAVE A GOOD DAY?
WHAT?
OH. RIGHT!
'COS OF THE, UH
THE THING.
HE LEFT ME A NOTE THIS MORNING.
STUCK TO MY FOREHEAD.
SAID HE WAS GOING IN TO THE CITY WITH YOU. TO THE COMIC STORES, HAVING LUNCH WITH YOU, ETC.
NEWS TO ME!

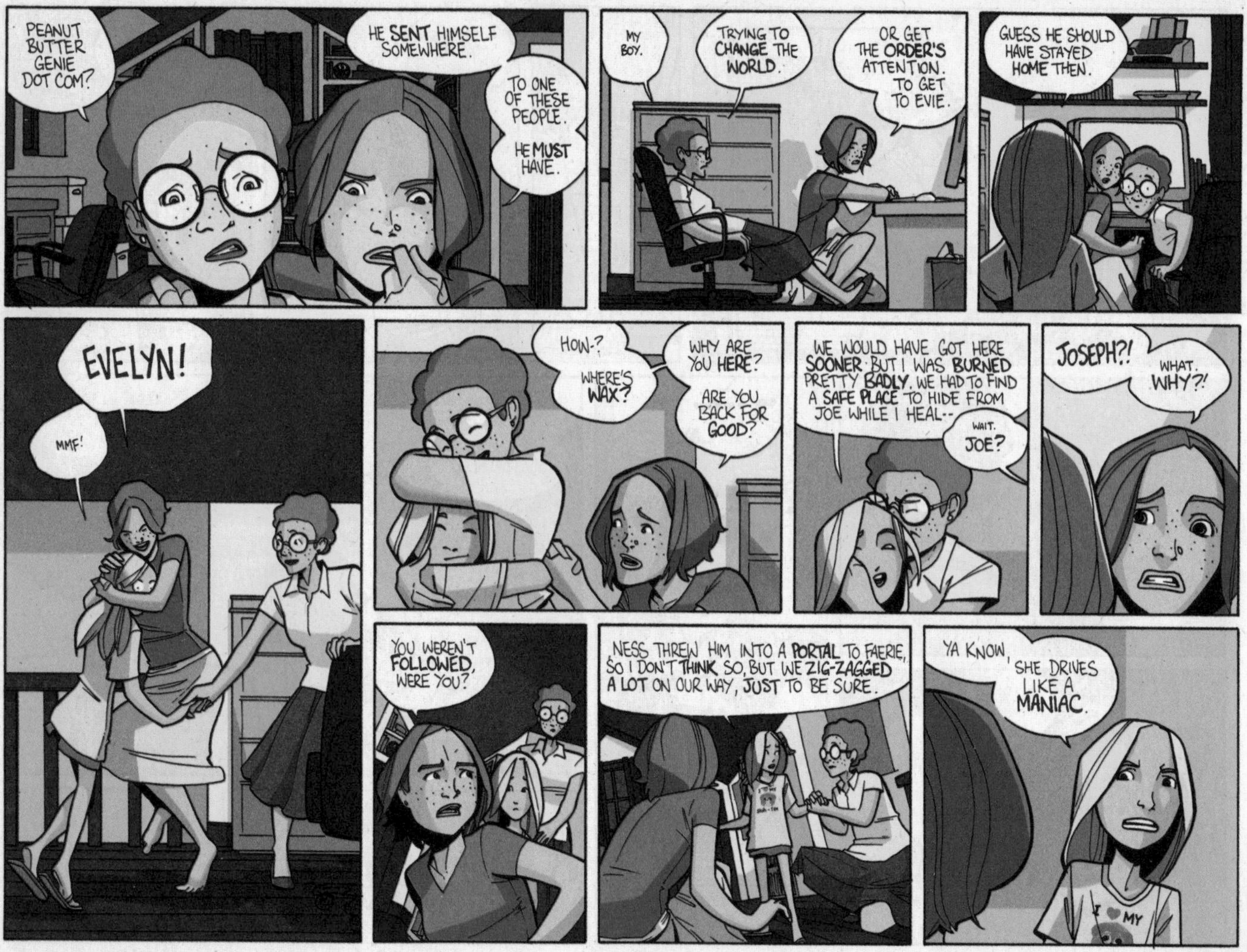
PEANUT BUTTER GENIE DOT COM?
HE SENT HIMSELF SOMEWHERE.
TO ONE OF THESE PEOPLE.
HE MUST HAVE.
MY BOY.
TRYING TO CHANGE THE WORLD.
OR GET THE ORDER'S ATTENTION. TO GET TO EVIE.
GUESS HE SHOULD HAVE STAYED HOME THEN.
EVELYN!
MMF!
HOW-?
WHERE'S WAX?
WHY ARE YOU HERE?
ARE YOU BACK FOR GOOD?
WE WOULD HAVE GOT HERE SOONER BUT I WAS BURNED PRETTY BADLY. WE HAD TO FIND A SAFE PLACE TO HIDE FROM JOE WHILE I HEAL--
WAIT. JOE?
JOSEPH?!
WHAT. WHY?!
YOU WEREN'T FOLLOWED, WERE YOU?
NESS THREW HIM INTO A PORTAL TO FAERIE, SO I DON'T THINK SO, BUT WE ZIG-ZAGGED A LOT ON OUR WAY, JUST TO BE SURE.
YA KNOW, SHE DRIVES LIKE A MANIAC.

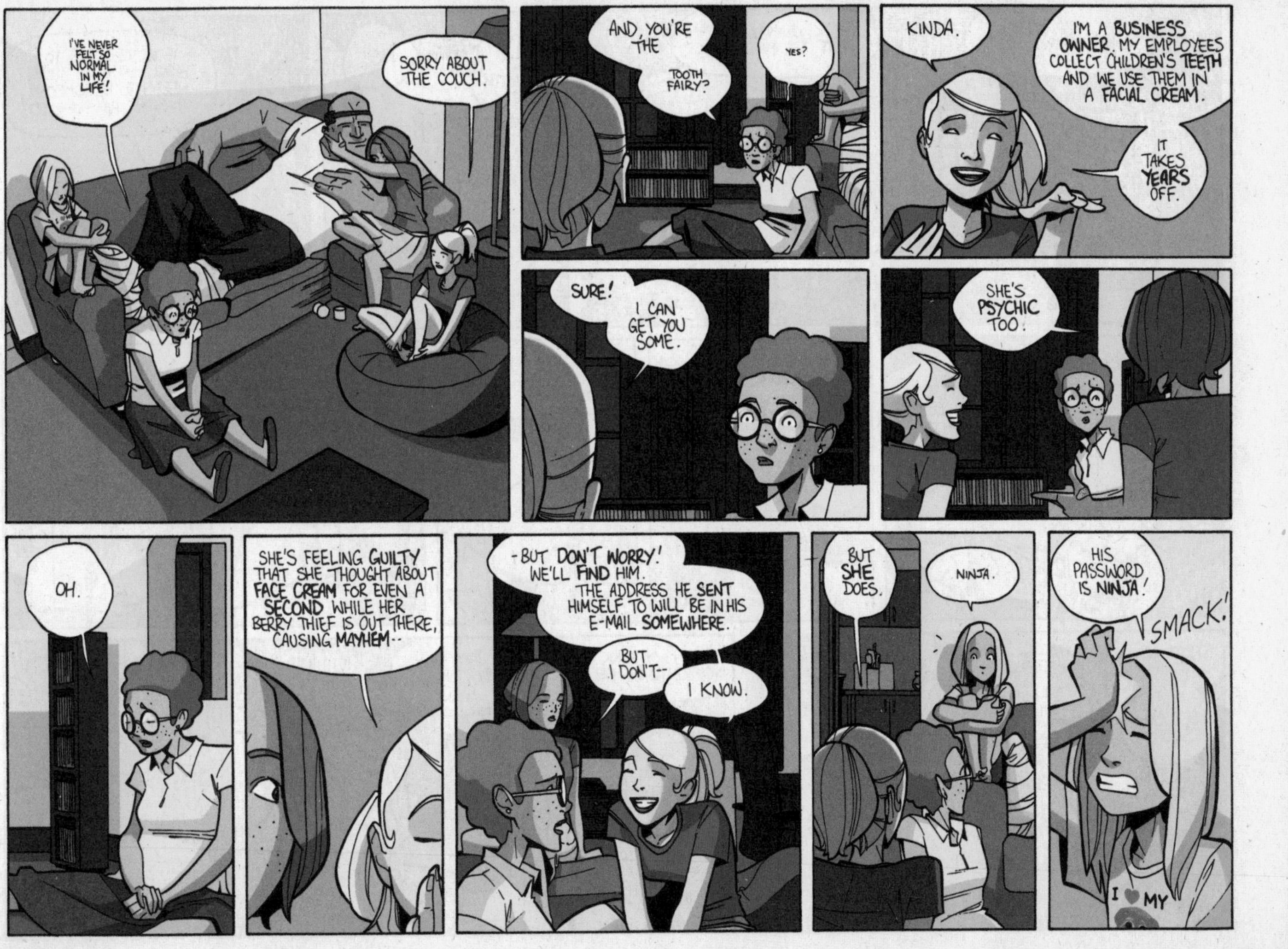
I'VE NEVER FELT SO NORMAL IN MY LIFE!
SORRY ABOUT THE COUCH.
AND, YOU'RE THE
TOOTH FAIRY?
YES?
KINDA.
I'M A BUSINESS OWNER. MY EMPLOYEES COLLECT CHILDREN'S TEETH AND WE USE THEM IN A FACIAL CREAM.
IT TAKES YEARS OFF.
SURE!
I CAN GET YOU SOME.
SHE'S PSYCHIC TOO.
OH.
SHE'S FEELING GUILTY THAT SHE THOUGHT ABOUT FACE CREAM FOR EVEN A SECOND WHILE HER BERRY THIEF IS OUT THERE, CAUSING MAYHEM--
-BUT DON'T WORRY! WE'LL FIND HIM.
THE ADDRESS HE SENT HIMSELF TO WILL BE IN HIS E-MAIL SOMEWHERE.
BUT I DON'T--
I KNOW.
BUT SHE DOES.
NINJA.
HIS PASSWORD IS NINJA!
SMACK!
I MY

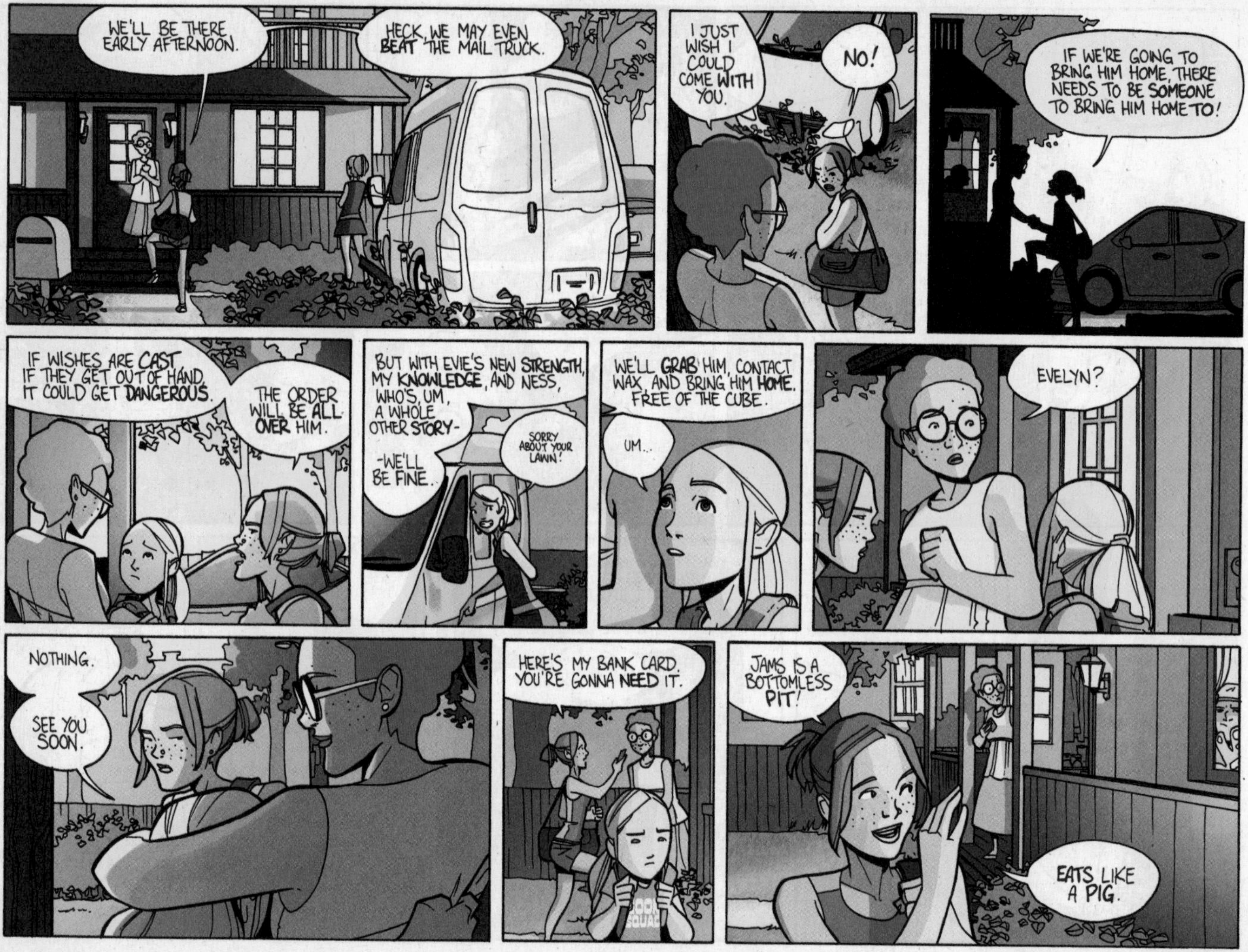
WE'LL BE THERE EARLY AFTERNOON.
HECK, WE MAY EVEN BEAT THE MAIL TRUCK.
I JUST WISH I COULD COME WITH YOU.
NO!
IF WE'RE GOING TO BRING HIM HOME, THERE NEEDS TO BE SOMEONE TO BRING HIM HOME TO!
IF WISHES ARE CAST, IF THEY GET OUT OF HAND, IT COULD GET DANGEROUS.
THE ORDER WILL BE ALL OVER HIM.
BUT WITH EVIE'S NEW STRENGTH, MY KNOWLEDGE, AND NESS, WHO'S, UM, A WHOLE OTHER STORY-
-WE'LL BE FINE.
SORRY ABOUT YOUR LAWN!
WE'LL GRAB HIM, CONTACT WAX, AND BRING HIM HOME. FREE OF THE CUBE.
UM...
EVELYN?
NOTHING.
SEE YOU SOON.
HERE'S MY BANK CARD. YOU'RE GONNA NEED IT.
JAMS IS A BOTTOMLESS PIT!
EATS LIKE A PIG.

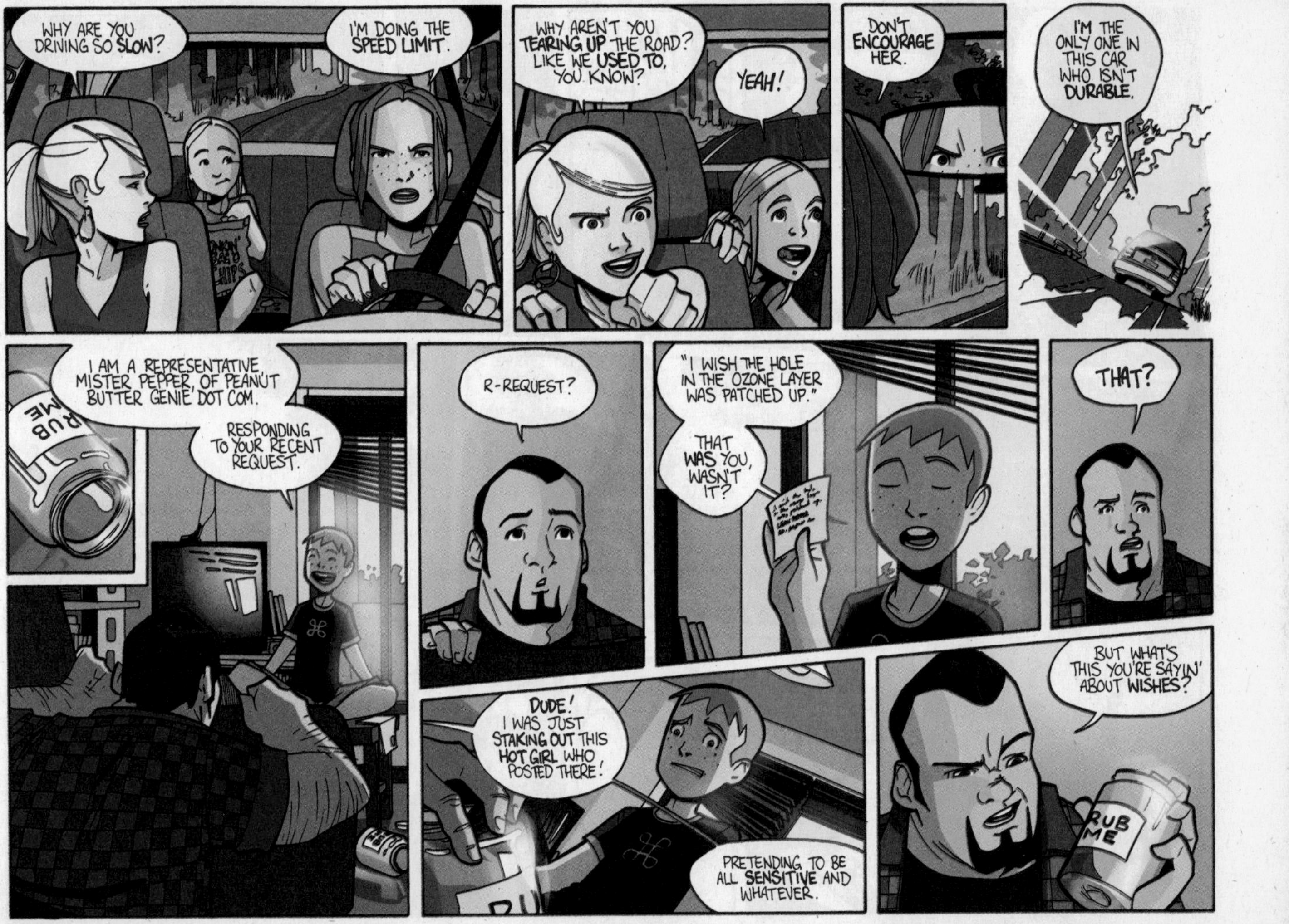
WHY ARE YOU DRIVING SO SLOW?
I'M DOING THE SPEED LIMIT.
WHY AREN'T YOU TEARING UP THE ROAD? LIKE WE USED TO, YOU KNOW?
YEAH!
DON'T ENCOURAGE HER.
I'M THE ONLY ONE IN THIS CAR WHO ISN'T DURABLE.
I AM A REPRESENTATIVE, MISTER PEPPER, OF PEANUT BUTTER GENIE DOT COM.
RESPONDING TO YOUR RECENT REQUEST.
RUB ME
R-REQUEST?
"I WISH THE HOLE IN THE OZONE LAYER WAS PATCHED UP."
THAT WAS YOU, WASN'T IT?
THAT?
DUDE! I WAS JUST STAKING OUT THIS HOT GIRL WHO POSTED THERE!
PRETENDING TO BE ALL SENSITIVE AND WHATEVER.
BUT WHAT'S THIS YOU'RE SAYIN' ABOUT WISHES?
RUB ME

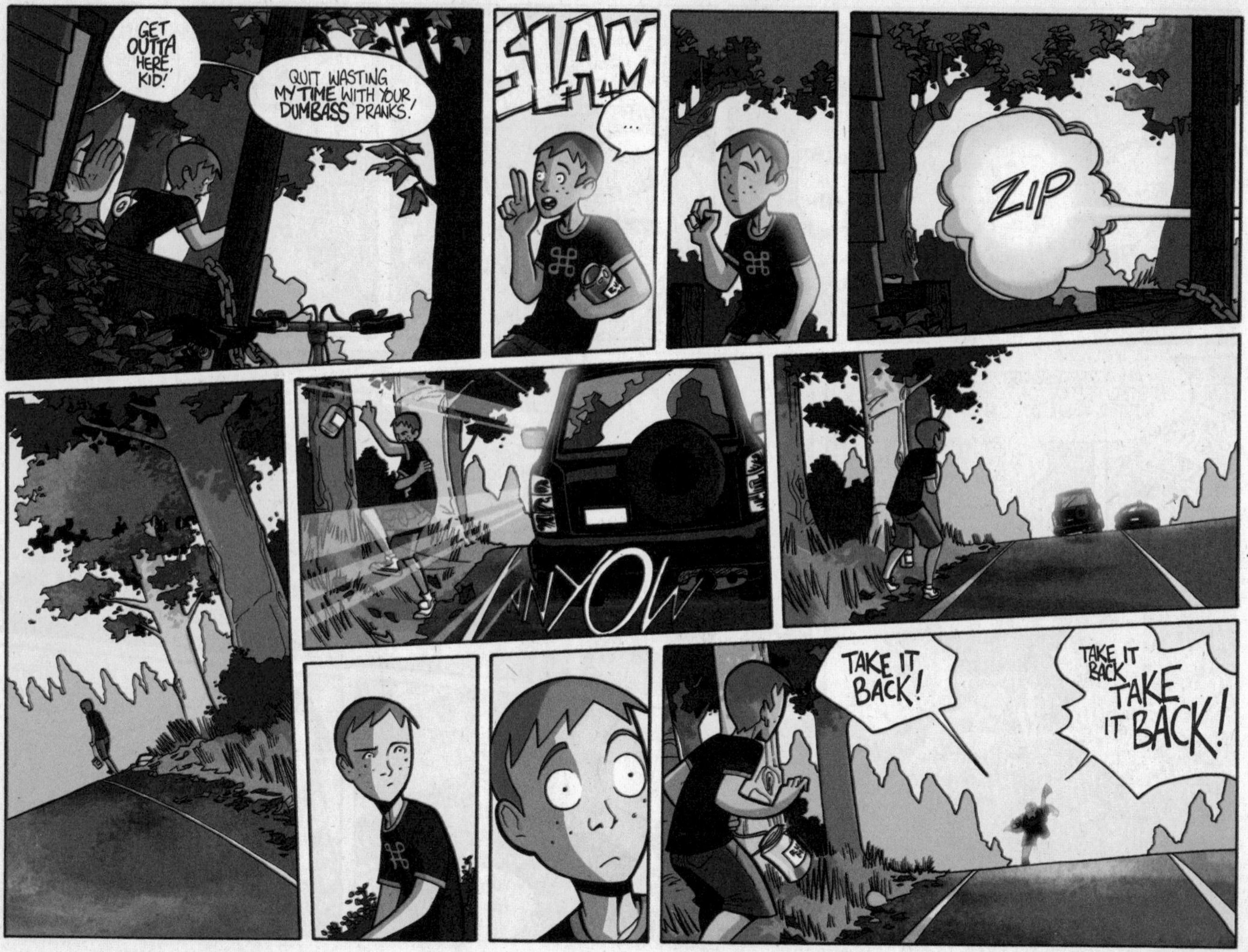
GET OUTTA HERE, KID!
QUIT WASTING MY TIME WITH YOUR DUMBASS PRANKS!
SLAM
...
ZIP
NNYOW
TAKE IT BACK!
TAKE IT BACK TAKE IT BACK!

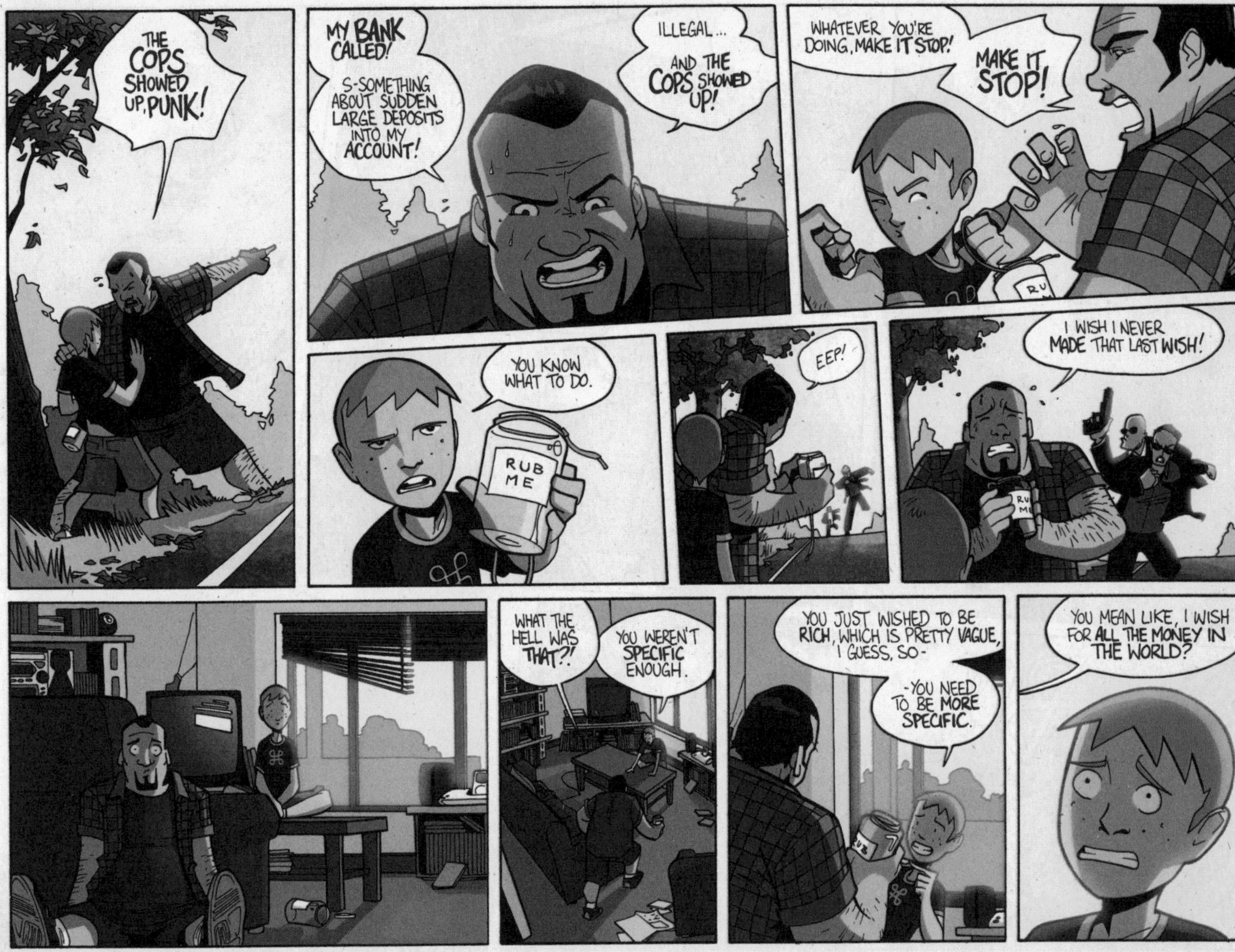
THE COPS SHOWED UP, PUNK!
MY BANK CALLED!
S-SOMETHING ABOUT SUDDEN LARGE DEPOSITS INTO MY ACCOUNT!
ILLEGAL...
AND THE COPS SHOWED UP!
WHATEVER YOU'RE DOING, MAKE IT STOP!
MAKE IT STOP!
YOU KNOW WHAT TO DO.
RUB ME
EEP!
I WISH I NEVER MADE THAT LAST WISH!
WHAT THE HELL WAS THAT?!
YOU WEREN'T SPECIFIC ENOUGH.
YOU JUST WISHED TO BE RICH, WHICH IS PRETTY VAGUE, I GUESS, SO-
-YOU NEED TO BE MORE SPECIFIC.
YOU MEAN LIKE, I WISH FOR ALL THE MONEY IN THE WORLD?

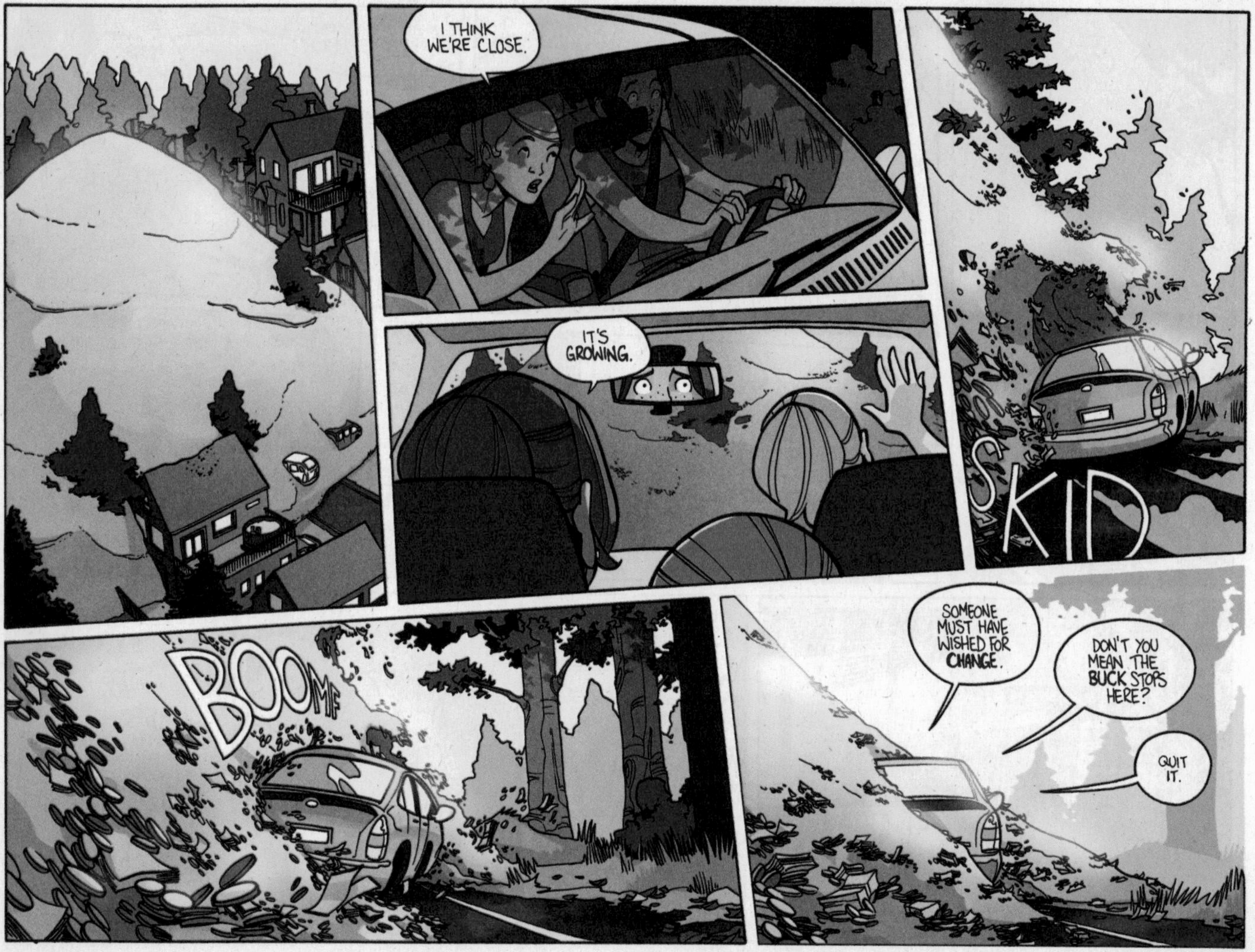
I THINK WE'RE CLOSE.
IT'S GROWING.
SKID
BOOMF
SOMEONE MUST HAVE WISHED FOR CHANGE.
DON'T YOU MEAN THE BUCK STOPS HERE?
QUIT IT.

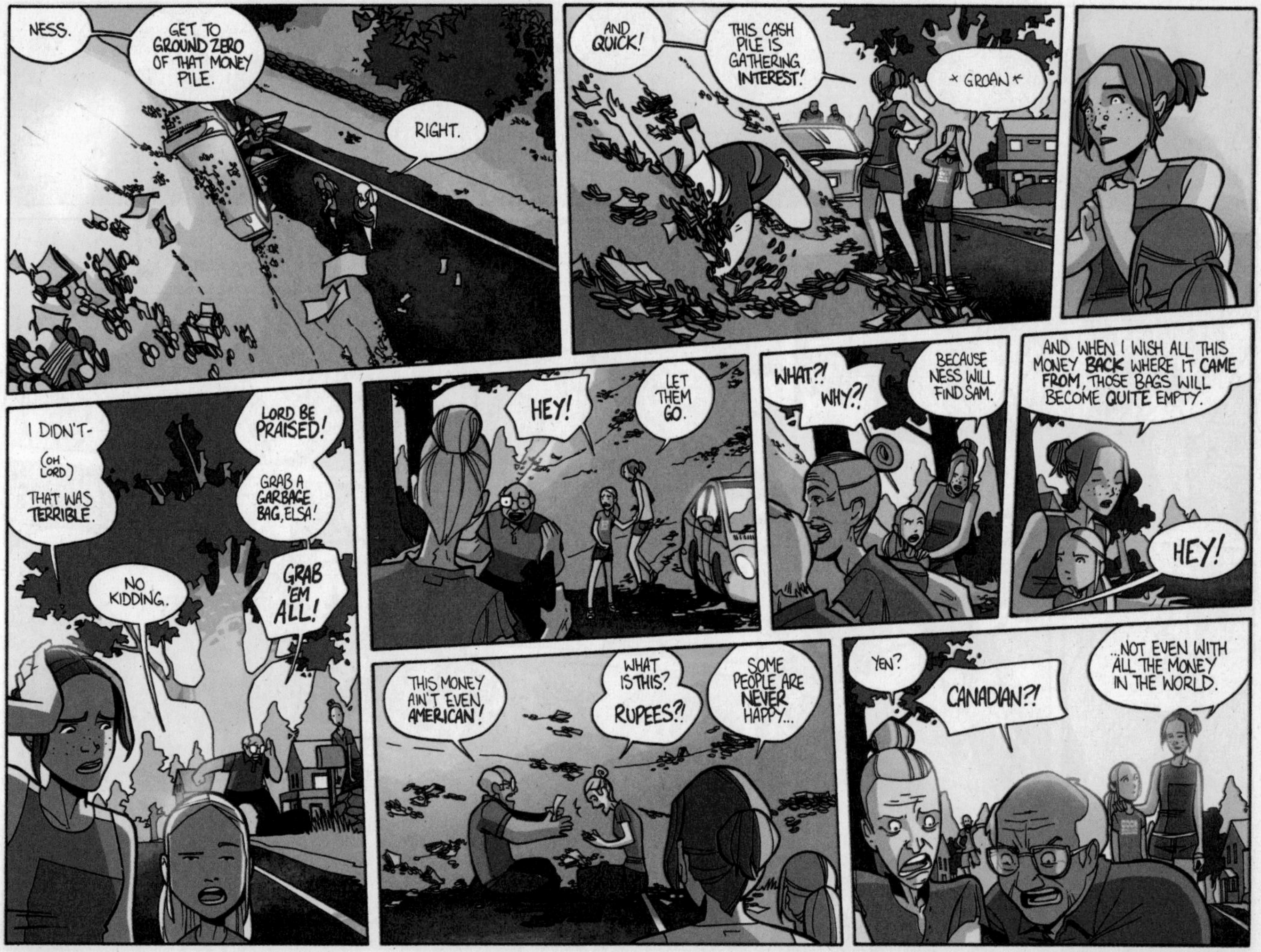
NESS.
GET TO GROUND ZERO OF THAT MONEY PILE.
RIGHT.
AND QUICK!
THIS CASH PILE IS GATHERING INTEREST!
GROAN
I DIDN'T-
(OH LORD)
THAT WAS TERRIBLE.
LORD BE PRAISED!
GRAB A GARBAGE BAG, ELSA!
NO KIDDING.
GRAB 'EM ALL!
HEY!
LET THEM GO.
WHAT?!
WHY?!
BECAUSE NESS WILL FIND SAM.
AND WHEN I WISH ALL THIS MONEY BACK WHERE IT CAME FROM, THOSE BAGS WILL BECOME QUITE EMPTY.
HEY!
THIS MONEY AIN'T EVEN AMERICAN!
WHAT IS THIS?
RUPEES?!
SOME PEOPLE ARE NEVER HAPPY...
YEN?
CANADIAN?!
...NOT EVEN WITH ALL THE MONEY IN THE WORLD.

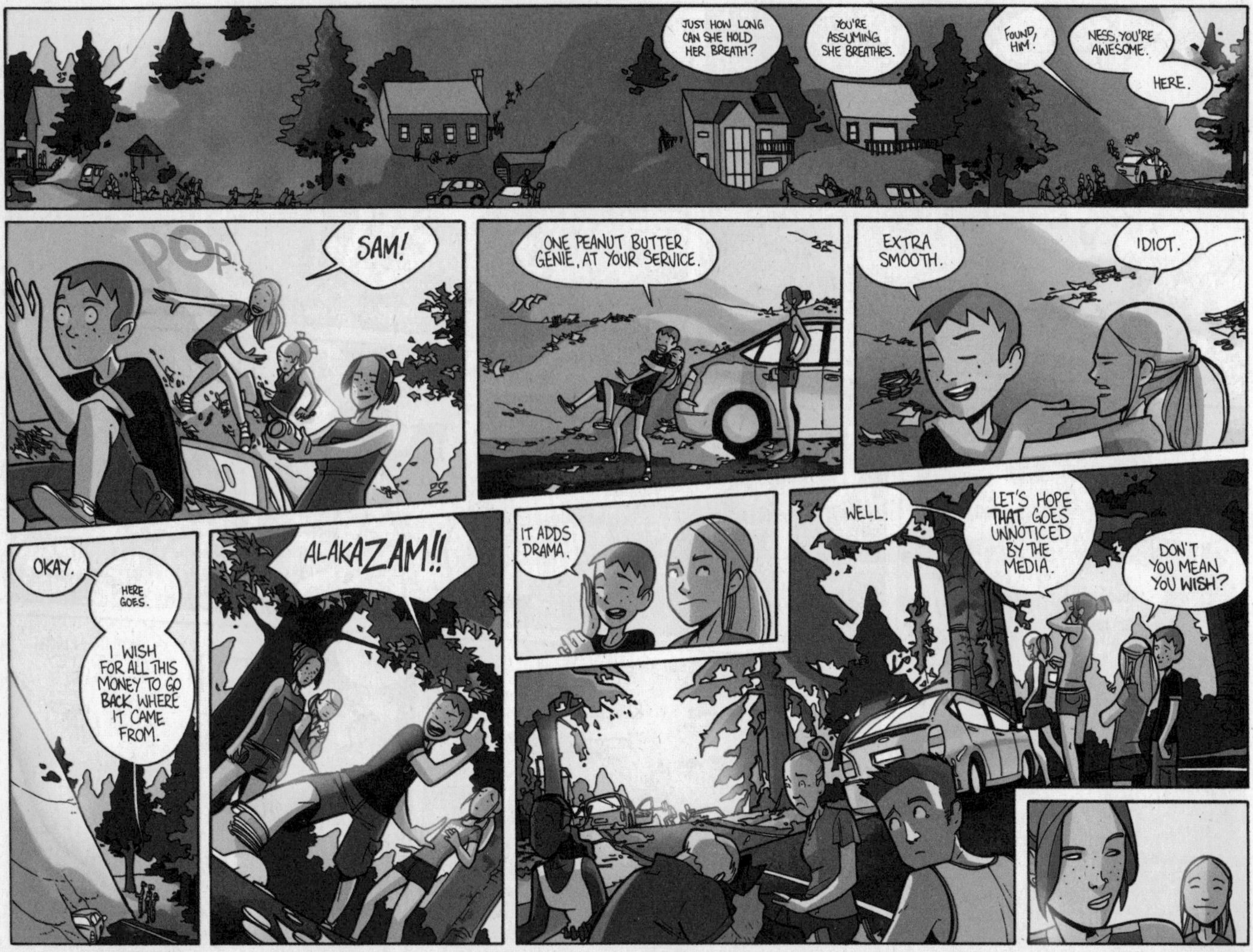
JUST HOW LONG CAN SHE HOLD HER BREATH?
YOU'RE ASSUMING SHE BREATHES.
FOUND HIM!
NESS, YOU'RE AWESOME.
HERE.
POP
SAM!
ONE PEANUT BUTTER GENIE, AT YOUR SERVICE.
EXTRA SMOOTH.
IDIOT.
OKAY.
HERE GOES.
I WISH FOR ALL THIS MONEY TO GO BACK WHERE IT CAME FROM.
ALAKAZAM!!
IT ADDS DRAMA.
WELL.
LET'S HOPE THAT GOES UNNOTICED BY THE MEDIA.
DON'T YOU MEAN YOU WISH?

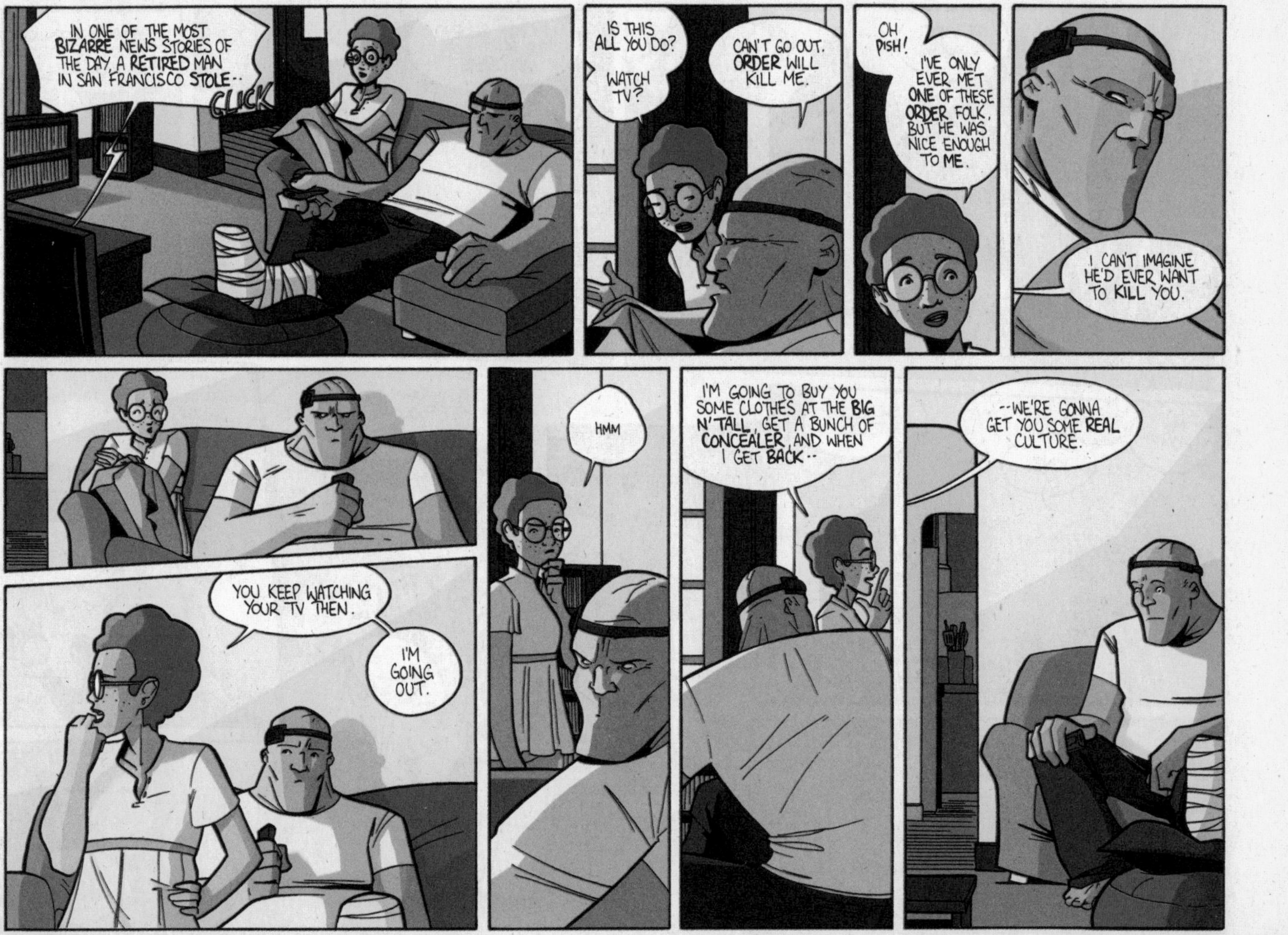
IN ONE OF THE MOST BIZARRE NEWS STORIES OF THE DAY, A RETIRED MAN IN SAN FRANCISCO STOLE--
CLICK
IS THIS ALL YOU DO?
WATCH TV?
CAN'T GO OUT. ORDER WILL KILL ME.
OH PISH!
I'VE ONLY EVER MET ONE OF THESE ORDER FOLK, BUT HE WAS NICE ENOUGH TO ME.
I CAN'T IMAGINE HE'D EVER WANT TO KILL YOU.
YOU KEEP WATCHING YOUR TV THEN.
I'M GOING OUT.
HMM
I'M GOING TO BUY YOU SOME CLOTHES AT THE BIG N'TALL, GET A BUNCH OF CONCEALER, AND WHEN I GET BACK--
--WE'RE GONNA GET YOU SOME REAL CULTURE.

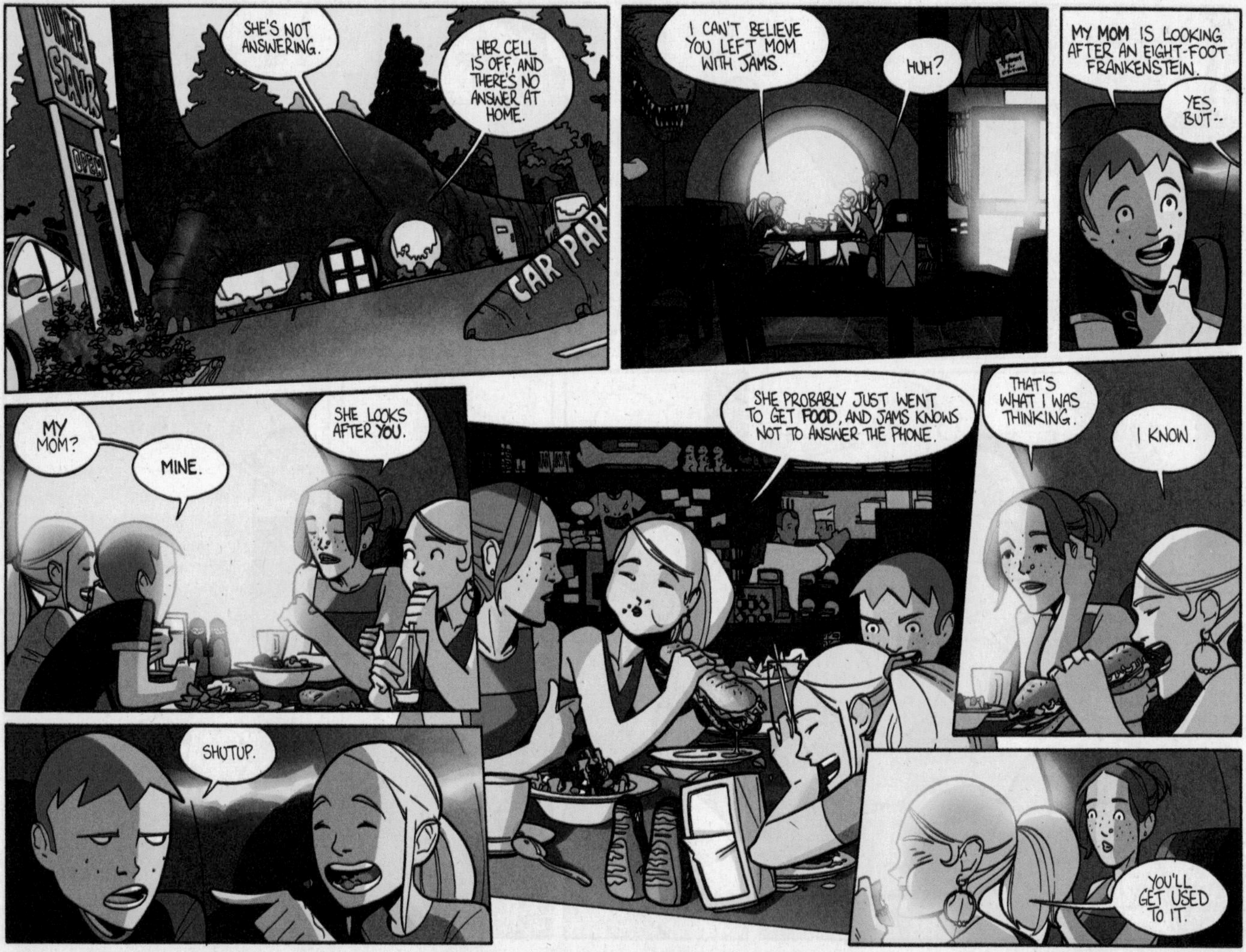

DINER SAUR
OPEN
SHE'S NOT ANSWERING.
HER CELL IS OFF, AND THERE'S NO ANSWER AT HOME.
CAR PARK
I CAN'T BELIEVE YOU LEFT MOM WITH JAMS.
HUH?
MY MOM IS LOOKING AFTER AN EIGHT-FOOT FRANKENSTEIN.
YES, BUT--
MY MOM?
MINE.
SHE LOOKS AFTER YOU.
SHE PROBABLY JUST WENT TO GET FOOD, AND JAMS KNOWS NOT TO ANSWER THE PHONE.
THAT'S WHAT I WAS THINKING.
I KNOW.
SHUTUP.
YOU'LL GET USED TO IT.

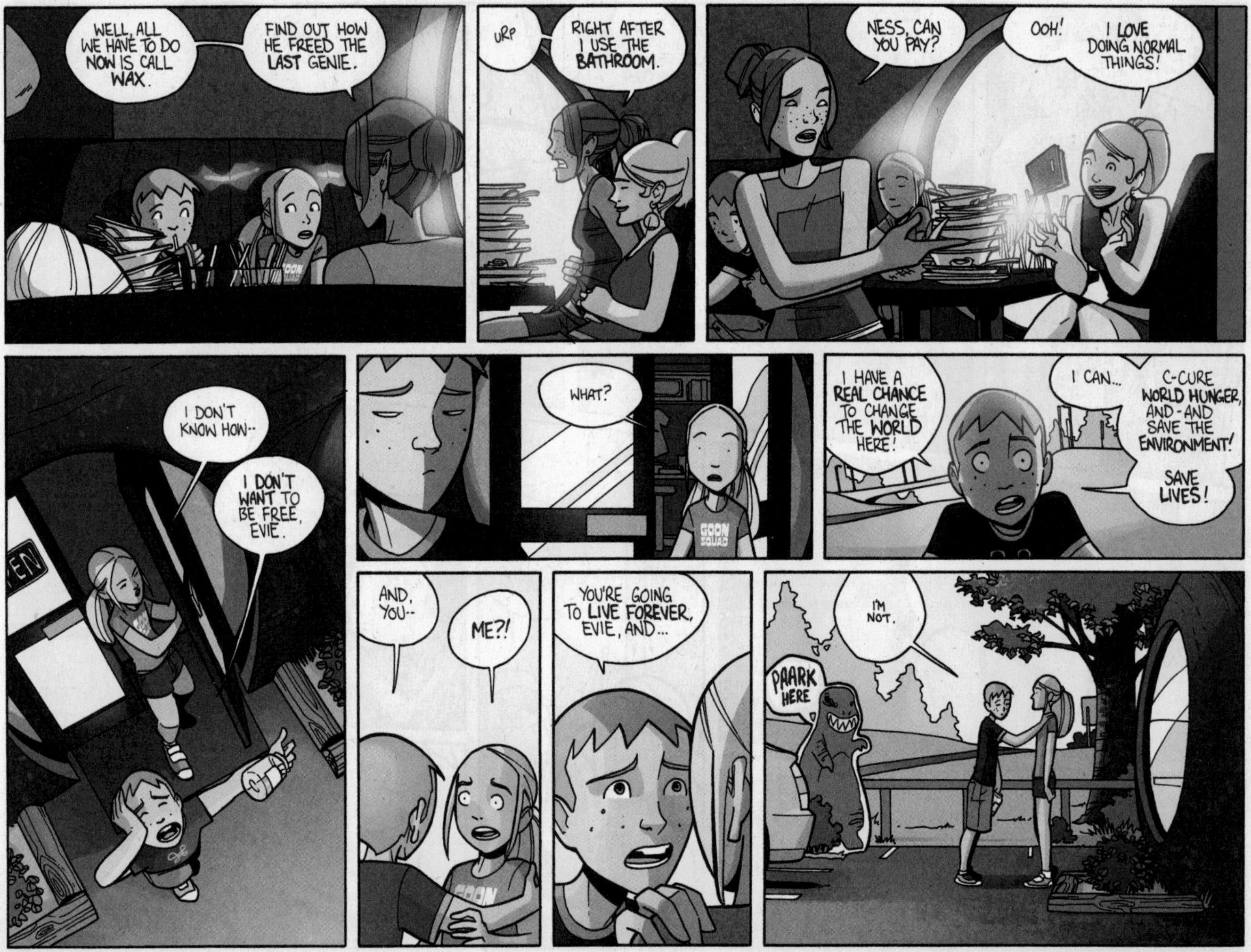
WELL, ALL WE HAVE TO DO NOW IS CALL WAX.
FIND OUT HOW HE FREED THE LAST GENIE.
URP
RIGHT AFTER I USE THE BATHROOM.
NESS, CAN YOU PAY?
OOH!
I LOVE DOING NORMAL THINGS!
I DON'T KNOW HOW--
I DON'T WANT TO BE FREE, EVIE.
WHAT?
I HAVE A REAL CHANCE TO CHANGE THE WORLD HERE!
I CAN...
C-CURE WORLD HUNGER, AND-AND SAVE THE ENVIRONMENT!
SAVE LIVES!
AND, YOU--
ME?!
YOU'RE GOING TO LIVE FOREVER, EVIE, AND...
I'M NOT.
PAARK HERE

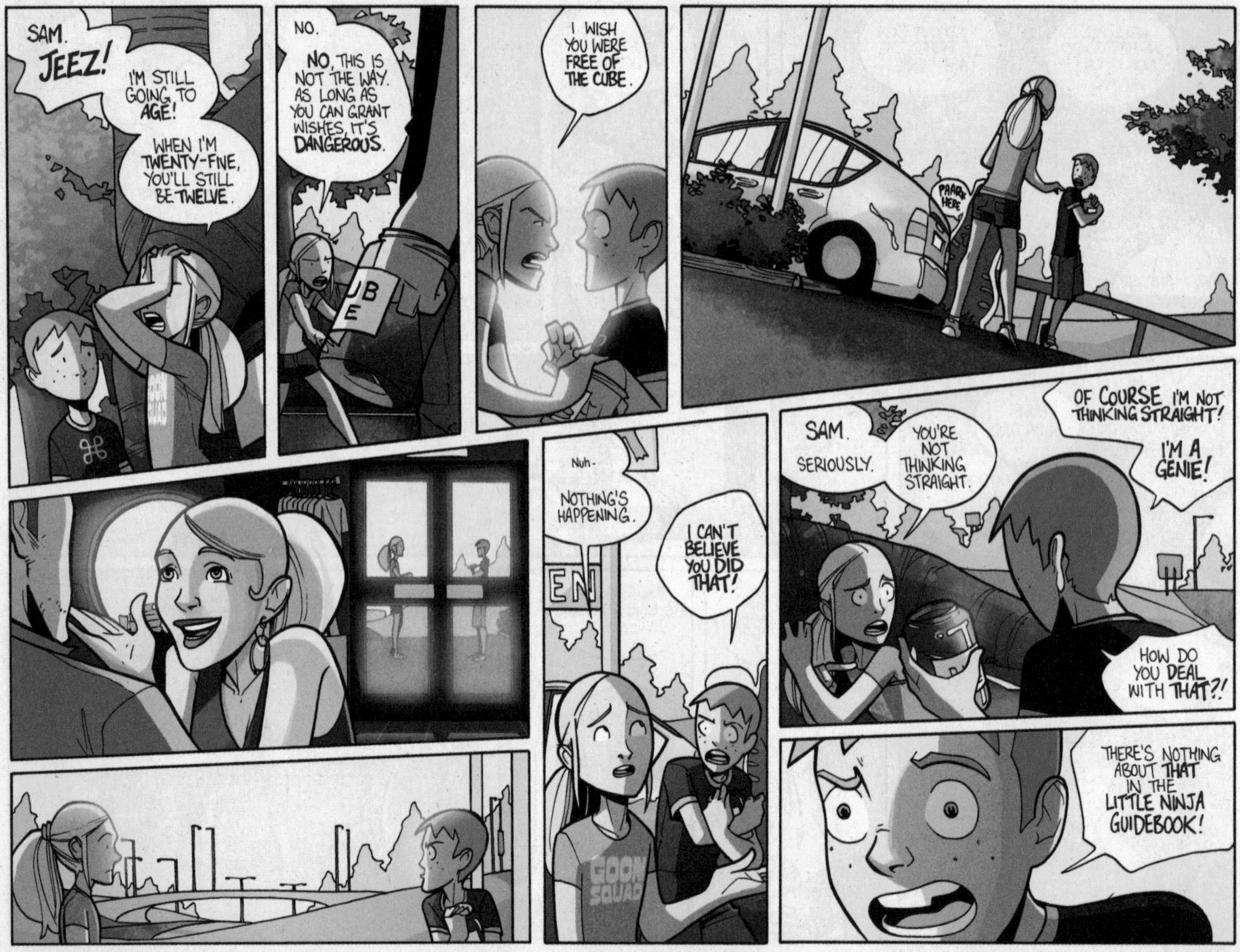
SAM.
JEEZ!
I'M STILL GOING TO AGE!
WHEN I'M TWENTY-FIVE, YOU'LL STILL BE TWELVE.
NO.
NO, THIS IS NOT THE WAY. AS LONG AS YOU CAN GRANT WISHES, IT'S DANGEROUS.
I WISH YOU WERE FREE OF THE CUBE.
Nuh-
NOTHING'S HAPPENING.
I CAN'T BELIEVE YOU DID THAT!
SAM.
SERIOUSLY.
YOU'RE NOT THINKING STRAIGHT.
OF COURSE I'M NOT THINKING STRAIGHT!
I'M A GENIE!
HOW DO YOU DEAL WITH THAT?!
THERE'S NOTHING ABOUT THAT IN THE LITTLE NINJA GUIDEBOOK!

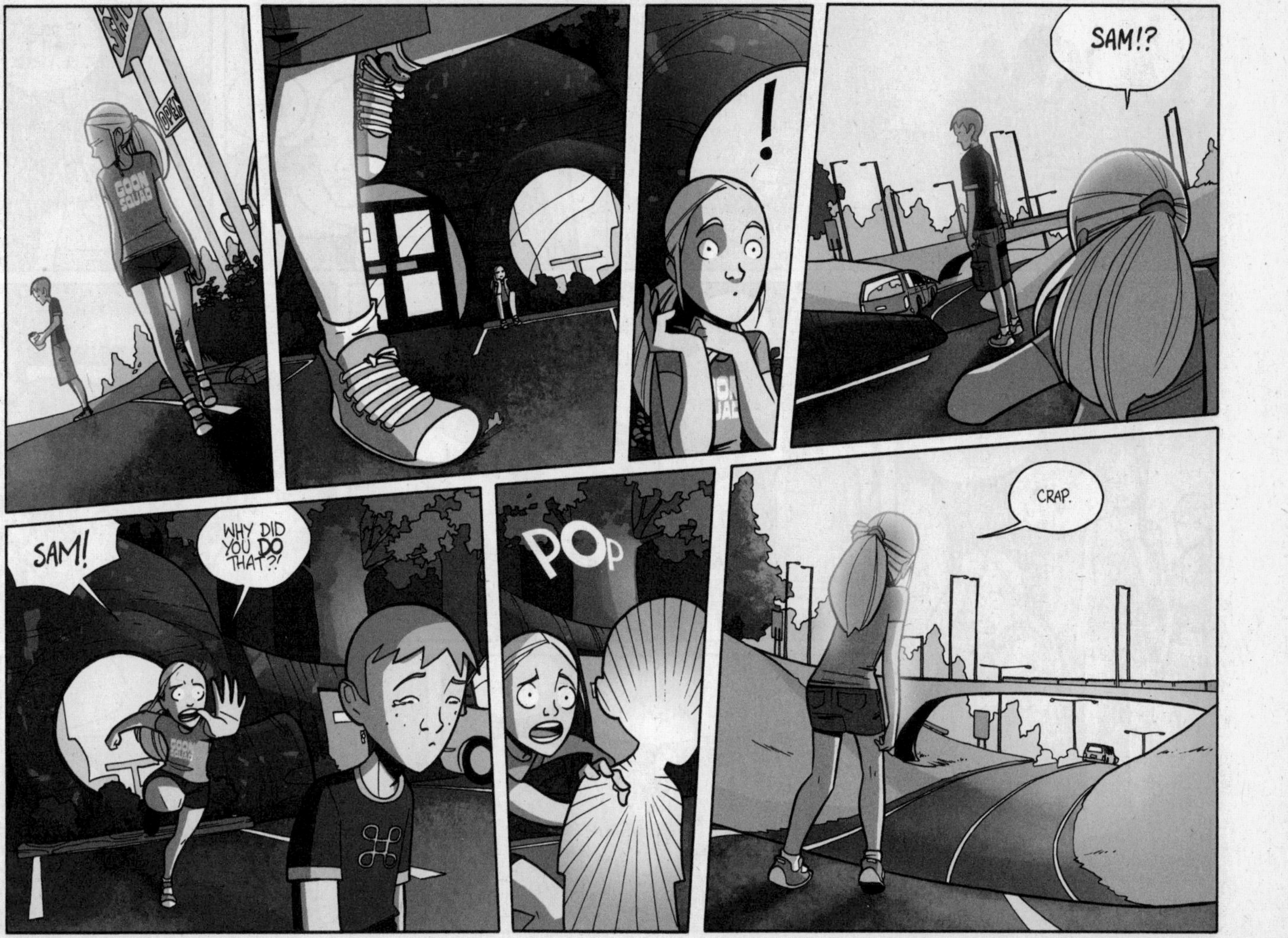

GOON SQUAD
OPEN
!
SAM!?
SAM!
WHY DID YOU DO THAT?!
POP
CRAP.

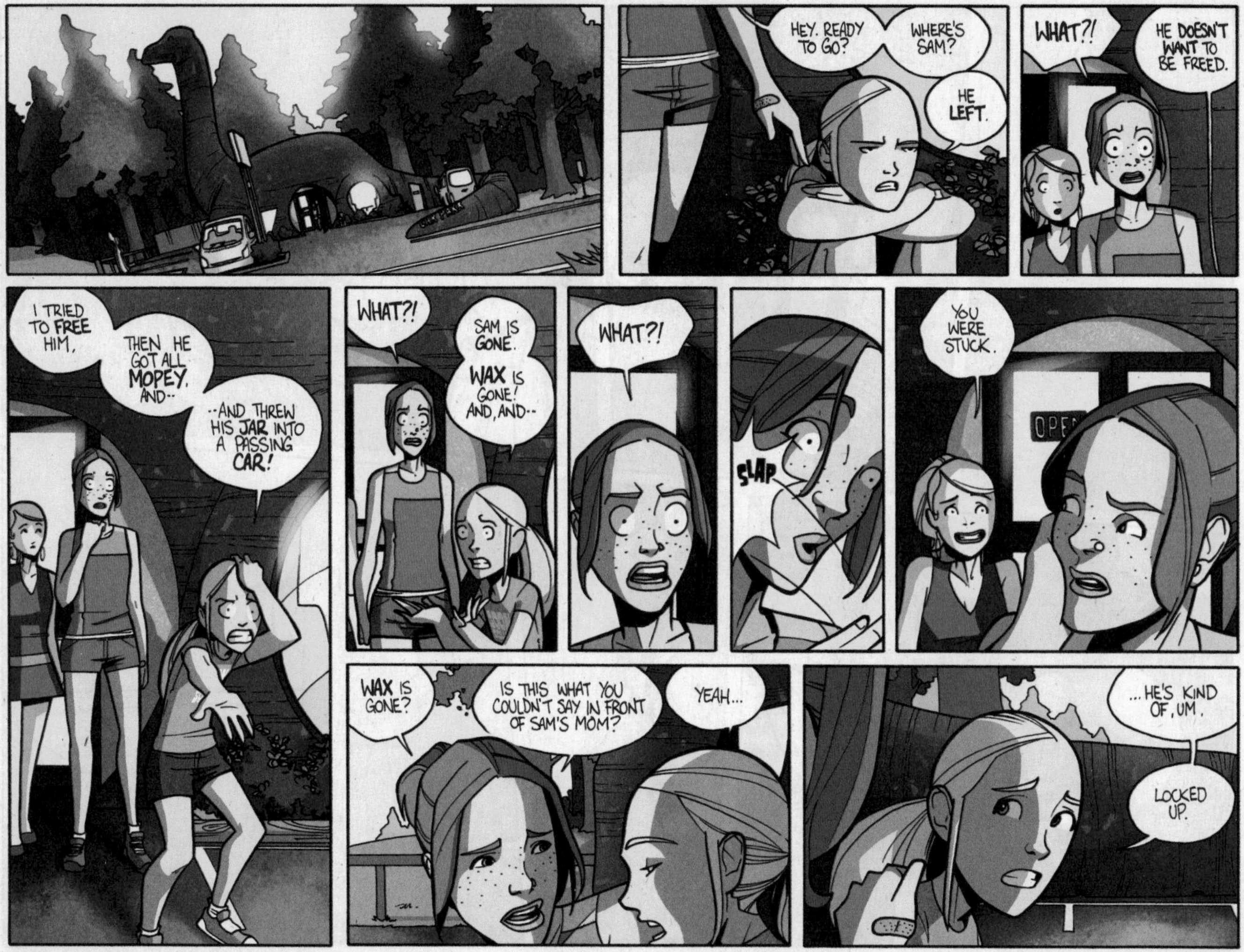
HEY. READY TO GO?
WHERE'S SAM?
HE LEFT.
WHAT?!
HE DOESN'T WANT TO BE FREED.
I TRIED TO FREE HIM.
THEN HE GOT ALL MOPEY. AND--
--AND THREW HIS JAR INTO A PASSING CAR!
WHAT?!
SAM IS GONE.
WAX IS GONE! AND, AND--
WHAT?!
SLAP
YOU WERE STUCK.
OPEN
WAX IS GONE?
IS THIS WHAT YOU COULDN'T SAY IN FRONT OF SAM'S MOM?
YEAH...
...HE'S KIND OF, UM.
LOCKED UP.

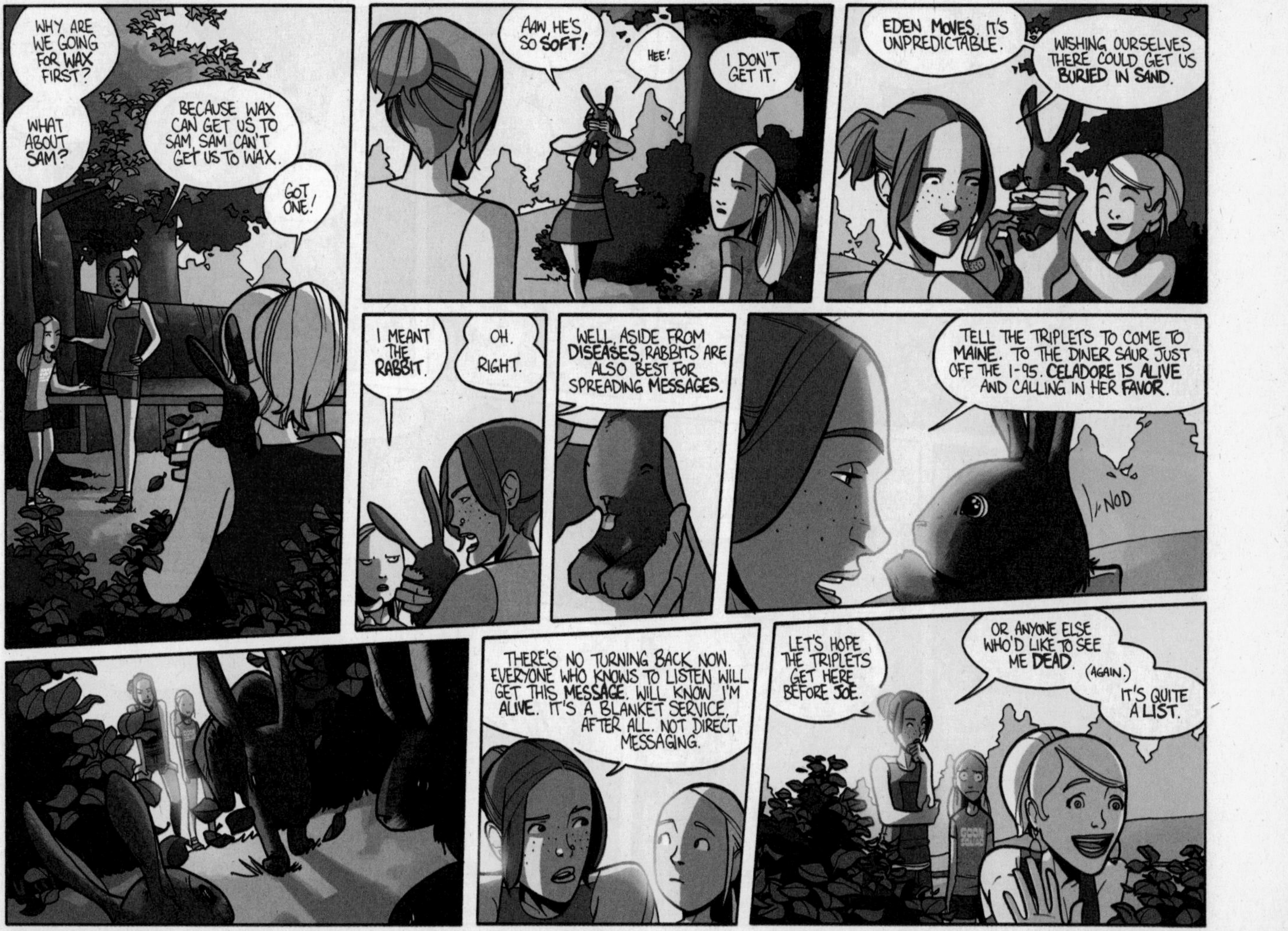
WHY ARE WE GOING FOR WAX FIRST?
WHAT ABOUT SAM?
BECAUSE WAX CAN GET US TO SAM, SAM CAN'T GET US TO WAX.
GOT ONE!
AAW, HE'S SO SOFT!
HEE!
I DON'T GET IT.
EDEN MOVES. IT'S UNPREDICTABLE.
WISHING OURSELVES THERE COULD GET US BURIED IN SAND.
I MEANT THE RABBIT.
OH.
RIGHT.
WELL, ASIDE FROM DISEASES, RABBITS ARE ALSO BEST FOR SPREADING MESSAGES.
TELL THE TRIPLETS TO COME TO MAINE. TO THE DINER SAUR JUST OFF THE I-95. CELADORE IS ALIVE AND CALLING IN HER FAVOR.
NOD
THERE'S NO TURNING BACK NOW. EVERYONE WHO KNOWS TO LISTEN WILL GET THIS MESSAGE. WILL KNOW I'M ALIVE. IT'S A BLANKET SERVICE, AFTER ALL. NOT DIRECT MESSAGING.
LET'S HOPE THE TRIPLETS GET HERE BEFORE JOE.
OR ANYONE ELSE WHO'D LIKE TO SEE ME DEAD.
(AGAIN.)
IT'S QUITE A LIST.

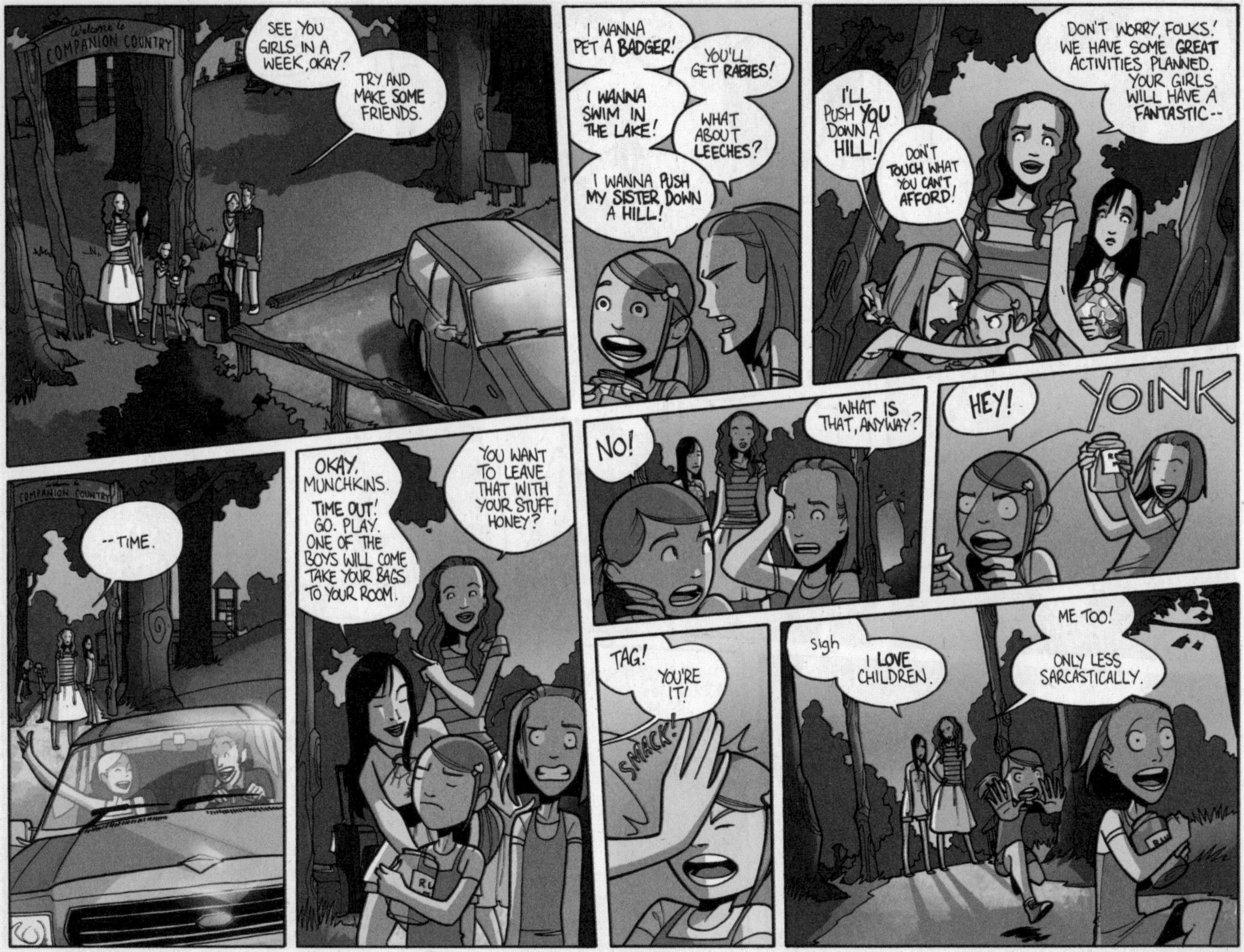
Welcome to COMPANION COUNTRY
SEE YOU GIRLS IN A WEEK, OKAY?
TRY AND MAKE SOME FRIENDS.
I WANNA PET A BADGER!
YOU'LL GET RABIES!
I WANNA SWIM IN THE LAKE!
WHAT ABOUT LEECHES?
I WANNA PUSH MY SISTER DOWN A HILL!
I'LL PUSH YOU DOWN A HILL!
DON'T TOUCH WHAT YOU CAN'T AFFORD!
DON'T WORRY, FOLKS! WE HAVE SOME GREAT ACTIVITIES PLANNED. YOUR GIRLS WILL HAVE A FANTASTIC--
COMPANION COUNTRY
--TIME.
OKAY, MUNCHKINS. TIME OUT! GO. PLAY. ONE OF THE BOYS WILL COME TAKE YOUR BAGS TO YOUR ROOM.
YOU WANT TO LEAVE THAT WITH YOUR STUFF, HONEY?
NO!
WHAT IS THAT, ANYWAY?
HEY!
YOINK
TAG! YOU'RE IT!
SMACK!
sigh
I LOVE CHILDREN.
ME TOO!
ONLY LESS SARCASTICALLY.

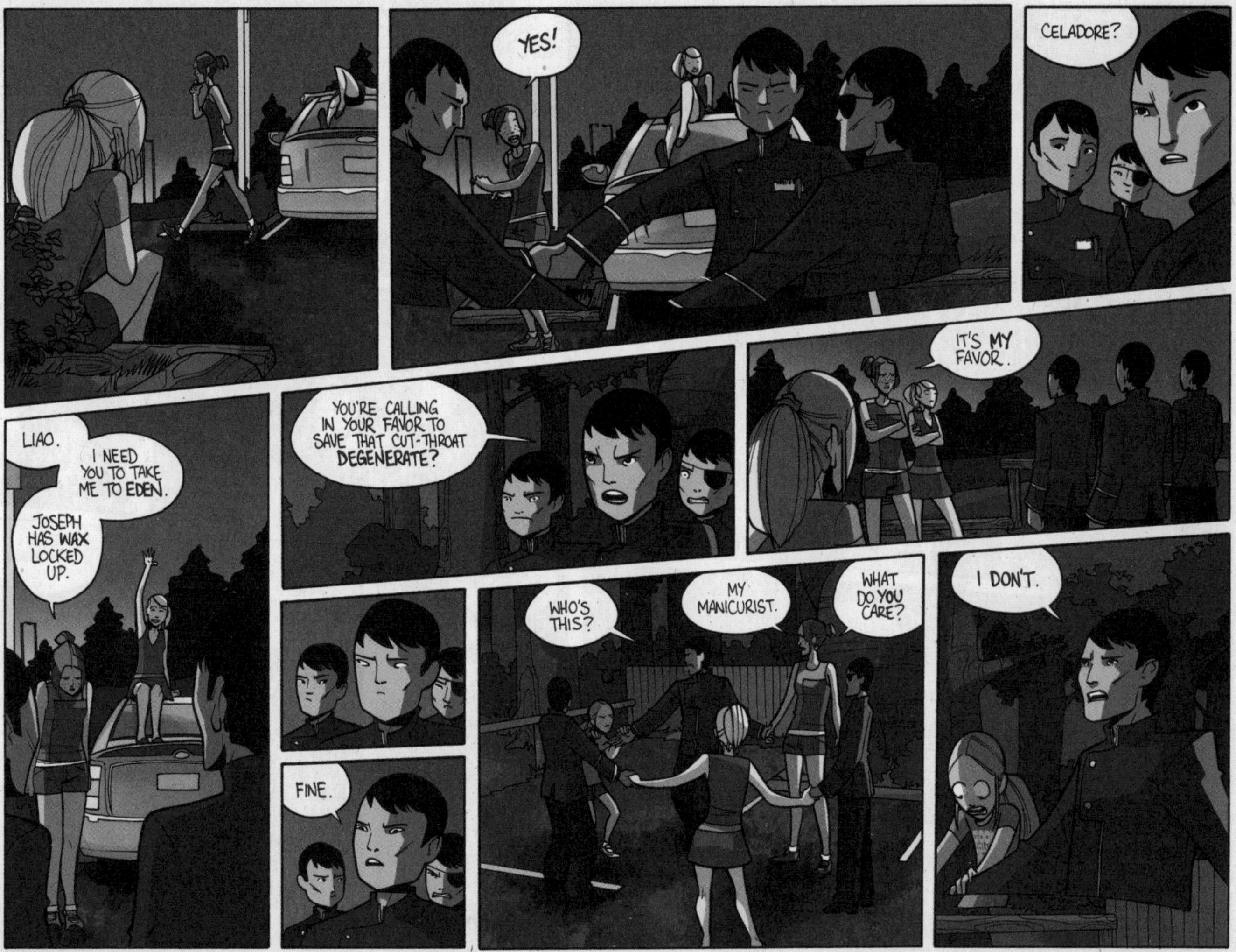
YES!
CELADORE?
LIAO.
I NEED YOU TO TAKE ME TO EDEN.
JOSEPH HAS WAX LOCKED UP.
YOU'RE CALLING IN YOUR FAVOR TO SAVE THAT CUT-THROAT DEGENERATE?
IT'S MY FAVOR.
FINE.
WHO'S THIS?
MY MANICURIST.
WHAT DO YOU CARE?
I DON'T.

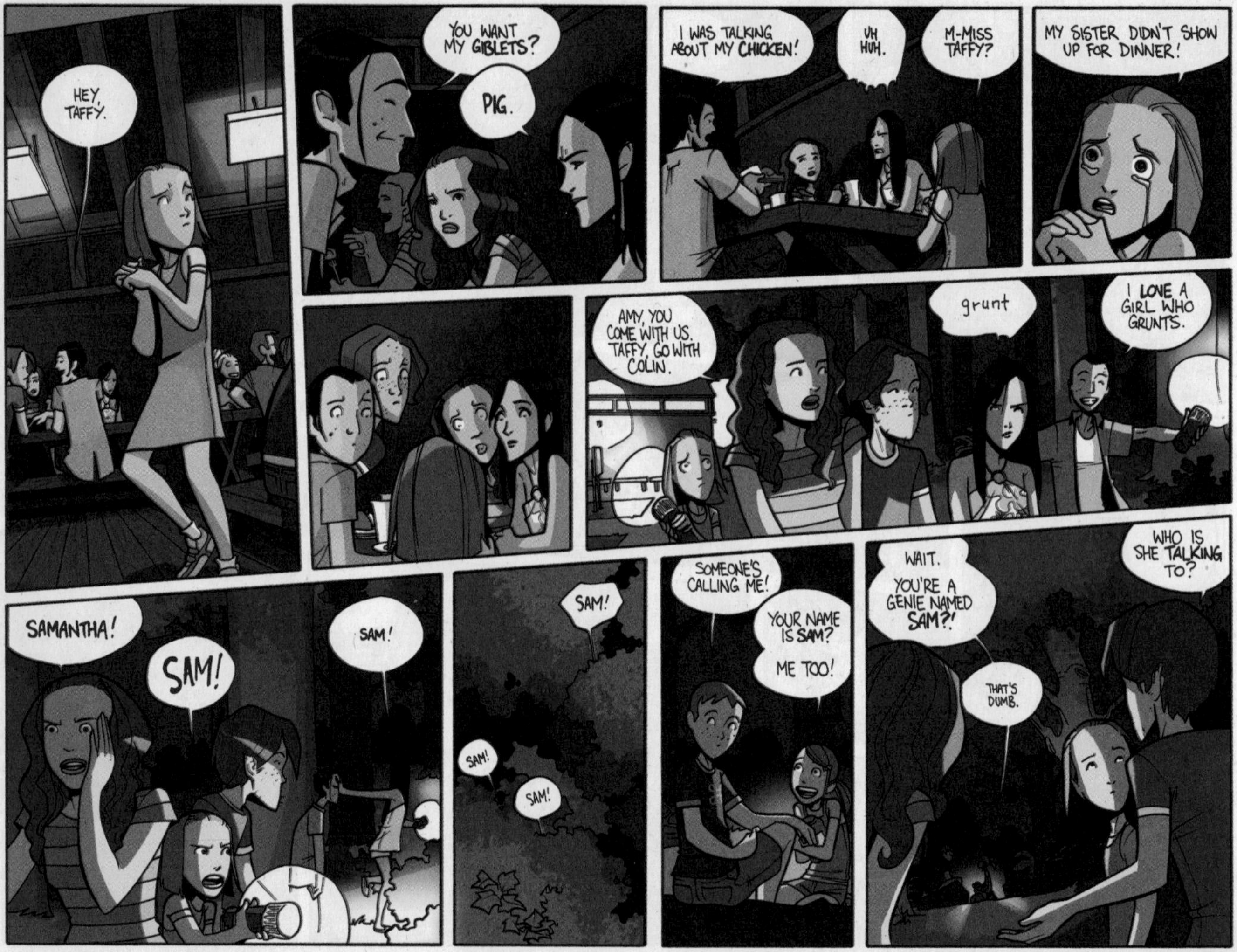
HEY, TAFFY.
YOU WANT MY GIBLETS?
PIG.
I WAS TALKING ABOUT MY CHICKEN!
UH HUH.
M-MISS TAFFY?
MY SISTER DIDN'T SHOW UP FOR DINNER!
AMY, YOU COME WITH US. TAFFY, GO WITH COLIN.
grunt
I LOVE A GIRL WHO GRUNTS.
SAMANTHA!
SAM!
SAM!
SAM!
SAM!
SAM!
SOMEONE'S CALLING ME!
YOUR NAME IS SAM?
ME TOO!
WAIT.
YOU'RE A GENIE NAMED SAM?!
THAT'S DUMB.
WHO IS SHE TALKING TO?

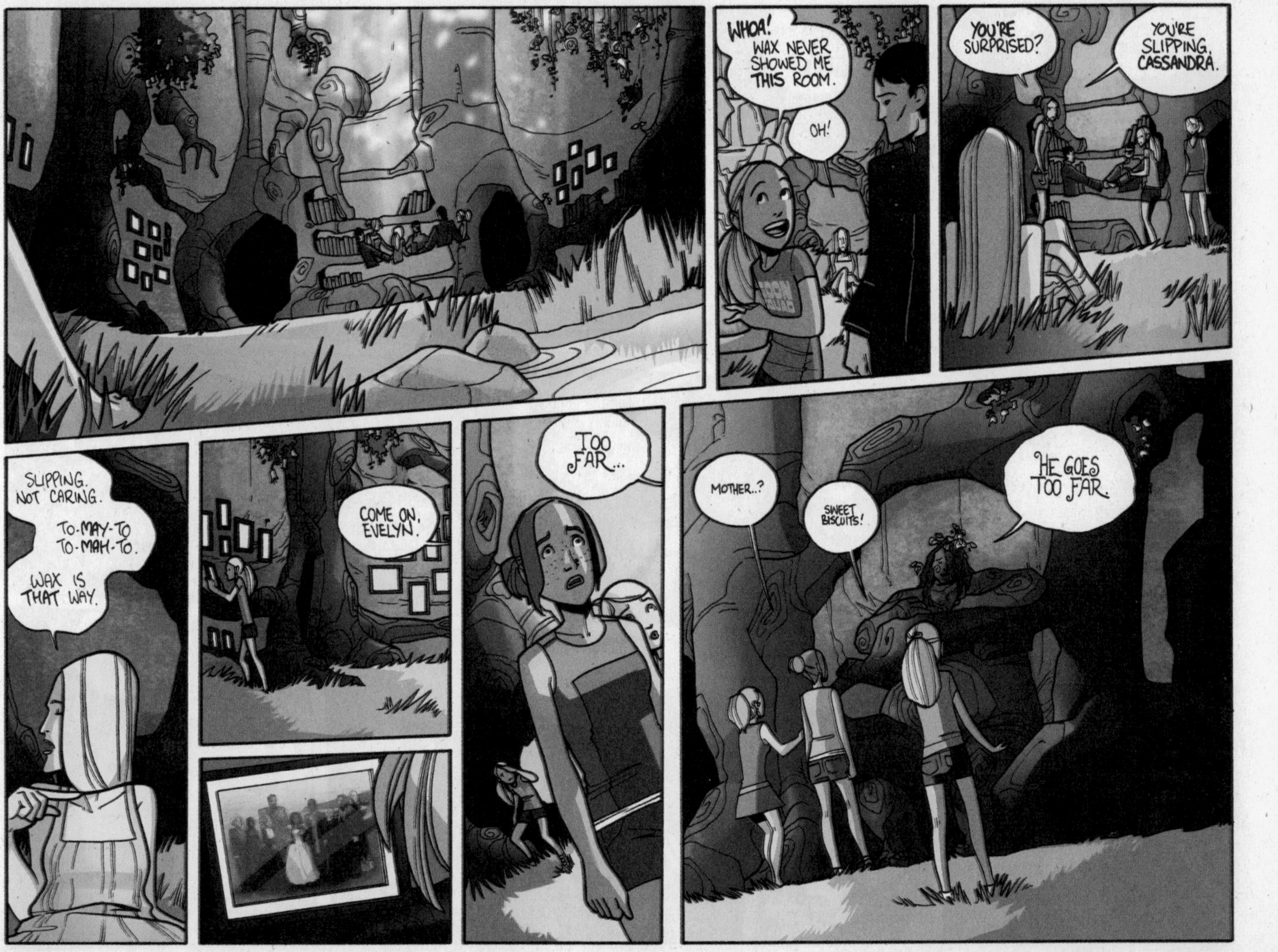
WHOA!
WAX NEVER SHOWED ME THIS ROOM.
OH!
YOU'RE SURPRISED?
YOU'RE SLIPPING, CASSANDRA.
SLIPPING. NOT CARING.
TO-MAY-TO TO-MAH-TO.
WAX IS THAT WAY.
COME ON, EVELYN.
TOO FAR...
MOTHER..?
SWEET BISCUITS!
HE GOES TOO FAR.

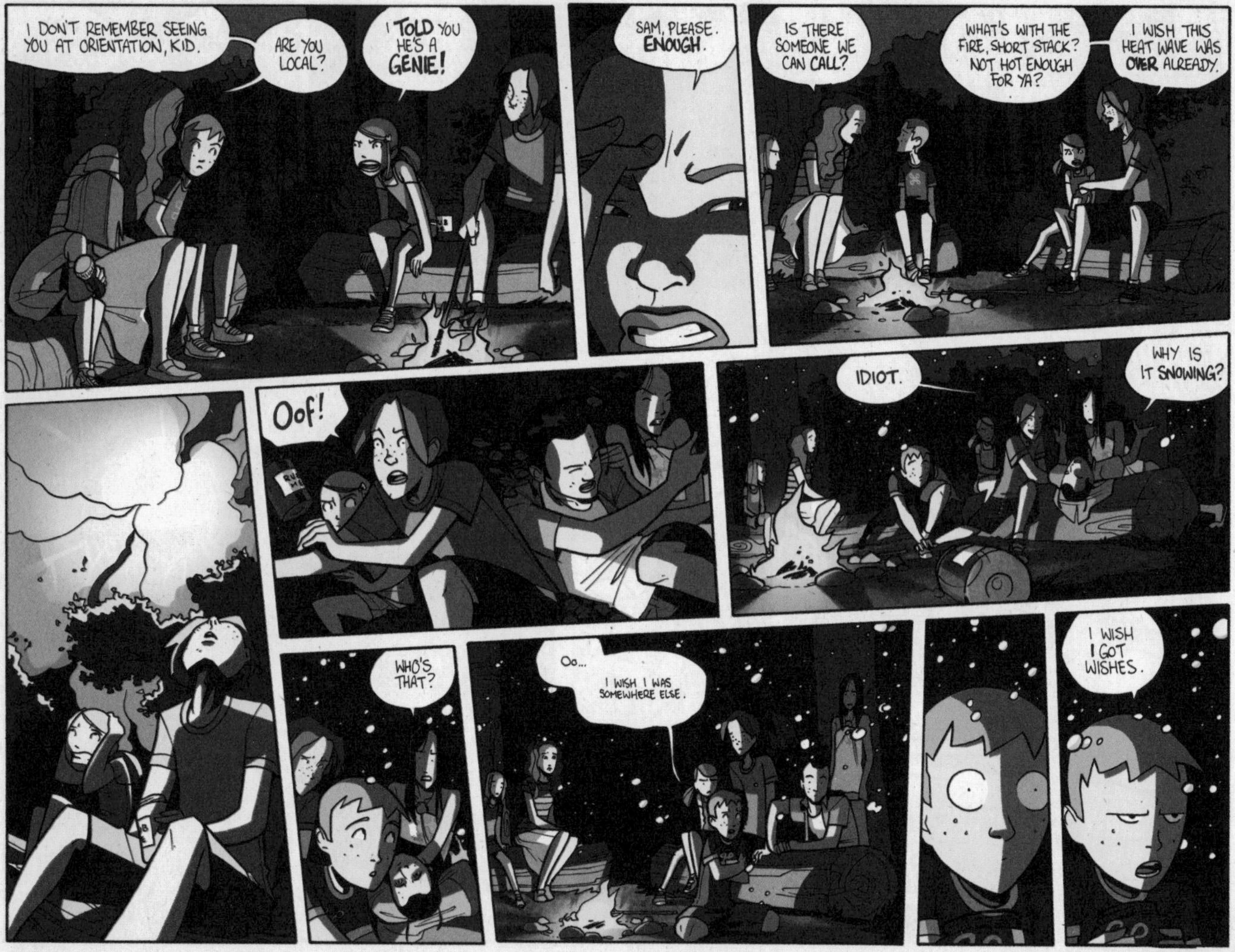
I DON'T REMEMBER SEEING YOU AT ORIENTATION, KID.
ARE YOU LOCAL?
I **TOLD** YOU HE'S A **GENIE**!
SAM, PLEASE. **ENOUGH**.
IS THERE SOMEONE WE CAN **CALL**?
WHAT'S WITH THE FIRE, SHORT STACK? NOT HOT ENOUGH FOR YA?
I WISH THIS HEAT WAVE WAS **OVER** ALREADY.
Oof!
IDIOT.
WHY IS IT **SNOWING**?
WHO'S THAT?
Oo...
I WISH I WAS SOMEWHERE ELSE.
I WISH **I** GOT WISHES.

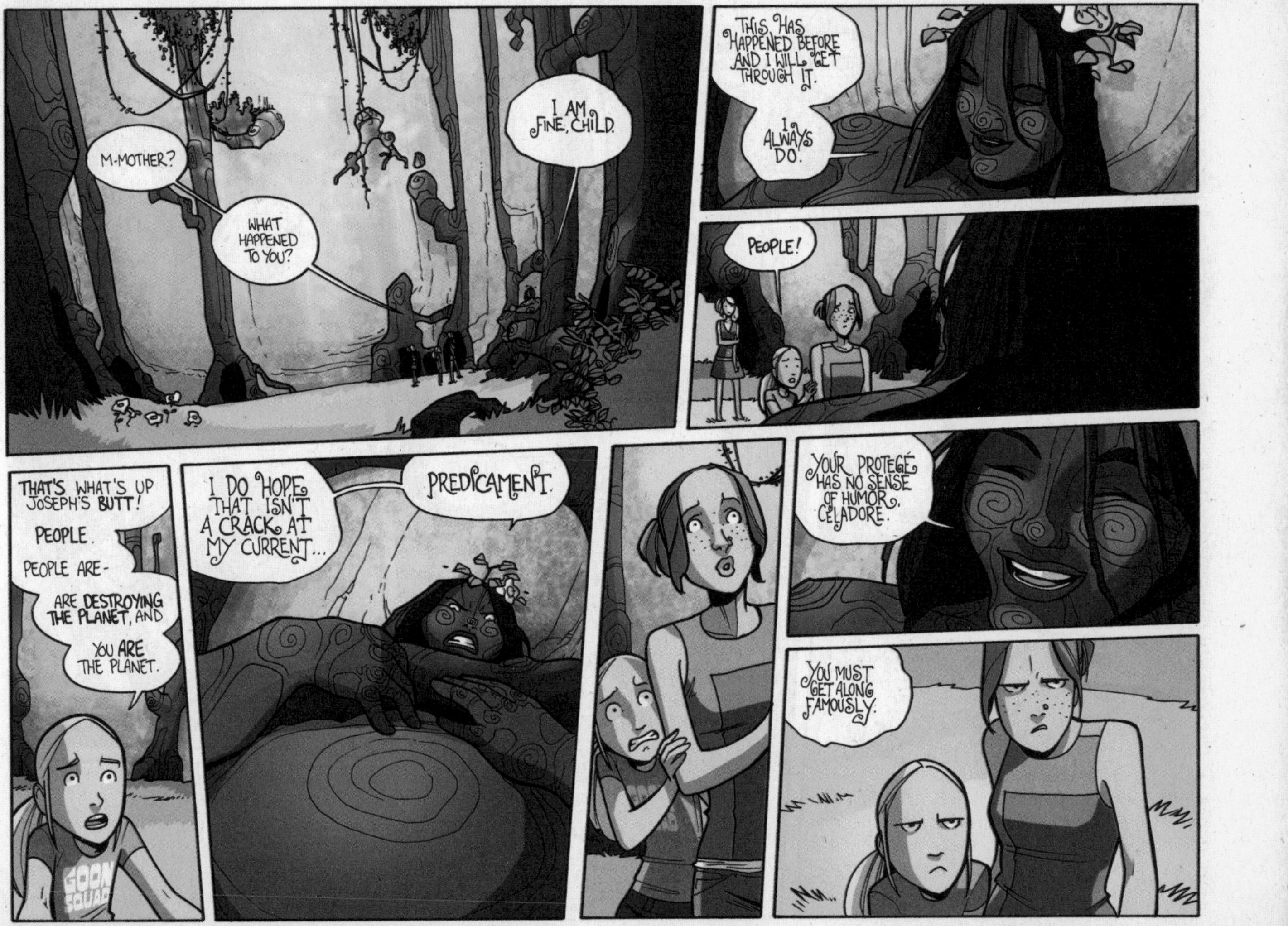
M-MOTHER?
WHAT HAPPENED TO YOU?
I AM FINE, CHILD.
THIS HAS HAPPENED BEFORE AND I WILL GET THROUGH IT.
I ALWAYS DO.
PEOPLE!
THAT'S WHAT'S UP JOSEPH'S BUTT!
PEOPLE.
PEOPLE ARE-
ARE DESTROYING THE PLANET, AND
YOU ARE THE PLANET.
I DO HOPE THAT ISN'T A CRACK AT MY CURRENT...
PREDICAMENT.
YOUR PROTEGÉ HAS NO SENSE OF HUMOR, CELADORE.
YOU MUST GET ALONG FAMOUSLY.
GOON SQUAD

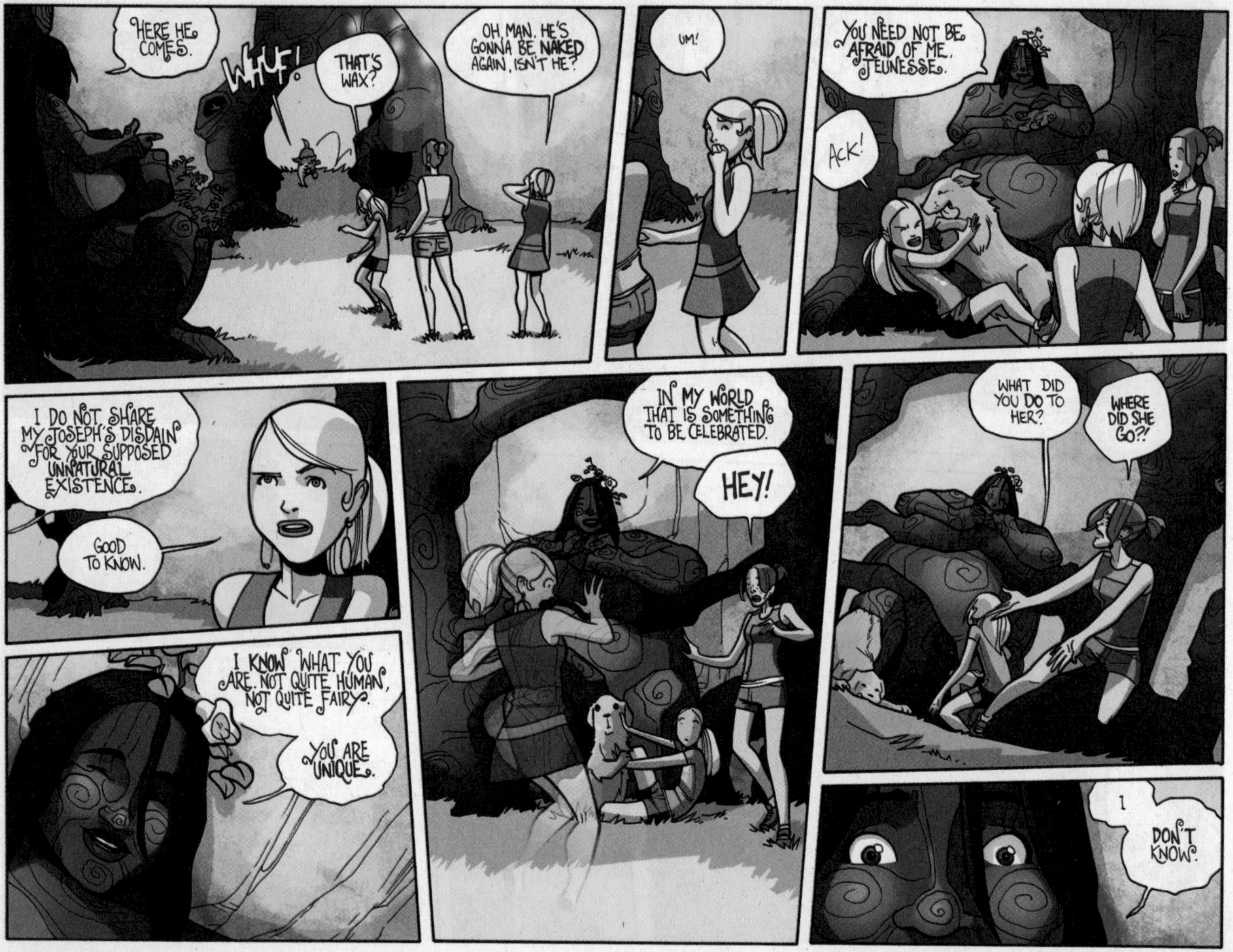
HERE HE COMES.
WHUF!
THAT'S WAX?
OH, MAN. HE'S GONNA BE NAKED AGAIN, ISN'T HE?
UM!
YOU NEED NOT BE AFRAID OF ME, JEUNESSE.
ACK!
I DO NOT SHARE MY JOSEPH'S DISDAIN FOR YOUR SUPPOSED UNNATURAL EXISTENCE.
GOOD TO KNOW.
I KNOW WHAT YOU ARE. NOT QUITE HUMAN, NOT QUITE FAIRY.
YOU ARE UNIQUE.
IN MY WORLD THAT IS SOMETHING TO BE CELEBRATED.
HEY!
WHAT DID YOU DO TO HER?
WHERE DID SHE GO?!
I
DON'T KNOW.

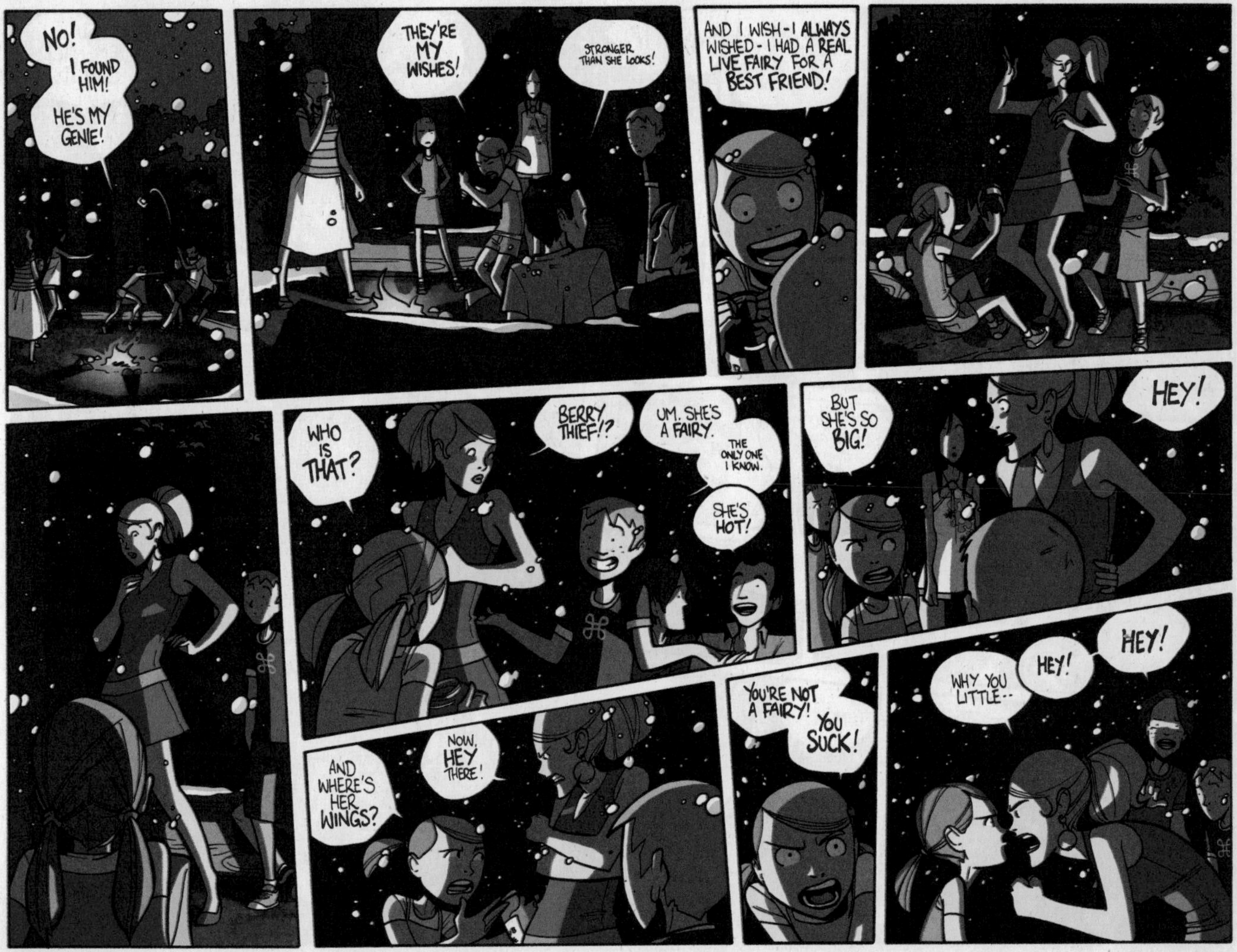
NO!
I FOUND HIM!
HE'S MY GENIE!
THEY'RE MY WISHES!
STRONGER THAN SHE LOOKS!
AND I WISH - I ALWAYS WISHED - I HAD A REAL LIVE FAIRY FOR A BEST FRIEND!
WHO IS THAT?
BERRY THIEF!?
UM. SHE'S A FAIRY.
THE ONLY ONE I KNOW.
SHE'S HOT!
BUT SHE'S SO BIG!
HEY!
AND WHERE'S HER WINGS?
NOW, HEY THERE!
YOU'RE NOT A FAIRY!
YOU SUCK!
WHY YOU LITTLE--
HEY!
HEY!

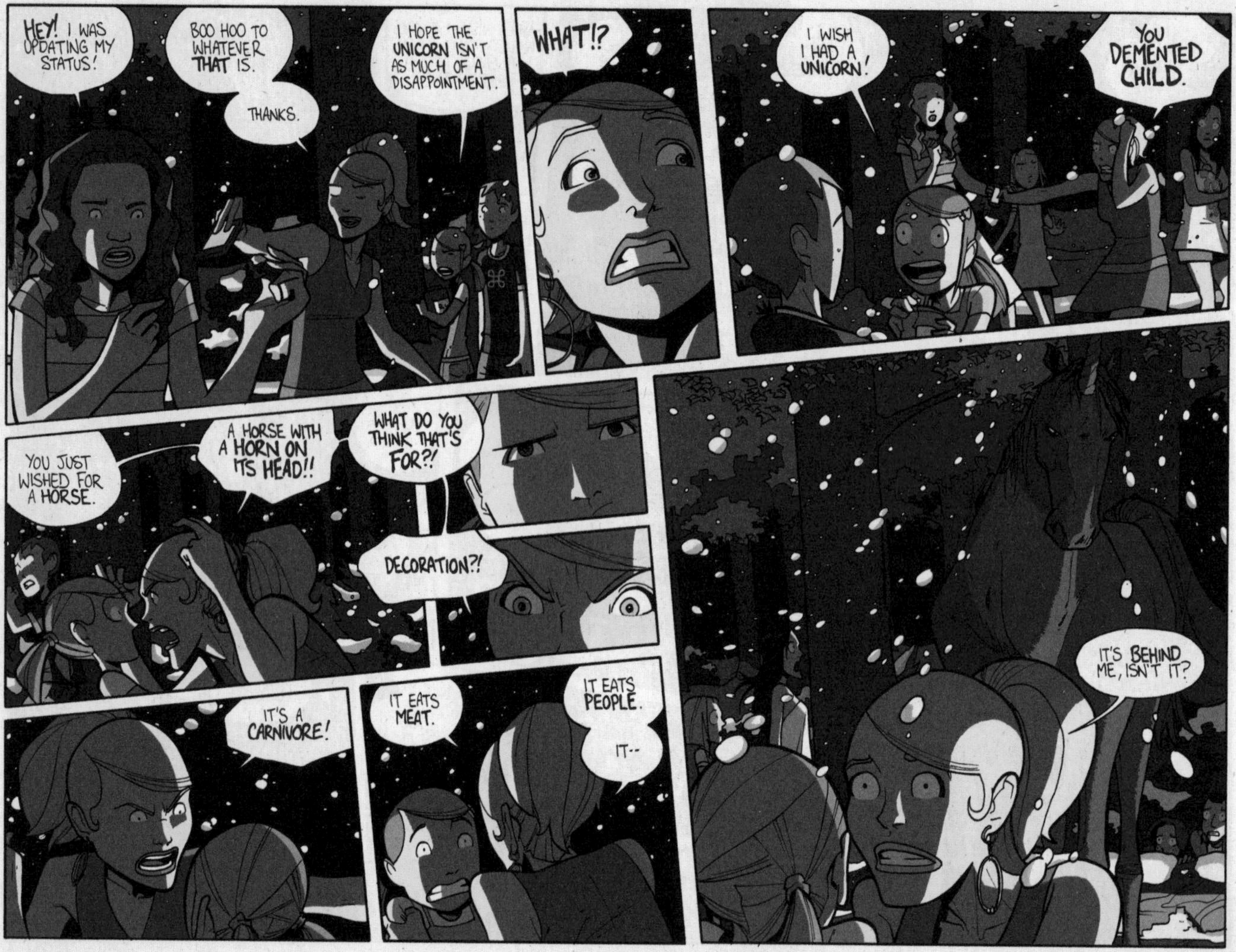
HEY! I WAS UPDATING MY STATUS!
BOO HOO TO WHATEVER THAT IS.
THANKS.
I HOPE THE UNICORN ISN'T AS MUCH OF A DISAPPOINTMENT.
WHAT!?
I WISH I HAD A UNICORN!
YOU DEMENTED CHILD.
YOU JUST WISHED FOR A HORSE.
A HORSE WITH A HORN ON ITS HEAD!!
WHAT DO YOU THINK THAT'S FOR?!
DECORATION?!
IT'S A CARNIVORE!
IT EATS MEAT.
IT EATS PEOPLE.
IT--
IT'S BEHIND ME, ISN'T IT?

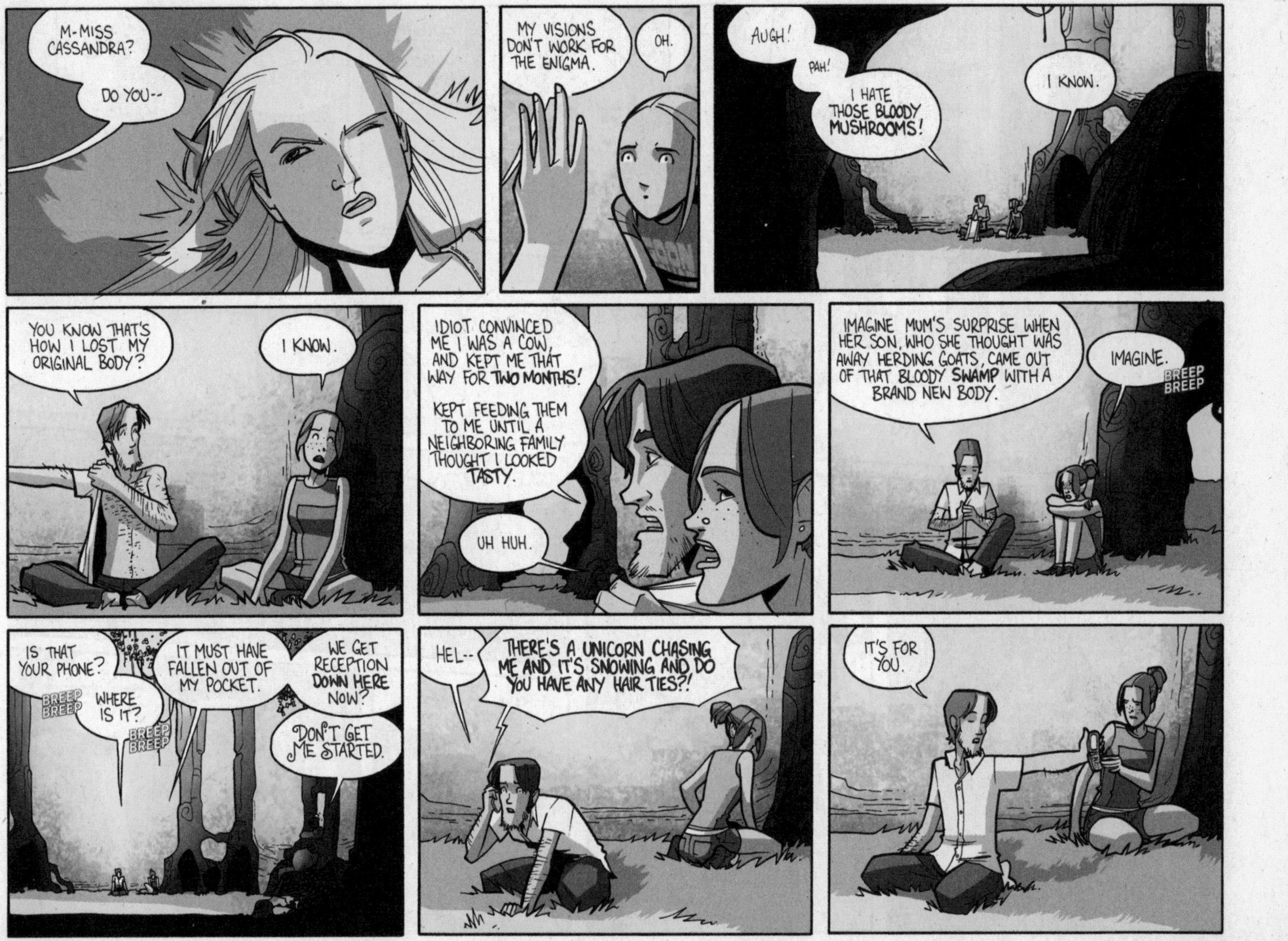
M-MISS CASSANDRA?
DO YOU--
MY VISIONS DON'T WORK FOR THE ENIGMA.
OH.
AUGH!
PAH!
I HATE THOSE BLOODY MUSHROOMS!
I KNOW.
YOU KNOW THAT'S HOW I LOST MY ORIGINAL BODY?
I KNOW.
IDIOT CONVINCED ME I WAS A COW, AND KEPT ME THAT WAY FOR TWO MONTHS!
KEPT FEEDING THEM TO ME UNTIL A NEIGHBORING FAMILY THOUGHT I LOOKED TASTY.
UH HUH.
IMAGINE MUM'S SURPRISE WHEN HER SON, WHO SHE THOUGHT WAS AWAY HERDING GOATS, CAME OUT OF THAT BLOODY SWAMP WITH A BRAND NEW BODY.
IMAGINE.
BREEP BREEP
IS THAT YOUR PHONE?
BREEP BREEP
WHERE IS IT?
BREEP BREEP
IT MUST HAVE FALLEN OUT OF MY POCKET.
WE GET RECEPTION DOWN HERE NOW?
DON'T GET ME STARTED.
HEL--
THERE'S A UNICORN CHASING ME AND IT'S SNOWING AND DO YOU HAVE ANY HAIR TIES?!
IT'S FOR YOU.

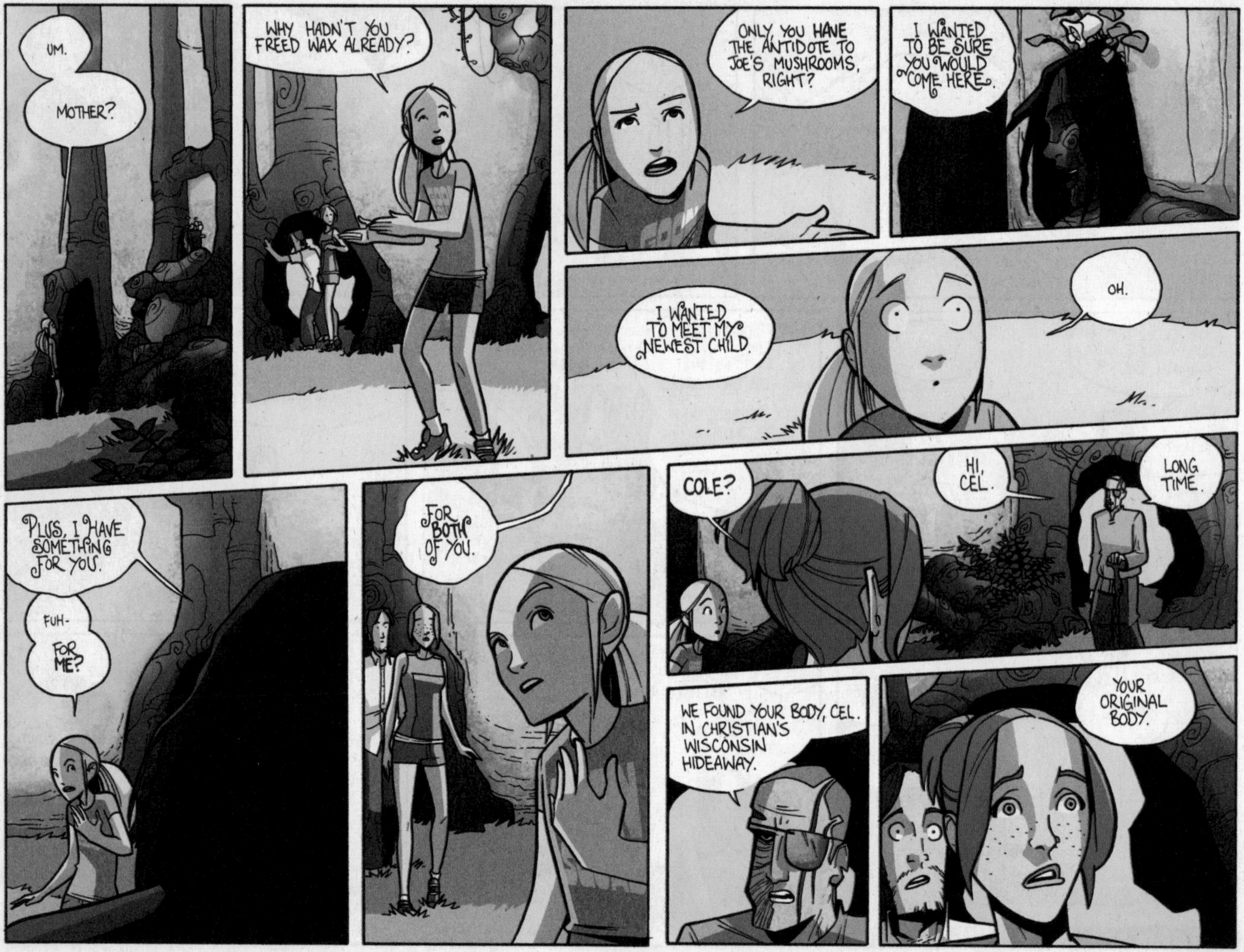
UM.
MOTHER?
WHY HADN'T YOU FREED WAX ALREADY?
ONLY YOU HAVE THE ANTIDOTE TO JOE'S MUSHROOMS, RIGHT?
I WANTED TO BE SURE YOU WOULD COME HERE.
I WANTED TO MEET MY NEWEST CHILD.
OH.
PLUS, I HAVE SOMETHING FOR YOU.
FUH-
FOR ME?
FOR BOTH OF YOU.
COLE?
HI, CEL.
LONG TIME.
WE FOUND YOUR BODY, CEL. IN CHRISTIAN'S WISCONSIN HIDEAWAY.
YOUR ORIGINAL BODY.

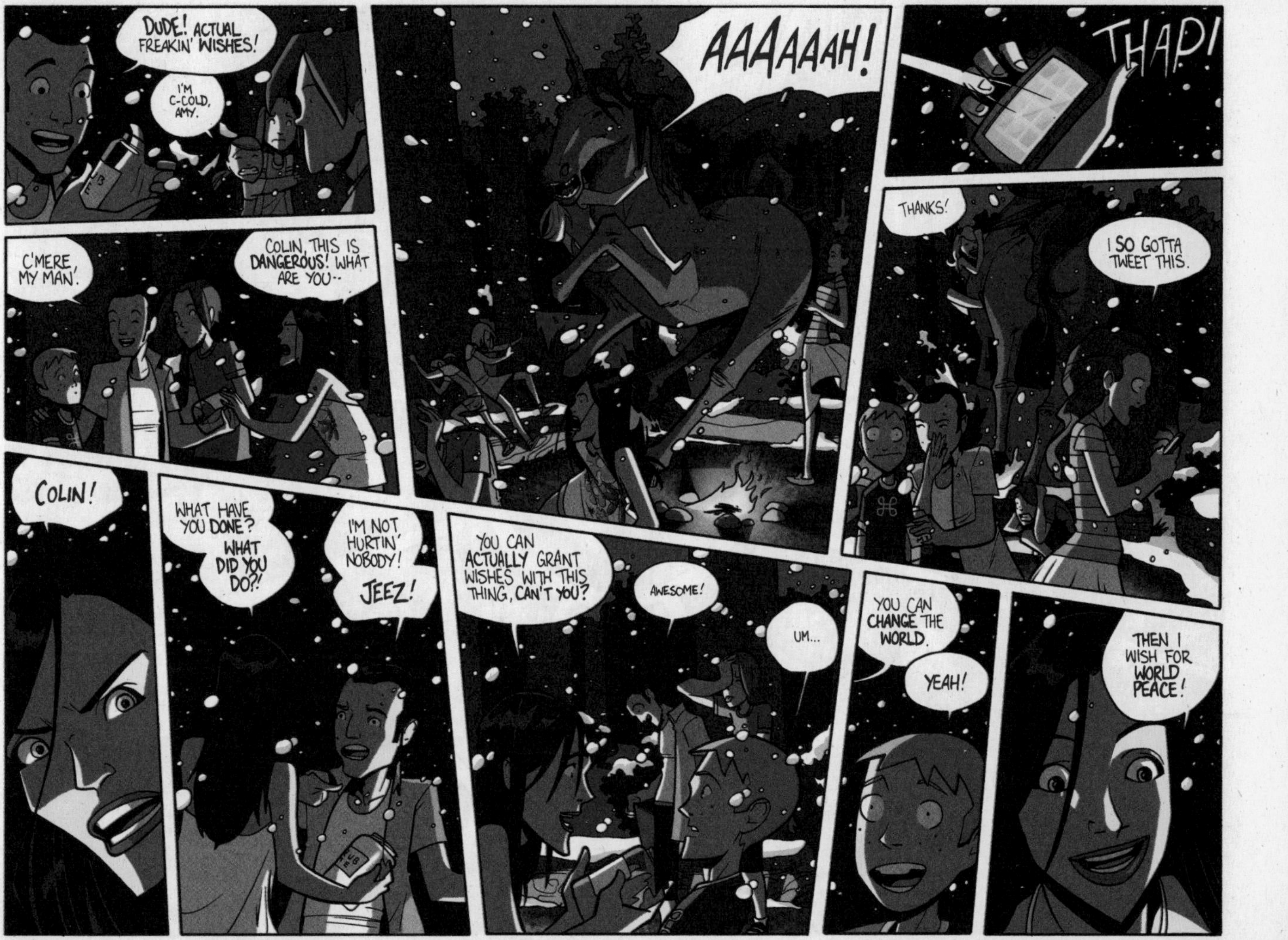
DUDE! ACTUAL FREAKIN' WISHES!
I'M C-COLD, AMY.
C'MERE MY MAN.
COLIN, THIS IS DANGEROUS! WHAT ARE YOU--
AAAAAAH!
THAP!
THANKS!
I SO GOTTA TWEET THIS.
COLIN!
WHAT HAVE YOU DONE? WHAT DID YOU DO?!
I'M NOT HURTIN' NOBODY!
JEEZ!
YOU CAN ACTUALLY GRANT WISHES WITH THIS THING, CAN'T YOU?
AWESOME!
UM...
YOU CAN CHANGE THE WORLD.
YEAH!
THEN I WISH FOR WORLD PEACE!

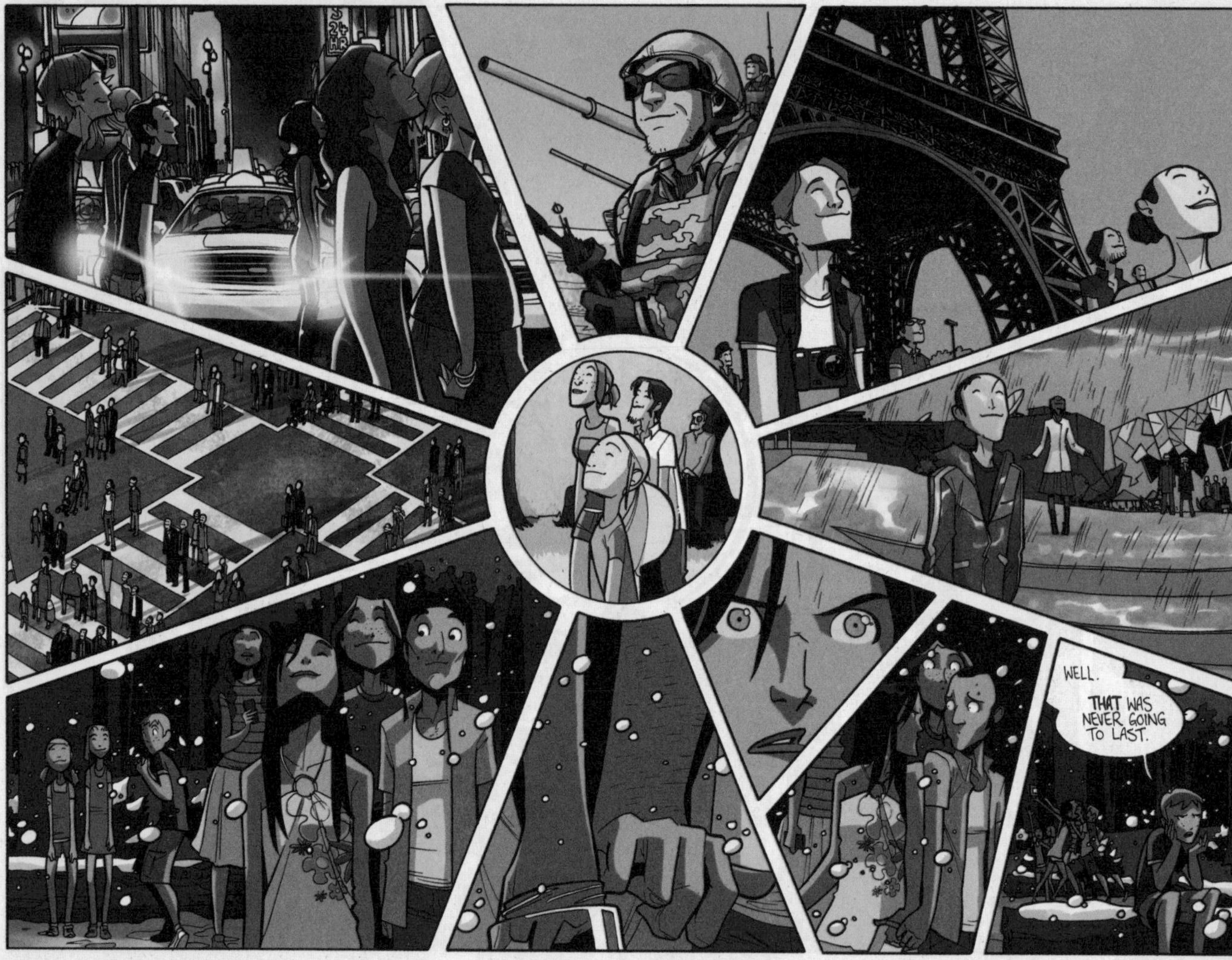
WELL.
THAT WAS NEVER GOING TO LAST.

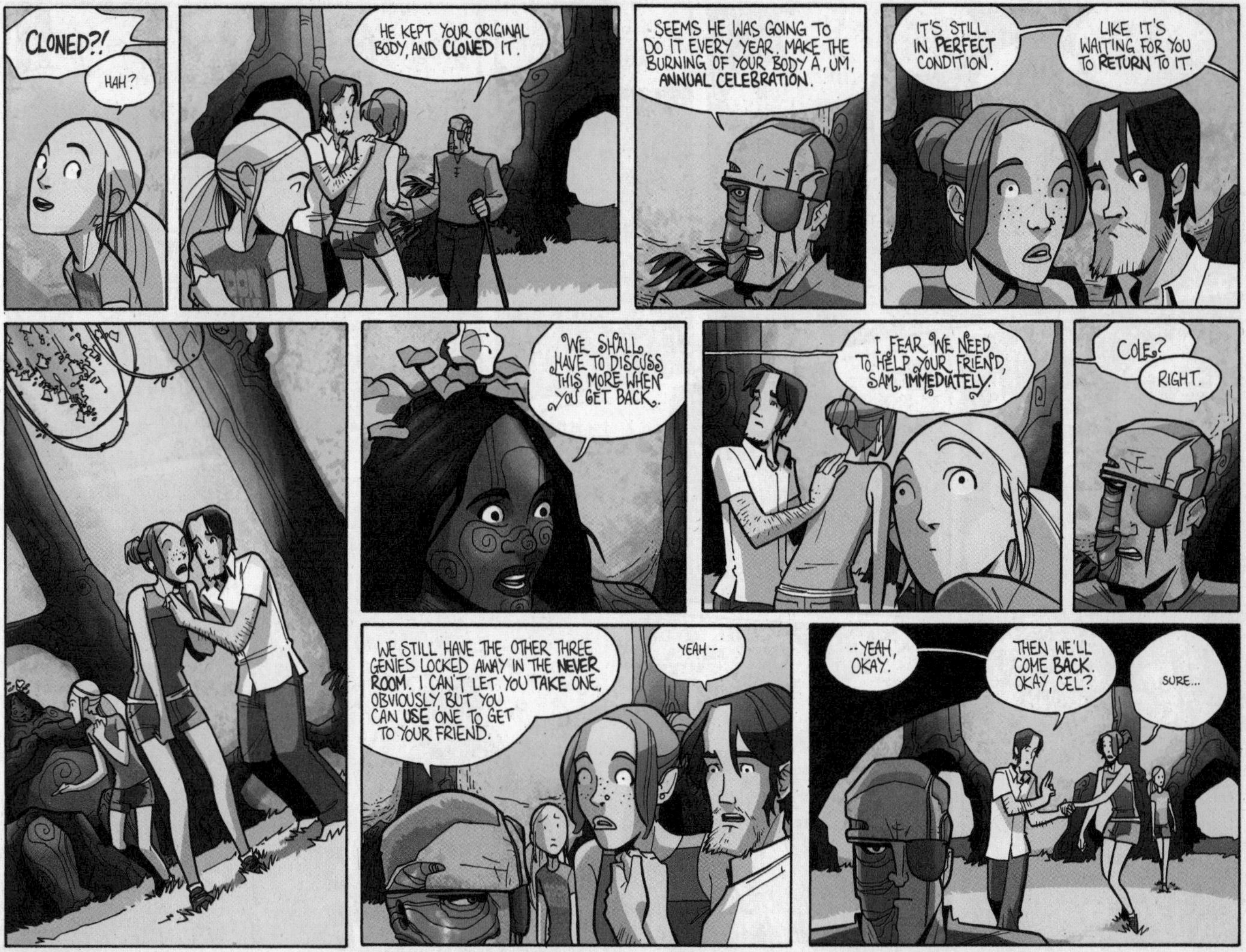
CLONED?!
HAH?
HE KEPT YOUR ORIGINAL BODY, AND CLONED IT.
SEEMS HE WAS GOING TO DO IT EVERY YEAR. MAKE THE BURNING OF YOUR BODY A, UM, ANNUAL CELEBRATION.
IT'S STILL IN PERFECT CONDITION.
LIKE IT'S WAITING FOR YOU TO RETURN TO IT.
WE SHALL HAVE TO DISCUSS THIS MORE WHEN YOU GET BACK.
I FEAR WE NEED TO HELP YOUR FRIEND, SAM, IMMEDIATELY.
COLE?
RIGHT.
WE STILL HAVE THE OTHER THREE GENIES LOCKED AWAY IN THE NEVER ROOM. I CAN'T LET YOU TAKE ONE, OBVIOUSLY, BUT YOU CAN USE ONE TO GET TO YOUR FRIEND.
YEAH--
--YEAH, OKAY.
THEN WE'LL COME BACK. OKAY, CEL?
SURE...

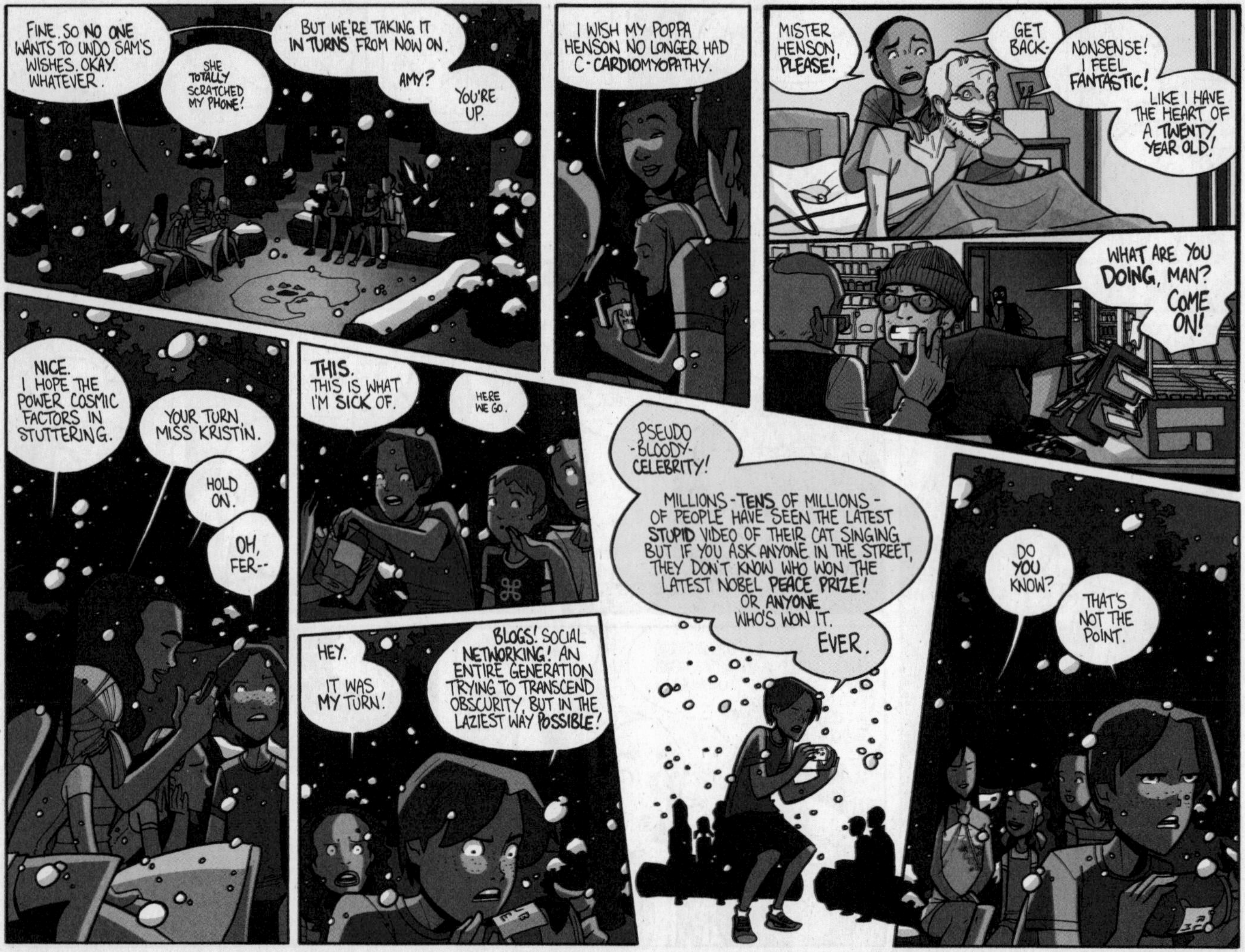
FINE. SO NO ONE WANTS TO UNDO SAM'S WISHES. OKAY. WHATEVER.
SHE TOTALLY SCRATCHED MY PHONE!
BUT WE'RE TAKING IT IN TURNS FROM NOW ON.
AMY?
YOU'RE UP.
I WISH MY POPPA HENSON NO LONGER HAD C-CARDIOMYOPATHY.
MISTER HENSON, PLEASE!
GET BACK-
NONSENSE! I FEEL FANTASTIC!
LIKE I HAVE THE HEART OF A TWENTY YEAR OLD!
WHAT ARE YOU DOING, MAN? COME ON!
NICE. I HOPE THE POWER COSMIC FACTORS IN STUTTERING.
YOUR TURN, MISS KRISTIN.
HOLD ON.
OH, FER--
THIS. THIS IS WHAT I'M SICK OF.
HERE WE GO.
HEY.
IT WAS MY TURN!
BLOGS! SOCIAL NETWORKING! AN ENTIRE GENERATION TRYING TO TRANSCEND OBSCURITY, BUT IN THE LAZIEST WAY POSSIBLE!
PSEUDO-BLOODY-CELEBRITY!
MILLIONS-TENS OF MILLIONS-OF PEOPLE HAVE SEEN THE LATEST STUPID VIDEO OF THEIR CAT SINGING BUT IF YOU ASK ANYONE IN THE STREET, THEY DON'T KNOW WHO WON THE LATEST NOBEL PEACE PRIZE!
OR ANYONE WHO'S WON IT.
EVER.
DO YOU KNOW?
THAT'S NOT THE POINT.

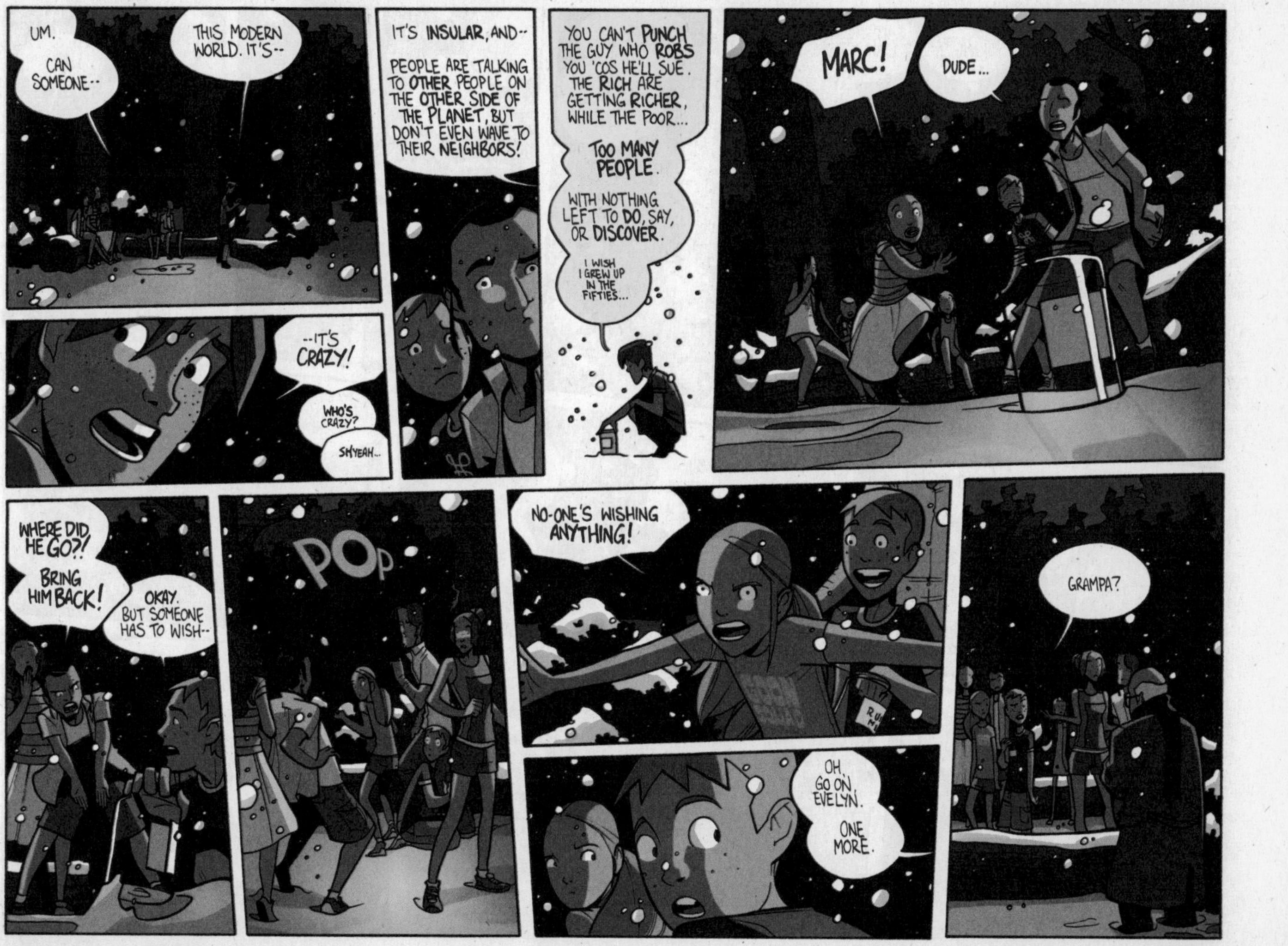
UM.
CAN SOMEONE--
THIS MODERN WORLD. IT'S--
--IT'S CRAZY!
WHO'S CRAZY?
SHYEAH...
IT'S INSULAR, AND--
PEOPLE ARE TALKING TO OTHER PEOPLE ON THE OTHER SIDE OF THE PLANET, BUT DON'T EVEN WAVE TO THEIR NEIGHBORS!
YOU CAN'T PUNCH THE GUY WHO ROBS YOU 'COS HE'LL SUE. THE RICH ARE GETTING RICHER, WHILE THE POOR...
TOO MANY PEOPLE.
WITH NOTHING LEFT TO DO, SAY, OR DISCOVER.
I WISH I GREW UP IN THE FIFTIES...
MARC!
DUDE...
WHERE DID HE GO?!
BRING HIM BACK!
OKAY. BUT SOMEONE HAS TO WISH--
POP
NO-ONE'S WISHING ANYTHING!
OH, GO ON, EVELYN.
ONE MORE.
GRAMPA?

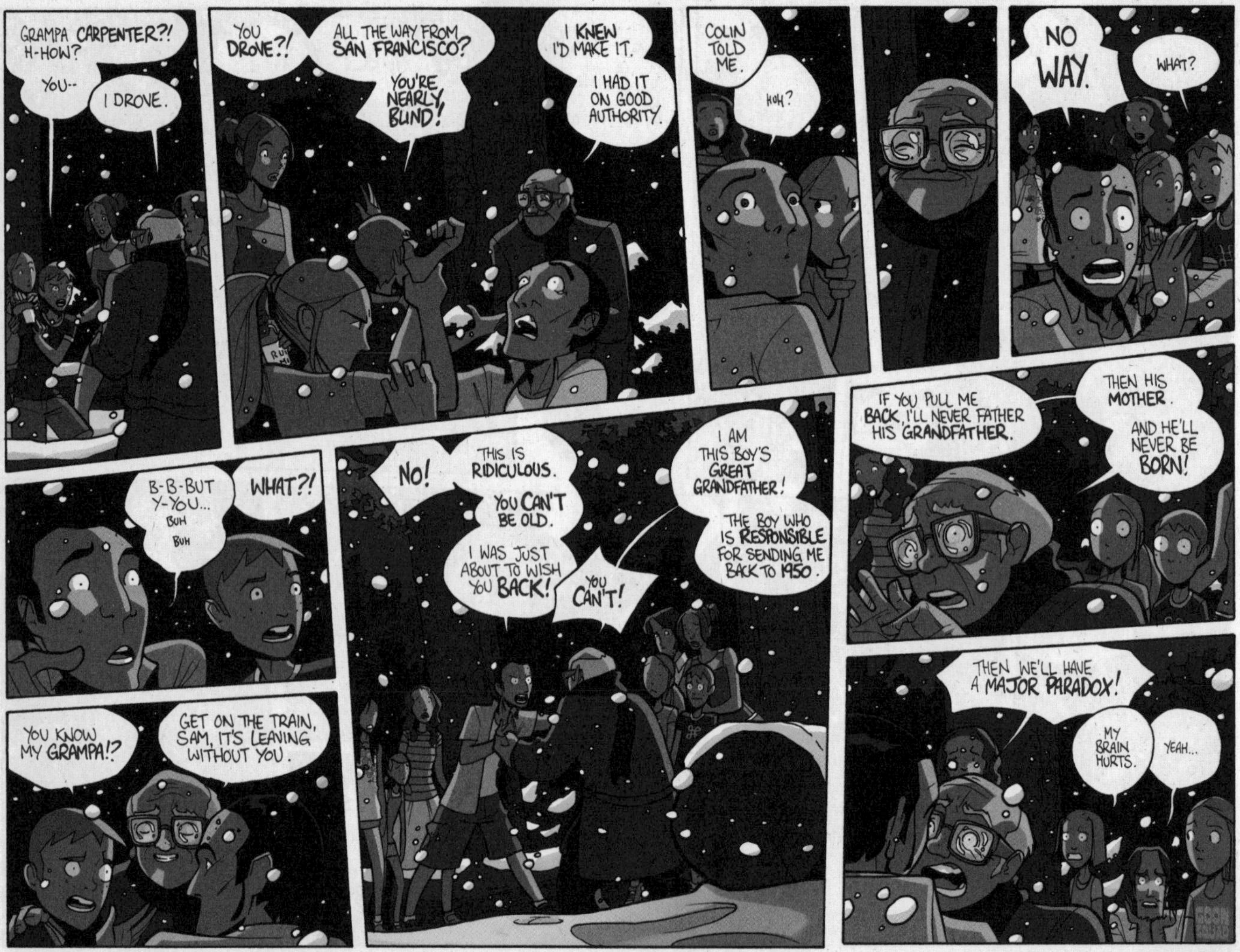
GRAMPA CARPENTER?! H-HOW?
YOU--
I DROVE.
YOU DROVE?!
ALL THE WAY FROM SAN FRANCISCO?
YOU'RE NEARLY BLIND!
I KNEW I'D MAKE IT.
I HAD IT ON GOOD AUTHORITY.
COLIN TOLD ME.
HUH?
NO WAY.
WHAT?
B-B-BUT Y-YOU... BUH BUH
WHAT?!
YOU KNOW MY GRAMPA!?
GET ON THE TRAIN, SAM, IT'S LEAVING WITHOUT YOU.
NO!
THIS IS RIDICULOUS.
YOU CAN'T BE OLD.
I WAS JUST ABOUT TO WISH YOU BACK!
YOU CAN'T!
I AM THIS BOY'S GREAT GRANDFATHER!
THE BOY WHO IS RESPONSIBLE FOR SENDING ME BACK TO 1950.
IF YOU PULL ME BACK, I'LL NEVER FATHER HIS GRANDFATHER.
THEN HIS MOTHER.
AND HE'LL NEVER BE BORN!
THEN WE'LL HAVE A MAJOR PARADOX!
MY BRAIN HURTS.
YEAH...

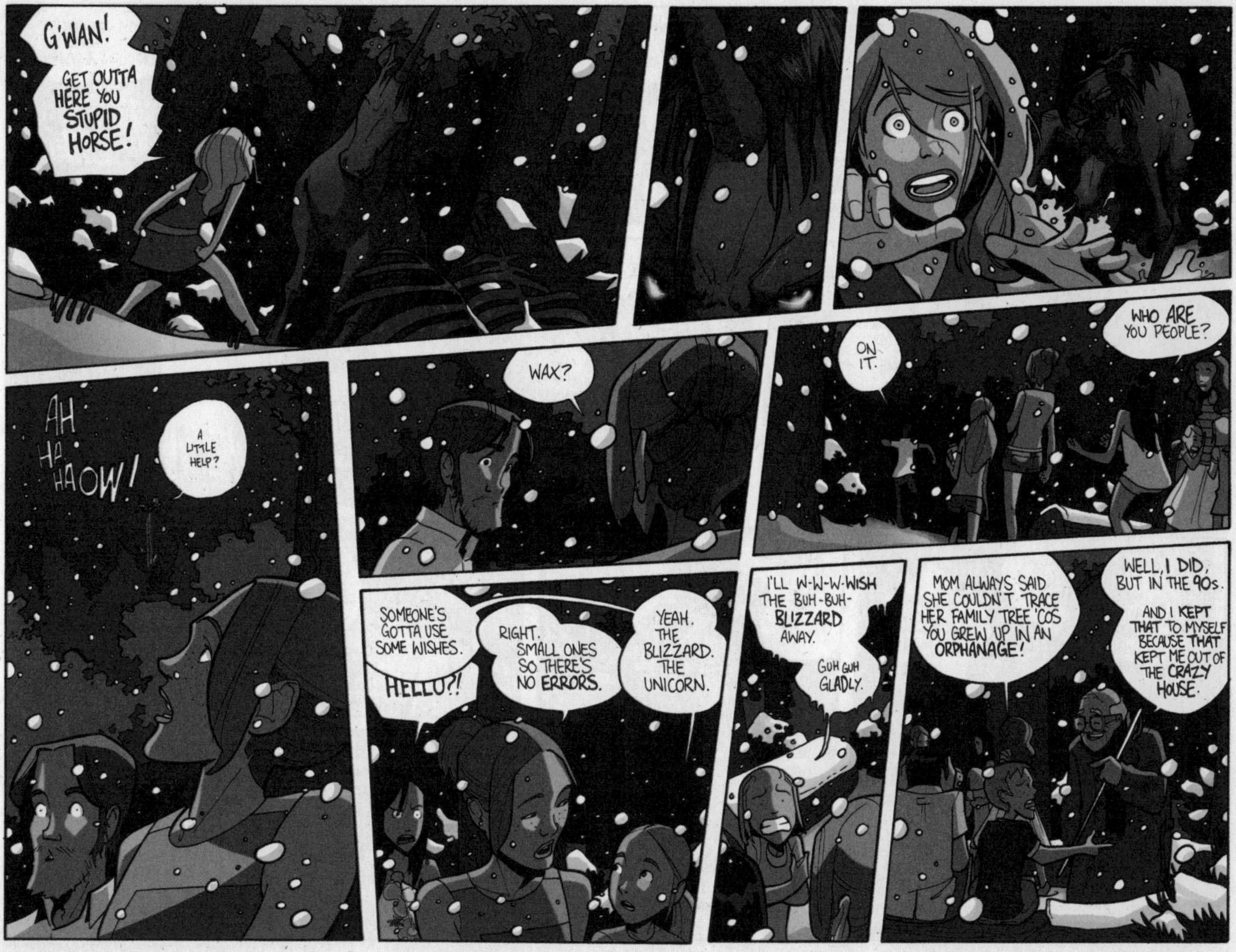
G'WAN!
GET OUTTA HERE YOU STUPID HORSE!
AH HA HAOW!
A LITTLE HELP?
WAX?
ON IT.
WHO ARE YOU PEOPLE?
SOMEONE'S GOTTA USE SOME WISHES.
HELLO?!
RIGHT. SMALL ONES SO THERE'S NO ERRORS.
YEAH. THE BLIZZARD. THE UNICORN.
I'LL W-W-W-WISH THE BUH-BUH-BLIZZARD AWAY.
GUH GUH GLADLY.
MOM ALWAYS SAID SHE COULDN'T TRACE HER FAMILY TREE 'COS YOU GREW UP IN AN ORPHANAGE!
WELL, I DID, BUT IN THE 90s.
AND I KEPT THAT TO MYSELF BECAUSE THAT KEPT ME OUT OF THE CRAZY HOUSE.

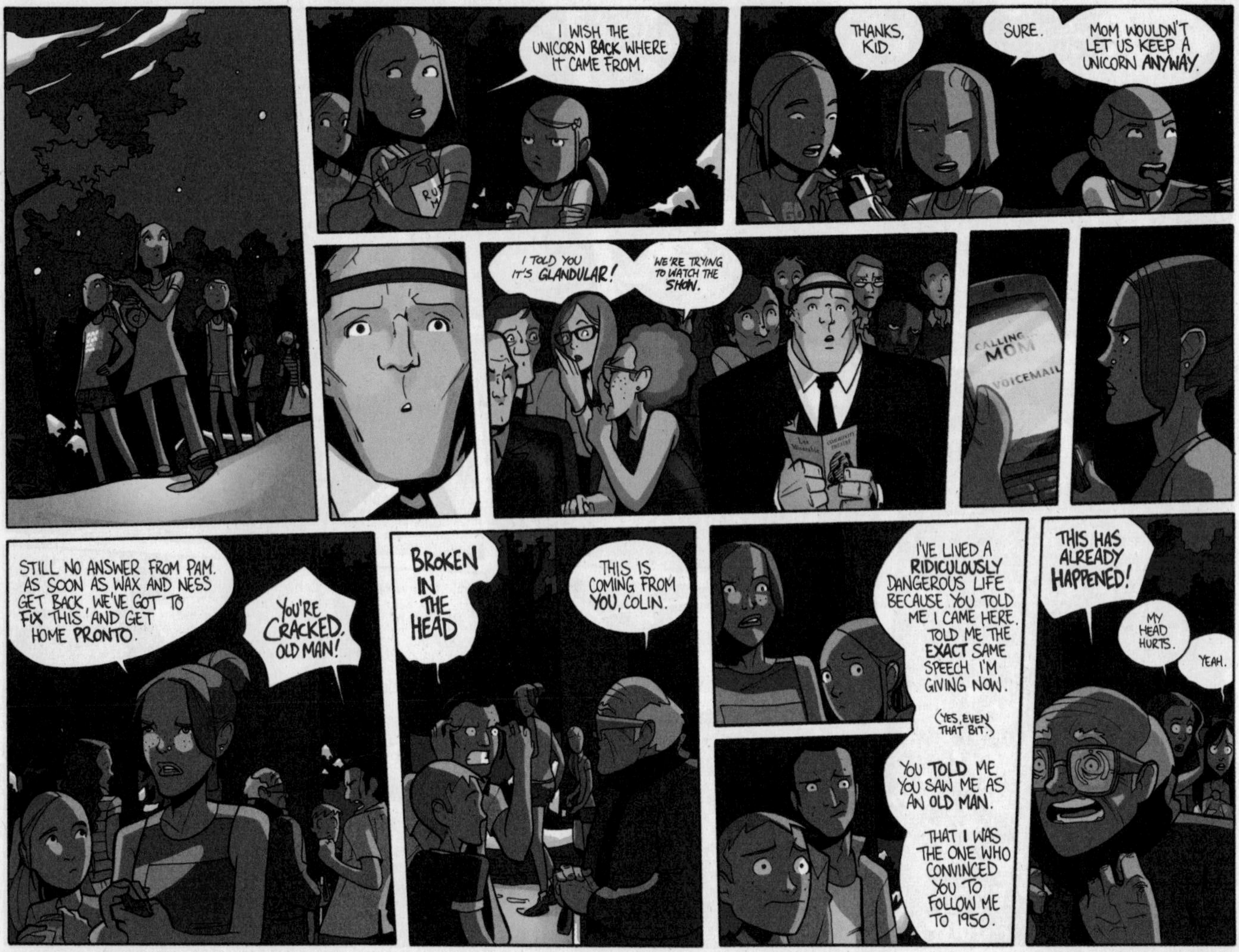
I WISH THE UNICORN BACK WHERE IT CAME FROM.
THANKS, KID.
SURE.
MOM WOULDN'T LET US KEEP A UNICORN ANYWAY.
I TOLD YOU IT'S GLANDULAR!
WE'RE TRYING TO WATCH THE SHOW.
CALLING... MOM
VOICEMAIL
STILL NO ANSWER FROM PAM. AS SOON AS WAX AND NESS GET BACK, WE'VE GOT TO FIX THIS AND GET HOME PRONTO.
YOU'RE CRACKED, OLD MAN!
BROKEN IN THE HEAD
THIS IS COMING FROM YOU, COLIN.
I'VE LIVED A RIDICULOUSLY DANGEROUS LIFE BECAUSE YOU TOLD ME I CAME HERE. TOLD ME THE EXACT SAME SPEECH I'M GIVING NOW.
(YES, EVEN THAT BIT.)
YOU TOLD ME YOU SAW ME AS AN OLD MAN.
THAT I WAS THE ONE WHO CONVINCED YOU TO FOLLOW ME TO 1950.
THIS HAS ALREADY HAPPENED!
MY HEAD HURTS.
YEAH.

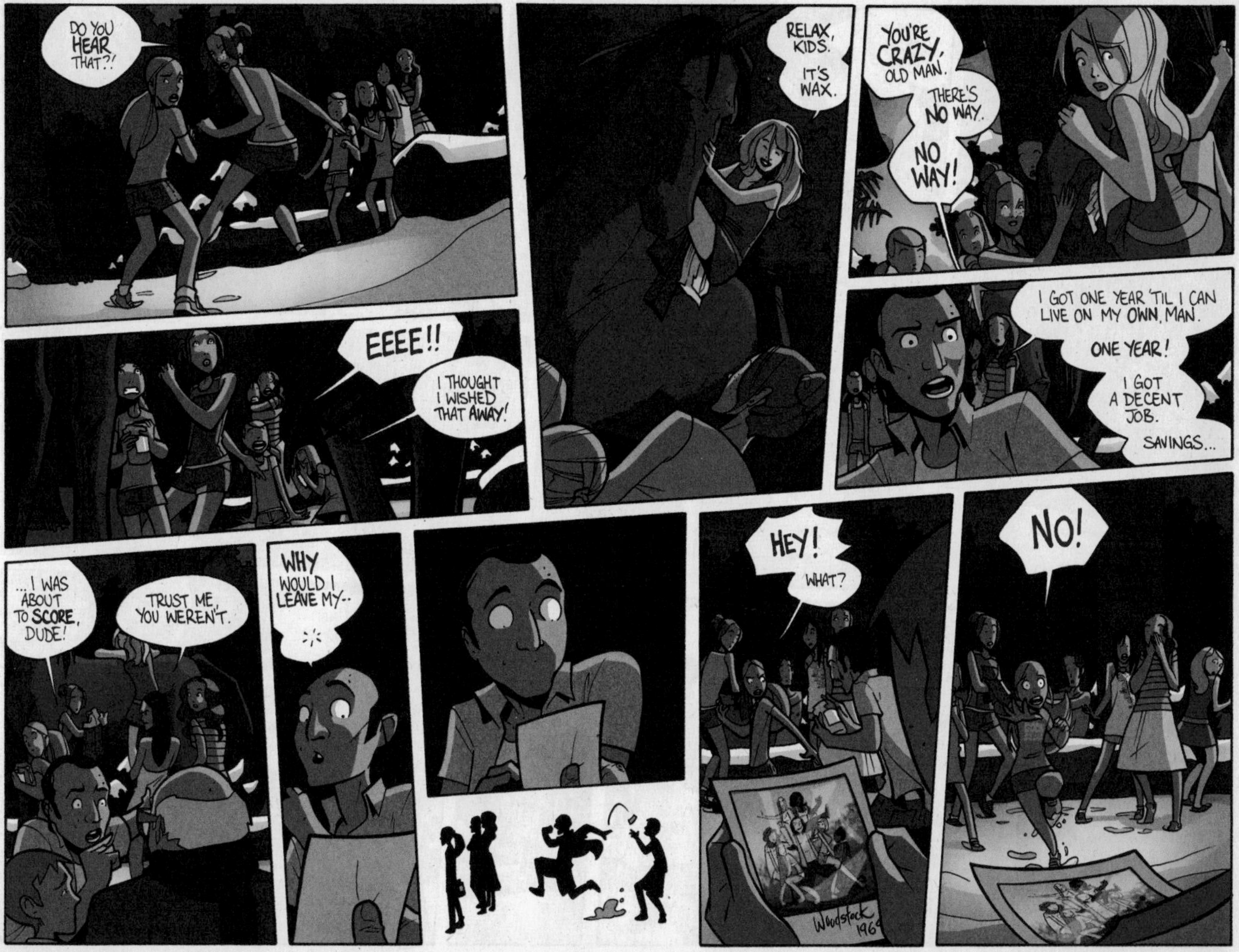

DO YOU HEAR THAT?!
RELAX, KIDS. IT'S WAX.
YOU'RE CRAZY, OLD MAN.
THERE'S NO WAY.
NO WAY!
EEEE!!
I THOUGHT I WISHED THAT AWAY!
I GOT ONE YEAR 'TIL I CAN LIVE ON MY OWN, MAN.
ONE YEAR!
I GOT A DECENT JOB.
SAVINGS...
...I WAS ABOUT TO SCORE, DUDE!
TRUST ME, YOU WEREN'T.
WHY WOULD I LEAVE MY--
HEY!
WHAT?
Woodstock 1969
NO!

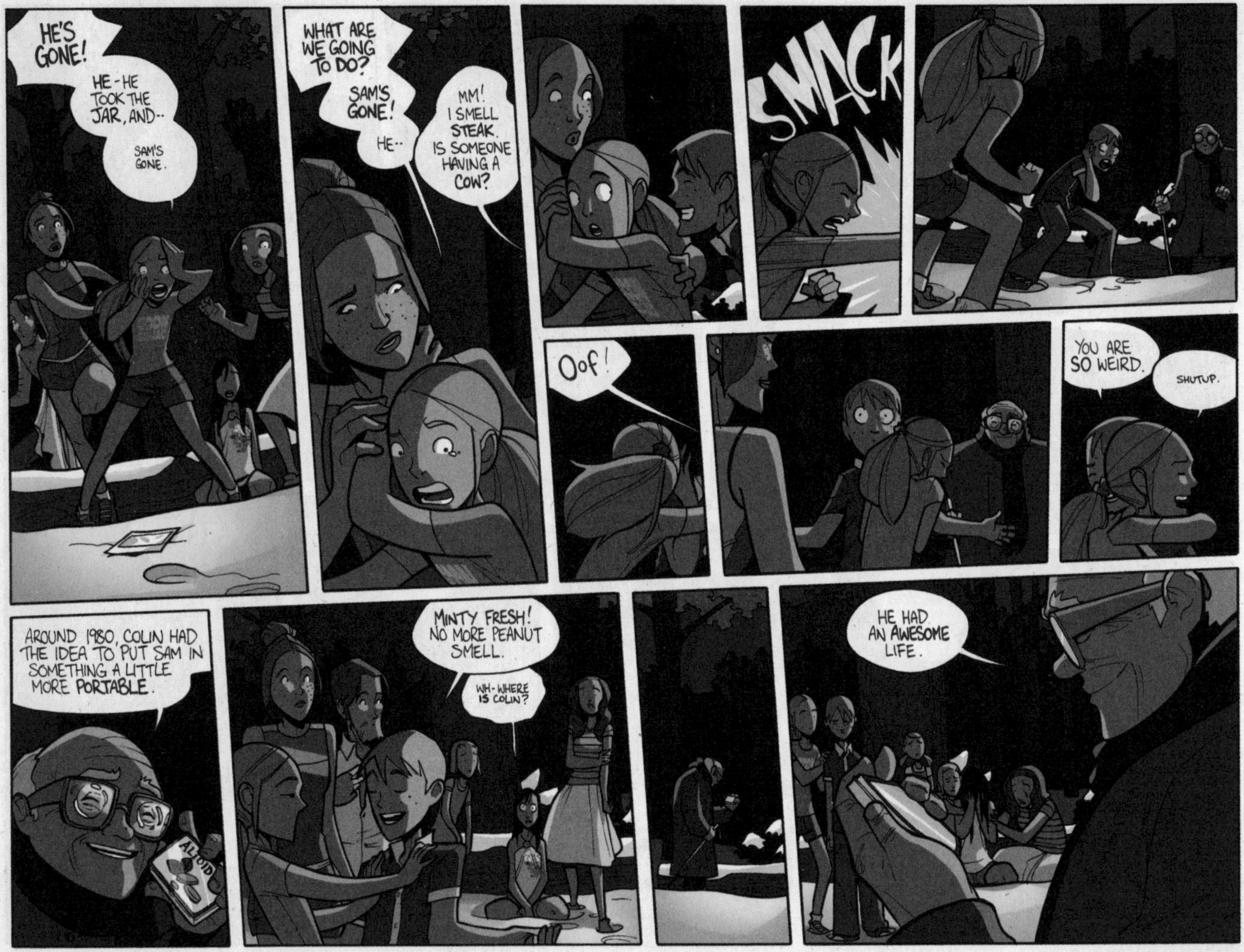
HE'S GONE!
HE-HE TOOK THE JAR, AND..
SAM'S GONE.
WHAT ARE WE GOING TO DO?
SAM'S GONE!
HE..
MM! I SMELL STEAK. IS SOMEONE HAVING A COW?
SMACK
Oof!
YOU ARE SO WEIRD.
SHUTUP.
AROUND 1980, COLIN HAD THE IDEA TO PUT SAM IN SOMETHING A LITTLE MORE PORTABLE.
ALTOID
MINTY FRESH! NO MORE PEANUT SMELL.
WH-WHERE IS COLIN?
HE HAD AN AWESOME LIFE.

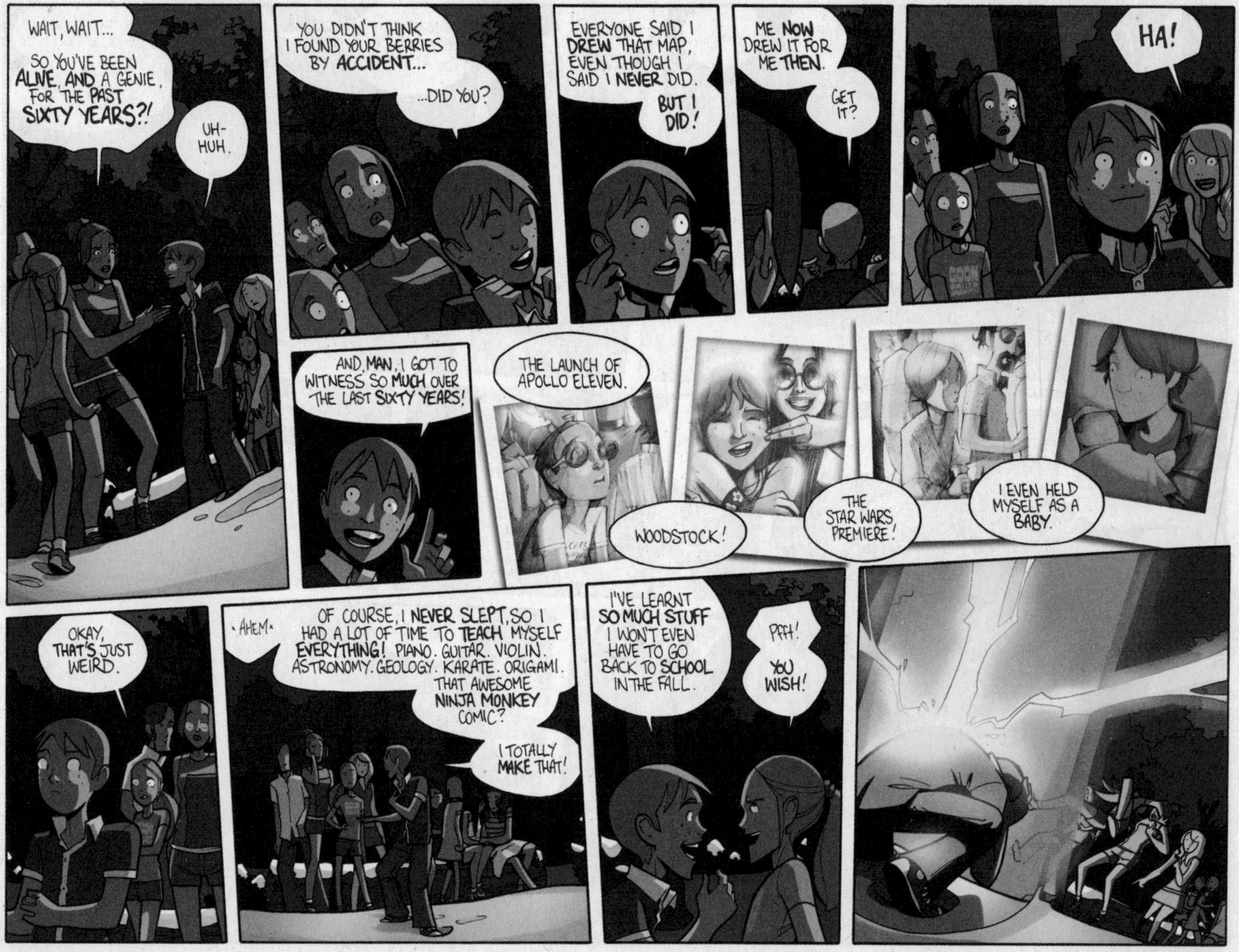
WAIT, WAIT...
SO YOU'VE BEEN ALIVE, AND A GENIE, FOR THE PAST SIXTY YEARS?!
UH-HUH.
YOU DIDN'T THINK I FOUND YOUR BERRIES BY ACCIDENT...
...DID YOU?
EVERYONE SAID I DREW THAT MAP, EVEN THOUGH I SAID I NEVER DID.
BUT I DID!
ME NOW DREW IT FOR ME THEN.
GET IT?
HA!
AND, MAN, I GOT TO WITNESS SO MUCH OVER THE LAST SIXTY YEARS!
THE LAUNCH OF APOLLO ELEVEN.
WOODSTOCK!
THE STAR WARS PREMIERE!
I EVEN HELD MYSELF AS A BABY.
OKAY, THAT'S JUST WEIRD.
AHEM
OF COURSE, I NEVER SLEPT, SO I HAD A LOT OF TIME TO TEACH MYSELF EVERYTHING! PIANO. GUITAR. VIOLIN. ASTRONOMY. GEOLOGY. KARATE. ORIGAMI.
THAT AWESOME NINJA MONKEY COMIC?
I TOTALLY MAKE THAT!
I'VE LEARNT SO MUCH STUFF I WON'T EVEN HAVE TO GO BACK TO SCHOOL IN THE FALL.
Pfft!
YOU WISH!

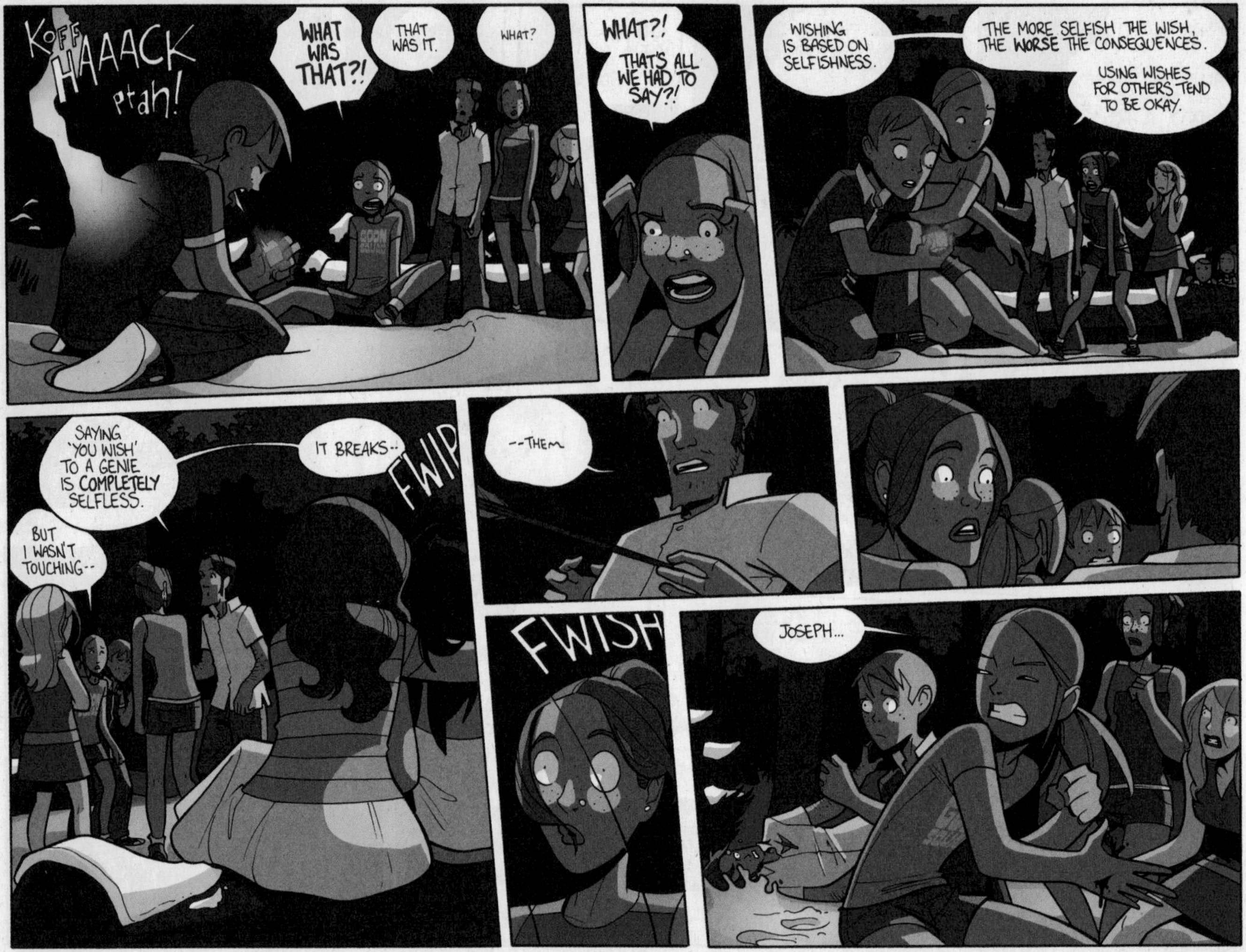
KOFF
HAAACK
ptah!
WHAT WAS THAT?!
THAT WAS IT.
WHAT?
WHAT?!
THAT'S ALL WE HAD TO SAY?!
WISHING IS BASED ON SELFISHNESS.
THE MORE SELFISH THE WISH, THE WORSE THE CONSEQUENCES.
USING WISHES FOR OTHERS TEND TO BE OKAY.
SAYING 'YOU WISH' TO A GENIE IS COMPLETELY SELFLESS.
IT BREAKS--
FWIP
BUT I WASN'T TOUCHING--
--THEM.
FWISH
JOSEPH...

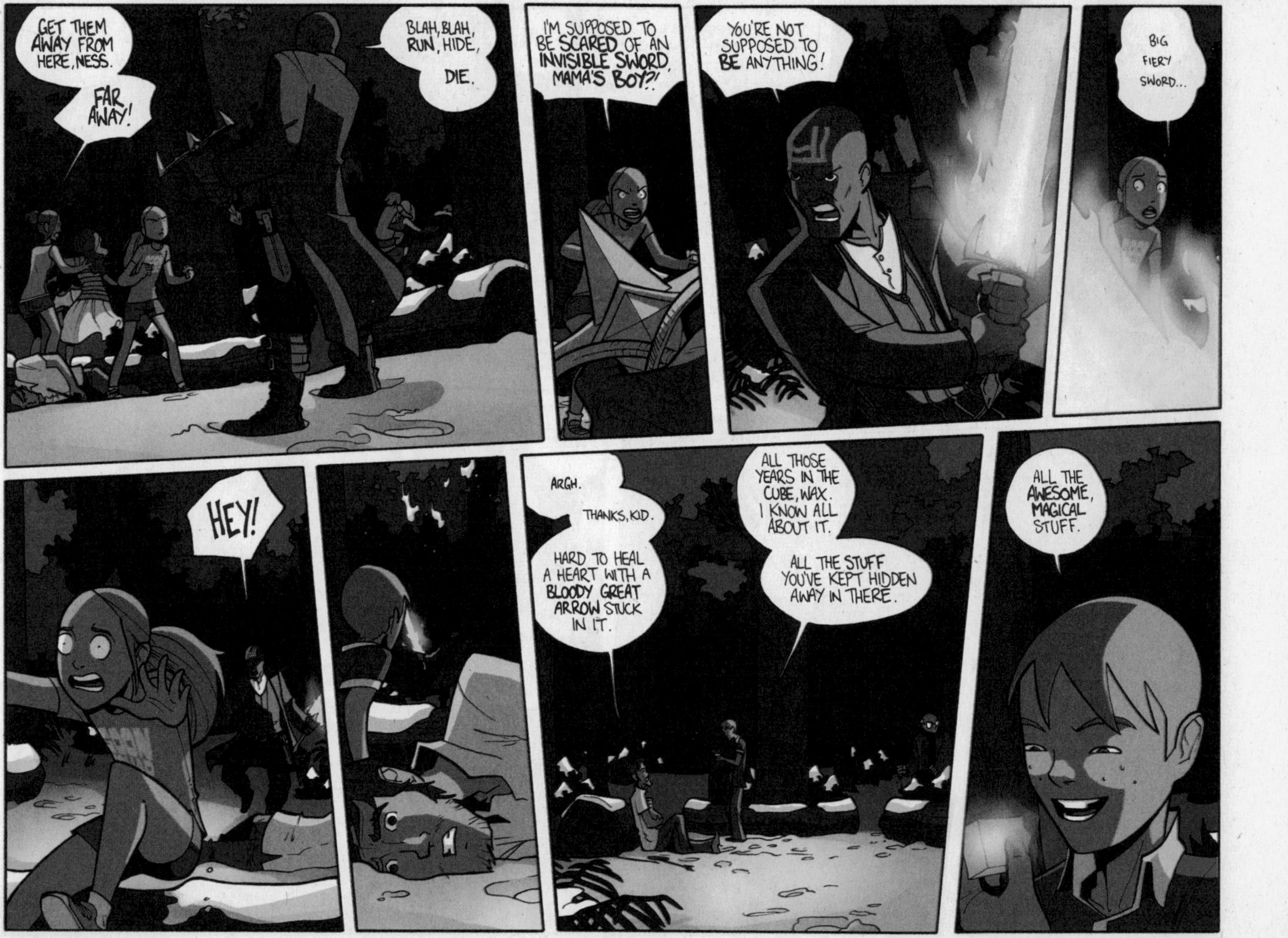
GET THEM AWAY FROM HERE, NESS.
FAR AWAY!
BLAH, BLAH, RUN, HIDE,
DIE.
I'M SUPPOSED TO BE SCARED OF AN INVISIBLE SWORD, MAMA'S BOY?!
YOU'RE NOT SUPPOSED TO BE ANYTHING!
BIG FIERY SWORD...
HEY!
ARGH.
THANKS, KID.
HARD TO HEAL A HEART WITH A BLOODY GREAT ARROW STUCK IN IT.
ALL THOSE YEARS IN THE CUBE, WAX. I KNOW ALL ABOUT IT.
ALL THE STUFF YOU'VE KEPT HIDDEN AWAY IN THERE.
ALL THE AWESOME, MAGICAL STUFF.

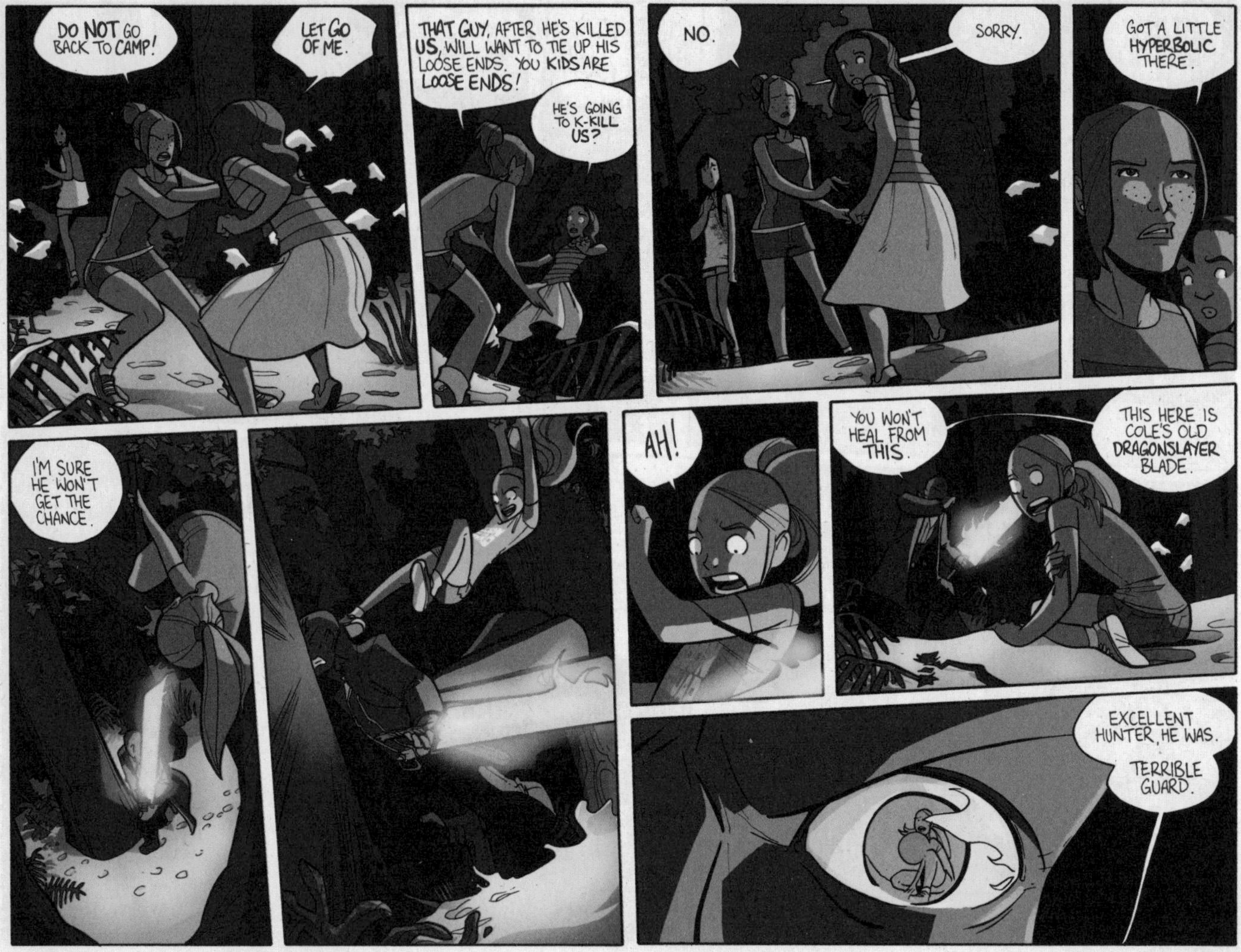
DO NOT GO BACK TO CAMP!
LET GO OF ME.
THAT GUY, AFTER HE'S KILLED US, WILL WANT TO TIE UP HIS LOOSE ENDS. YOU KIDS ARE LOOSE ENDS!
HE'S GOING TO K-KILL US?
NO.
SORRY.
GOT A LITTLE HYPERBOLIC THERE.
I'M SURE HE WON'T GET THE CHANCE.
AH!
YOU WON'T HEAL FROM THIS.
THIS HERE IS COLE'S OLD DRAGONSLAYER BLADE.
EXCELLENT HUNTER, HE WAS.
TERRIBLE GUARD.

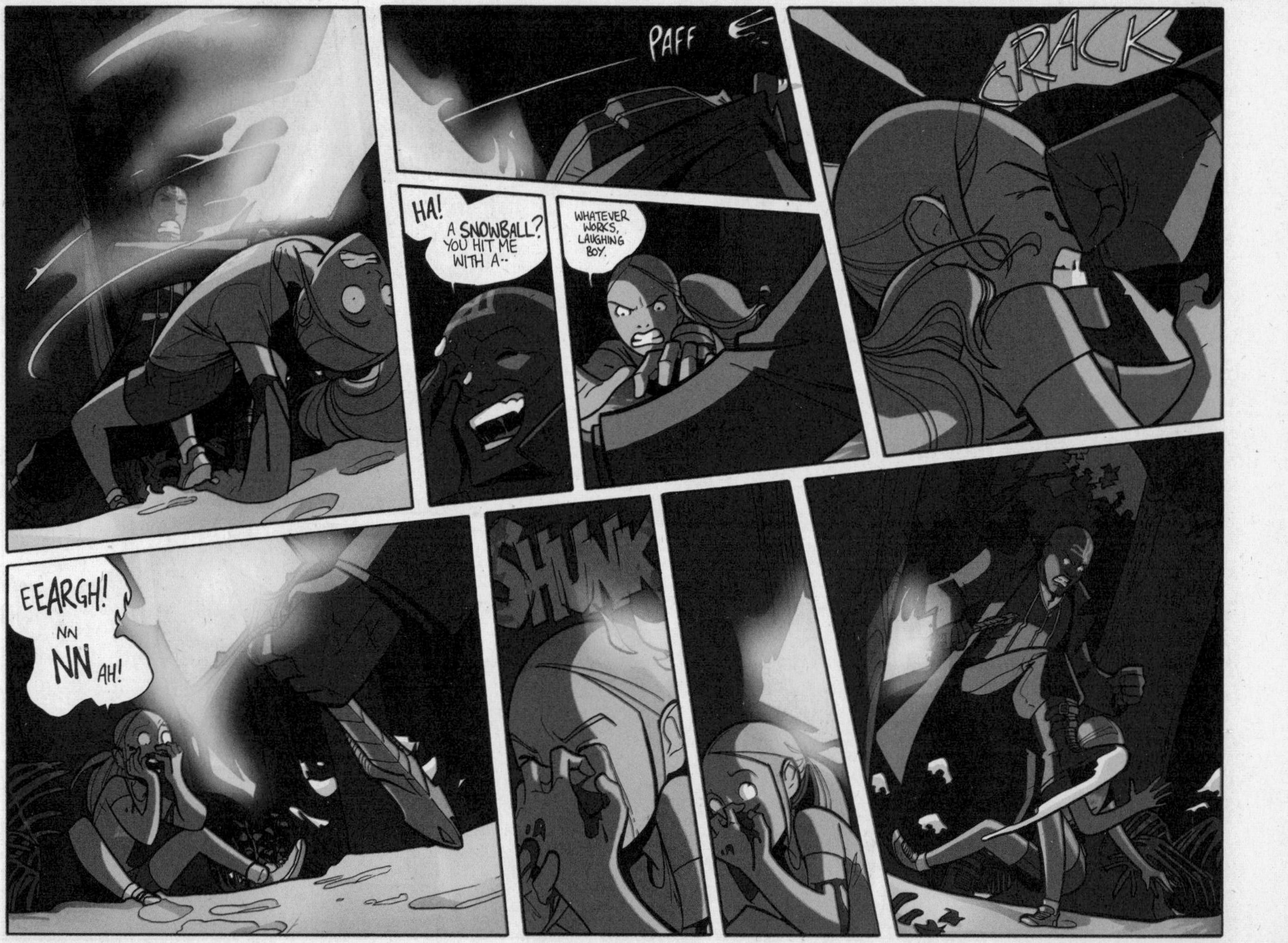
PAFF
CRACK
HA!
A SNOWBALL? YOU HIT ME WITH A--
WHATEVER WORKS, LAUGHING BOY.
EEARGH! NN NN AH!
SHUNK

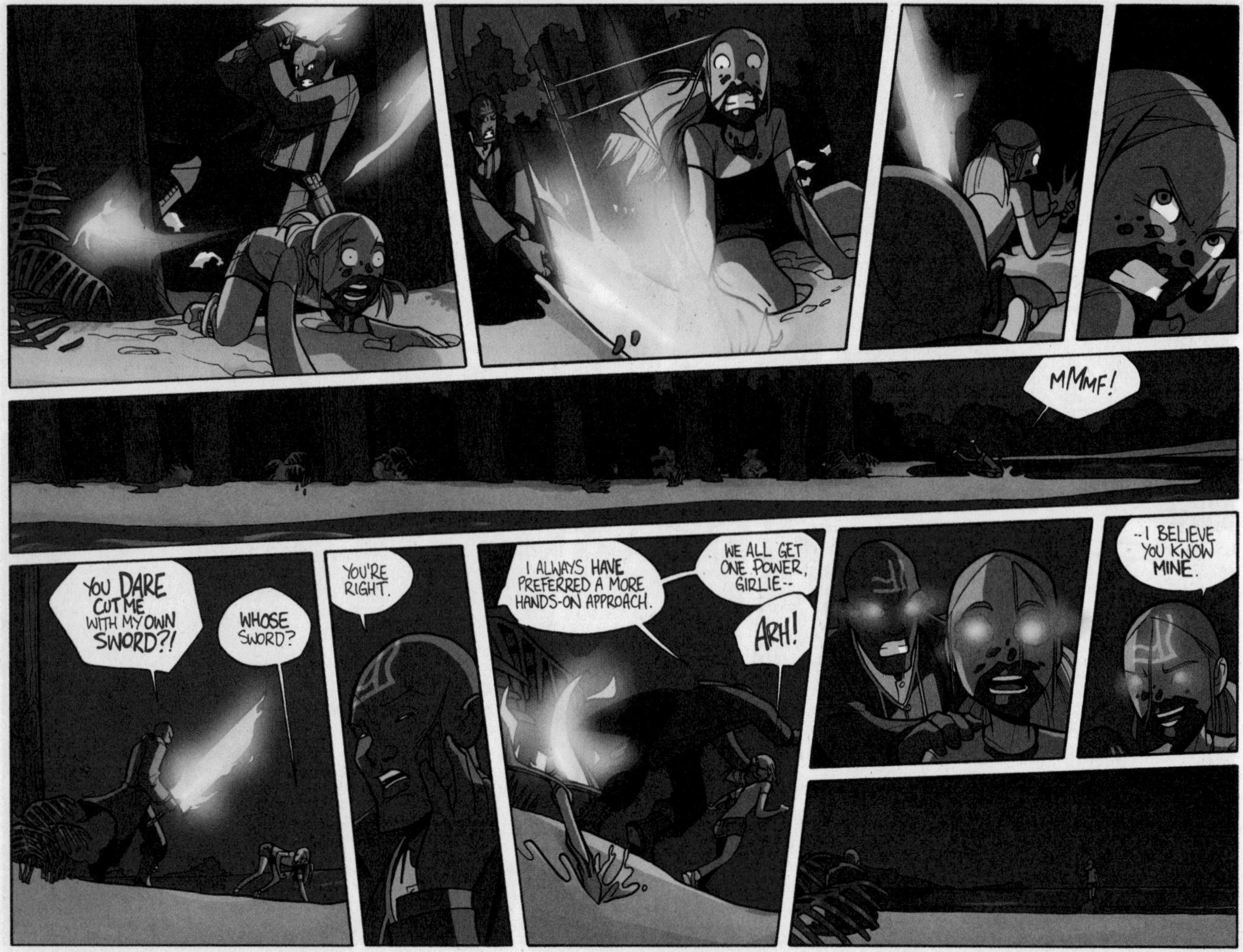
MMMF!
YOU DARE CUT ME WITH MY OWN SWORD?!
WHOSE SWORD?
YOU'RE RIGHT.
I ALWAYS HAVE PREFERRED A MORE HANDS-ON APPROACH.
WE ALL GET ONE POWER, GIRLIE--
ARH!
--I BELIEVE YOU KNOW MINE.

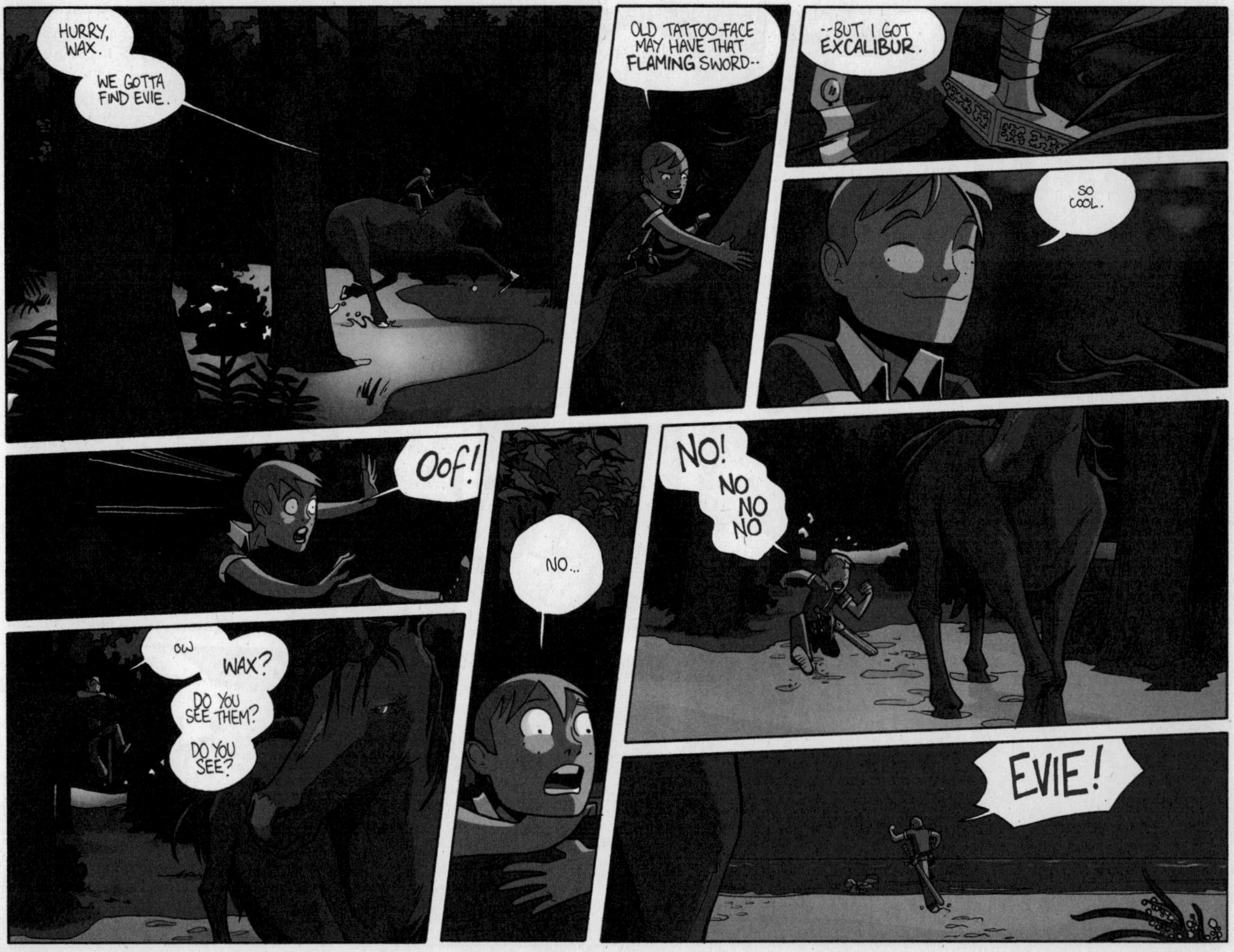
HURRY, WAX.
WE GOTTA FIND EVIE.
OLD TATTOO-FACE MAY HAVE THAT FLAMING SWORD--
--BUT I GOT EXCALIBUR.
SO COOL.
Oof!
OW
WAX?
DO YOU SEE THEM?
DO YOU SEE?
NO...
NO!
NO NO NO
EVIE!

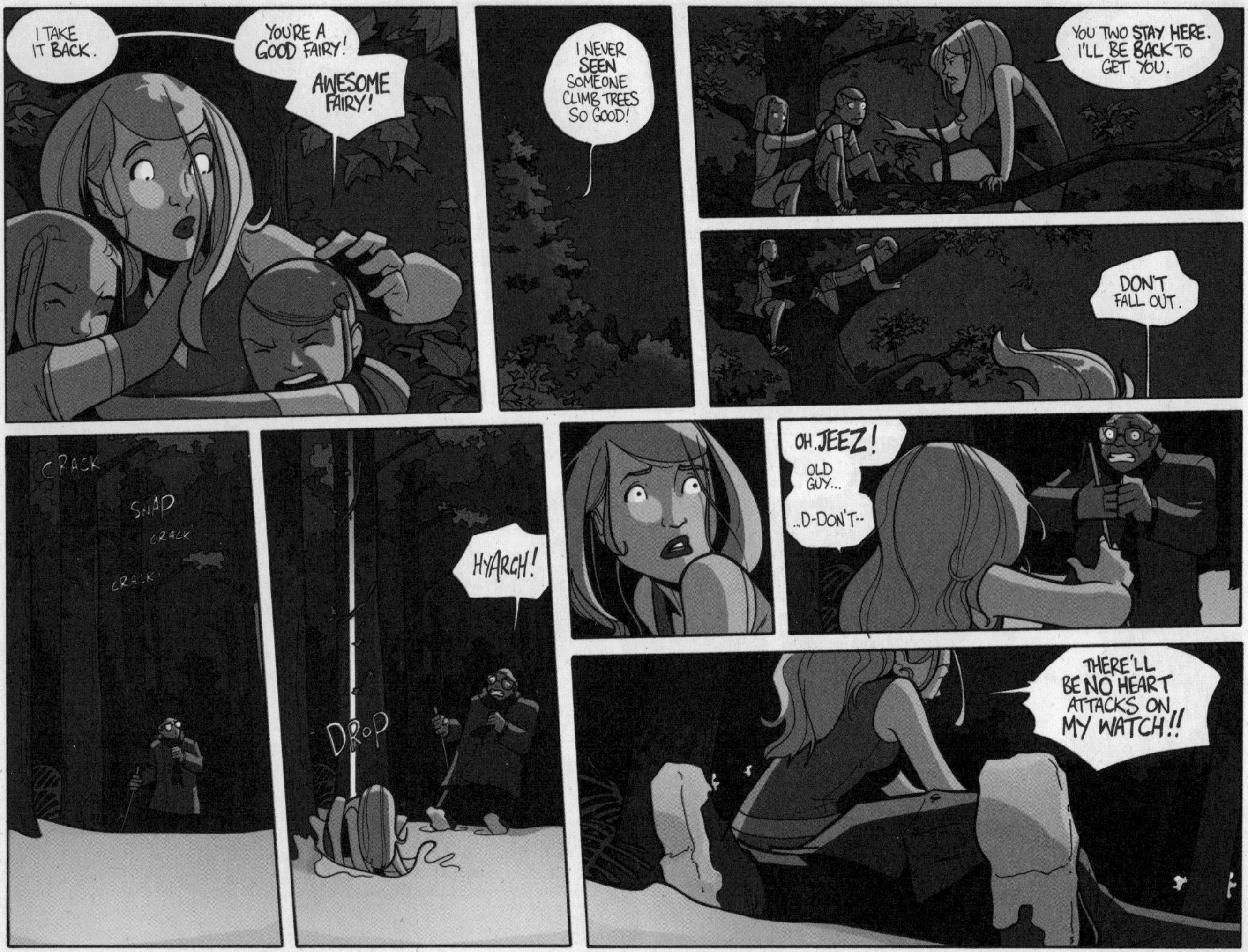
I TAKE IT BACK.
YOU'RE A GOOD FAIRY!
AWESOME FAIRY!
I NEVER SEEN SOMEONE CLIMB TREES SO GOOD!
YOU TWO STAY HERE. I'LL BE BACK TO GET YOU.
DON'T FALL OUT.
CRACK
SNAP
CRACK
CRACK
DROP
HYARGH!
OH. JEEZ!
OLD GUY...
..D-DON'T--
THERE'LL BE NO HEART ATTACKS ON MY WATCH!!

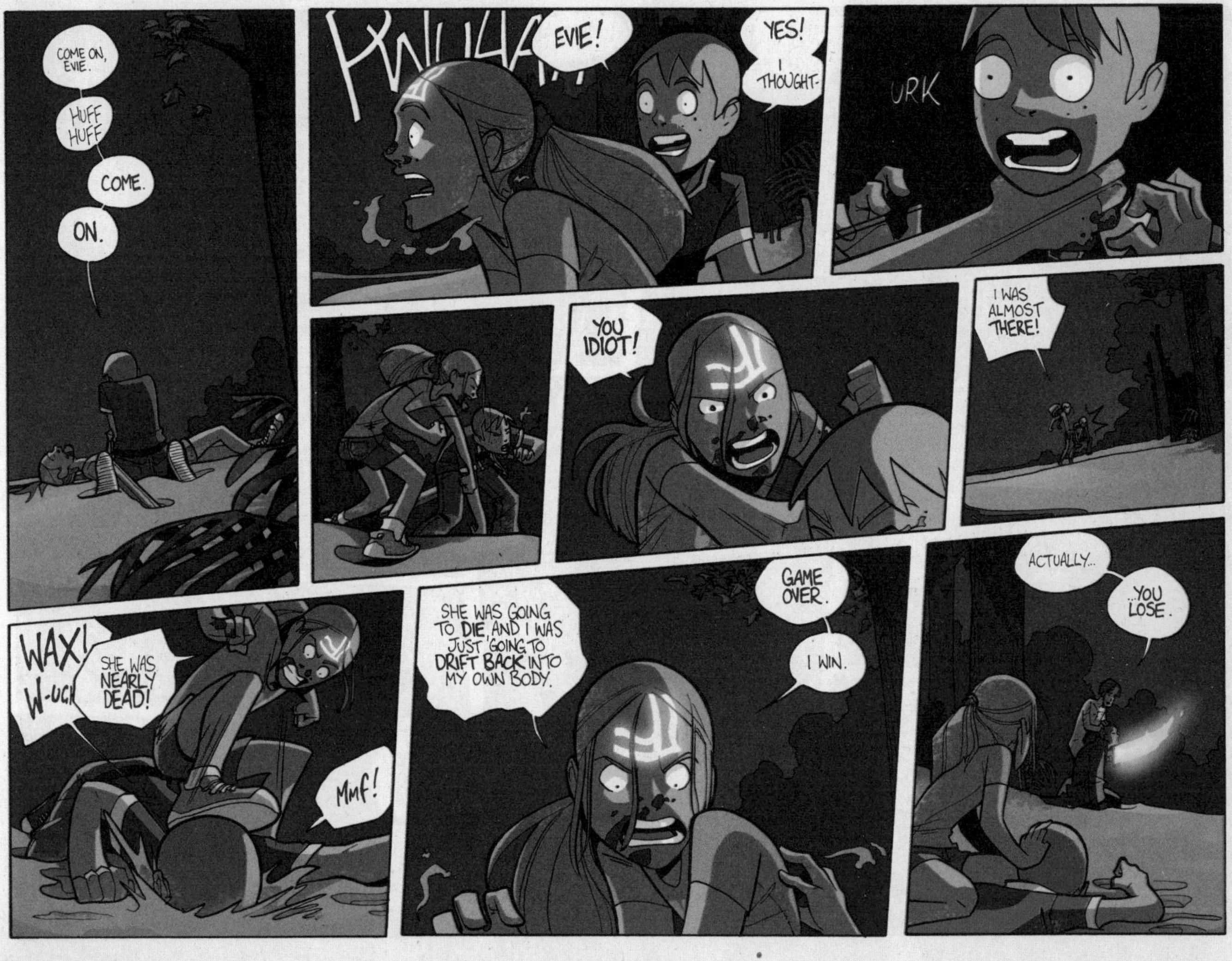
COME ON, EVIE.
HUFF HUFF
COME.
ON.
EVIE!
YES!
I THOUGHT-
URK
YOU IDIOT!
I WAS ALMOST THERE!
WAX!
SHE WAS NEARLY DEAD!
Mmf!
SHE WAS GOING TO DIE, AND I WAS JUST GOING TO DRIFT BACK INTO MY OWN BODY.
GAME OVER.
I WIN.
ACTUALLY...
...YOU LOSE.

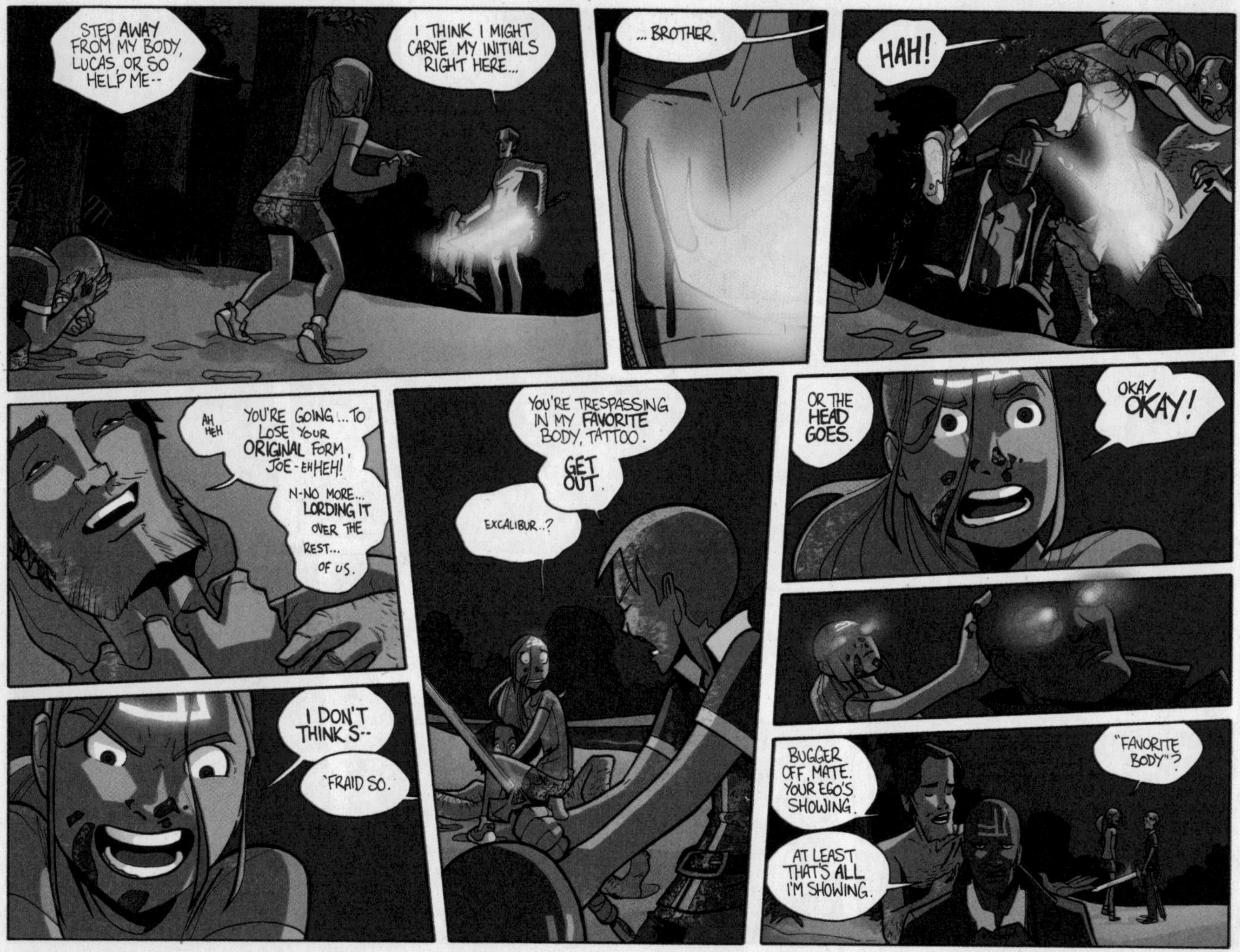
STEP AWAY FROM MY BODY, LUCAS, OR SO HELP ME--
I THINK I MIGHT CARVE MY INITIALS RIGHT HERE...
...BROTHER.
HAH!
AH HEH
YOU'RE GOING...TO LOSE YOUR ORIGINAL FORM, JOE-EHHEH!
N-NO MORE... LORDING IT OVER THE REST... OF US.
I DON'T THINK S--
`FRAID SO.
YOU'RE TRESPASSING IN MY FAVORITE BODY, TATTOO.
GET OUT.
EXCALIBUR..?
OR THE HEAD GOES.
OKAY OKAY!
BUGGER OFF, MATE. YOUR EGO'S SHOWING.
"FAVORITE BODY"?
AT LEAST THAT'S ALL I'M SHOWING.

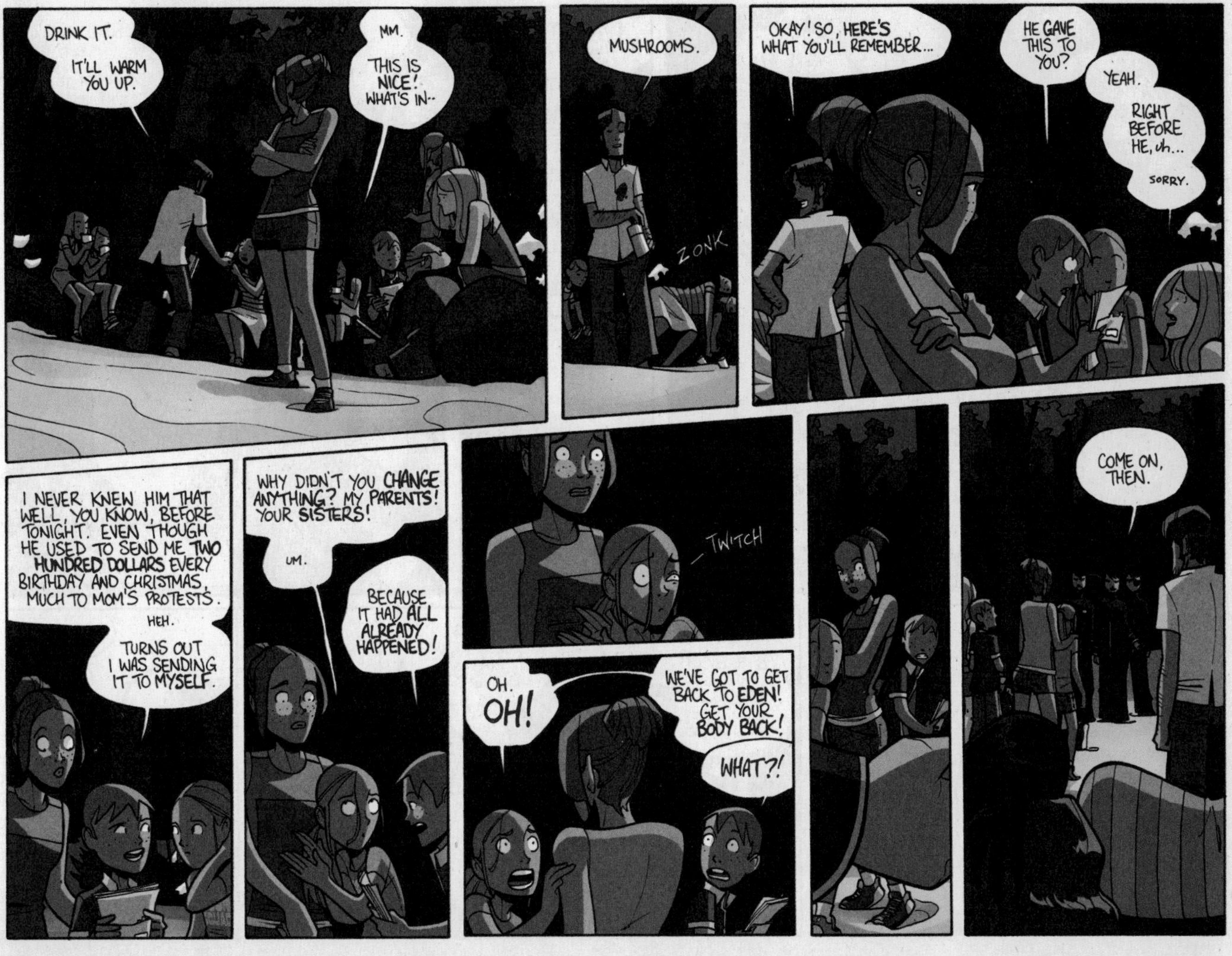
DRINK IT.
IT'LL WARM YOU UP.
MM.
THIS IS NICE! WHAT'S IN--
MUSHROOMS.
ZONK
OKAY! SO, HERE'S WHAT YOU'LL REMEMBER...
HE GAVE THIS TO YOU?
YEAH.
RIGHT BEFORE HE, uh...
SORRY.
I NEVER KNEW HIM THAT WELL, YOU KNOW, BEFORE TONIGHT. EVEN THOUGH HE USED TO SEND ME TWO HUNDRED DOLLARS EVERY BIRTHDAY AND CHRISTMAS, MUCH TO MOM'S PROTESTS.
HEH.
TURNS OUT I WAS SENDING IT TO MYSELF.
WHY DIDN'T YOU CHANGE ANYTHING? MY PARENTS! YOUR SISTERS!
UM.
BECAUSE IT HAD ALL ALREADY HAPPENED!
TWITCH
OH.
OH!
WE'VE GOT TO GET BACK TO EDEN! GET YOUR BODY BACK!
WHAT?!
COME ON, THEN.

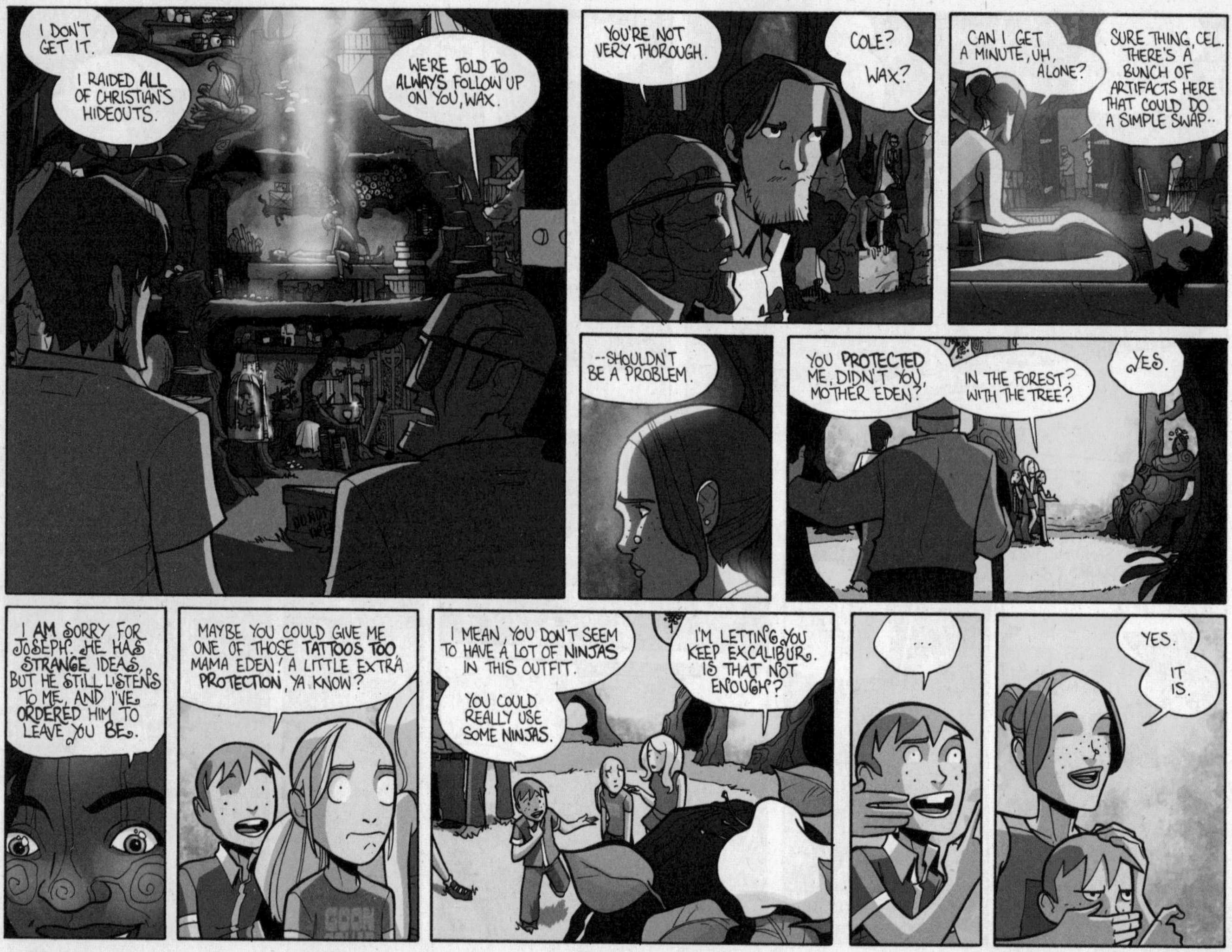
I DON'T GET IT.
I RAIDED ALL OF CHRISTIAN'S HIDEOUTS.
WE'RE TOLD TO ALWAYS FOLLOW UP ON YOU, WAX.
YOU'RE NOT VERY THOROUGH.
COLE?
WAX?
CAN I GET A MINUTE, UH, ALONE?
SURE THING, CEL. THERE'S A BUNCH OF ARTIFACTS HERE THAT COULD DO A SIMPLE SWAP..
--SHOULDN'T BE A PROBLEM.
YOU PROTECTED ME, DIDN'T YOU, MOTHER EDEN?
IN THE FOREST? WITH THE TREE?
YES.
I AM SORRY FOR JOSEPH. HE HAS STRANGE IDEAS, BUT HE STILL LISTENS TO ME, AND I'VE ORDERED HIM TO LEAVE YOU BE.
MAYBE YOU COULD GIVE ME ONE OF THOSE TATTOOS TOO MAMA EDEN! A LITTLE EXTRA PROTECTION, YA KNOW?
I MEAN, YOU DON'T SEEM TO HAVE A LOT OF NINJAS IN THIS OUTFIT.
YOU COULD REALLY USE SOME NINJAS.
I'M LETTING YOU KEEP EXCALIBUR. IS THAT NOT ENOUGH?
...
YES.
IT IS.

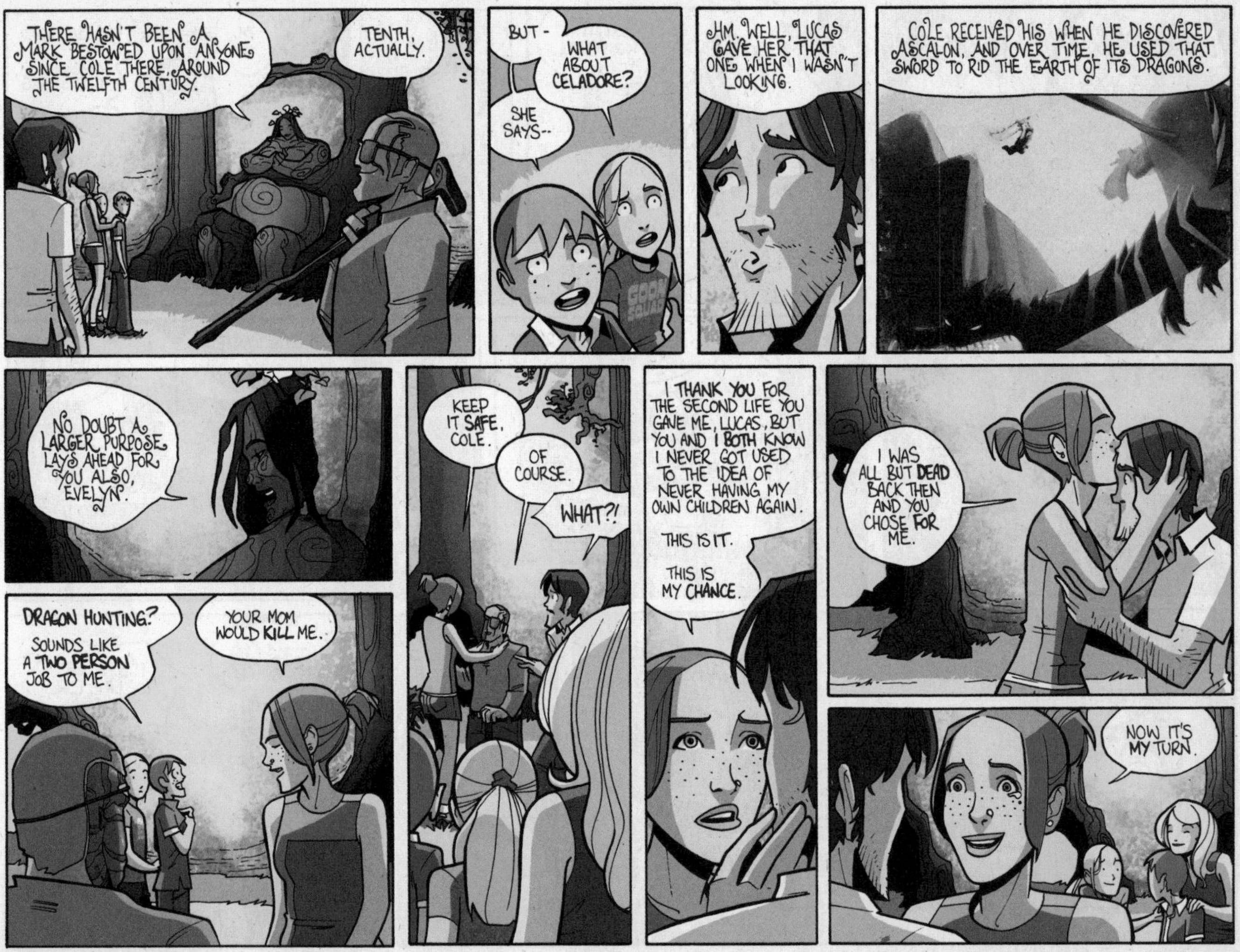
THERE HASN'T BEEN A MARK BESTOWED UPON ANYONE SINCE COLE THERE, AROUND THE TWELFTH CENTURY.
TENTH, ACTUALLY.
BUT -
WHAT ABOUT CELADORE?
SHE SAYS--
HM. WELL, LUCAS GAVE HER THAT ONE WHEN I WASN'T LOOKING.
COLE RECEIVED HIS WHEN HE DISCOVERED ASCALON, AND OVER TIME, HE USED THAT SWORD TO RID THE EARTH OF ITS DRAGONS.
NO DOUBT A LARGER PURPOSE LAYS AHEAD FOR YOU ALSO, EVELYN.
KEEP IT SAFE, COLE.
OF COURSE.
WHAT?!
DRAGON HUNTING?
SOUNDS LIKE A TWO PERSON JOB TO ME.
YOUR MOM WOULD KILL ME.
I THANK YOU FOR THE SECOND LIFE YOU GAVE ME, LUCAS, BUT YOU AND I BOTH KNOW I NEVER GOT USED TO THE IDEA OF NEVER HAVING MY OWN CHILDREN AGAIN.
THIS IS IT.
THIS IS MY CHANCE.
I WAS ALL BUT DEAD BACK THEN AND YOU CHOSE FOR ME.
NOW IT'S MY TURN.

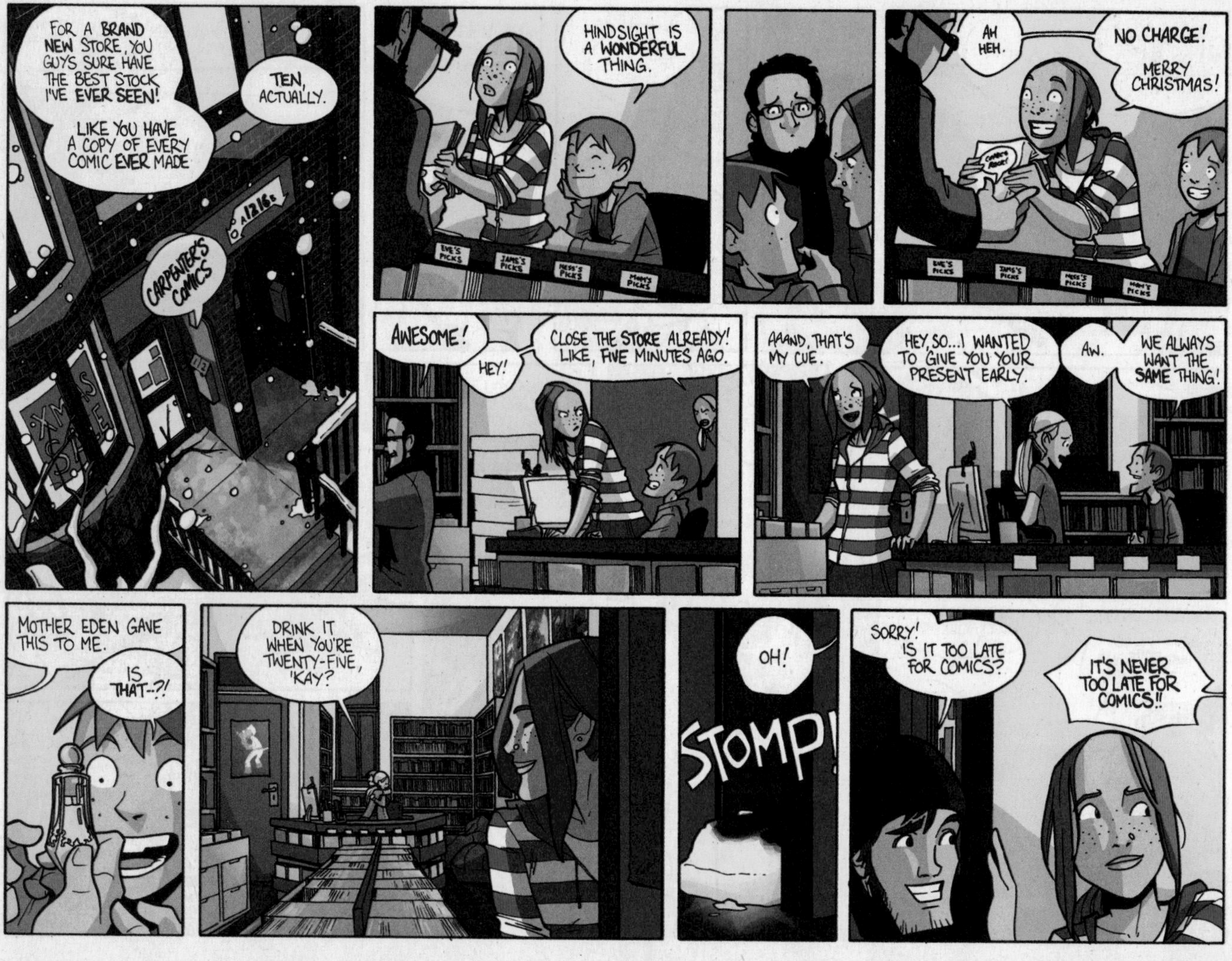
FOR A BRAND NEW STORE, YOU GUYS SURE HAVE THE BEST STOCK I'VE EVER SEEN!
LIKE YOU HAVE A COPY OF EVERY COMIC EVER MADE
TEN, ACTUALLY.
CARPENTER'S COMICS
HINDSIGHT IS A WONDERFUL THING.
EVE'S PICKS
JAMS'S PICKS
NESS'S PICKS
AH HEH.
NO CHARGE!
MERRY CHRISTMAS!
AWESOME!
HEY!
CLOSE THE STORE ALREADY! LIKE, FIVE MINUTES AGO.
AAAND, THAT'S MY CUE.
HEY, SO...I WANTED TO GIVE YOU YOUR PRESENT EARLY.
AW.
WE ALWAYS WANT THE SAME THING!
MOTHER EDEN GAVE THIS TO ME.
IS THAT--?!
DRINK IT WHEN YOU'RE TWENTY-FIVE, 'KAY?
OH!
STOMP!
SORRY! IS IT TOO LATE FOR COMICS?
IT'S NEVER TOO LATE FOR COMICS!!

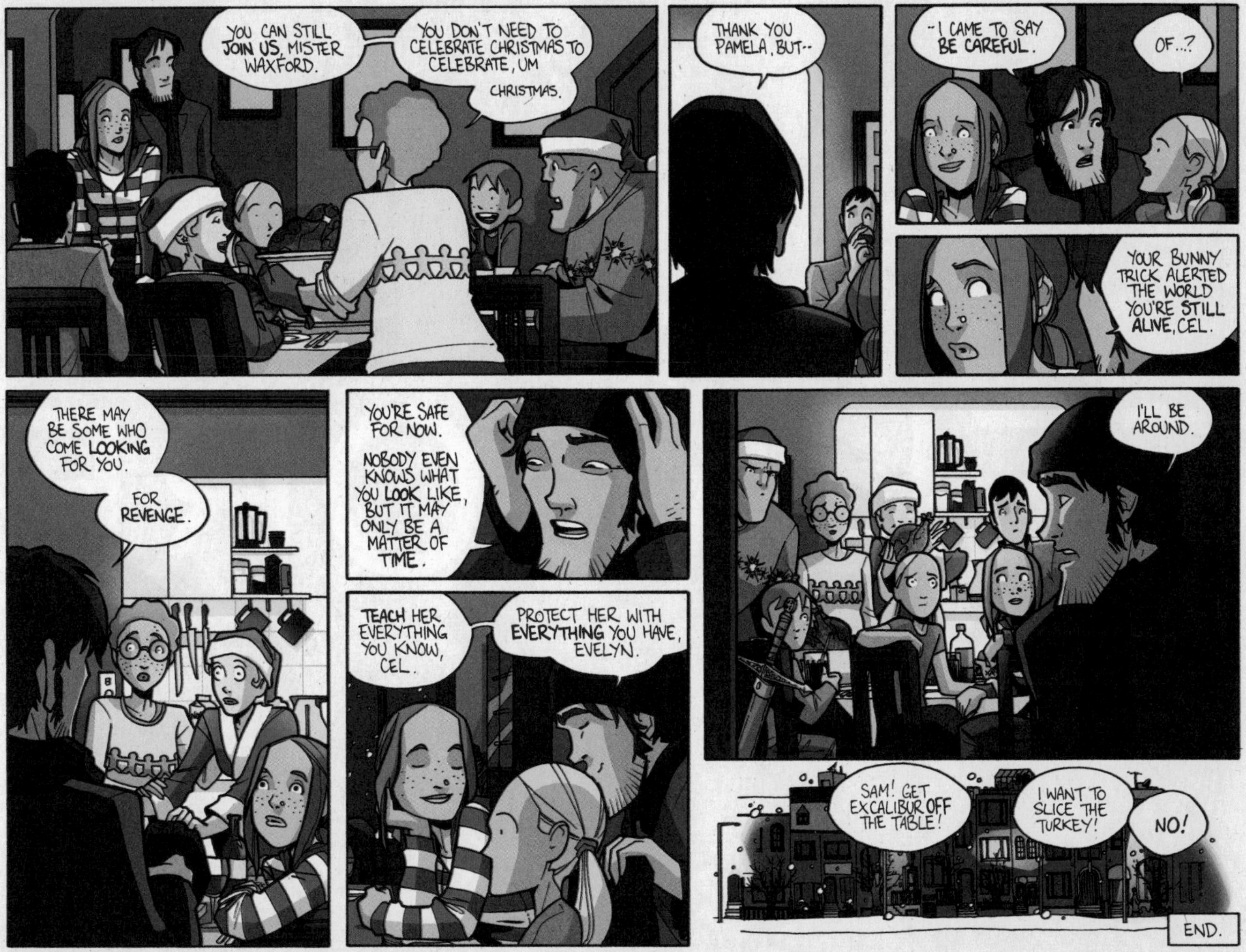
YOU CAN STILL JOIN US, MISTER WAXFORD.
YOU DON'T NEED TO CELEBRATE CHRISTMAS TO CELEBRATE, UM
CHRISTMAS.
THANK YOU PAMELA, BUT--
--I CAME TO SAY BE CAREFUL.
OF...?
YOUR BUNNY TRICK ALERTED THE WORLD YOU'RE STILL ALIVE, CEL.
THERE MAY BE SOME WHO COME LOOKING FOR YOU.
FOR REVENGE.
YOU'RE SAFE FOR NOW.
NOBODY EVEN KNOWS WHAT YOU LOOK LIKE, BUT IT MAY ONLY BE A MATTER OF TIME.
TEACH HER EVERYTHING YOU KNOW, CEL.
PROTECT HER WITH EVERYTHING YOU HAVE, EVELYN.
I'LL BE AROUND.
SAM! GET EXCALIBUR OFF THE TABLE!
I WANT TO SLICE THE TURKEY!
NO!
END.

CELADORE

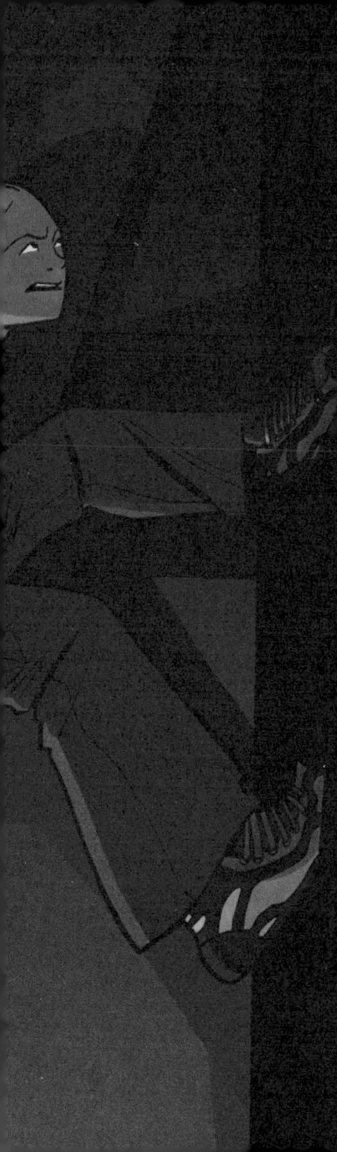

Caanan is an Australian cartoonist living in Nova Scotia, Canada. He has a B.A. in advertising — as well as a strong desire never to use it. Instead, he prefers the imaginative landscape of comics. In Australia, he adapted several fairy tales into online comics for ziptales.com, illustrated for Cambridge Press and Oxford Press, storyboarded for ad companies, and self-published mini-comics that were strongly regarded by about 30 people. CELADORE is his first major story.

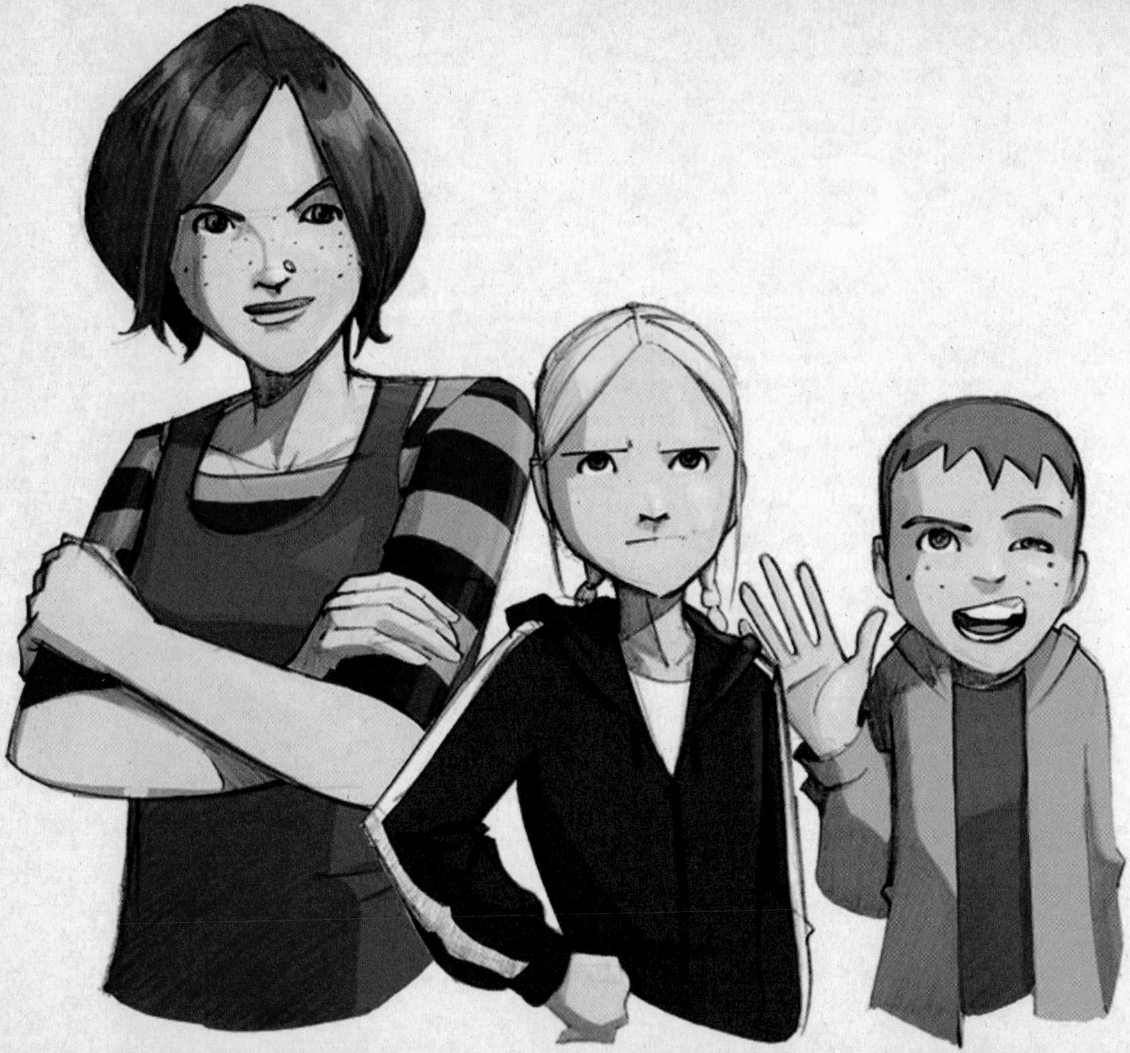

Celadore (as Jay St. George) Eve Sam

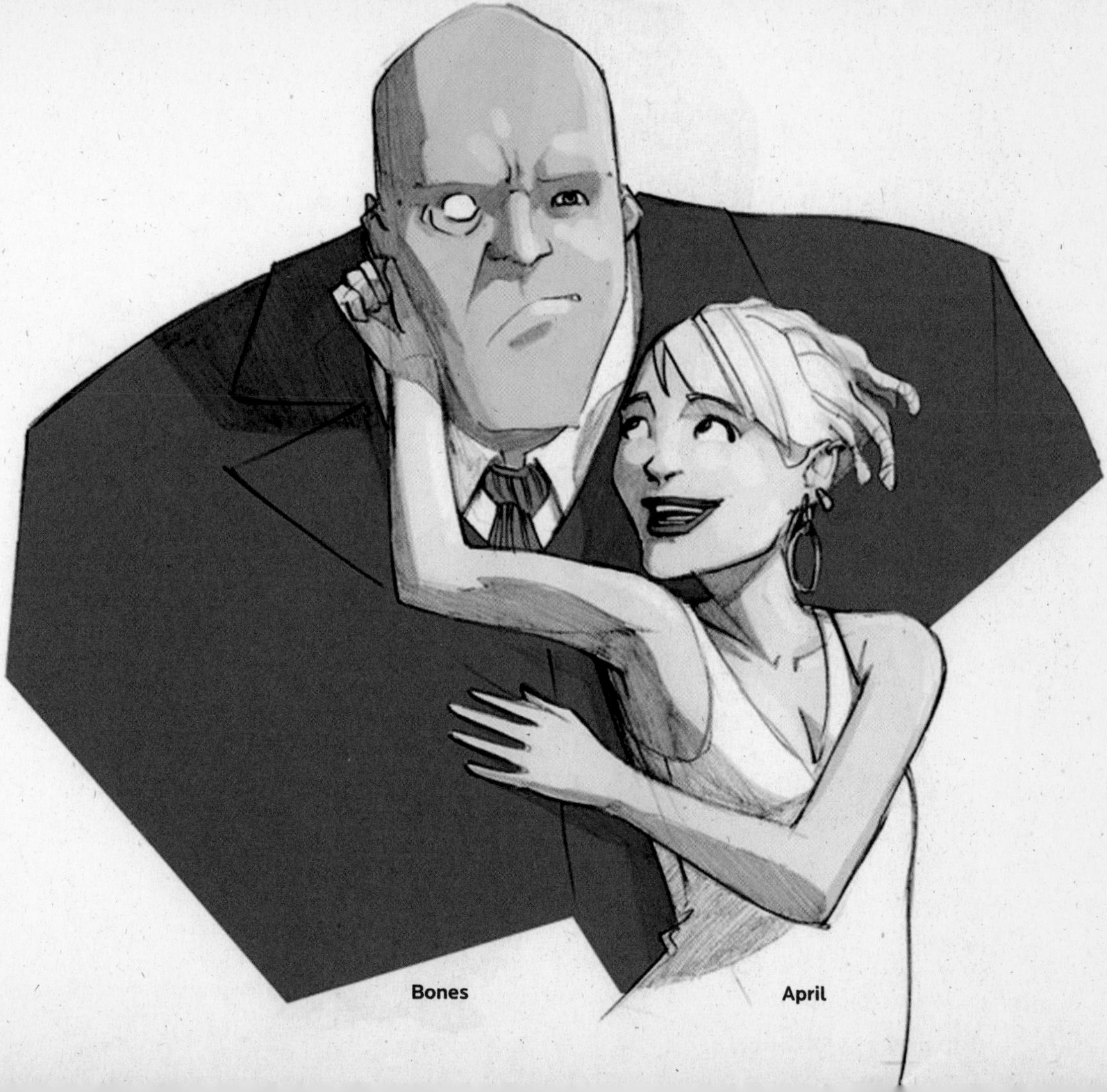
Bones
April

Wax

BAYOU

By Jeremy Love

Winner of a record-breaking five Glyph Awards, BAYOU is a critically acclaimed masterpiece.

Eisner-nominated for best digital comic and named great graphic novel for teens by the American Library Association.

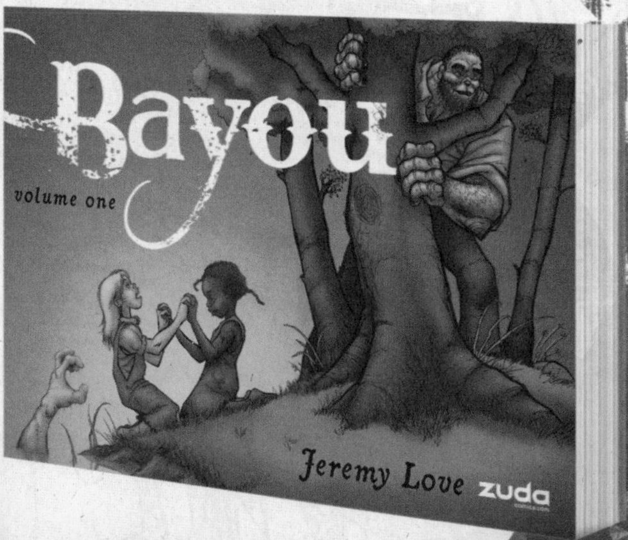
Bayou
volume one
Jeremy Love
zuda

IN STORES NOW

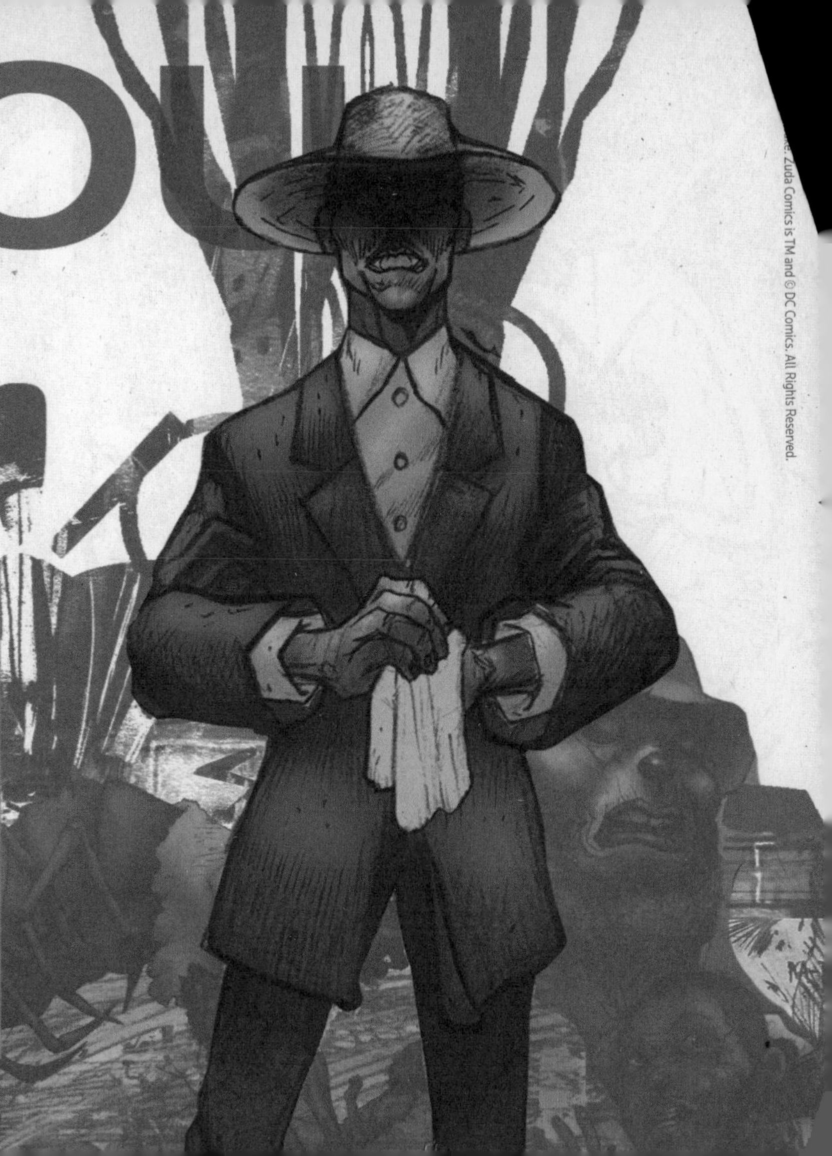

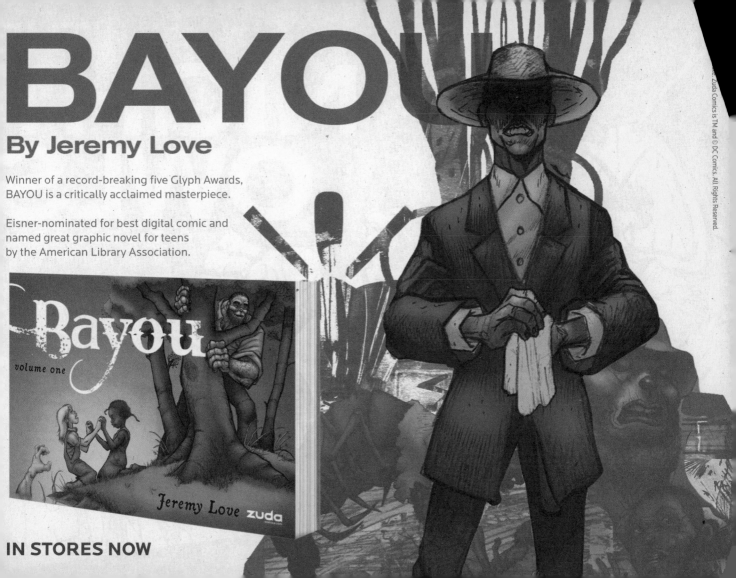

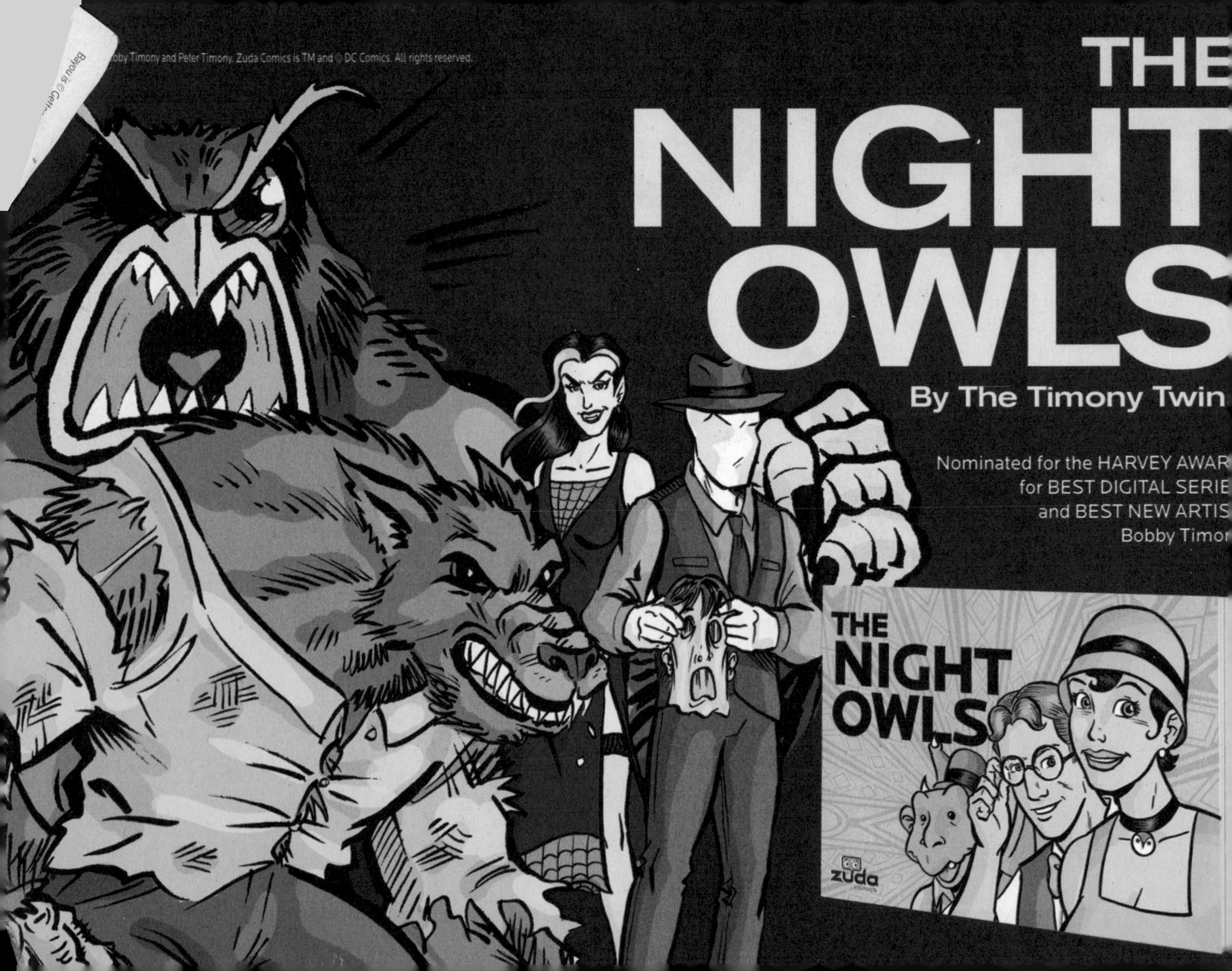
bby Timony and Peter Timony. Zuda Comics is TM and © DC Comics. All rights reserved.
Bayou is ©
THE NIGHT OWLS
By The Timony Twin
Nominated for the HARVEY AWAR
for BEST DIGITAL SERIE
and BEST NEW ARTIS
Bobby Timor
THE NIGHT OWLS
zuda comics

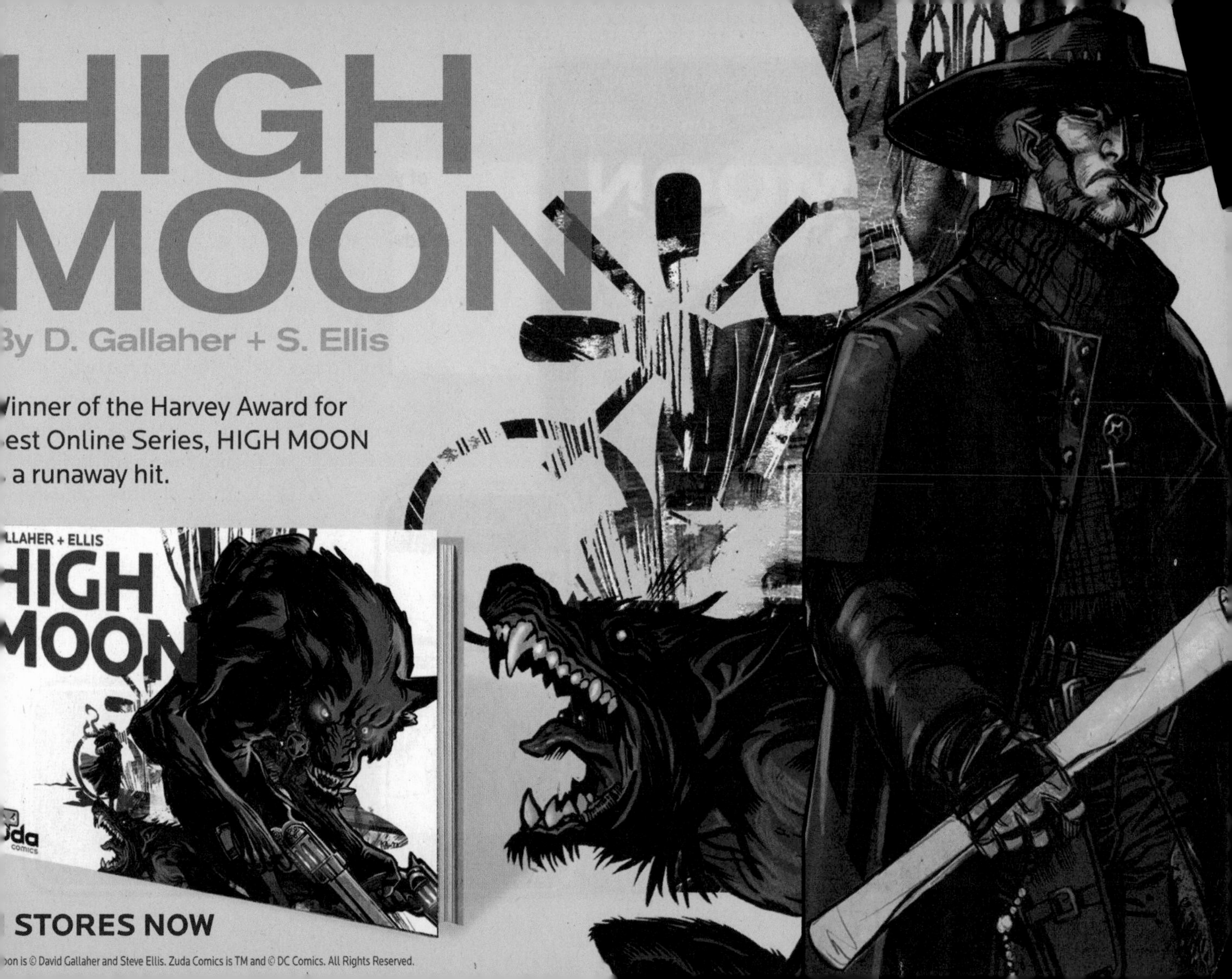
HIGH
MOON
3y D. Gallaher + S. Ellis
Vinner of the Harvey Award for
est Online Series, HIGH MOON
a runaway hit.
LLAHER + ELLIS
HIGH
MOON
uda
comics
STORES NOW
oon is © David Gallaher and Steve Ellis. Zuda Comics is TM and © DC Comics. All Rights Reserved.

With the official DC COMICS App, you can download BAYOU, HIGH MOON, THE NIGHT OWLS, CELADORE and the rest of your favorite ZUDA COMICS. Powered by ComiXology, this app enables you to take advantage of a unique Guided View reading experience or enjoy the pristine, classic full-page view. What's more, you'll be able to conveniently manage and read your entire collection anytime, whether you're at your desk computer, laptop or on the move using your iPhone, iPod Touch or iPad. Experience the amazing world of DC Comics wherever you are!